David Lehman

the last
avant-garde

David Lehman is the author of *Sign of the Times: Deconstruction and the Fall of Paul de Man*, several books of poetry, and is Series Editor of *The Best American Poetry*. His essays, poems, and reviews have appeared in all the major literary publications, from the *Times Literary Supplement* to *The New Yorker* to *The Paris Review*. He is the recipient of numerous prizes and fellowships, including a Guggenheim and the Award in Literature from the American Academy and Institute of Arts and Letters. He lives in New York City.

the last
avant-garde

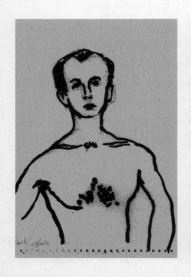

the making of the new york school of poets

by David Lehman

Anchor Books
A Division of Random House, Inc.
New York

First Anchor Books Edition, December 1999

The Library of Congress has cataloged the Doubleday edition as follows:
Lehman, David, 1948–
    The last avant-garde: the making of the New York School of Poets
/ by David Lehman.—1st ed.
      p. cm.
    Includes bibliographical references and index
    1. American poetry—New York (State)—New York—History and
criticism. 2. Experimental poetry, American—History and criticism.
3. Avant-garde (Aesthetics)—New York (State)—New York.
4. American poetry—20th century—History and criticism.
5. New York (N.Y.)—Intellectual life—20th century. 6. City and
town life in literature. I. Title.
PS255.N5L45 1998
811′.540997471—dc21   98-16249
                                         CIP

Anchor ISBN 0-49533-1

www.anchorbooks.com

Author Photograph © Star Black

Printed in the United State of America
10 9 8 7 6 5 4 3 2 1

for Joe

contents

the last avant-garde

The interest in language so dominant in modern art is not an interest in semantics *per se*: it is a continual interest in making language (whatever the medium) to fit our real feelings better, and even to be able to express true feelings that had never been capable of expression before. How much more humanistic in the end is this effort on the part of solitary individuals than that of those who throw a collective ideology at one and say, that is the obvious truth, now express it! It is only authoritarian groups, whether political or religious, who can determine by pressure the *future* of their arts. To us who are freer individually, the future is a wide-open adventure of unimagined possibilities, and of hundreds of booby-traps.

—ROBERT MOTHERWELL, LETTER TO FRANK O'HARA,
AUGUST 18, 1965

Our idea is to do something with language
That has never been done before
Obviously—otherwise it wouldn't be creation
We stick to it and now I am a little nostalgic
For our idea, we never speak of it any more, it's been
Absorbed into our work, and even our friendship
Is an old, rather fragile-looking thing.
Maybe poetry took the life out of both of them,
Idea and friendship.

—KENNETH KOCH, "DAYS AND NIGHTS"

The story of the New York School of poets is a study in friend-ship, artistic collaboration, and the bliss of being alive and young at a moment of maximum creative ferment. It is also the story of the last authentic avant-garde movement that we have had in American poetry.

When John Ashbery, Kenneth Koch, Frank O'Hara, and James Schuyler first lived in New York, the Korean War was in progress and McCarthyism was the scourge of freethinking intel-lectuals. It was the era of Levittown and the "silent generation," when the original *Guys and Dolls* was on Broadway, suburban flight was in progress, New York had three baseball teams and at least one of them played in the World Series every year. In an age of split-level conformism, the poets of the New York School put their trust in the idea of an artistic vanguard that could sanction their deviations from the norm. The liberating effect of their writing became increasingly evident in the passionate, experi-mental, taboo-breaking early 1960s, when the nation's youngest president was in office, men discarded their hats, women started using the Pill, the acceleration in the speed of social change seemed to double overnight, and America finally left the nine-teenth century behind.

In his book *The Banquet Years*, Roger Shattuck characterized the avant-garde in Paris in the golden period before World War I as an "artistic underground" dedicated to "heterodoxy and oppo-sition." The artists maintained "a belligerent attitude toward the world and a genuine sympathy for each other." They lived and worked "in an atmosphere of perpetual collaboration." The avant-garde "was a way of life, both dedicated and frivolous," generating tremendous excitement. Guillaume Apollinaire, a poet, was the "impresario of the avant-garde," the champion of Cubism and the man who gave Surrealism its name. Apollinaire's "magnetic presence" and his "expansive, volatile nature flowed inexhaustibly on and left behind it poems and lyric texts which seemed to flower effortlessly out of his enthusiasms."

Substitute Frank O'Hara for Apollinaire and Abstract Expressionism for Cubism, and you get an eerie fit. The poets of the New York School were as heterodox, as belligerent toward the literary establishment and as loyal to each other, as their Parisian predecessors had been. The 1950s and early '60s in New York were their banquet years. It is as though they translated the avant-garde idiom of "perpetual collaboration" from the argot of turn-of-the-century Paris to the roughhewn vernacular of the American metropolis at midcentury.

While the four core members of the New York School did not set out to recruit disciples, never issuing public statements or devising a group program in the manner of the French Surrealists, they had a close sense of community and an awareness that their destinies as poets were intertwined. They shared much else besides, including the conviction that they were heading for greatness. Witnesses to what Robert Motherwell called "the greatest painting adventure of our time," they strove for the same excitement in poetry, looking to the painters as the agents of artistic change. "New York poets, except I suppose the color blind, are affected most by the floods of paint in whose crashing surf we all scramble," Schuyler wrote in 1959, summing up a decade and more of unprecedented artistic turbulence. "In New York the art world is a painters' world; writers and musicians are in the boat but they don't steer."

The poets took their lead from the Abstract Expressionists

(also known as the Action Painters and as the New York School of painting) in several key respects. From Jackson Pollock and Willem de Kooning, they learned that it was okay for a poem to chronicle the history of its own making—that the mind of the poet, rather than the world, could be the true subject of the poem—and that it was possible for a poem to be (or to perform) a statement without making a statement. From the painters, too, they understood that acceptance was not necessarily a blessing, nor rejection a curse. "The literary establishment cared as much for our work as the Frick cared for Pollock and de Kooning," O'Hara wrote defiantly, pushing the analogy between poets and painters. Like painting, writing was properly understood to be an activity, a present-tense process, and the residue of that activity could not help referring to itself. All poetry was the product of a collaboration with language. While mimesis, the imitation of nature, remained a goal of art, the abstract painters had redefined the concept by enlarging the meaning of nature; "I am nature," Pollock said. This, too, was a liberty the poets could take. Like abstract paintings, their poems originated not in a Platonic conception of their final form but in an engagement with the medium of expression itself.

Still, the poets meant to honor the great example of Abstract Expressionism not only by absorbing its principles but also by veering from them as their own development required. In this exact regard, they paralleled their closest friends among the so-called Second Generation of New York School painters—Fairfield Porter, Jane Freilicher, Nell Blaine, and Larry Rivers among them—who strove to learn from Pollock, de Kooning, and the rest, without the slavish fidelity of epigones. The Second Generation painters veered by returning to figuration at the very moment when the critic Clement Greenberg, the ayatollah of Abstract Expressionism, declared that painting had to be abstract and "flat." The poets veered in an equally fundamental way. In

3

place of the high seriousness that engulfed the Abstract Expressionists, they opted for aesthetic pleasure. They were ironists, not ecclesiasts. They favored wit, humor, and the advanced irony of the *blague* (that is, the insolent jest or prank) in ways more suggestive of Jasper Johns and Robert Rauschenberg than of the New York School painters after whom they were named. About everything, including the ideals and pretensions of the avantgarde, the poets could be jubilantly irreverent, as when Frank O'Hara collaborated with Larry Rivers on "How to Proceed in the Arts," their satirical "study of the creative act" (1961): "Youth wants to burn the museums. We are in them—now what? Better destroy the odors of the zoo. How can we paint the elephants and hippopotamuses? Embrace the Bourgeoisie. One hundred years of grinding our teeth have made us tired. How are we to fill the large empty canvas at the end of the large empty loft? You do have a loft, don't you, man?"

The poets liked hoaxes and spoofs, parodies and strange juxtapositions, pseudotranslations and collages. On the ground that the rules of all verse forms are at base arbitrary, they created ad hoc forms (requiring, say, an anagram or the name of a river in every line) and unconventional self-assignments ("translate a poem from a language you do not understand; do not use a glossary or dictionary"). They adapted the Cubist collage and the Surrealist "exquisite corpse" (a one-line poem composed by a group of poets, each of whom contributes a word without knowing what the others have written). Apollinaire's café poems, "Les Fenêtres" and "Lundi rue Christine," taught them that a poem could originate in snatches of overheard conversations. You could cull lines at random from books. Or you could scramble the lines in an already written poem to produce a disjunctive jolt. Many works would be improved if you simply deleted every second word. Poems didn't have to make sense in a conventional way; they could discover their sense as they went along. The logic of a dream or a word game was as valid as that of empirical science as a means of arriving at poetic knowledge.

Freely experimental and fiercely intellectual, the poets were at the same time resolutely antiacademic and antiestablishment even as they began to win acceptance in establishment circles. Some of their more radical productions neither looked like nor sounded like poems. Since acceptance or rejection of these works was an indication neither of success or failure, the poets looked to each other as ultimate arbiters. "John and Frank and I were almost like a mutual admiration society," Schuyler said. But they also competed fiercely, each trying to outdo the other. "It's wonderful," Koch said many years later, "to have three good friends that you think are geniuses." The poets were "like the members of a team, like the Yankees or the Minnesota Vikings," Koch elaborated. "We inspired each other, we envied each other, we emulated each other, we were very critical of each other, we admired each other, we were almost entirely dependent on each other for support. Each had to be better than the others but if one flopped we all did." They were prolific. In addition to their own work in several genres, they collaborated with painter pals on collages and lithographs and comic strips. Collaborating with each other, they produced poems, plays, a novel, and four issues of a literary magazine they called *Locus Solus*, the very model of an avant-garde journal, which they named after a prose masterpiece by Raymond Roussel, the ultimate avant-garde writer. The whole period was, in Koch's phrase, "fizzy with collaboration."

All this activity was predicated on the idea that poetry could be reinvented from top to toe. Everything was up for grabs. "It came to me that all this time / There had been no real poetry and that it needed to be invented," Koch writes in "Days and Nights," one of several of his poems that look back to the seminal 1950s. The approved American poetry of the time was crusty with convention. "There was no modern poetry in the sense that there was modern painting," Ashbery asserted. The avant-garde writer had the advantage of beginning with a clean slate (or the illusion of one). The rejection of the acceptable poetry of the age made it possible to pursue a grander ambition: "to write poetry that is better than poetry," in Koch's words. It is not that Ashbery, Koch, O'Hara, and Schuyler were ignorant of poetic tradition. On the contrary, they were voracious readers. But they recognized that tradition is a vast passing-away and renewal, and they had enough respect for the past not to copy it lazily but to adapt, alter, and adjust the tradition through the application of their individual talents. They understood, too, that a poem no less than a picture could be "a hoard of destructions," in Picasso's phrase. And so they favored avant-garde methods of composition that inverted the received order of things. The aim was the liberation of the imagination, and any and all means to this end were valid.

Forty years after Pound and Eliot made the first modernist revolution in poetry, the New York poets were the first to extend that new frontier. They were intent on widening the framework of American poetry; they wanted to be read not in the narrow context of the Anglo-American poetry of midcentury but with reference to other arts, earlier periods, alternative traditions. The poets were unusually responsive to modern music and to poetry in other languages as well as to modern art. They favored a tradition of literary outsiders—what Ashbery has called "an other tradition"—and felt that, in Ashbery's words, "modern poetry gave the poet the license to be strange." They admired the deliberate "derangements" of Arthur Rimbaud, the artificial contrivances of Raymond Roussel, the peripatetic musings of Guillaume Apollinaire; they learned from the expatriate experiments of Gertrude Stein and Laura Riding as well as from such neglected homespun originals as David Schubert, Delmore Schwartz, and John Wheelwright. French poetry since Baudelaire and the Symbolists put it through the paces of the modernist revolution had a particularly salubrious effect on the New York poets. By adopting unconventional methods and models, they were able to reject the academic orthodoxies of the New Criticism, then the dominant mode of literary interpretation, which seemed to have a stranglehold on midcentury verse. Enlarging the sphere of the poetic, they revitalized poetry at a moment when it seemed that everything that could be done had been done. (It always seems that way.) They took Pound's old dictum to heart: They made it new.

The New York School of poets—though it wouldn't be named that until 1961—can be said to have begun operations on the June day in 1948 that Ashbery, completing his junior year at Harvard, wrote "The Painter" and mailed it to Koch, who had already graduated from Harvard and migrated to New York. "The Painter," a sestina, was the first of many poems in which these poets aligned themselves with modern painters in their crises, their conflicts, and their sense of artistic aspiration and romantic possibility. A pretty good idea of the aesthetics of the New York School could be gleaned from such works as Koch's "The Artist," Ashbery's "The Painter" and "Self-Portrait in a Convex Mirror," and O'Hara's "Memorial Day 1950" and "Why I Am Not a Painter," all of which treat the visual arts as a kind of allegorical surrogate for poetry. It seems both just and inevitable that Ashbery, O'Hara, Koch, and Schuyler gave their first public readings at the Club, the nondescript Eighth Street loft where the Abstract Expressionists gathered weekly to hash out aesthetic issues.

The poet at the vital center of the New York School was O'Hara. The group did not gel, Ashbery observed, until O'Hara arrived in New York in 1951 "to kind of cobble everything together and tell us what we and they were doing." O'Hara, who did much to promote the Abstract Expressionists in his curatorial position at the Museum of Modern Art, was also the nearest thing to an action painter in verse. Blessed with tremendous personal magnetism, O'Hara lived the life of a poet in New York, and chronicled it. The painters adored him; Philip Guston called him "our Apollinaire." O'Hara's death in a freak accident on Fire Island in July 1966 removed the group's dominant personality. But by then the New York School had established a sphere of influence beyond its initial milieu. That influence has ramified over the years, and today the impulses and strategies of the school have less to do with the specific geography of New York than with a state of mind in which the capacity for wonderment is matched by the conviction that poems are linguistic engines rather than repositories of felt experience.

In contrast to their painter namesakes, the New York School of poets did not quite conquer the world of poetry; the recognition they won came grudgingly and belatedly. Koch was the first to achieve a national reputation. His innovative techniques for teaching poetry to schoolchildren—as described in *Wishes, Lies, and Dreams* (1970) and *Rose, Where Did You Get That Red?* (1973)—made him the most famous poetry teacher in America. O'Hara's posthumous apotheosis came in 1972, when his *Collected Poems* won the National Book Award in poetry. Ashbery, though a darling of the international avant-garde, was still a well-kept secret until 1976, the year his *Self-Portrait in a Convex Mirror* was the dark horse that won the Triple Crown—the Pulitzer Prize, the National Book Award, and the National Book Critics Circle Prize. Overnight Ashbery became an inescapable presence in American poetry, provoking seminars, debates, essays in criticism, a fair amount of attention in the national press, more prizes and honors, a great many imitators, and a slew of never-say-die critics bent on denigrating their favorite bête noir. Schuyler, the last of the four core members of the New York School to come to prominence, did so when his *Morning of the Poem* won the Pulitzer in 1980, due in part to the efforts of Ashbery, who was one of the judges that year.

What makes the New York poets exemplary at this time is

that they managed to be not only avant-garde writers but literary artists. They experimented not for experimentation's sake but for the sake of writing great poems. Their idea of innovation was very different from a value placed on novelty. They wanted to be original in the sense recommended by Emerson: "Why should not we also enjoy an original relation to the universe?" While they could be silly, they were artful in their silliness; they used playful means to arrive at high aesthetic ends. They formed a movement not by design but by a kind of group momentum fostered by friendship and propelled by their growing confidence in the value of their works. Eventually it would be seen that the poems they wrote and the magazines they edited had casually performed the task of manifestos and pronouncements. Without searching for them, the poets attracted apostles, who understood that their works implied a collective point of view and a finely honed sense of taste embodying that point of view. It was not the most heralded movement of the 1950s; the Beats made more noise. But it will have the most lasting significance.

Like the Beats, who were intent on bringing Hebraic chants, Eastern mysticism, and "bop prosody" into their writing, Ashbery, O'Hara, and company tapped sources beyond the strictly literary: movies, comic books, music, avant-garde drama, and, above all, modern art. Like the Beats, too, they were determined to be poetically incorrect; their work is full of provocative gestures and violations of decorum. Unlike the Beats, however, the poets of the New York School pursued an aesthetic agenda that was deliberately apolitical, even antipolitical. The rebellion they conducted had to do with poetry: how to write it, how to read it. Their idea, as Koch put it, was "to do something with language / That [had] never been done before."

The Last Avant-Garde aspires to combine cultural history, biography, and literary analysis. In the first half of the book, I profile Ashbery, O'Hara, Koch, and Schuyler singly and as a group. I mean to show that this remarkable gang of four, though different from one another in ways that I will make clear, should be considered in the light of what they shared. Contemporary critics tend to treat Ashbery as an isolated case. Without wishing to diminish Ashbery's great singularity, I believe that the spirit of collaboration and the sense of common cause linking these poets are too important to be minimized or ignored.

I also want to communicate what Lionel Trilling called the "hum and buzz of cultural implication" in New York during the group's glory years—the years between the Marshall Plan and the escalation of the war in Vietnam. What was it like to start out in the early 1950s? Though received wisdom has it that the decade was a dead zone, the period was in fact a major moment for the imagination, an exciting episode in the cultural history of New York City, and it wasn't all that long ago, though it seems nostalgically far away: a time when the life of the artist had a certain seedy glamour, rents were cheap, the subway safe, and the art market had not yet become the plaything of the very rich. Hoping to convey the aura of the era, I will interrupt my narrative as needed to introduce the reader not only to painters, critics, and gallery directors but to other totemic figures who turn up because they populated the literary landscape (W. H. Auden, Robert Lowell, Jack Kerouac, Allen Ginsberg), because they helped define the intellectual currents of the time (Clement Greenberg, Lionel Trilling, Susan Sontag, Norman Mailer), or simply because Frank O'Hara wrote about them in his poems (Jackson Pollock, Miles Davis, Lana Turner, Billie Holiday, James Dean) as versions of the same American dream that inspired and consumed him.

The poets of the New York School were avant-garde at a time when that designation meant something. They are not the last avant-garde movement we will ever have. But at the moment the conditions surrounding art and literature are anything but favorable to the idea of an avant-garde. The problem has something to do with the decline of the public intellectual and the corresponding expansion of the purview of academe; the idea that something can be at once avant-garde and academic would seem a contradiction in terms. Gertrude Stein summarized a second problem in "Composition as Explanation," a lecture she delivered at Oxford and Cambridge in 1926. "For a long time everybody refuses and then almost without a pause almost everyone accepts," Stein wrote. "In the history of the refused in the arts and literature the rapidity of the change is always startling."

The interval between rejection and acceptance has steadily grown shorter since Stein wrote those words. The consequence is that the avant-garde's incursions into the temple of art have become ritualized as the predictable gestures of postmodernism. Kafka's succinct parable "Leopards in the Temple" seems to apply: "Leopards break into the temple and drink up the contents of the sacrificial pitchers; this is repeated again and again; finally it can be calculated in advance, and it becomes part of the ceremony." If we are all postmodernists, we are none of us avant-garde, for postmodernism is the institutionalization of the avant-garde.

In the second half of this book, I raise the question of whether the avant-garde as an abstract concept or a practical idea is finished. It is a question that leads to others, or requires the answer to others, before it can be settled. What does (or did) *avant-garde* mean, and how did it come to have that meaning? What exactly are the requirements of an avant-garde art movement? What lessons do the movements of the past have to teach us? The argument against the viability of the avant-garde today rests on the assumption that there is no real resistance to the new, no stable norm from which the defiant artist may depart. While I find this to be a convincing argument, I would sooner help quicken a new avant-garde than pronounce the demise of an old one. In any event, my book means to stand or fall not on speculation regarding the future of the avant-garde but on the job that it does of presenting four major poets, defining their importance, examining the way their friendships entered their art, and depicting the milieu in which they lived and worked.

I consider the death of O'Hara to signal the end of the first phase of the New York School as an avant-garde movement. It is possible, even probable, that the three surviving poets did their best work after O'Hara's untimely demise. Still, I would argue, it was the work the poets produced between 1948 and 1966—when the spirit of collaboration and friendly competition was at its most intense—that made their individual breakthroughs possible. In concentrating on Ashbery, Koch, O'Hara, and Schuyler, I know I must necessarily stint other admirable writers in their circle, such as Edwin Denby, Kenward Elmslie, Barbara Guest, and Harry Mathews. It is no slur on these writers to observe that they do not seem nearly as central to the New York School in the 1950s as the quartet I have chosen to emphasize. This was the "secret" conviction of the poets themselves. In 1959, when they were planning the magazine they came to call *Locus Solus*, James Schuyler wrote to John Ashbery, "Secretly, I don't think K. [Koch] believes anybody except you, he, Frank & me has anything to offer." Schuyler added, "While I am of this opinion too, of course, it seems rather limiting for a magazine."

When I lecture on the New York School, I am sometimes asked why relatively few women were involved in the movement. I reply that this is not true of its later manifestations. In the 1960s and '70s, when St. Mark's Church in the Bowery served as headquarters for a second generation of New York School poets, the leading exponents of the style included Anne Waldman, Bernadette Mayer, Maureen Owen, and Alice Notley no less than Ted Berrigan, Ron Padgett, Joe Brainard, Tony Towle, and Michael Brownstein. Women figure even more prominently on any list of contemporary poets for whom the New York School influence has been decisive. In this way, the demographics of the New York School have accurately reflected a larger sociological pattern. But the predominantly masculine identity of the New York School in its formative years does have a crucial, and crucially ironic, significance. Masculine the poets were, but they deviated boldly from the prevailing idea of masculinity. In their aestheticism, the New York poets presented an alternative to the aggressive heterosexualism of an era whose celebrations of manhood were themselves signs of a high anxiety. "That was the year everybody in the United States was worried about homosexuality," John Cheever wrote in his journal in 1959. "They were worried about other things, too, but their other anxieties were published, discussed, and ventilated while their anxieties about homosexuality remained in the dark: remained unspoken. Is he? Was he? Did they? Am I? seemed to be at the back of everyone's mind. A great emphasis, by way of defense, was put upon manliness, athletics, hunting, fishing, and conservative clothing, but the lonely wife wondered, glancingly, about her husband at his hunting camp, and the husband himself wondered with whom he shared a rude bed of pines. Was he? Did he? Had he? Did he want to? Had he ever? But what I really mean to say is that this is laughable. Guilty man may be, but only an absurdly repressed people would behave this way." Not the least attractive thing about the poets of the New York School is the freedom from guilt that their celebration of the imagination entailed. And while I would not want to overemphasize their homosexuality as an element of their aesthetic practice, it does seem to me that one question some of these poets are asking some of the time is whether the American pursuit of happiness may be consistent with a poetics of gaiety in both the traditional and modern senses of the word.

"The regularity of my design / Forbids all wandering as the worst of sinning," Lord Byron wrote at the beginning of *Don Juan*, the most digressive of English poems. My design in *The Last*

Avant-Garde is not nearly as regular as Byron's but favors some of the same narrative and rhetorical strategies, including digressive sidebars and the abrupt insertion of the first-person point of view. As a poet who came under Koch's spell at Columbia and later became a colleague of Ashbery's at Brooklyn College and at *Newsweek*, I have not hesitated to draw on my own experiences as they relate to the history, the methods, and the personalities of the New York School.

I began writing *The Last Avant-Garde* in a studio I was renting at the Chelsea, the venerable bohemian hotel on Twenty-third Street in Manhattan, where James Schuyler resided during the last twelve years of his life. When I turned in the manuscript, I was living in a small apartment on MacDougal Street, just a few paces from the old San Remo café, long gone, where Schuyler, Ashbery, O'Hara, and Koch used to initiate evenings with drinks and an exchange of poems. The unmarked site of the Cedar Tavern, the fabled "painters' bar," where the poets bent elbows with Franz Kline and Willem de Kooning, was a short walk away on the corner of Eighth Street and University Place. (The current incarnation of the Cedar a few blocks north on University Place bears no relation to the dive of Abstract Expressionist legend.) In the course of researching this book, I frequented other locales dear to the hearts of the New York School of poets: the Museum of Modern Art, where O'Hara (and briefly Schuyler) worked; the New School for Social Research and Columbia University, where Koch quickened the enthusiasm of several generations of New York poets; and the Tibor de Nagy Gallery, now on Fifth Avenue and Fifty-seventh Street, which, at a previous location in the early 1950s, had sponsored the first publications of the New York poets and celebrated their collaborative forays with painters.

It is no secret that our own times are inimical to the imagination. Technology has put art to the rout. The concept of fame has been degraded, replaced by the notion of celebrity, and poetry is recognized as an expedient and sometimes eloquent way to hasten the aims of social justice on the one hand and of marketing strategies on the other. Poetry consists of irreproachable sentiment rendered in bite-sized pieces, doggerel for an inaugural. Or it is a rhymed injunction to the jury, or a rock singer's wail. Or perhaps it is something in the air of a hip, dark underground café that can help sell blue jeans. How precious at such a time is true poetry, which resists the blandishments of the celebrity culture, is impatient with pretense and piety, and remembers that the gratuitousness of a work of art is its grace. If reality is indistinguishable from the consumerism and mass thinking that the mass media foster, there is an urgent need for a poetry that can press back against the pressures of reality, and I would argue that the example of the New York School may best show the way.

We are so often told that poetry plays a marginal role in our culture that most of us accept this as a fact without ever considering that its position on the periphery may be what gives American poetry the freedom in which it has flourished. I am convinced not only of the high quality and enduring value of our best poetry but of its importance in helping us to understand some of the major aesthetic and cultural issues of our time. I believe this to be especially true of the New York School, and I hope that the sense of romantic possibility that charged the lives of these poets may prove as inspiring to my readers as it has been in my own life and work.

part

one

the poets

the pursuit of happiness

In the beginning there are those who don't quite fit in
But are somehow okay. And then some morning
There are places that suddenly seem wonderful:
Weather and water seem wonderful,
And the peaceful night sky that arrives
In time to protect us, like a sword
Cutting the blue cloak of a prince.

—JOHN ASHBERY,
"A SNOWBALL IN HELL"

(I)

The "New York School of Poets" was always, on the face of it, an incongruous label. Here was a group of poets who were born elsewhere, went to college elsewhere, and contrived—all except Frank O'Hara—to abandon New York City for long stretches in Europe. In the poems that poured out of him in the 1950s, O'Hara wrote with incessant exuberance about New York; his buddies rarely did. Yet for all of them the artistic life of the city seemed to function as a stimulus and a necessary backdrop. The poets had the good fortune to live in New York at the moment when it was displacing Paris as the world capital of modern art, and something of New York's metropolitan energy and sass made its way into their writing. It is there in the wit, humor, and irony that they favored; no group or movement of poets was ever so intent on appropriating comic devices for purposes serious and sometimes sublime. It is equally there in the sheer verbal excitement that gave some of their early poems a rough resemblance to the abstract painting that was taking New York—and the world—by storm. That Ashbery, Koch, O'Hara, and Schuyler launched their careers in New York can hardly have been a geographical accident; if anything, the confluence was overdetermined. This fact alone makes the "New York School" an attractive name, and by now a historically inevitable one, for the band of outsiders who brought the avant-garde revolution to American poetry.

John Bernard Myers, the flamboyant director of the Tibor de Nagy Gallery, came up with the New York School moniker in 1961, hoping to cash in on the cachet of the world-conquering Abstract Expressionists. "The idea was that, since everybody was talking about the New York School of painting, if he created a New York School of poets then they would automatically be considered important," Ashbery commented without enthusiasm. But the importance of the Tibor de Nagy Gallery in the careers of the New York poets goes well beyond Myers's promotional skills. It was here that the poets were validated as part of the avant-garde enterprise; it was here that the idea of a concord among poets and painters enjoyed a practical demonstration. When the poets were without a perch in the literary world, Myers teamed them up with the painters in his gallery and published them. In 1952 and '53, Myers—"an ageless, hulking Irishman with the self-image of a pixie," as James Merrill described him—printed fine, limited-edition chapbooks of O'Hara, Ashbery, and Koch, with drawings or prints by their painter friends Larry Rivers, Jane Freilicher, and Nell Blaine, all of whom the Tibor de Nagy Gallery represented. O'Hara's *A City Winter* in 1952 was followed by Koch's *Poems* (1953) and Ashbery's *Turandot and Other Poems* (1953): in each case it was the poet's first book publication.

An unabashed advocate of avant-garde causes from the time he was managing editor of the surrealist magazine *View* in the 1940s, Myers aspired to be the Diaghilev of the New York School, orchestrating the mutual adoration of poets and painters and imploring them to make artistic collaborations of all shapes and sizes. In 1950 he set up shop with his partner Tibor de Nagy, a trim and elegant man who had been a banker in his native Hungary, and the suave European was content to let the gallery bear his name while the flamboyant American ran the show. Myers was well connected. "We were all name-droppers, but he really was the king," Rivers remarked. No less an authority than Clement Greenberg told Myers which artists to show, and he had the good sense to listen when Greenberg, or such a painter as Willem de Kooning, handed out advice. The younger painters to whom Greenberg gave his stamp of approval included Rivers, Grace Hartigan, Helen Frankenthaler, Alfred Leslie, Robert Goodnough, and Harry Jackson. All went to the Tibor de Nagy Gallery in one fell swoop. When de Kooning touted Fairfield Porter, Myers signed him up for a show, sight unseen.

"Every artist likes to have a house poet," the composer Virgil Thomson, another Myers intimate, told him. Myers went out and acted on the notion, and when Ashbery, O'Hara, Koch, Schuyler, and Barbara Guest "were in the studios being petted and adored," he could sincerely say that "no one was more euphoric about this than I." In 1954 Myers began publishing a four-page broadside entitled *Semi-Colon*, his "newspaper" as he called it, and crammed it full of his favorite poets' latest experiments, garnered from them at the Cedar Tavern, the painters' hangout. One issue consisted exclusively of poems and collaborations by Koch and O'Hara. Included were the former's "Collected Poems"

(one-line poems, each with its own title), the latter's "Collected
Proses, an Answer" (one-line poems using Koch's titles), a Koch
sestina in which every line ends with the word *point*, and a collaborative poem that Koch and O'Hara created one afternoon on a
midtown street corner. The last mentioned consists of the stanza

> Sky
> woof woof!
> harp

repeated twelve times. Roughly three hundred copies of each
issue of *Semi-Colon* were printed and sold for twenty cents each
at the painters' Eighth Street Club and at the Cedar Tavern as
well as at the Tibor de Nagy Gallery. It wasn't the size of the
circulation that mattered; it was something very different and
perhaps incompatible with a sizable audience. It was the pleasure
of being in on the secret, among the select, in the know, ahead
of the game: the pleasure of being avant-garde.

Myers, who had once made a living as a professional puppe-
teer, had a strong showman's streak, and he promoted "his" artists tirelessly. When O'Hara and Grace Hartigan collaborated on
poem-posters in 1953, Myers showed the results at his gallery.
He would wax rhapsodic about a Larry Rivers costume ball, with
"vast paper murals" painted by Alfred Leslie and Joan Mitchell,
in which "poets were dressed in fabulous costumes by painters"
and Bunny Lang "as a louche *femme-fatale*" stole the show. Myers
lived with the theater director Herbert Machiz, and the two men
put on one-act plays by Ashbery (*The Heroes*, 1954, with sets by
Nell Blaine), Koch (*Red Riding Hood*, 1953, with sets by Grace
Hartigan), O'Hara (*Try! Try!*, 1953, with sets by Larry Rivers),
Schuyler (*Presenting Jane*, 1953, with sets by Elaine de Kooning),
Barbara Guest (*The Lady's Choice*, 1954, for which Jane Freilicher
painted the back wall of the Comedy Club stage), and James

Merrill (*The Bait*, 1954, with sets by Al Kresch). "John and Herbert wanted to produce Plays by P*O*E*T*S, with Sets by P*A*I*N*T*E*R*S—not that mere asterisks can render the starry-eyed emphasis John brought to the plan," Merrill wrote.

A born matchmaker, Myers introduced James Schuyler to O'Hara and Ashbery. Schuyler had published some work in a magazine called *Accent*. On the phone Myers complimented Schuyler ("My dear, you're a poet!"), who replied that a poem he had admired in the same magazine was Frank O'Hara's "The Threepenny Opera." "Frank O'Hara is right *here* in the *room* with *me*," Myers crowed. Schuyler met O'Hara and Ashbery soon after, at a party given by Myers after a Larry Rivers opening. At another such gathering, Myers tried to get a play out of James Merrill. "Sweetie," he cried, darting forward on tiptoe, "you must write something wonderfully, perfectly, divinely beautiful for our Artists Theater. Hush! Don't say a word, just let it happen!"

Myers was living in the Hamptons in the summer of 1952 when Ashbery, Koch, O'Hara, and Jane Freilicher rented a small cottage for a month. "I asked Elaine [de Kooning] one morning if I could introduce some friends who wrote poetry to her and Bill de Kooning," Myers writes in *Tracking the Marvelous*, his lively art-world memoir. "I was aware that Bill did not like to be disturbed while he was working. After a short consultation with Bill, Elaine gave the green light. I then went to the door of the studio and shouted 'Poets!' Immediately O'Hara, Koch, and Ashbery emerged from the bushes where they were hiding and walked through the door. Their sudden appearance hit Bill as very funny; from then on they all became good friends, especially O'Hara, on whom de Kooning doted."

It is easy to spoof Myers with his hyperbolic manner and his devotion to a grand artistic alliance of poets and painters presided over by himself in the role of ringmaster. In person he was exaggerated, obvious, over the top, as if consciously playing the part of a lip-pursing, eye-rolling, wrist-flicking fruitcake. "No gathering was complete without poets," he gushed in *Tracking the Marvelous*, recalling those "halcyon" days in New York City. He had placed himself "in the very center of this literary gold mine" and was sure he was envied on all sides: " 'John constantly worries about being the hostess with the mostest,' bitched one of my dearest friends." Here is how O'Hara and Rivers render Myers in their play, *Kenneth Koch: A Tragedy*, which they wrote in 1954, aping Koch's style to parody the whole crew of Cedar Tavern regulars:

> JOHN MYERS: Why, my dear, haven't you heard? I have a gallery of the liveliest, most original, and above all youngest, painters in America, and for every painter there's a poet. You know, we've discovered something called "the figure" that's exciting us enormously this season. I don't quite understand it myself, but it has something terribly pertinent to do with the past. It's called "Painting Divine" and includes the black laugh of surrealism, and the pile-strewn sobs of suprematism, and lots of boffing. Waldemar [Myers's dog] hates it. . . .

But Myers's achievement is not to be written off. He brought the poets together in his gallery, his theater, and again in *The Poets of the New York School*, an anthology he edited in 1969. Besides his passion for collaboration and his delight in the spirit of play, he never stopped believing in the artists and poets whose cause he made his own. "John came out of the Paris occupation of New York the way Motherwell did," Barbara Guest said. "In the end, they deserted him, I think—his painters left him, his poets laughed at him. But he was an essential figure of our time, absolutely essential to our cultural inheritance." "He was a marvelous, intelligent, sensitive, nutty, sad man, and there was something in him which could never really put out that special flame of his," Rivers said.

Myers took risks. He was on a perpetual crusade for the avant-garde, yet in exhibiting figurative painters such as Rivers, Blaine, Freilicher, and Porter, he risked being branded an apostate. "Whether the Tibor de Nagy Gallery in those years represented a continuation of the American avant-garde or a recoil from it was often a subject of lively debate," Hilton Kramer recalls. "In that period, when Abstract Expressionism dominated the contemporary American art world, exhibiting figurative painting of any sort could be taken as a sign of defection from the movement that was just beginning to win acclaim for American art on the international scene, and the Tibor de Nagy Gallery exhibited a lot of figurative painting."

The poets instinctively resisted Myers's "New York School" label. It was a misnomer on several counts. If schools are "static and classical" while movements are "dynamic and romantic," the poets surely constituted a movement. That is a semantic problem. More important, the relation of the poets to New York City was not exactly unambiguous. Ashbery, who grew up on a farm near Rochester, New York, left New York City for Paris in 1955 and lived there for most of the next ten years, which happened to be the glory years of the New York School. Schuyler, also from western New York but nearer Buffalo, spent the better part of a decade escaping the city to live with Fairfield Porter's family in Southampton and in Maine; Anne Porter, the painter's widow, quipped that Schuyler came to lunch one day and stayed for eleven years. Many of Schuyler's poems have a pastoral Long Island setting. Koch, a Cincinnati native, flourished in New York, earning a doctorate at Columbia and becoming an acclaimed teacher there. But among his most fruitful years as a poet were the fellowship years that he and his wife spent in Paris and Florence in the 1950s. The setting of his poems, such as "The Circus" and "The Railway

Stationery," is an America that doesn't exist except in Koch's vivid imagination. Neither for him nor for Ashbery or Schuyler was the city a dominant theme or a recurrent setting. Only O'Hara among them celebrated self and metropolis in the manner of Walt Whitman. True, O'Hara's poems are so full of Manhattan, the horns honking, the heels clicking—and his friendship was so central to the group—that perhaps his example is sufficient to justify the New York part of the "New York School" label. In his poetry one feels the romance of cheap digs in Greenwich Village, chinos and sneakers, a constant flow of adrenaline, taxis, drinks, an opening at the Museum of Modern Art, a party at a painter's loft, poems written on the run between the San Remo bar and the New York City Ballet. In the perennial literary debate pitting the virtues of town against those of country, O'Hara came down hard for the former. "One need never leave the confines of New York to get all the greenery he wishes," he wrote in "Meditations in an Emergency," his best prose poem. "I can't even enjoy a blade of grass unless I know there's a subway handy, or a record store or some other sign that people do not totally *regret* life." This sentence was engraved on a railing of Battery Park in Manhattan in 1989.

If O'Hara loved Gotham and saw its romantic possibilities in and for art, Ashbery has always had a particular animus against the "New York School" label. New York, for him, was just a convenient place to be, or not to be. The "New York School" term "designates a place, whereas New York is really an anti-place, an abstract climate, and I am not prepared to take up the cudgels to defend such a place especially when I would much rather be living in San Francisco," Ashbery said in 1968. He made the same point in conversation with me nine years later, though this time the comparison with San Francisco ("where everybody is congratulating themselves on what a wonderful place they're in") worked out to the advantage of New York. "It was the value of the metropolis that once one was there one didn't have to think about where one was," Ashbery said. "One could think of oneself as living in 'the world,' whereas in Key West, let's say, one is all too aware of being in Key West." To an Australian interviewer, Ashbery conceded that he, Koch, O'Hara, and Schuyler had important things in common, notably the "experimental approach," but maintained that the New York School "didn't really come into existence until after the fact"; he was living in Paris when Myers came up with the label in an article in a California magazine named *Nomad* in 1961.

Paradoxically, one of the ways the New York School of poets was avant-garde was in resisting the "movement" mentality with its inevitable solemnity and penny-ante philosophizing. In 1968, an article about Ashbery, Koch, and O'Hara appeared in the *New York Times Book Review* with the effect, Ashbery said, that "a lady wrote Kenneth Koch asking for the address of the New York School of Poets because she wanted to enroll in it." A second effect was that Ashbery was asked to speak on a panel as a representative of the New York School. He spent most of his speech explaining his objections to the term. As he saw it, New York had little to do with it. His narrative was simplicity itself. It was the story of three pals, Koch and O'Hara and himself, who met at Harvard and wrote poetry, and each differed from the others but all were united in feeling that "modern French poetry, modern music, and modern painting" seemed "much more congenial to us than the American and English poetry we knew." Later they came to New York, an antiplace, a convenient crossroads, accessible to concerts and galleries, and there they met other poets such as James Schuyler, Barbara Guest, and Kenward Elmslie, and though they were all very different from one another, they were called the New York School because they were friends. "We also got to know some artists and a few of us began to write about art in *Art News*, because poets are always broke and the editor

[Thomas B. Hess] is a nice man who happens to like poets." In his *Paris Review* interview, Ashbery restated this general position: "We were a bunch of poets who happened to know each other; we would get together and read our poems to each other and sometimes we would write collaborations." These activities may well constitute sufficient grounds for considering them a movement even if, as Ashbery also said, they never planned to "take over the literary world."

Once the "New York School" entered the lexicon, there was no stopping anyone from formulating a rationale for the term. The great dance critic Edwin Denby, an underrated poet whose marvelous metropolitan sonnets O'Hara championed, considered the term to be a sophisticated double joke. He understood that the painters who drank at the Cedar bar had been dubbed the New York School in opposition to the School of Paris, which had itself earned its name as a modern successor to the earlier schools of Florence and Venice. As Denby saw it, the "New York School of poetry" was the poets' homage to the "people who had de-provincialized American painting" and who were incidentally rubbing shoulders with them at the Cedar. "It wasn't a question of New York subject matter," Denby said. "But just as Paris broke through in opposition to, say, the School of Florence, New York was where it was happening and it was these people living in New York who said 'That's what we want to do.' "

In the end, the New York School of poetry has less to do with the city than with a state of mind to which the poet would like to travel. "The Instruction Manual," the most admired poem in Ashbery's first book, *Some Trees,* tells of this state of mind. The poem records a daydream about escaping from a boring office in New York City, where the task of writing a manual "on the uses of a new metal" faces the dreamer, a professional writer, who succeeds in willing himself—temporarily—to sunny Guadalajara. Guadalajara—"City I most wanted to see, and most did not see, in

Mexico"—is described with a kind of naïve delight. The dreamer beholds a storybook spectacle whose charms are all on the surface. It is as if he has entered a painting, a place where he can observe, himself unobserved, housed defined by their colors and people by their habitual actions:

> There is the rich quarter, with its houses of pink and white,
>   and its crumbling, leafy terraces.
> There is the poorer quarter, its homes a deep blue.
> There is the market, where men are selling hats and
>   swatting flies
> And there is the public library, painted several shades of
>   pale green and beige.
> Look! There is the square we just came from, with the
>   promenaders.
> There are fewer of them, now that the heat of the day has
>   increased,
> But the young boy and girl still lurk in the shadows of the
>   bandstand.
> And there is the home of the little old lady—
> She is still sitting in the patio, fanning herself.
> How limited, but how complete withal, has been our
>   experience of Guadalajara!

The poem is not really about Guadalajara at all. It is rather a parable of the imagination with its power to fulfill desire and supply any lack. The imagination provides a vehicle of escape into a Guadalajara better than the real thing if only because the mental traveler is spared the inconveniences of packing bags, booking rooms, exchanging currency, and suffering from indigestion. But the vision also has a tragic propensity for vanishing. "What else is there to do but stay, and that we cannot do," Ashbery writes in a modern restatement of the pathos at the end of the departed vision in Keats's "Ode to a Nightingale" ("Adieu! The fancy cannot cheat so well / As she is famed to do, deceiving elf"). Elsewhere, in his poem "A Last World," Ashbery identifies death as "a new office building filled with modern furniture." If the office building is a metonymy for New York City and the viewless wings of poetry afford the means to escape and liberation, one can see how uncomfortable with the concept of a New York School Ashbery would be. For Ashbery, perhaps even more than his fellows, is at heart a Romantic poet, who conceives of the Imagination as a realm apart from experience, or reality, or time, to which it lends the redemptive enchantment that we seek in art and that may come closer to fulfilling the promise of happiness than any other form of human activity.

(II)

James Schuyler viewed John Ashbery as the last word on matters of artistic taste. Ashbery "can sort of make taste a matter of ethics," Schuyler said. The terms of the compliment hint at something fundamental not only about Ashbery but about the whole circle of friends. The poets of the New York School were aesthetes, not moralists, but they pressed their taste in modern poetry, painting, and music with the force of ethical injunctions. As Frank O'Hara wryly observed in a letter to Larry Rivers, "In our own discursive way we are getting to be the moralists of our time, since we are always trying to tell people how to act." Though their work was long on irony and short on rhetoric, and didacticism was the last thing that could be imputed to them, they were dead serious about their poems, which they well understood to

be incompatible with the orthodox verse of the 1950s. Determined to mount an avant-garde assault on the proprieties of literary America, they conceived themselves as outsiders and
consciously looked to foreign climes for alternative models to try
on for size. Already as a Harvard undergraduate, O'Hara had
raved about Samuel Beckett, Jean Rhys, Flann O'Brien, Ronald
Firbank, and other writers who were little known in the late
1940s. O'Hara and friends set store by their taste, which they
raised to a major imperative. Taste meant sensibility, and sensibility meant freedom from the dogmas of the day. An anecdote
in Schuyler's "The Morning of the Poem" illustrates:

> When I first knew John Ashbery he slipped me
> One of his trick test questions (we were looking at a window
> full of knitted ribbon dresses): "I don't think
> James Joyce is any good: do you?" Think, what did I think! I
> didn't know you were *allowed* not to like James
> Joyce. The book I suppose is a masterpiece: freedom of
> choice is better. Thank you, "Little J. A. in a
> Prospect of Flowers."

The New York School's emphasis on taste was part of a
larger aesthetic strategy resting on three major precepts of avant-
garde practice as Fairfield Porter formulated them in 1959. "Art
does not stand for something outside itself," Porter wrote, summarizing one lesson he derived from the nonobjective painting
of the time. A second lesson concerned the "organic use of accident" in works of art: "When an artist pays the closest possible
attention to the work as it goes along, it does not escape his
attention that the accident may have a place." A third lesson was
to be "playful about work," as if the composition of a painting
resembled in its processes those of a game.

Poetry, too, was autonomous. A poem had its own organic

life that the poet discovered rather than imposed. The element of chance and the element of play could be determining factors. After all, it was T. S. Eliot himself who proved, in *The Waste Land*, that a great poem can be organized in the manner of a crossword puzzle in which literary quotations and fragments serve as the clues. If the poets of the New York School were inclined to screen out the political aspects of our common reality, they could argue that they did so for the sake of something deeper, truer, more beautiful and more urgent—"the real reality beyond truer imaginings," as Ashbery put it in a diabolically clever double paradox. It was not the business of art to instruct but to provide a species of redemptive enchantment. The dialect of the tribe was meant to be not purified but perpetuated, warts and all, without apology or attack. Poetry was the music of Orphic praise or it was nothing. The aim was not to upbraid the reader but to communicate aesthetic experiences that stand in relation to poetry as the phrase "the pursuit of happiness" stands in relation to the Declaration of Independence.

More and more it seems to me that this Jeffersonian phrase is what we think about when we think about the American dream. Ashbery, Koch, O'Hara, and Schuyler were of that postwar generation of young men that regarded the pursuit of happiness as their inalienable right. The Allied triumph in World War II had created a state of intellectual euphoria, short-lived but intense. With the defeat of the Nazis came the loosely held belief that civilization was perfectible and that America was poised to lead the way. After all, we had won the war, defeated fascism, endured and survived the Great Depression. Now peace and prosperity were here. There was nothing we couldn't do. "New York City had never been so attractive," Anatole Broyard wrote in his memoir of postwar New York, *Kafka Was the Rage*. "The postwar years were like a great smile in its sullen history. The Village was as close in 1946 as it would ever come to Paris in the twenties. Rents were cheap, restaurants were cheap, and it seemed to me that happiness itself might be cheaply had. The streets and bars were full of writers and painters and the kind of young men and women who liked to be around them. In Washington Square would-be novelists and poets tossed a football near the fountain and girls just out of Ivy League colleges looked at the landscape with art history in their eyes. People on the benches held books in their hands."

The adventures of art and education were a reward for having fought the good war. Yet a current of foreboding and dread disturbed this brave optimism. For the first time people had to reckon with the human race's ability to wipe itself out—and with the knowledge of the horrors perpetrated by supposedly civilized people during the war. The populace had to make sense of an incongruous montage of images: pictures of skeletons in concentration camps, cities laid to waste, churches bombed, the mushroom cloud following the explosion of an atomic bomb. And now the era of good feelings between wartime allies had come to an abrupt end. Winston Churchill decried the "iron curtain" that had fallen across Eastern Europe, and a new condition of perpetual belligerency set in as a seemingly irreversible state of affairs that did last forty years. Among the educated classes, Freudian psychoanalysis achieved a sudden popularity that gave rise to the suspicion that neurosis was the universal human condition. W. H. Auden dubbed the era "the age of anxiety." "Along with so much that weighs on our minds there is perhaps even more that grates on our nerves," Louis Kronenberger commented. "Has there ever been an age so rife with neurotic sensibility, with that state of near shudders, or near hysteria, or near nausea, much of it induced by trifles, which used to belong to people who were at once ill-adjusted and overcivilized? Has there ever before been such an assortment of people who have found such an assortment of things to set their teeth on edge?"

The work of the New York poets was haunted by Freudian daydreams and nightmares; Ashbery wrote a poem entitled "Civilization and Its Discontents," Koch weighed in with "The Interpretation of Dreams," and both tried their hand at "The Problem of Anxiety." The specter of nuclear Armageddon hung over their lives, "like the gigantic specter of a cat towering over tiny mice / About to adjourn the town meeting due to the shadow," to use a simile from an Ashbery poem entitled "The Pursuit of Happiness." But their way of dealing with the anxiety of the age was to invest their energy fully in the avant-garde projects of experimentation, collaboration, and artistic liberty applied to artistic ends. They were strict with themselves. They felt that the value of a poem rested not in the nobility of the sentiment behind it but in the pleasure it gave to the reader. Agreeing with Oscar Wilde that "All bad poetry springs from genuine feeling," they guarded vigilantly against sentimentality in their work. They took it to be a self-evident truth that, as Koch observed of O'Hara, "the silliest idea actually in his head was better than the most profound idea actually in somebody else's head." Poetry did not have to be limited by the life experience of the poet; it could be generated linguistically, conjured up via innovative methods of composition. Poetry was not life, but it did suggest—and embody—an aesthetic form of life, liberty, and the pursuit of happiness. And this pursuit was chronicled, explored, memorialized, and enacted in their poems.

Happiness, wrote O'Hara when his friends Jane Freilicher and Joe Hazan were married in 1957, is "the least and best of human attainments." Not that it was guaranteed, just that one was free to pursue it like "a promise / and if it isn't kept that doesn't matter," as Schuyler put it with much pathos in his poem "December." The irony the poets favored was a saving grace under pressure. Ashbery, speaking to himself across pronominal borders, referred to "your fragile dream of happiness," knowing that the fragility of the dream is what renders the pursuit so poignant. "And surely we shall not continue to be unhappy," wrote O'Hara, arguing with himself at the close of his poem "Adieu to Norman, Bon Jour to Joan and Jean-Paul":

> we shall be happy
> but we shall continue to be ourselves everything continues
>   to be possible
> René Char, Pierre Reverdy, Samuel Beckett it is possible
>   isn't it
> I love Reverdy for saying yes, though I don't believe it

When I say that happiness is a central preoccupation in the work of these poets, and that by temperament and inclination they favored the joyful mood of Milton's "L'Allegro" rather than the dour spirit of his "Il Penseroso," I must make it clear that this was no superficial pursuit. It was a daring thing to insist on the happiness of the autonomous individual in the teeth of all that would militate against it in a decade notable for kitsch, consumerism, and the herd mentality. It was equally daring to insist on the primacy of the imagination in its mission to press back against a view of reality that would ground itself in the worship of material wealth.

In their treatment of the themes of happiness, pleasure, and joy, the last conceived as a state of creative inspiration, the New York School was another new manifestation of the Romanticism that had raged onto the scene in the early 1800s, was checked by various reactions, but always seemed to spring back in some wholly unanticipated form. It was in the high Romanticism of the first decades of the nineteenth century that human happiness emerges as the preeminent goal of the individual, and that pleasure, bliss, joy, and delight are depicted as supreme aesthetic goods. Wordsworth insisted that pleasure was the animating principle of literature. "The Poet writes under one restriction only, namely, the necessity of giving immediate pleasure," he wrote in his preface to the *Lyrical Ballads* (1800). And as pleasure is to the realm of sensations, so is joy to the life of the spirit. Joy, we understand from Coleridge's "Dejection Ode," is the enabling condition of the human imagination. It transforms loneliness into the "bliss of solitude" in Wordsworth's "I Wandered Lonely as a Cloud"; it is the "deep delight" that would empower Coleridge to build a pleasure-dome in air in "Kubla Khan." Joy is to be understood less as an end in itself than as the means by which the poet may escape the vale of tears and enter an imaginative realm where love—"More happy love! More happy, happy love!"—is "Forever warm and still to be enjoyed, / Forever panting, and forever young." At the heart of Keats's mighty odes, not only the "Ode on a Grecian Urn," from which I have been quoting, but the "Nightingale" and "Melancholy" odes as well, is this vision of happiness. It is, however, a happiness that is precarious—a moment, and it's gone. The vision cannot last, and even when in its throes the poet can never quite overcome his consciousness of its imminent loss. No doubt it is this sense of precariousness that explains why the Romantic poets so rarely contemplate joy without facing its opposite. Thus Keats finds melancholy in "the very temples of delight." It is precisely in his "Ode on Melancholy" that he summons up "Joy, whose hand is ever at his lips, / Bidding adieu; and aching Pleasure nigh, / Turning to poison where the bee mouth sips."

For the New York poets, too, joy was synonymous with the imagination, and the pursuit of happiness indistinguishable from the relentless search for what Wallace Stevens called a "supreme fiction"—something constructed or imagined to take the place of an absent deity. As aesthetes, the New York poets expected as much from art as intellectuals had previously expected from politics and religion. Nietzsche's view that Art was needed "in order that we may not perish from Truth" was paraphrased by Ashbery introducing Koch at a poetry reading in New York City in the late 1960s. Escapism, Ashbery said, "is a very pejorative word, but I believe it is wrongly understood. When we escape life into literature, we are actually substituting something real for something unreal. It is what we think of as literature that is clean, definite, solid and meaningful. Through the years there has been a confusion, nurtured by literature, that life is what is outside and that what is inside is fantasy, so that the two terms have actually gotten substituted for each other. Kenneth Koch has redressed the balance. As you listen to him I think you will begin to realize that you are escaping to what you should never have been allowed to escape from." On another occasion, Ashbery made the same point more pithily. "I am aware of the pejorative associations of the word 'escapist,' " he said, "but I insist that we need all the escapism we can get and even that isn't going to be enough."

The New York poets did not set out simply to accentuate the positive and eliminate the negative. As good as Schuyler is at capturing a moment of warmth and comfort, or O'Hara one of buoyancy and glee, or Koch one of orgasmic delight, or Ashbery one of spiritual exaltation, there is an air of profound sadness in Schuyler, of melancholy in O'Hara, of incurable nostalgia in Koch, and of wry resignation in Ashbery. What they were seeking was not an artificial paradise but a new mode of writing to chart out the progression of their hearts, and the movement of their minds, without the sentimentality that customarily imperils such efforts. The project was not made easier by the poets' personal circumstances, which could be difficult in the extreme.

Schuyler, who was prone to psychotic fits, spent much of his adult life in and out of psychiatric institutions. His "Payne Whitney Poems" are quietly harrowing:

Wigging in, wigging out:
when I stop to think

the wires in my head
cross: kaboom. How
many trips
by ambulance (five,
count them five),
claustrated, pill addiction,
in and out of mental
hospitals,
the suicidalness (once
I almost made it)
but—I go on?
Tell you all of it?
I can't. When I think
of that, that at
fifty-one I,
Jim the Jerk, am
still alive and breathing
deeply, that I think
is a miracle.

It is a terrific anomaly that a man so tormented by demons would be, in his best poems, so skillful at conveying what happiness feels like.

Although none of the other three poets suffered from a condition as alarming as Schuyler's, all three were risk takers, betting everything on their art and willing to endure ridicule and neglect. O'Hara lived his life with a kind of lyric desperation. "I often wish I had the strength to commit suicide, but on the other hand, if I had, I probably wouldn't feel the need," he wrote in his journal while in college. "God! Can't you let us win once in a while?" Morbidly affected by the deaths of other artists, O'Hara was convinced that he, too, would die young. Once, in a game of Twenty Questions, somebody asked him what he was most afraid of. "Living beyond forty," he answered, and failed to survive his fortieth year.

Ashbery underwent a different trial. Going to Paris to find his way in poetry, he deliberately isolated himself from friends, family, home, and the pleasures of the American vernacular for ten years; he abandoned New York City at the very moment when the avant-garde reigned triumphant in art. Lacking any institutional backing or anything resembling a regular job until he lucked into the position of art critic for the *International Herald Tribune*, Ashbery understood that his whole career was a spectacular gamble. "Recklessness is what makes experimental art beautiful," he reasoned, "just as religions are beautiful because of the strong possibility that they are founded on nothing. We would all believe in God if we knew He existed, but would this be much fun?"

As for Koch, he took a terrible risk in making his poems unabashedly funny; the critical and academic prejudice against humor in poetry runs deep. Koch could have been speaking for all the friends when he objected to a conception of seriousness that left it indistinguishable from dire solemnity. "I grew up in a time when T. S. Eliot was, as Delmore Schwartz said, the literary dictator of the West, and not only were you supposed to be serious, you were supposed to be a little depressed," Koch remarked. "You could read through the quarterlies—the *Kenyon Review*, the *Partisan Review*, the *Sewanee Review*—all the big journals of those days, and nobody was seeing anything at the end of that tunnel. They were not even seeing the tunnel. I remember being exhilarated when I read Nietzsche. He said you should be very careful how long you look into the abyss because the abyss is also looking into you. I was very grateful to William Carlos Williams because he seemed happy so much of the time. And to the French poet Saint-John Perse, because he looked at the waves rolling in over the ocean and he saw blue enchantresses, kings, mountains, decades—it was wonderful. So many poets have the courage to look into the abyss, but Perse had the courage to look into happiness."

(III)

Writing about this quartet of poets, one is struck by how often a useful generalization fits three of the four principals, with O'Hara the one constant in all.

Three of the four poets served in the armed forces during World War II, Koch in the army, O'Hara and Schuyler in the navy. The experience of war instilled in each a reverence for peace and the civilian life. For O'Hara, who joined the naval reserve in June 1944, the three months he spent in boot camp were "probably the most depressing months of my life," he wrote in his application to Harvard after the war had ended. Assigned to Fleet Sonar School in Key West, he gradually adjusted to navy routine, and when he went overseas in February 1945, his duties with the Third Fleet—which included transporting the signers of the peace treaty to the U.S.S. *Missouri*—awakened in him "a keen feeling about the peace." But disillusionment was immediate. "Watching the botching of military governments, the crippling of the U.N., the ineffectual expediency of our national policies, and the mis-handling of the atomic bomb, has been a bitter experience." O'Hara put some of that bitterness in his breakthrough poem, "Memorial Day 1950," in which the poet finds his paternity in the modern artist who appropriates the engines of destruction for his art:

Picasso made me tough and quick, and the world;
just as in a minute plane trees are knocked down
outside my window by a crew of creators.
Once he got his axe going everyone was upset
enough to fight for the last ditch and heap
of rubbish.

Like O'Hara, Schuyler went to Sonar School in Key West, where he learned to be, in naval slang, a "ping jockey." He was assigned to convoy duty on a destroyer in the North Atlantic, and when he was discharged he got a job with the Voice of America. "I did stand by in the studio when they broadcast the first atom bomb test after the war, and a lot of people were afraid it would set off a chain reaction that would destroy the world," Schuyler told an interviewer. "I was to take this record, if the world wasn't destroyed, and run with it down to the studio." How did this make him feel? "Well," Schuyler said, "my heart was in my mouth." The paradigmatic title in the Schuyler oeuvre is "Hymn to Life," which is also a hymn to peace and its pleasures, including the tranquil pleasures of observation and meditation:

> All jays are one to me. But not the sun which seems at
> Each rising new, as though in the night it enacted death and
>   rebirth,
> As flowers seem to. The roses this June will be different
>   roses
> Even though you cut an armful and come in saying, "Here
>   are the roses,"
> As though the same blooms had come back, white freaked
>   with red
> And heavily scented.

Koch did his basic training in Camp Hood, Texas. He saw combat in the Philippines and would have fought at Okinawa, the bloodiest battle of the Pacific war, if a providential case of jaundice hadn't sidelined him in Guam. Asked about his army experiences, Koch remarked that he had "never figured out how to use a Browning Automatic Rifle," and that this had "probably saved my life," since the average life of a Browning Automatic Rifleman was "four minutes and twenty seconds." Though spared from Okinawa, where the casualty rate approached 100 percent, Private Koch came through a trauma of his own. On a jungle march in the Philippines during typhoon season, the nineteen-year-old poet stumbled and fell; helped to his feet, he could not find his eyeglasses. The loss left him virtually blind. Koch's account of the episode has his characteristic comic edge. "We were supposed to take a hill, Catmont Hill, where the Japanese had just wiped out a battalion of U.S. soldiers," Koch recalled. "Luckily the Japanese had left. Otherwise I wouldn't be here. I had my bayonet fixed. I was very lazy and had the rifle slung over my shoulder. My bayonet hit a hornet's nest, and a stream of hornets went after me. I screamed and fell down. My glasses flew off, I knew not where, in the dense jungle foliage. We were thirty feet in the air, walking on the tops of trees. The only person behind me in the company was a hillbilly corporal from Oklahoma. 'C'mon Cock'—they all pronounced my name *Cock*—'get your fuckin' ass outta here.' 'But my glasses . . .' 'I don't care about your mother-fuckin' glasses. Get up or you're dead.' He was right." Later Koch reported to the commander of the company, "the only one in the whole battalion who called me *Coke* instead of *Cock*," and explained that he couldn't see without his glasses. Might his next combat assignment be deferred until a replacement pair could be obtained? "Sorry, we're under strength," the commander of F Company replied. "Dismissed." "But—" "Dismissed!" "So I fought the whole campaign without being able to see," Koch mused. "I don't know what he thought I'd accomplish. Maybe he thought I'd write another *Iliad.*"

In his Harvard application, Koch was asked to write about his service experiences. He complained that "the army had done a masterful job of misclassification" in assigning him as a rifle-man in the infantry. The unpleasantness and the constant sense of danger were, however, "ameliorated by the *esprit de corps* of the company." He felt "unbelievable relief" at the end of the campaign. Where he was instructed to list his chief interests, Koch wrote "peace" right after "creative writing (poetry and prose)" and just before "philosophy" and "psychiatry" in his Harvard application. Certainly Koch's imagination is one that is wholly oriented toward the shield of Achilles and away from the field of human conflict. At the height of the Vietnam War, Koch wrote not an antiwar poem but "The Pleasures of Peace," the central poem of his career and a title that could embrace all of his work before and since. In the course of the poem, one of its putative readers—Koch was an avatar of postmodernism before there was such a thing—interprets the work as satire, and is roundly rebuffed:

> "You don't get it," I said. "I like all this. I called this poem *Pleasures of Peace* because I'm not sure they will be lasting."

That sums it up. Koch likes his subjects, his characters, and the things he puts into poetry: blouses and earrings, locks ("the lock of the life raft when I was taking a bath instead of drowning"), lunch ("Let us give lunch to the lunch— / But how shall we do it?"), and the forty-eight contiguous states: all are pleasures to be approved, not criticized or castigated. The irony is there to keep sentimentality at bay, not to inject a barb or insinuate a critique. Koch's element is that of comedy, not satire; his work constantly illustrates the difference between these modes.

Three of the four poets were homosexual; Koch was not, and was even mocked by the others for his "homosexual dread," though the cheerfully bisexual Larry Rivers ("Frank [O'Hara] one night and, if I could manage it, a woman the next. I was so convinced of being heterosexual I could be homosexual") recalls that Koch talked and acted as gay as the rest. A critic could make the plausible claim that what I have been calling the pursuit of happiness is code for the celebration of a gay sensibility—an assertion of otherness, a deviation from accepted norms. Ashbery has always maintained a reticence about his sexual preference (though one of his poems does begin "Once I let a guy blow me"), but O'Hara wrote many frankly homosexual love poems, and Schuyler—especially from the 1970s on—gives voice to what he calls "East Fifties queen / taste."

Homosexuality was not a subject that O'Hara shied from. A poem he wrote in 1954 finds pleasure in "tallying up the merits of each / of the latrines" where a gay liaison may take place:

> 14th Street is drunken and credulous,
> 53rd tries to tremble but is too at rest. The good
>
> love a park and the inept a railway station,
> and there are the divine ones who drag themselves up
>
> and down the lengthening shadow of an Abyssian head
> in the dust, trailing their long elegant heels of hot air
>
> crying to confuse the brave "It's a summer day,
> and I want to be wanted more than anything else in the
>   world."

The poem is entitled "Homosexuality"—its original title was "The Homosexuals"—and perhaps the most striking thing about it is its opening: "So we're taking off our masks, are we, and keeping / our mouths shut?" Though the poet may still "pull the shadows around me like a puff," he recommends self-admiration "with complete candor." This was, in 1954, a remarkably prescient declaration of gay pride, an unmasking that heralded others to come in which the participants would not be content to keep their mouths shut.

It is possible to discern in O'Hara's *Collected Poems* a movement "from does she love me to do I love him," as he puts it in "Ode to Michael Goldberg('s Birth and Other Births)." Generally, O'Hara opted for the gender-free pronoun "you" in his love poems to Larry Rivers ("To the Harbormaster") and the dancer Vincent Warren ("Having a Coke with You"), yet he sprinkles hints that the beloved is a male ("in your orange shirt you look like a better happier St. Sebastian," he writes to Warren). Schuyler is even less inhibited—he came into his own as a poet in the 1970s, after Stonewall and Gay Liberation had begun to have their transforming effect on public consciousness. The "you" in this passage is explicitly male:

> It's
> not that I
> think of you all
> the time. But
> I think of you
> a lot. The air
> is still. Per-
> haps tomorrow
> you'll scud
> before a breeze.
> You're physical
> and need that
> breeze. Breeze,
> blow for one
> I love, stretch

his muscles as
he needs and wants.

Three of the four poets of the New York School were professional art critics, and the fourth (Koch) wrote plays partly for the
pleasure of collaborating with the painters who did the sets.
O'Hara was the groundbreaker. He got a job at the front desk at
the Museum of Modern Art—in order, he explained, to be able to
see Alfred Barr's monumental Matisse show as often as he liked—
and wound up becoming a curator of exhibitions. O'Hara made
painting the central focus of his professional life; neither Ashbery nor Schuyler did, but both wrote with authority about contemporary art. Ashbery made his living as an art critic for the
better part of twenty-five years; his pieces in the *International
Herald Tribune*, *New York*, and *Newsweek* would fill several tomes
beyond *Reported Sightings*, the collection of his art criticism that
he published in 1989. Schuyler worked at the Museum of Modern
Art, albeit briefly, and wrote on painting for *Art News*, as did
O'Hara, Barbara Guest, and Ashbery, which came about not just
because the editor was a "nice man who happens to like poets,"
but because *Art News* was the house organ of Abstract Expressionism and Tom Hess's taste and sensibility matched that of the
poets—they were all in awe of de Kooning.

The poets found their own aesthetic notions articulated in
the paintings they admired, and this makes their art criticism
doubly significant. James Schuyler understood his own predilec-
tions when he was confronted with Jane Freilicher's paintings, in
which a still life may be combined with an interior and a landscape. Like Freilicher, Schuyler was determined to let order
emerge from a faithful rendering of a scene rather than from an
exercise of the artist's will. He and she had in common the ability
to be satisfied, aesthetically, with one view from one window at
different times of day, in changing light. For Ashbery, too, Frei-

licher was a major inspiration. Among the most beautiful passages in *Reported Sightings* is the paragraph Ashbery devotes to Freilicher's *The Painter's Table*, a reproduction of which adorns the book's cover. (The painting hangs in Ashbery's living room.) It is a still life in which cans and tubes of paint and brushes in jars of water substitute for flowers in vases or fruits in bowls. The painting, Ashbery writes, "is a congeries of conflicting pictorial grammars"—a "mellow realism" punctuated by various departures from realism. The result is "a little anthology of ways of seeing, feeling and painting" that puts Ashbery in mind of his own "fondness for a polyphony of clashing styles, from highbred to demotic, in a given poem." Ashbery seems again to be adverting to his own strategies when he writes appreciatively of R. B. Kitaj's allusive paintings, which are "exemplary" because they are full of contradictory aims and are "beautiful because exemplary." O'Hara, on the other hand, saw an image of himself in Action Painting as practiced by Jackson Pollock and Franz Kline. O'Hara's panegyric to Pollock's *The Deep* (1953)—"an abyss of glamour encroached upon by a flood of innocence"—sounds rather like a self-description. Pollock, O'Hara wrote in accents as heroic as he could make them, "was totally conscious of risk, defeat, and triumph. He lived the first, defied the second, and achieved the last."

Three of the four poets had the benefit of a Harvard education. Schuyler, the odd man out, remembered thinking of the others as "the Harvard wits." Koch, O'Hara, and Ashbery all were undergraduates in 1947 when Secretary of State George Marshall came to Harvard Yard and used his commencement address to unveil the European Recovery Program that would bear his name. It was another landmark piece of legislation, the G.I. Bill, that had enabled O'Hara and Koch to go to college there. It was a wonderful time to be at Harvard. Thanks to the G.I. Bill—which may have been as vital an initiative on the domestic front as the

Marshall Plan was in foreign policy—elite institutions like Harvard were, it seemed, democratized overnight as urban Jews (like Koch), blue-collar Irish Catholics (like O'Hara), and working-class veterans entered the colleges with the confidence of conquering heroes.

Harvard had institutionalized anti-Semitism with a quota system in force since the early 1920s. Now, as the evidence of mass murder mounted at the Nuremberg Trials, anti-Semitism stood repudiated. In 1947, Laura Hobson's popular novel *Gentlemen's Agreement* made a stirring movie, with Gregory Peck as a magazine writer who impersonates a Jew for six months to unmask the anti-Semitic code of privilege and prejudice. Other films, notably *The Best Years of Our Lives* (1946), dramatized the plight of veterans returning to civilian life. Hollywood and Harvard were in this instance in step. The conception of Harvard as a gentlemen's club with restricted access gave way rapidly to a model of the university as an intellectual center that doubled as a site for advanced social change. Jewish students were admitted in record numbers; by 1948, one quarter of Harvard's total enrollment was Jewish. And one quarter of the student body came from working-class households with incomes below $5,000.

The veterans transformed Harvard. In a class on Chaucer, a young prep-school graduate might find himself sitting next to a twenty-five-year-old who had been an army major in Italy. Robert Bly, who had served in the navy, entered in 1947. "We were arrogant," Bly says, relishing the memory of making Archibald MacLeish miserable when he came to Harvard to teach. "MacLeish was used to yes men from his years as Librarian of Congress. We veterans treated him like a sergeant." Donald Hall, a Harvard undergraduate from 1947 to 1951, recalls an openness about heterodox ideologies and unconventional behavior when he arrived in Cambridge. But the golden moment was fleeting. Koch (graduating in 1948), Ashbery (1949), and O'Hara (1950) appear to have left just in time. By Hall's senior year, the Korean War had broken out, the House Un-American Activities Committee was in high gear, and Truman's loyalty oaths were the law of the land. "I went into the Harvard of Norman Mailer, and the Harvard I left was John Updike's," Hall says. "Instead of talking about capitalist exploitation or imperialist machinations, people were now talking about original sin."

Harvard in the late 1940s was aswarm with young writers. Besides Koch, Ashbery, and O'Hara, the list of Harvard and Radcliffe students with high literary aspirations included Bly, Harold Brodkey, Robert Creeley, Hall, John Hawkes, Alison Lurie, and Adrienne Rich. Richard Wilbur, Richard Eberhart, and Ruth Stone were among the slightly older poets living in Cambridge. Two highly literary bookstores, the Grolier and the Mandrake, catered to the poets' taste. Violet ("Bunny") Lang, O'Hara's confidante and for a time his muse, was busily setting up the Poets' Theatre to produce plays by her poet friends. A typical program of four one-act plays included Ashbery's masque *Everyman*, with music composed by O'Hara, and O'Hara's *Try! Try!* with Ashbery playing the part of "John" and Bunny Lang herself in the role of "Violet." Daniel Ellsberg, who became famous twenty years later for leaking the Pentagon Papers to the press, reviewed the evening for the *Harvard Crimson*. Ellsberg reported that the playwright Thornton Wilder berated the audience for having had the bad manners to laugh out loud during O'Hara's play; Wilder had, Ellsberg correctly observed, "misjudged" both play and audience—the laughter was the point.

T. S. Eliot, Marianne Moore, William Carlos Williams, and Wallace Stevens were among the eminences who came to Harvard to read their poems when Ashbery, Koch, and O'Hara were students there. In 1946, W. H. Auden delivered the university's Phi Beta Kappa poem, which he had written for the occasion. "Under Which Lyre" concludes with Auden's "Hermetic Decalogue" of advice to the graduates. They were told not to be "on friendly terms / With guys in advertising firms" and were encouraged to "Read *The New Yorker*, trust in God; / And take short views."

The chain of friendships that turned into the New York School began the year Auden read these lines in Harvard Yard. Ashbery, the first to arrive, entered Harvard in 1945, fresh out of Deerfield Academy; he had turned eighteen the summer of Hiroshima and Nagasaki. Koch came a year later, a combat veteran at twenty-one. The two became fast friends upon meeting in the offices of Harvard's literary magazine, the *Advocate*. The intellectually precocious Ashbery, skinny and shy, had gone on national radio as a "quiz kid" the week after Pearl Harbor was bombed; he lived in Dunster House in the same rooms that Norman Mailer had occupied a few years earlier. The tall, bespectacled Koch, an A student who breezed through the rigorous academic requirements, had a talent for improvising blank verse in conversation and wrote his class notes in unrhymed iambic pentameter in Werner Jaeger's course on Greek culture. Each liked the native craziness to be found in the other's poems.

Koch joined the editorial board of the *Advocate* soon after arriving in Cambridge. Three of his works, including his "Poem for my Twentieth Birthday," had appeared in print in the November 1945 issue of *Poetry*, then the nation's most important venue for verse, and this gave the ex-rifleman from the 96th Infantry Division additional clout with his peers. Koch wanted Ashbery as a colleague and was willing to sponsor him at the *Advocate*, but the nomination ran into a snag Koch had not anticipated. At the time, the *Advocate* was short of funds. A donor had been found but had attached the stipulation that Jews, homosexuals, and alcoholics be barred from the editorial board. "I don't know where you'd find such a magazine," Koch recollected. "Maybe at Brigham Young. Everyone on the *Advocate* was either a Jew or a drunkard or a gay. Someone had proposed me for the *Advocate*. I was merely a Jew, the least objectionable of the three things." Koch never realized that Ashbery was homosexual. "I wasn't sure I knew what to look for," he told me. "I was very naïve in those days. Someone could be as queer as, what's the expression, a three-dollar bill, and I wouldn't necessarily have known it." And Ashbery did not flaunt his sexual preference. "John thought that neither I nor any other heterosexual would like him if they knew he was gay." At the *Advocate*, Koch maintained that his friend wasn't homosexual and threatened to quit if he weren't appointed to the board. The gesture worked. Ashbery became a regular contributor to the *Advocate* and was named "class poet" of his graduating class. And his friendship with Koch was cemented. The solidarity with Koch was all the more valuable to Ashbery in that its originating gesture indicated a blithe indifference to conventional taboos surrounding sexual preference. At the same time, the incident reinforced Ashbery's anxiety that his reputation as a poet would be seriously compromised if his homosexuality were a public fact.

Koch described the impact that Ashbery's first poems had on him at Harvard: "To read them was like falling in love with some thrilling young person from Mars." He and Ashbery would pool their enthusiasms. "I just read somebody named Alfred Jarry," Ashbery announced, referring to the notorious author of *Ubu Roi*, a play that opened with an obscenity that shocked the bourgeoisie of Paris in 1896. "Well?" Koch replied expectantly. "I think," Ashbery said, "we should be a little crazier." The words fell on glad ears; Koch was always inspired by examples of literary outrageousness. The companions were also rivals, competing for Harvard's most prestigious poetry prize. Koch was visiting a girlfriend at Smith College when the results of the Garrison poetry competition were announced in 1948. The prize had gone to Koch for his "Entr'acte for a Freak Show," a dramatic monologue to be spoken by a bearded lady. Ashbery wired the news to Northampton, borrowing the first line of one of Stephen Spender's best-known poems. "You won STOP I got honorable mention STOP I think continually of those who are truly great."

The friendship between O'Hara and Ashbery began at the Mandrake Book Shop in the spring of 1949. Ashbery was about to graduate. (Koch had already left for New York the previous June.) The pivotal event was a reception in honor of an exhibition of watercolors by Harvard undergraduate Edward Gorey. Gorey's roommate was there. Ashbery knew who Frank O'Hara was; O'Hara's poems and stories had appeared in the *Advocate*. But he was startled when he overheard "a ridiculous remark such as I liked to make uttered in a ridiculous voice that sounded to me like my own." The voice said: "Let's face it, *Les Sécheresses* is greater than *Tristan*." Elevating a vocal work by Poulenc above Wagner's opera was an intellectual provocation that Ashbery enjoyed. Loaded with irony, it seemed to him to sum up his own aesthetic attitude. "I knew instinctively that Frank didn't really believe that *Les Sécheresses* was greater than *Tristan*, and that he wanted people to understand this, but at the same time he felt it important to make that statement, possibly because he felt that art is already serious enough; there is no point in making it seem even more serious by taking it too seriously." The episode became part of the New York School's group lore. In 1956 O'Hara, spending time in Cambridge, wrote to Schuyler in New York that he had "been having a terribly spiritual morning bathing on Poulenc songs, 2 piano concertos and *Les Sécheresses*." He added: "It *is* greater than *Tristan*, so there!"

Donald Hall has vivid recollections of Koch, Ashbery, and O'Hara as Harvard undergraduates. Koch was "terribly literary, terribly sophisticated, terribly strong-minded and certain," and consistently contemptuous of the younger man. When a poem of Hall's was accepted for publication in the *Advocate*, Koch said that he had been absent from the meeting and that it would not have happened had he been there. He was, Hall summed up, a "primary Harvard type: sober, grim-faced, and eager to denigrate everything else." Hall found it easier to get along with Ashbery. He admired Ashbery's facility and wit, both of which were evident in "The Return of the Screw," a parody of Henry James that Ashbery wrote when he was elected to Signet, the campus literary society. By this time Hall had himself joined the editorial board of the *Advocate*. Just as an issue was closing, the editors noticed a half-page gap in the magazine, room for one last-minute poem. Ashbery said he thought he might have one. Leaving the office, he walked to his rooms at Dunster House—the most geographically distant of the Harvard houses and therefore sometimes called the "Sphinx on the Charles"—and returned thirty minutes later with the requested work, a poem beginning with the phrase "Fortunate Alphonse, the shy homosexual." It was clear that he had written the poem on the spot. Reminded of the incident forty years later, Ashbery quoted the first four lines of the poem from memory. "Admit it, John, you wrote the poem in twenty minutes," Hall exclaimed. Sighing, Ashbery replied, "Yes, I took longer then."

O'Hara, meanwhile, was already possessed of the charisma that made him the natural center of attention in a room. According to Hall, O'Hara and Ted Gorey threw "the best parties" at Harvard. "Frank was the funniest man I ever met, utterly quick-witted and sharp with his sarcasm. Once in his presence I made some sort of joshing reference, comparing him to Oscar Wilde. Being gay was relatively open, even light, in the Harvard of those years. One of Frank's givens was that *everybody* was gay, either in or out of the closet. He answered me with a swoop of emphasis: '*You*'re the type that would sue.'" The witty comeback likened O'Hara's "joshing" accuser to "Bosie," Lord Alfred Douglas, who urged Wilde to sue Douglas's father, the Marquess of Queensberry—disastrous advice that led to Wilde's downfall.

O'Hara's father died while he was at Harvard, and his journals of the period show him in a soul-searching mood. Already he had developed his nervous "loophole for life" as a way of talking himself out of suicide: "I refuse to be a slave; if life were merely a habit I should commit suicide; but even now, more or less desperate, I cannot but think, 'Something wonderful may happen.' It is not optimism, it is a rejection of self-pity (I hope) which leaves a loophole for life." He added, "I merely choose to remain living out of respect for possibility." O'Hara's poetry is well described as the noble "possibility" justifying the pains of existence. The poems he wrote in his senior year at Harvard already contain the note of gently self-lacerating irony that makes his work so distinctive and so unprecedented in American poetry. Entering Harvard as Francis O'Hara, a music major, he graduated as Frank O'Hara, the English major and fearless poet whose exuberant poems transmuted the stuff of self-pity into an exclamation of wonderment. He wrote his "Autobiographia Literaria" in his senior year:

When I was a child
I played by myself in a
corner of the schoolyard
all alone.

I hated dolls and I
hated games, animals were
not friendly and birds
flew away.

If anyone was looking
for me I hid behind a
tree and cried out, "I am
an orphan."

And here I am, the
center of all beauty!
writing these poems!
Imagine!

Koch, the first of the "Harvard wits" to graduate, lit out for New York City in 1948. After living in a rooming house, he soon found more commodious digs in a three-story building on Third Avenue at Sixteenth Street. A painter named Jane Freilicher lived upstairs. She was a tall brunette with oval eyes, very funny and very smart. Koch was crazy about her: "I never enjoyed conversing with anyone so much in my life." Through Freilicher, Koch met other painters, including Nell Blaine and Larry Rivers. All were or had been students of Hans Hofmann. Each would try to absorb the lessons of Abstract Expressionism, as Hofmann propounded them, while remaining committed to the representation of figures and landscapes. Each had tremendous energy and the desire to lead a life in which work and play were as nearly continuous as possible. It was understood that poets and painters formed the natural audience for each other's work and that the audience's role included that of participation. One could lead one's life as if it were a poem, always in motion, in a continual process of revision, and obeying aesthetic principles of composition and structure while eliminating as nearly as possible the model of human consciousness that could be extrapolated from the front pages of the *New York Times, Boston Globe,* and *Wall Street Journal.*

A man of irrepressible high spirits, Koch liked playing practical jokes on his pals. "Kenneth was a cutup, a joker," Nell Blaine said when I visited her at her Riverside Drive apartment in 1994. One day in 1949 Blaine was having lunch with Freilicher on the roof terrace of the building Freilicher and Koch lived in. "Kenneth came up and locked us out," Blaine said. "He put on his monkey head. It was more than a mask; it covered the whole head. But he was charming." Koch sported the rubber ape mask as he leaned out the window of his apartment to greet the passengers on the Third Avenue El outside. He did this only once or twice, he maintains, but the stunt made an indelible impression on his friends.

In 1949, fate in the form of the graduate school admissions office at Harvard lent literary history a hand. Ashbery, who had won departmental honors in his senior year at Harvard with a well-received thesis on W. H. Auden, was nevertheless denied admission to the university's graduate program in English. Luckily for the future New York School, the Columbia English department accepted Ashbery, which gave him an excuse to join Koch in the city. Koch introduced Ashbery to all his new painter friends, and Ashbery had the exhilaration of a rapid immersion in modern art, which was largely ignored in the art history courses Ashbery had taken at Harvard. "I had come down from Cambridge to catch the historic Bonnard show in the spring of 1948, unaware of how it was already affecting a generation of young painters who would be my friends, especially Larry Rivers, who turned from playing jazz to painting at that moment in his life," Ashbery wrote. "And soon there would be equally breathtaking shows of Munch, Soutine, Vuillard and Matisse, in each of whom—regardless of the differences that separate them—one finds a visceral sensual message sharpened by a shrill music or perfume emanating from the paint that seemed to affect my painter friends like catnip." The one thing missing "in our privileged little world (privileged because it was a kind of balcony overlooking the interestingly chaotic events happening in the bigger worlds outside) was the arrival of Frank O'Hara to kind of cobble everything together and tell us what we and they were doing," Ashbery continued. "This happened in 1951, but before that Jane [Freilicher] had gone out to visit him in Ann Arbor [where O'Hara spent a year in graduate school following his Harvard graduation] and painted a memorable portrait of him, in which Abstract Expressionism certainly inspired the wild brushwork rolling around like so many loose cannon, but which never loses sight of the fact that it is a portrait, and an eerily exact one at that."

It was at a cocktail party thrown by Ashbery that O'Hara met Larry Rivers. "I thought he was crazy and he thought I was even crazier," O'Hara noted, explaining their mutual attraction. "I was very shy, which he thought was intelligence; he was garrulous, which I assumed was brilliance—and on such misinterpretation, thank heavens, many a friendship is based." "We shook hands and talked our heads off for two hours," Rivers recalled. "At one point Frank and I went behind some curtains and he said, 'Let's see what a kiss feels like.' It was as if we were experiencing a kiss for the first time." Rivers, who had conducted a passionate affair with Freilicher, for the love of whom he would one day slash his wrists, became O'Hara's lover, collaborator, and confidant. In a memoir O'Hara likened Rivers to "a demented telephone. Nobody knew whether they wanted it in the library, the kitchen, or the toilet, but it was electric." In a more recent memoir Rivers described O'Hara as a "charming madman, a whoosh of air sometimes warm and pleasant, sometimes so gusty you closed your eyes and brushed back the hair it disarranged."

The question that has vexed the New York School for thirty years is what O'Hara would have been like if he had lived. "It's a real question, because he always wrote at the edge of discovery, with enthusiasm," Rivers said. "It was always as if something was happening to him for the first time. He was always a little out of breath and amazed at how beautiful things were. There's a lot of amazement in his poetry." It is because of his capacity for amazement and wonderment that the exclamation point was O'Hara's punctuation mark of choice.

Koch was initially resistant to O'Hara's charms. When Ashbery copied several of O'Hara's poems for Koch, the latter had reservations. He felt that O'Hara's poems weren't lofty enough and were marred by colloquial expressions. But the poems had made enough of an impression on Koch that he packed them along when he went off to Europe for a year. In Vienna he reread O'Hara's poem "Today":

> Oh! Kangaroos, sequins, chocolate sodas!
> You really are beautiful! Pearls,
> harmonicas, jujubes, aspirins! all
> the stuff they've always talked about
>
> still makes a poem a surprise!
> These things are with us every day
> even on beachheads and biers. They
> do have meaning. They're strong as rocks.

"The lights went on," Koch recalled. "Immediately exclamation points, aspirin tablets, harmonicas, kangaroos, and jujubes appeared in my poetry. It was a real conversion experience." O'Hara was amazed when word of Koch's conversion reached him in Ann Arbor. He confided to Jane Freilicher that he had made up a list of "Kenneth Koch words," with *castrated, upset, problems, hostile, anxiety* and *the country* among them. "Alack aday, who has changed Kenneth Koch's mind about my poetry?" he asked Freilicher. "Is it you Tabby? I pinch *your* paws. Anyhow, I was thinking perhaps I shouldn't like him if he didn't because Paul G. [Goodman] said there was no line between the artist and his work, do you think this is true? what is art? what is life? who is Koch? I hear he writes his lyrics on human skin, is this correct? HOW ARE WE GOING TO ARRANGE IT SO WE WON'T HAVE TO BE ALWAYS SEPARATED THIS WAY?" When O'Hara's *Lunch*

Poems appeared in 1964, he dedicated Koch's copy "in memory of the conversion in Vienna."

Freilicher was the poets' muse of adoration. She is the Jane of Schuyler's "Looking Forward to Seeing Jane Real Soon" and "Presenting Jane," of O'Hara's "Chez Jane," "Jane Awake," "Jane Bathing," and "Jane at Twelve." In a home movie that the librettist John Latouche made in 1952, Freilicher was given the power to walk on water—which pretty much sums up the regard in which the poets held her. The Freilicher mystique began with her dry wit. Encountered in the street she might say, "I just stepped out for a breath of fresh fallout," on a day when radioactive fallout had been reported in the New York atmosphere. A visit with the composer Virgil Thomson was like being "locked in the office with the school principal." Robert Motherwell and Helen Frankenthaler had married and were now "the Irene and Vernon Castle of Abstract Expressionism." Freilicher used her irony and wit to keep melancholia at bay, and her letters to Ashbery—they corresponded voluminously when he lived in Paris—are full of mischievous turns of phrase. "Please write again," she implored in one missive, "and help cheer me through these next months of post-show depression until it's time for pre-show depression again." On the occasion of what she called "my summer of the seventeenth injustice," she owned up to feeling that "there is a world-wide grass roots movement against me." She was not above kidding Ashbery, congratulating him on "his recent elevation to the position of Art Buchwald of the art world," when he began writing art criticism for the *International Herald Tribune*. But when the poet was in a funk because of the hostile reception of his book *The Tennis Court Oath* in 1962, Freilicher came through marvelously for him. "I know I am the last person in the world to talk," she wrote, "but I think you are being a silly goose. You know you are a grand poet and in fact I have never heard anybody say a negative thing about your work. Just in the last week I heard

Fairfield, Jimmy and Bill Berkson give your book the highest praises (if that is not the audience you were necessarily aiming at at least it will give you a little insight into one girl's social life). Of course it is caviar for the general and there are very few generals but I'm sure you know how very superior and distinguished your work is and I just wish I were as certain of my own talents as I am of yours, you schnook." Freilicher's ironically self-deprecating style was widely imitated. The painter Al Leslie, complaining that a show of his work had failed to garner a desired review, evoked a Freilicher quip: "At moments like this I like to think of what Jane would have said: 'Luckily there are other things more important than my life.' "

The writer Joe LeSueur, who lived with O'Hara for ten years, remembers thinking that O'Hara, Freilicher, Ashbery, Schuyler, and Koch were "like a high school clique." They constantly used words and phrases "as if italicized," as if theirs were a secret society with a code language available to none but the elect. Freilicher and O'Hara were particularly famous for their repartee; their routine conversation seemed to have been spontaneously scripted. They were, as LeSueur put it, "like the smartest kids in school." Barbara Guest recalls having been, in effect, recruited to the school by Freilicher. "I published a poem in *Partisan Review*—Delmore Schwartz was the poetry editor then—that was startlingly like what the New York poets were doing. I remember Jane saying, 'We were so excited we wanted to know where you lived.' "

It was because of Freilicher that Larry Rivers—at the time a twenty-year-old tenor saxophonist—took up painting in the first place. It was in the summer of 1945 in Old Orchard Beach, Maine. Rivers and Freilicher's first husband, Jack Freilicher, had gone there to play jazz in the evening and poker in the afternoon. But seeing Jane's painting and watching her work changed Rivers utterly. "After a week or two I began thinking that art was an activity on a 'higher level' than jazz," Rivers writes in his memoir

What Did I Do? From his "romance with jazz, blues, drugs, and night," he turned now to the pleasure of painting in daylight. "Music was like sex. I wouldn't want it all the time. Painting was like living, a little lower-keyed than the life I lived, but something I wanted to hang on to." Rivers stoutly maintains that Freilicher "had more integrity than anyone I have ever known": "In the beginning she made paintings looking at what was in her studio. Later she painted looking out the window. It took years of sticking to her quiet guns to overcome the power of the avant-garde. The power of her own aesthetic created a place for her art outside the narrow judgment of the day. For me she personifies Ezra Pound's dictum 'Art is character.' " Freilicher's courage in resisting Abstract Expressionism went together with her ability to take what she needed from it as from any movement or style she might be rejecting. Her quirky kind of realism—a "slightly rumpled realism," Ashbery once called it—made her as much a maverick in her quiet way as Rivers more loudly was.

A long and intense love affair between Rivers and Freilicher, who had divorced her husband in the interim, came to an end in 1952 when she left him for another man. Rivers, distraught, responded to this cardiac crisis in characteristically wild style. One evening he launched a new affair, this one a short-lived romance with the poet Jean Garrigue. Another day he decided to lose himself in his work. Intending to copy a Titian at the Metropolitan Museum of Art, Rivers took pad, pencils, and a razor blade for sharpening those pencils but decided to stop at Jane's apartment first. There Freilicher was busy painting a portrait of O'Hara. "They were sipping and smoking," Rivers remembered. "Frank was dishing a lot of Johns: John Ashbery, John Myers, John Button, John Honsbeen (out of Hollywood's *Lives of a Bengal Dancer* to the directorship of Peggy Guggenheim's museum in Venice), and Jasper Johns." Depressed at the sight of his friends enjoying themselves, Rivers left in a huff. After working on his Titian project at the museum, Rivers returned to his studio, emptied out his drawing paraphernalia, and applied the razor blade to his wrists. Seconds later he phoned O'Hara for help. O'Hara took him to the emergency room of Beth Israel Hospital. O'Hara also arranged for Rivers to convalesce at Fairfield Porter's house in Southampton. Porter's portrait of Rivers shows him with his bandaged wrists.

Many pages could be devoted to the romantic triangle that Freilicher, O'Hara, and Rivers formed. O'Hara's role in the triangle—as Rivers's lover and Freilicher's intimate—was the stuff French novels are made of. "Somehow, you couldn't tell if he was a very good friend of Jane's so he could keep in contact with me, or a good friend of mine, so he could keep in contact with Jane," Rivers remarked. Reading Marcel Proust's masterpiece prodded O'Hara to see his own romantic relationships in the paradigm of *A la recherche du temps perdu.* As he wrote in a letter to Schuyler in 1956, "I think Proust is ruining me, since when one is not actively reading him one seems to be unconsciously scrutinizing one's own experiences and particularly one's motives (ugh!) and finding them unworthy. For example it may be that where I acted like Marcel with Larry, I acted like Albertine with [the pianist] Bobby [Fizdale,] and with Jane continue to act like the Prince de Guermantes to her Oriane, unconsciously heightening my own vulgarity to make clear to others my admiration and appreciation of her superior sensibility, sensitivity and wit (superior to my own, that is)."

The other painter that Larry Rivers credits with his conversion from jazz musician to visual artist was Nell Blaine. Blaine was, in Freilicher's words, "our Joan of Arc." Slightly older than the others, she had her own loft on West Twenty-first Street, whose walls all were painted white. "I maintain that she started the whole New York School," the playwright Arnold Weinstein has observed. "It started at her place. That was the Big Bang—the place where everybody met. Her loft, with everything painted white, was the place. It was the first time any of us saw everything painted white. Remember, we came from pink walls." Rivers and Freilicher were frequent visitors. Sometimes they brought jazz musicians with them for impromptu jam sessions with Rivers on saxophone and Blaine on drums. Grass was inhaled. "Nell made me feel comfortable," Rivers wrote. "I admired her. I must have asked hundreds of questions, all of them giving her the role of a practicing expert." On Blaine's walls, Rivers saw his first modern paintings. And through Blaine, he met artists, writers, and photographers, and found himself initiated into a homosexual milieu: "The few ideas I had about homosexuality were quickly adjusted to my new experiences." Here is how Rivers recreates a typical conversation *chez* Nell:

> "My dear, I've been reading Dostoyevski's *Raw Youth.* It's marvelous. I found the spirit of the book to be—"
>
> "Spirit, my ass," someone interrupts. "He filched it all from Dickens, who has everything Dostoyevski has, plus being—"
>
> "What, a social historian? How about the honorable Honoré? You're not telling me that Dickens had more balls than Balzac."
>
> "Ronald Firbank held more balls than Balzac."
>
> "Where?"
>
> "In a ballroom, honey. Where do you hold balls?"
>
> "I hold them in a men's room," someone chirps up from the end of the couch.
>
> "Anyone know a nice quiet spot where I can finish part twelve of *Swann's Way*?"
>
> "Sure. Try the San Remo Bar."

A photograph of a costume party Blaine gave in 1949 shows her dancing with John Ashbery. "Larry Rivers was in the picture, dressed as an opium smoker," she pointed out. "John was dressed in a kilt like a Scot. I was dressed like a whorehouse madam from the time of Marie Antoinette. I went to Brooks costume place and rented a real frou-frou costume." The friends went places as a group. "We'd go, six or eight of us, to hear Judy Garland together," Blaine remembered. "Very late at night frequently we'd go out, walking from my place down to the Village. We'd be at Jane's house sometimes with John and Frank. We'd be dancing. There was a lot of dancing. Then when it got very late, one or two at night, the gay boys would go off to a bathhouse. I had so much energy then that I needed to get rid of some before I could paint. I'd come home and paint at two in the morning and sometimes all night." Blaine's spirit held her in good stead. Despite a crippling attack of polio in 1959, she continued to paint brilliantly—gardens in a riot of bloom, the Hudson River as seen from her eighth-floor apartment—until her death in November 1996.

I asked Blaine for her impressions of Ashbery and O'Hara when they were new to New York. "John was very sweet and a little sad and always very warm to me." What was he sad about? "His love life. He was lonely. Frank was more outgoing and aggressive. He used to say he could write a poem during a commercial break on TV. John was someone who wanted to be comforted and held. He used to cry on your shoulder. I had that feeling anyway. But Frank was the cock of the walk. He was somewhat vain. He didn't mind stripping and posing for us. I saw them a couple of times a week. That was in the early 1950s. We were all very young, very wild, and very innocent."

the band of rivals

Watch, then, the band of rivals as they climb up and down
Their steep stone gennels in twos and threes,
sometimes
Arm in arm, but never, thank God, in step. . . .

—W. H. AUDEN,
"IN PRAISE OF LIMESTONE"

(I)

In the floating bohemia of Manhattan, where life sometimes
seemed like a party and art an aphrodisiac, the young poets began
their evenings at the Cedar Tavern or a few blocks away at the
San Remo bar, where they would pull out their latest poems from
their coat pockets and show them to each other. Located at University Place and Eighth Street, the Cedar was the painters' bar,
legendary even then for marathon boozing and brawling, for the
parthenogenesis of the beautiful art groupie, and for the darkly
unconventional behavior of its habitués. Attractive women of independent means went there, as one of them put it, to "play the
game of 'pickup artists.'" The artists themselves were on "a decade-long bender," as the painter and critic Elaine de Kooning

called the 1950s. "We go there," Ad Reinhardt said, "to meet the very people we hate most, the other painters." The Cedar was where Elaine de Kooning and Franz Kline knocked back multiple shots of scotch, sometimes accompanied by Frank O'Hara; where Elaine's husband Bill once socked Clement Greenberg in the jaw; and where Jackson Pollock regularly picked fights and sometimes smashed glass and china, then played with the fragments, making designs with his blood on the tabletop. The peace was kept by Kline, who was big, comradely, well respected, and who "always got there before you did and was still there after you left," as Rivers remarked.

The Cedar consisted of a long narrow bar up front with partitioned booths in the back. The walls were plastered a color that has been described as "interrogation green." It was "a dive of no distinction—which was its distinction," as the critic Mark Stevens has written. The smoke-filled bar had no jukebox, no television. The bartenders were indifferent, and the hamburgers weren't especially good, though they were cheap. Rivers did paintings of the menu at the Cedar not because it was distinguished in any way but because it was so authentically ordinary. The painters liked the drab decor, because it seemed true to their experience of urban anonymity. It was a sign of their seriousness, and it seemed somehow in keeping with the discrepancy between their aspirations as artists and the belated public recognition of their art. There were advantages in being anonymous. When the Cedar became known as the painters' bar, tourists came in to gawk. On a night in the early 1950s, Pollock, de Kooning, and Kline were at the bar when a couple of spectators came in, took a look, and left. "This is the place where the painters are supposed to come," one of them said knowingly. "But there's no one here tonight."

It stands to reason that there are more Cedar Tavern anecdotes illustrating scandalous behavior than there are recorded instances of the excitement of ideas, since people went there primarily to drink and get drunk. Pollock, in particular, constantly tested the limits of acceptable behavior. "He was the most radical alcoholic I ever met," Greenberg said admiringly. When Pollock ripped the men's room door off its hinges, "it was something he just did and was interesting, not an annoyance," O'Hara wrote. "You couldn't see into it anyway, and besides there was then a sense of genius. Or what Kline called 'the dream.' " Young writers flocked to Kline for tutelage. "I sat for hours on end listening to Franz Kline in the Cedar Bar, fascinated by literally all that he had to say," Robert Creeley wrote. "Kline could locate the most articulate senses of human reality in seemingly casual conversation, as I remember he once did, painfully, moving, by means of the flowers, from a flower shop a friend had just opened to the roses he had brought to the pier to welcome his bride—to find that she had had a breakdown in passage. Those flowers gave us both something to hold on to." When somebody badgered him about what he wanted to communicate in his paintings, Kline gave an answer that poets like Creeley felt applied to them as well. "Well, look," Kline said, "if I paint what *you* know, then that will simply bore you, the repetition from me to you. If I paint what I know, it will be boring to myself. Therefore I paint what I *don't* know." Somebody at the Cedar complained that all of Barnett Newman's pictures looked alike—they all had a vertical stripe dividing two fields of color. Newman was too simple, the man said. Kline quietly asked whether all the stripes were the same size. No. Same color? Different colors. Same width? Not exactly. Was the stripe painted on top of the background color or had it been done the other way around? Hard to tell. "Well, I don't know," Kline said, "it all sounds damn complicated to me."

The charismatic de Kooning was another center of attention. De Kooning once punctuated a barroom argument about atheism by exclaiming that "it's like an empty lot between warehouses where they've just torn down the buildings"—a hard-

boiled urban image with the complexity of a metaphysical conceit. "I have to change to stay the same," he said, commenting
on his penchant for painting over an already painted canvas, an
aesthetic strategy that appealed to the New York poets. One evening Kenneth Koch came to the Cedar, saw de Kooning, and excitedly told him about a new O'Hara poem, "Radio," in which the
poet complains about the quality of the selections on the classical
station. Koch quoted the poem's conclusion:

> Well, I have my beautiful de Kooning
> to aspire to. I think it has an orange
> bed in it, more than the ear can hold.

The painter, pleased, told Koch that mattresses had always interested him because they were pulled together in some places and
puffed out in others, "like the earth." De Kooning loved American idioms and slang. "Terrific," he would say. A visitor from
Venice came to the Cedar for the express purpose of meeting
him. After the introductions were made, William Barrett enthusiastically pointed out the symbolic importance of the event. Pil-
grims had once flocked to Venice to pay homage to art; now a
Venetian had come to New York to meet de Kooning. "De Kooning blinked for a moment, trying to take in the full sweep of the
idea, and then his face lit up with a grin: 'Gee!'"
    If the Cedar Tavern was, in Larry Rivers's words, "the
G-spot of the whole art scene," the San Remo, on the northwest
corner of Bleecker and MacDougal streets, was the Xanadu of the
young writers. "I used to go there every night, as did most of my
friends," John Ashbery recalled. It was, he added, a little "like a
Paris café." Dating from 1925, the San Remo was a neighborhood
dive, a working-class bar with wooden booths, black-and-white
tiled floors, and a backroom restaurant. It was the sort of "unliterary" place, James Merrill wrote, in which literary types like

himself could feel "protected from encounters they perhaps desired with other customers by the glittering moat, inches deep, of their allusive chatter." It was at the San Remo that Merrill first met David Jackson, who became his lifelong companion.

The San Remo was a shrine of the Beat movement. In Jack Kerouac's novel *The Subterraneans* (1958), which he wrote over the course of three days and nights, the San Remo is transposed to San Francisco and rechristened the Black Mask. In the "spontaneous" prose that made Allen Ginsberg salute "the rhythm of the mind at work at high speed" while Truman Capote wondered whether it wasn't an example of typing rather than writing, Kerouac evoked the San Remo:

> Beginning as usual in the Mask.
>
> Nights that begin so glitter clear with hope, let's go see our friends, things, phones ring, people come and go, coats, hats, statements, bright reports, metropolitan excitements, a round of beers, another round of beers, the talk gets more beautiful, more excited, flushed, another round, the midnight hour, later, the flushed happy faces are now wild and soon there's the swaying buddy da day oobab bab smash smoke drunken latenight goof leading finally to the bartender, like a seer in Eliot, TIME TO CLOSE UP—in this manner more or less arriving at the Mask. . . .

Like other underground secrets that do not remain secret long, the San Remo soon attracted "wannabeats" of both sexes, clad in dungarees and work shirts, the women scandalously braless. "You were headed for the Remo," Ronald Sukenick writes in his memoir *Down and In*, "where you'd try to look old enough to be in an actual Village-Bohemian-literary-artistic-underground-mafioso-pinko-revolutionary-subversive-intellectual-existentialist-anti-bourgeois café. Real life at last." An article by Mary McCarthy in the *New York Post* spread the Remo's fame. McCarthy wrote not to praise but to denigrate the bar and its habitués, whom she compared unfavorably to an older generation of New York intellectuals; the latter fought "the battle of ideas and standards," McCarthy wrote, while the former seemed to radiate a sort of blithe apathy. But just as *Life* in 1949 had intended to mock but had effectively publicized the possibility that Jackson Pollock was America's greatest living painter, so on a local level McCarthy's article resulted in a publicity boon for the aging Village hangout. From the perspective of 1997, McCarthy's resistance to what Sukenick calls "the San Remo underground" suggests nothing so much as a generational divide between the intellectuals of the 1930s (whose center was *Partisan Review*) and a new, eclectic generation whose gurus ranged from John Cage to John Coltrane. Moral earnestness was out; existential cool, in. But this is easily said in retrospect; for the writers who gravitated to the Remo, it was not a symbol of anything but a convenient meeting place where they could go to be themselves and encounter like-minded souls.

"It is hard for someone born after 1950 to understand the edgy excitement of the city's low bars nearly a half-century ago, from the equivocal San Remo on MacDougal Street to the alien, but finally friendly glass-fronted Wellworth Cafe in the heart of Harlem," the translator William Weaver recalls. A visit to the San Remo might punctuate an evening that also included an opera or ballet and an impromptu party. On Election Day 1952, when the electorate cast its ballots for either Republican Dwight Eisenhower or Democrat Adlai Stevenson, Weaver and Frank O'Hara met to attend the opening night of the New York City Ballet season. The two men planned to go to Weaver's apartment afterward to celebrate a Stevenson victory with Black Velvets (champagne and Guinness stout). But when the news of a likely Eisenhower landslide was announced by the ballet's tuxedo-clad house manager, O'Hara decided to head home. "I don't feel like a party," he said. Neither did anyone else. Chester Kallman phoned Weaver from the San Remo: "Everybody down here is crying," he said.

(II)

One winter twilight in the early 1950s, Schuyler and O'Hara, heading toward the San Remo, talked about their poems as they walked in the slush of Washington Square. "Let's face it," O'Hara abruptly said, "John's the poet." The line infuriated Schuyler, who was acutely conscious of being the New York School's Fourth Musketeer. He was the last of the group to have a book published and the first to be overlooked; he was the one who hadn't gone to Harvard but to an obscure college in West Virginia, where he had spent the time mastering bridge. "I thought I was a poet, too," Schuyler fumed but didn't say. He noticed the uncharacteristic bitterness in O'Hara's voice: "John's the poet," as if there could be only one, and Ashbery came closest to approaching the ideal.

Of the competitiveness that underscored the friendships among these poets, this anecdote speaks volumes. The competition was friendly, laced with admiration and respect, but it was as fierce as only a match between close friends can be, and it brought out the best in them, just as the great Wimbledon matches between John McEnroe and Bjorn Borg made both of them better tennis players. It was, in fact, competition as much as collaboration that linked Ashbery and O'Hara and Schuyler and Koch so tightly that they acquired a group identity with a collective force. "Collaboration, a direct extension of O'Hara's mode of living, is a good metaphor for the manner of his relationships—an intimate competition in which each participant goads the other toward being at his best," the poet and art critic Peter Schjeldahl perceptively noted. Or as Koch advised the young poets who came to him for instruction at Columbia, "Have some friends who are so good it scares you."

But the anecdote also says something about the private mythology of this elite company of poets. If each of the four had a definite role to play, Ashbery's was that of the Poet, the first among his peers. O'Hara was the hero, the great *animateur,* the catalyst of the New York School and the social force connecting it all together, poetry and action painting and jazz and cocktails and afternoon tabloids with a social conscience. The force of O'Hara's personality, his infectious enthusiasm, and his seemingly limitless capacity for the enjoyment of art made him the natural center of attention. Envy and resentment are the common lot of authors, whose unhappiness is made complete by a contemporary's success. How unusual was O'Hara, whose generosity was matched only by his incisive wit and charm. It is this combination that made O'Hara the poet that younger poets chose to emulate. Not just his peripatetic poems but his stylish manner of being was imitated. "If I have a hero it is Frank O'Hara," the painter Joe Brainard wrote. "Because Frank really lived life. Which, as you know, is not so easy. You can get hurt that way. It's very time consuming. And, at least for me, it's hard to be that uninhibited. When Frank got mad at somebody he lost his temper. When Frank was unhappy he cried. If Frank loved you you knew it. Frank had a natural gift (I assume it was natural) of being able to *be* himself."

Brad Gooch, O'Hara's biographer, dwells on the poet's ability to "become blind drunk" at night and function successfully as a curator by day. "For a creative, ambitious alcoholic he was a perfect role model," a friend of the poet told Gooch. But for most of O'Hara's fans, and especially the poets, alcohol had little to do with it. The hyperactive poetry scene at St. Mark's Church in the Bowery in the 1960s took O'Hara's taste as Gospel. The untranslated works of the French poet Pierre Reverdy were tracked down, read, and translated because O'Hara once ended a poem, "My heart is in my / pocket, it is Poems by Pierre Reverdy."

O'Hara's ironically self-deprecating tone was much imitated. "I am the least difficult of men. All I want is boundless love," he wrote. He kiddingly called his own poems "the by-product of exhibitionism" and wrote constantly about his daily life. It was O'Hara who initiated the policy of dropping names in his poems, a habit that became a New York School trademark. O'Hara peppered his work with references to his painter friends—Freilicher, Rivers, Mike Goldberg, Joan Mitchell, Norman Bluhm, Grace Hartigan, Al Leslie—with perfect indifference to whether readers would recognize their names. That indifference argued a certain confidence in the poet's ability to make the details of his autobiography-in-progress so irresistible that the reader feels flattered to be regarded as the poet's intimate. O'Hara's celebration of friendship in poetry represented an ideal that second-generation New York School poets, such as Bill Berkson, Ted Berrigan, Joe Brainard, Ron Padgett, and Anne Waldman, emulated in the 1960s. Everyone wanted to be, as Berrigan put it, "perfectly frank." James Schuyler has a marvelous riff in a letter to Berkson urging him to "be frank (if you can't be frank, be john and kenneth). Say," Schuyler continues, "maybe our friends' names would make good verbs: to kenneth: emit a loud red noise; to ashbery: cast a sidewise salacious glance while holding a champagne glass by the stem; to kenward: glide from the room and not make waves; to brainard: give a broad and silent chuckle; to machiz, shower with conversational spit drops—but I said friends, didn't I—cancel the last. To berkson and to schuyler I leave to you."

Koch was the madcap spirit of the New York School, quick

with a jest, a pun, or a brilliant idea for a multimedia art project. Eager to collaborate on poems with whoever might be willing, he had the gift of making people see that poetry could be funny *and* serious, sublime *and* ridiculous. Having diligently completed his doctorate at Columbia, he infiltrated academic headquarters to wage his antiacademic campaign and in the process transformed the art of teaching poetry writing. The role of the professor came naturally to him. As a twenty-year-old in the army he developed a sideshow act for a USO show touring the Pacific in which he billed himself "The Rhyming Professor" and offered to make up poems on the spot on the subjects of the soldiers' choice. ("It was easy," Koch reflected. "I knew what they were going to say: Red Cross Girls, Sergeants, Going Home, Japs. So I made up poems in advance.") In 1960 Koch joined the faculty at Columbia, where he attracted followers like a pied piper in his classes in "imaginative writing" (he never called it a workshop, and he disliked the words "creative writing"). Hilarity and high jinks came naturally to this enormously animated man who had a slight stutter and was always liable to do something unexpected, like break into a German accent and walk around the room impersonating a mad dictator. An aesthetic hard-liner, with a very limited tolerance for poetry that he regarded as solemn or sentimental or old hat—*poésie*, he called it—Koch did more than anyone to promulgate the group aesthetic of the New York School.

Schuyler was the editor par excellence, the ideal reader, the one you wanted to show your poems to first, not only because his taste was said to be flawless, but because he expressed his views with tact and skill. "James Schuyler is the person whose word I would always value almost as much as my own opinion," Ashbery remarked in 1977. "He always has a sure sense of what is wrong and right in poetry, of what belongs and what doesn't in a given poem. And if there's something he doesn't like, he very seldom says something negative; I can tell, however, from his silences when he's not carried away by the writing." Koch dropped the verse preface to his epic poem *Ko, or, A Season on Earth* because Schuyler told him to do so. On the other hand, Koch knew that a parody of Gerard Manley Hopkins had succeeded when Schuyler reacted by crossing himself.

Schuyler felt he had a vocation as an editor. He, Koch, and Ashbery took turns as editors of the individual issues of *Locus Solus*, but Schuyler was the most avid for the task. Only five numbers were published; Schuyler was responsible for the first and fifth. The contents of the first issue go far to define or at least illustrate a group identity. Kenneth Koch is represented with a prose piece, a spoof of Jack Kerouac entitled "On the Go," and two seminal poems, "The Circus" and "The Railway Stationery." Ashbery has nine poems, including one, "Idaho," that resembles nothing so much as a half-wrecked, half-erased story. O'Hara has ten, including "Adieu to Norman, Bonjour to Joan and Jean-Paul," one of the most affecting of what he called his "I do this I do that" poems. There are also nine sonnets by Edwin Denby, four poems by Fairfield Porter, seven by Barbara Guest, Schuyler's story "Current Events," the first section of Harry Mathews's novel *The Conversions*, and a poem by Anne Porter. The second issue of *Locus Solus*, under Kenneth Koch's direction, was wholly devoted to the art of literary collaboration and included examples of seventeenth-century Japanese linked verse, poems and prose by the French Surrealists, half a dozen poems that Koch and Ashbery had produced collaboratively, and a portion of the novel Schuyler and Ashbery had begun under the title *A Nest of Ninnies*. Perhaps no better introduction to the poetry of the New York School exists than these two issues of *Locus Solus*.

As late as 1971, nine years after *Locus Solus* had last appeared, Schuyler was still hoping to publish a one-shot revival. During the previous year Schuyler had proved his mettle by brilliantly editing two important prose works by his friends:

Ashbery's introduction to O'Hara's *Collected Poems* and Koch's essay on teaching children to write poetry in *Wishes, Lies, and Dreams*. These were major publications for the poets involved. *Wishes, Lies, and Dreams* was Koch's breakthrough book, establishing his fame as an educator. O'Hara's *Collected Poems* won the National Book Award in 1972 and suddenly O'Hara began to be read by poets far from the aesthetic maelstrom of New York City.

Schuyler's letter to Ashbery advising him on the first draft of his O'Hara essay is a masterpiece of editorial acumen. Dated December 29, 1970, this typed five-page letter is full of insights into O'Hara ("Don't forget that, much as Frank liked to play the film fan with the gifted great, at heart, he preferred a setting in which he was the star") and shrewd suggestions for revision. It is here that Schuyler produced the phrase the "intimate yell" to characterize what O'Hara had picked up from Mayakovsky. Throughout the letter Schuyler never forgets that Ashbery is "in the unenviable situation of trying to explain to strangers someone you love and understand so intimately." But he impresses upon Ashbery the importance of the occasion. "A review or an article appears and disappears, and if it doesn't turn out to be one of one's best, well, they can't all be," he sums up. "But Frank's poems are going to be in print for a long time, and so will the introduction, and for some readers, it will be not just an introduction to Frank's work, but their introduction to you. This seems to me one of several reasons for taking pains." Schuyler's letter is signed "Cynthia Westcott, The Rose Doctor" and addressed to "Miliza Gorgeous"—he and Ashbery always used camp names in their letters. Schuyler typed in a postscript concluding: "Now to decide whether I should not perhaps tear this up."

If Koch was the professor and Schuyler the editor, Ashbery was simply "the Poet." He was the one who was not there—the one who had gone away to Paris, like the hero in a medieval romance embarking on a test, a quest, and an adventure. Ashbery left for France in 1955 and stayed in Paris on and off for the next ten years. His Parisian sojourn is one of Ashbery's enigmas. Why did he abandon New York for Paris at the very instant that New York displaced Paris as the international art capital? Wasn't it precisely in order to vacate the center, to take up a position on the periphery, on the conviction that the avant-garde calling requires nothing so much as the spirit of individualism and nonconformism? "In both art and life today we are in danger of substituting one conformity for another, or, to use a French expression, of trading one's one-eyed horse for a blind one," Ashbery wrote in his important essay "The Invisible Avant-Garde" (1968). To be in "the center of a cheering mob" is no better for the artist than "creating in a vacuum." Ashbery's absence was a central presence for the three poets who remained in New York: Their transoceanic correspondence was frequent and voluminous, and the fact that Paris was one of the cardinal points on the New York School compass was a bulwark against provincialism, a reminder that this American poetry movement defined itself in a broad international context. Ashbery's absence also endowed him with a certain mystery for younger poets attracted to the New York School aesthetic who had encountered his work only on the page. When Koch set up a poetry reading in New York for the visiting Ashbery in 1963, it was a triumph for the self-exiled artist who spoke cryptic truths and perpetrated mysterious disjunctions in his poems.

None of the poets was satisfied with a notion of poetry limited to one form, the lyric. None felt inhibited from making the occasional foray into another art form or from engaging in group collaborations. In the early 1950s, Ashbery (who had initially wanted to be a painter) and O'Hara (who had started out as a composer) acted in each other's plays. O'Hara collaborated with Rivers on lithographs, with Grace Hartigan on paintings, with Alfred Leslie on films, with Joe Brainard on drawings, collages, and comic strips, and with Norman Bluhm on "poem paintings." The collaborations with Bluhm took place in October 1960. "Each one was different," Bluhm commented. "Frank would write something on a sheet of paper while I was in another part of the studio, making a gesture on the paper. It was all instantaneous, like a conversation between friends. You know, going back and forth. Quick and playful. There were no big thoughts, no idea that anyone would be interested in it or that it would ever be shown or published. We were just having fun on what had started out as a dismal Sunday afternoon." In one of the poem-pictures, O'Hara's words appear against a backdrop of drips: "Help! I am alive! / I was having such / a good sleep / no / I was awake."

For his part, Koch collaborated with Larry Rivers in 1961 on a series of maps, a second series about women's shoes, and other more abstract creations. They used oil paint, pastel, pen, pencil, and charcoal directly on paper or canvas. Speed and excitement were two of the desired results, and the presence of the second person gave each the feeling that there was nothing to lose. "If my words weren't perfect, Larry could fix them with some red or yellow; the same for his brushstrokes and pictures, I could amend them with adjectives and nouns," Koch recalls. Koch liked all manner of collaboration—simultaneous, as with Rivers, or in sequential order, as when he created texts to accompany the drawings Alex Katz made for a book they called *Interlocking Lives.* Most of all Koch liked collaborating with artists on plays. Koch's *George Washington Crossing the Delaware*, with sets by Katz, was staged in March 1962, and two months later *The Construction of Boston*, on which Koch collaborated with Niki de Saint-Phalle, Jean Tinguely, and Robert Rauschenberg, went up at the Maidman Playhouse in New York, directed by Merce Cunningham. "They were all battling till the very moment the curtain went up about what direction it was going to take," O'Hara commented. "And I don't mean in an unpleasant way, but they were—you know, it really was a collaboration in the sense that nobody had, absolutely, made themselves the key figure in it."

Inspired by the poets, a number of young painters doubled as writers. Joe Brainard, who arrived in New York in the early 1960s, not only provided the cover art for many poetry books but also wrote poems and at least one prose masterpiece, *I Remember*. Alfred Leslie was another painter who refused to limit himself to a single art form. O'Hara put Leslie in his play, *Awake in Spain*, a comic extravaganza: When a landscape architect describes "an orange sky, with a white band about its throat, and perhaps a sunken pool of black," a tourist replies, "It's another case of nature imitating Alfred Leslie!" In addition to painting, Leslie made movies, wrote plays, and, in 1961, published *The Hasty Papers*, a one-shot avant-garde review that included works by Ashbery, Koch, O'Hara, and Schuyler as well as a speech by Fidel Castro at the United Nations and a curator's assessment of Churchill, Hitler, and Eisenhower as painters. As for Rivers, on top of painting, playing saxophone, appearing on TV quiz shows, designing the sets for some of his friends' plays and the jackets for some of their books, and conducting a highly active amorous life, he had enough manic energy left over to write poems and to collaborate with O'Hara on plays *(Kenneth Koch: A Tragedy)* and mock manifestos ("How to Proceed in the Arts").

To collaborate on a work of art or a "happening"—a word coming into use in the early 1960s—was the height of avant-garde glamour. "One of the most wonderful ways in the world to be with someone's sweetness and brilliance is to collaborate with that person," Koch reminisced. "I liked collaborating the way people like drinking. Collaborating was making a game out of social life." And poetry? "Poetry was like stolen kisses—you could do it fast." In Europe when their Fulbright years coincided, Koch and Ashbery collaborated on poems while visiting such places as the Luxembourg Gardens and the Rodin Museum in Paris. The avant-garde tradition of the *blague* energized them. They arbitrarily adopted a set of exigent requirements contrived for the occasion. In Florence, they wrote a sestina that, in addition to fulfilling the exacting requirements of the form, includes the name of a flower, a tree, a fruit, a game, and a famous old lady, as well as the word *bathtub*, in every one of its thirty-nine lines. (A sample line: "Forget me not, as Laura Hope Crewes once spelt out in anagrams while we were all eating honeydew melon. I write you this from the bathtub and from a willow chair.") They called it "Crone Rhapsody," after a German circus, Krone Rhapsody, that was playing in Florence when they wrote the poem. In Paris, after playing pinball in a café, they wrote "Gottlieb's Rainbow," each line of which contains the words *bonus* and *bumper*, a color, a season, and the name of a philosopher:

> The red winter ball hit the Plato bonus bumper
> Whose indigo bonus killed the spring Bertrand Russell
> bumper.
> The Aristotle bonus kept the autumn inside an orange
> bumper awaiting the big rollover.
> Autumn ("the bonus season") colored the Harry Emerson
> Fosdick bumper yellow,

and so on for twelve additional lines. The repetition of the words mimes the action of the ball bouncing off the bonus bumpers in a pinball machine. You might think that the poem's title was a nod to the Abstract Expressionist painter Adolph Gottlieb. Not so; it was a reference to the Gottlieb company in Chicago, a prime manufacturer of the pinball machines of Paris.

The most extended collaboration produced by the poets was the novel that Ashbery and Schuyler began in the backseat of a car returning to New York City from the Hamptons on a summer day in 1952. Looking for a way to lessen the boredom of the ride,

Schuyler suggested that they write a novel. "How can we do that?" Ashbery asked. "Oh, it's very simple," Schuyler said and pulled out a pad. "Think of a first line." Driving past a house in Smithtown, Long Island, they decided that it would be a good place for the characters to live. They took turns writing sentences, striving to outdo one another in deadpan social wit, and gathered inspiration from the suburban countryside as seen through a car's windows. It is worth pausing over *A Nest of Ninnies*, the comic tour de force they began that day and completed seventeen years later.

Nothing much happens in *A Nest of Ninnies*. The novel's suburban characters travel a lot—to the city, to Europe—and the weather is usually terrible. "The topers by the fire became aware that the blizzard had changed to a torrential downpour," the authors write in a characteristic sentence. Characters marry, but there is nothing extraordinary about that; there is no depth of character, no psychological complexity, no moral upheaval in this book. The authors' intent, however, is not to condemn the characters for their vacuousness but to delight in them and rejoice in their clichés: " 'I'm afraid I'm that rare bird, a born New Yorker,' Mr. Kelso said. 'Personally, I'd like to try the suburbs, but it wouldn't suit Mother. You see, I live with my mother and she's getting on.' "

Character is a subordinate function of dialogue in *Nest*, and dialogue is a celebration of the American suburban vernacular, which is accurately mimed in the spirit not of ridicule but of "respect for things as they are," in Fairfield Porter's phrase. As in the novels of Henry Green, which Ashbery had made the subject of his master's thesis at Columbia, *A Nest of Ninnies* is 90 percent dialogue. The novel's technical debt to Green is great, but its tone couldn't be more different. In his master's thesis Ashbery had saluted the "strangeness and the strange despair" he found in Green's novel *Concluding*, which differed from Kafka's despair inasmuch as Green "still finds an occasional and nervous beauty in the world he is describing." Green's despair and "nervous beauty" are conspicuously absent from *A Nest of Ninnies*. It is as though Ashbery and Schuyler had taken Green's distinctive narrative manner and fused it with the arch spirit of Ronald Firbank: "Marshall observed Alice's knitted brow with alarm, and found himself in the unenviable position of one who is trying to change a subject that has not yet been broached." The art of the non sequitur finds its perfect expression here:

> "In the fall," Mrs. Turpin said, her voice rising excitedly, "when the chestnuts are ripe, hogs are driven up the hills. With sticks, by boys. Later they are driven down again."
>
> Though the others waited, this was the end of her tale.

The style of arch ventriloquism that Ashbery and Schuyler adopted in *A Nest of Ninnies* had the virtue of allowing each of the two to escape from his personality, to lose himself in his work, in the sense commended by T. S. Eliot, who had argued that "poetry is not a turning loose of emotion, but an escape from emotion" and that "only those who have personality and emotions will know what it means to want to escape from these things." Perhaps the most extraordinary thing about *A Nest of Ninnies* is that the two poets have dissolved their own personalities and merged so entirely into a common style that it can be said that the book's author is neither Ashbery nor Schuyler but a third entity fashioned in the process of collaboration. They had transformed a game into a form of literary creation. "It was written all over the place, in cars, over martinis, any place," Schuyler told an interviewer. They did it for fun, "but John and I were always serious about our fun" and "were always trying to cap each other as it went on." The novel would have been finished sooner except that the collaboration worked best when the two poets were in the same room while writing, and Ashbery was away in France for ten years of that period. Collaborating by correspondence was not nearly as rewarding. As Ashbery put it in a letter to Schuyler, "I liked your 'page' for the Nest, but somehow it seems to lack the nubbly, handwoven texture that we can probably only get by pitting our respective 'wits' against each other, which I think is the principal thing to be said in favor of the book, although no one else may ever say it. So I think we should probably finish the book that way, endless as the road may be." A collaboration so faithfully sustained in the face of such frequent and prolonged interruptions cannot but be seen as the fruit and testament of a friendship grounded in love—or even as a form of literary lovemaking.

In effect, the poets got a contact high from one another. Koch reports that he and O'Hara repaired to his apartment one day, set up two typewriters, and sat writing with their backs to each other for an hour. Ashbery persuaded Koch that "shapely as an ameba" was a better simile than "shapeless as an ameba." Koch improved O'Hara's most famous prose poem by talking him out of "Meditations on an Emergency" and into "Meditations in an Emergency" as its title. On several occasions, Koch and Ashbery sat down with the day's *New York Times* and made poetry out of it. The paper of October 25, 1953, yielded thirty items like this one:

EISENHOWER SURE PROGRAM WILL GIVE FARMER A FAIR SHAKE

His books get under my wheels,
Scratchy dust not pollen,
Pressure not seaworthiness
Omphale not certain of birthmark
Gasping not shyly swimming ably to a bruise
O last labor-cut adjective!

"I was attracted to the Dadaists and the Surrealists," Koch told me. "I liked their wildness and funniness, the complete irrationality. I liked the social aspect of it, poets and painters hanging out together in cafés. They really exposed their lives. The only collaborations I knew about at first were the *cadavres exquis*. With John our first collaborations were our sestinas. The poems with amusing intricate rules came later. I was usually the aggressor in such matters. I was always the one who did the physical writing. I loved collaborations as much as anyone in our gang and probably more." In a letter from Paris in 1963, Ashbery told Koch he was "enclosing a few poems more out of a sense of duty than pride—I think they show how sadly I need an injection of vitamin KK."

To an important extent, the spirit of collaboration was the flip side of the poets' intense competitiveness. In 1953 Koch began writing a long poem entitled *When the Sun Tries to Go On* ("There is a big airplane running O my / Blimp, across the defeated Mexicos of aspirin!"), and O'Hara answered with *Second Avenue* ("Blue negroes on the verge of a true foreignness / escape nevertheless the chromaticism of occidental death / by traffic, oh children bereaved of their doped carts / and priests with lips like mutton in their bedrooms at dawn!"). The poets telephoned each other nightly with the day's results. Soon after, Koch recalls, "John wrote 'The Japanese Houseboy,' his entry in our unofficial long poem contest. He was piqued that we were writing long poems. His first response was to write a one-line poem. Then he wrote 'The Japanese Houseboy.' " Ashbery may have judged "The Japanese Houseboy" a dud; he never published it. But "Europe" in *The Tennis Court Oath* might be regarded as a belated entry in the long-standing "long poem contest." Deploying the techniques of the collage and the cutup, this 111-part poem goes even further than *When the Sun Tries to Go On* and *Second Avenue* in fracturing syntax and turning the page into a field resembling an abstract canvas. Here is section 79 of "Europe," entire:

To stroll down Main Street
the dignified and paternal image
telegraph—magnificent

            dump

porch
    flowers store
weed local relatives
            whine

The sense of competition seems to have enhanced the poets'
pleasure in each other's productions. When Ashbery sent "Europe" to Koch in 1960, Koch was bowled over. "EUROPE is so
beautiful and exciting that I can hardly think of anything to say
about it," he wrote back. "It seems to me that you finally succeeded in doing what Apollinaire said he & the Cubists had to do,
destroy everything so it can be put back together again in a new
way. Seems to me your poetry's been going in this direction (of
EUROPE) for years, especially lately, but gish you did it (I meant
gosh). Gish! wow! Help! It's wonderful. I haven't been so excited
about poetry in years (I mean someone else's); and I believe the
last time I was or anyway the time before it was about yours too."
Koch reported similar thumbs-up verdicts from O'Hara and
Schuyler: "Frank says, 'You must change your life' (I wonder
where he got that phrase!). Jimmy says 'Beautiful and inscrutable.
Europe is a great masterpiece.'"

Competitiveness provided an incentive to excel. The pleasure of being one another's first reader would have been greatly
diminished if any of the poets felt that the others' approbation
were automatic. True, a condition of their candor was the fraternal sympathy underlining it; tact and sensitivity were required,
and when praise was earned it was to be hyperbolic in its expres-

sion. Nevertheless, the enthusiasm they fired in one another—Koch to Ashbery: Your poems are "just beautiful and even crazier than life itself"—could not be faked.

Disciplined by friendship, the internal competitiveness among the poets gave way to a united front when the world outside the chosen circle had to be faced. When Koch's poetry was attacked by a critic in *Poetry* magazine in 1955, O'Hara rushed in with a ringing defense. Koch (who returned the favor in *Partisan Review* six years later) was unstinting in his efforts to promote Ashbery, O'Hara, and their movement. At a poetry reading at Yale in December 1961 Koch read some of the poems he and Ashbery had written collaboratively in Europe five years earlier. "Gottlieb's Rainbow" had the audience in stitches. Returning to New York, Koch introduced his Columbia students not only to specific poems by O'Hara ("Blocks") and Ashbery ("Our Youth") but to the whole bag of New York School tricks, from cutups and collages to collaborations and comic-book narratives. The excitement was contagious: This was what it meant to be avant-garde.

Koch played an instrumental part in bringing Ashbery's second book, *The Tennis Court Oath*, to the notice of John Hollander, then a judge of the Wesleyan poetry series, which published it in 1962. Koch also lobbied his senior Columbia colleague, Frederick Dupee, an editor of *Partisan Review*, on behalf of his friends. According to a letter Koch sent to Ashbery, Dupee was "writing an article about you & me & Frank & Jimmy & Harry [Mathews] & our wonderful movement & everything else that is wonderful about us for either *Esquire* or *PR* (I have explained to him at length our wonderful aims, & perhaps you can add a few rusted platinum pointers)." The article didn't come off, though Dupee did write an admiring piece on Koch's collection *Thank You* in *Partisan Review*. "If, like Marianne Moore, he is always springing surprises, he does not spring them as if he were handing you a cup of tea," Dupee wrote. "For him, the element of surprise, and the excitement created by it, are primary and absolute."

A public poetry reading could be a private competition, and so could a conversation. In the early 1960s, Koch and Ashbery got together at Jane Freilicher's summer house in the Hamptons to conduct a mutual interview. The outcome is a rare document in the annals of literary conversations. Koch: "Have your speculations about ambiguity produced any result as yet?" Ashbery: "Only this: that ambiguity seems to be the same thing as happiness—or pleasant surprise, as you put it. I have a feeling that since I am assuming that from the moment that life cannot be one continual orgasm, real happiness is impossible and pleasant surprise is promoted to the front rank of the emotions." (Only a true aesthete would formulate the matter thus.) The entire conversation is like a prolonged fencing match. At one point, Koch interrupts the verbal jousting by blurting out, "You're a wit and I see that you are obviously going to win this interview." I have heard Koch use this same locution to characterize poetry readings he and Ashbery have given together. When I proposed that the two of them read under the auspices of the Academy of American Poets in New York in 1994, Koch said that the last time they had been paired on the same program was at St. Mark's Church in the Bowery: "Was it ten years ago? I forgot who won." He paused, then added, "We're very competitive. I want to win by winning. John wants to win by not trying."

The sense of competition between Ashbery and O'Hara was, if anything, more intense. In 1955, both O'Hara and Ashbery submitted manuscripts for the Yale Younger Poets Prize, then as now the nation's most prestigious competition for a first book of poems. When Ashbery's *Some Trees* was chosen over O'Hara's *Meditations in an Emergency*, O'Hara swallowed his disappointment and hastened to be the first to laud his friend's accomplishment. In *Poetry* magazine, one of the few places where poetry criticism was done seriously, O'Hara called *Some Trees* "the most beautiful first book to appear in America since *Harmonium*." I cite this statement not only as a characteristic instance of

O'Hara's generosity but because, forty years on, the comparison of Ashbery's first book to Wallace Stevens's seems not wild but apt. Indeed, according to several of his most ardent critics, Ashbery is precisely the inheritor of Stevens's mantle. But O'Hara's gesture redounds in significance when you consider the terms of his friendship with Ashbery and the unusual circumstances of the Yale competition in 1955.

The rivalry between Ashbery and O'Hara was based on mutual sympathy to the point of identity (as defined by Wallace Stevens: "the vanishing point of resemblance"). It is tempting to regard the pair as fraternal twins. Ashbery has recalled that O'Hara's voice and his own "were all but indistinguishable" over the telephone. They sounded so alike that on different occasions both Ashbery's mother and O'Hara's companion Joe LeSueur were fooled into thinking that one was the other. Once, Ashbery said, "when Frank came to visit my parents' farm in upstate New York he walked into the kitchen one evening when my mother was washing dishes and asked if he could help; without turning 'round from the sink my mother said, 'No, John, go back in and talk with your friends.' " The poets had, in Ashbery's words, the "same flat, nasal twang, a hick accent so out of keeping with the roles we were trying to play that it seems to me we probably exaggerated it, later on, in hopes of making it seem intentional."

If the Yale contest was a perfect venue for a fraternal clash, that is because the competition's judge was W. H. Auden, the father (or, in camp slang, mother) figure for an entire generation of gay male poets. And Auden was in the curious position of choosing not from a stack of anonymous manuscripts (as is usually the case in the Yale contest) but between the collections of two young men whose identities were well known to him. Both were late entries. This state of affairs would not have come about had Auden been satisfied with the regular submissions. None of these, however, struck him as worthy of the award. When Chester

Kallman, Auden's companion, explained the situation to his close friend James Schuyler, the latter channeled the manuscripts of *Some Trees* and *Meditations in an Emergency* to Auden via Kallman. Auden "didn't think either of them was very good, and he chose John's *faute de mieux*," Schuyler confided to Koch. Auden's lack of enthusiasm is clear from his preface to *Some Trees*, which expresses some concern about the "calculated oddities" of Ashbery's poetry. Nevertheless Auden's imprimatur, grudging or not, remained the great prize for a young poet, not only because of the attention the Yale book customarily received but because Auden's selections were distinguished by a shrewdness that subsequent decades of critical judgment have confirmed. (Among Auden's choices for the Yale prize in the 1950s were Adrienne Rich, W. S. Merwin, Daniel Hoffman, and John Hollander, in addition to Ashbery.) Choosing between Ashbery and O'Hara, Auden was as though thrust into the position of God choosing between the gifts of Cain and Abel—at least that is the allegorical psychodrama that the competing poets seem to have instinctively apprehended in the situation. The competition for Auden's nod stands somewhere behind the epistolary quarrel between O'Hara and Ashbery on the question of which of the two was more like the James Dean figure in Elia Kazan's *East of Eden* (1955).

James Byron Dean was an instant sensation in *East of Eden*, which was the only one of his three films to be released when he was alive. The specter of young death hangs over Kazan's movie. It also pervades the next movie Dean was in: Nicholas Ray's *Rebel Without a Cause* (1955), in which a guy in a game of chicken drives a car off a cliff to his death—a film that no viewer could have seen without being aware that the leading actor had just died in a high-speed car crash. Both movies gave vent to an inchoate protest against conventionality; *Rebel Without a Cause* in particular anticipated the youth culture of the 1960s when there were more than enough causes for rebels to take up. But Dean's persona in these movies was more ambiguous and more complex than this reduction to type would suggest. *East of Eden*, Pauline Kael observed, is "an enshrinement of the mixed-up kid. Here and in *Rebel Without a Cause* Dean seems to go just about as far as anybody can in acting misunderstood." Dean seemed to combine the wounded vulnerability of Montgomery Clift with the savage aggression of Marlon Brando. Dean well understood the appeal of his persona. On the set of *Giant*, his last movie, he told Dennis Hopper: "Y'know, I think I've got a chance to really make it because in this hand I'm holding Marlon Brando, saying 'Fuck you!' and in the other hand, saying, 'Please forgive me,' is Montgomery Clift. 'Please forgive me.' 'Fuck you!' 'Please forgive me.' 'Fuck you!' And somewhere in between is James Dean." On September 30, 1955, Dean died the tragic death of choice of the 1950s. He was on his way to a car race in Salinas when he crashed his silver Porsche into a Ford on Highway 466 and broke his neck. He was twenty-four.

O'Hara identified himself strongly with Dean. He wrote half a dozen heartfelt elegies to the young actor, a fellow metropolitan soul, who had arrived in New York City in 1951, as had O'Hara himself, and had lived there until heading out to Hollywood in 1954. In "For James Dean" O'Hara addresses the gods with uncharacteristically shrill anger. "I speak as one whose filth / is like his own, of pride / and speed and your terrible / example nearer than the sirens' speech, / a spirit eager for the punishment / which is your only recognition." O'Hara presents himself as the "ambassador of a hatred," the voice of a man who is doomed but defiant. "Men cry from the grave while they still live / and now I am this dead man's voice, / stammering, a little in the earth." In "Obit Dean, September 20, 1955," O'Hara presents Dean to the actress Carole Lombard in heaven: "I hope / you will be good to him up there." Dean, he explains, "rocketed to stardom" in *East of Eden*, "playing himself and us / 'a brooding, inarticulate adolescent.' "

East of Eden, based on the John Steinbeck novel of the same name, is a loose and finally somewhat incoherent retelling of the Cain-Abel story in Genesis. It is set around the time of America's entry into World War I. Cal Trask (Dean) and his brother Aaron (Richard Davalos) vie for their father's approval. For the old man's birthday, Cal gives him the money he has made speculating on bean futures. But Adam Trask (Raymond Massey), who works on the local draft board, refuses to be a war profiteer and rejects the present. A stern moralist, he prefers Aaron's gift: the announcement that he and his girlfriend Abra (Julie Harris) are engaged to be married. Just as Adam is God and Aaron is Abel, Cal is Cain, and just as the biblical Cain murders his brother, so Cal sees to it that Aaron suffers a similar fate. Aaron had been told that his sainted mother was deceased; Cal has learned that she is, in fact, the madam of a brothel in a nearby town. After Cal brings his brother to see her, the disillusioned boy gets drunk and enlists in the army. The action is, in the film's vocabulary, tantamount to suicide. The father has a stroke and with Abra's intercession accepts Cal as his caregiver.

The hero of *East of Eden* is the alienated Cain, not the sanctimonious Abel. "James Dean is decorated with all sorts of charming caucheries; he's sensitive, defenseless, hurting," Pauline Kael commented. "Maybe his father doesn't love him, but the camera does, and we're supposed to." The film conceives of Cain as misunderstood rather than wicked, desperate for the love his unforgiving father withholds from him until the end. This interpretation of the first fratricide had a strong appeal for O'Hara. "I have seen *East of Eden* 4 times and loved it more each. It is the *La Strada* of our set," O'Hara wrote to Kenneth Koch's wife, Janice. To Fairfield Porter, O'Hara explained his self-identification with the "naughty boy wondering why he's different." And if he was Cal, Ashbery was Aaron. "I think one of the things about *East of Eden* is that I am very materialistic and John is very spiritual, in our work especially," O'Hara wrote. "John's work is

full of dreams and a kind of moral excellence and kind sentiments. Mine is full of objects for their own sake, spleen and
ironically intimate observation which may be truthfulness (in the
lyrical sense) but is more likely to be egotistical cynicism mas-
querading as honesty."

Ashbery, as devoted to moviegoing as his friend, went to see
A l'Est d'Eden in Paris and was unimpressed. "I've decided that
your liking [it] is the flaw in your character which insures your
greatness," he wrote to O'Hara from Paris. But he was unwilling
to yield to O'Hara's claim to the spirit of James Dean. "Don't
think I've forgotten, either, that you said I was like R. Davalos"—
the actor who plays Aaron—"the most mealy-mouthed sissy the
screen has ever dared to exhibit," Ashbery wrote. "You're quite
wrong, Frank, it's I and not you who am like James Dean." I
wondered, after I came across this letter tucked away in a file of
papers in Kenneth Koch's New York apartment, why Ashbery felt
so strongly about the matter. Then I remembered that Ashbery
had lost a younger brother, Richard, to leukemia at the age of
nine. Richard was John's opposite, athletic and active as his
brother was bookish and introverted. If Richard had survived,
perhaps John would have felt less keenly the pressure of parental
expectation and the guilt of disappointing his father. Chester
Ashbery, a rugged outdoors type who had taken an agricultural
degree at Cornell and bought some farmland near Lake Ontario,
was forever trying to get his son to help out with farm chores.
Was he, in the young poet's mind, like the disapproving father
played by Raymond Massey in the movie? Perhaps. "My father
had a violent temper," Ashbery told a reporter from *New York*
magazine in 1991. "My mother was very sweet and timid. He and
my mother were always quarreling. He would wallop me. It was
like living in a volcano. I never knew what would precipitate an
eruption."

"I was always getting kicked out of the house by my parents," Ashbery told another interviewer. " 'You've always got your nose in a book—go out and get some fresh air. You won't be healthy if you continue like this.' They were right, I suppose." Ashbery associated the memory with a phrase he recalled in a story by Mary Butts, a writer he had discovered in the early 1950s, whose work he characterized admiringly as "very weird, rather like Djuna [Barnes], but tight-lipped and suppressed hysteria." The heroine of the story encounters a man in a public place, has a brief conversation with him, and thinks, "He was of the majority who disapprove." Ashbery said, "I seem to have grown up surrounded by this majority."

The need to escape took Ashbery to Deerfield, Harvard, New York City, and Paris—an itinerary of places progressively more distant from his father's farm—where he could be, at last, the poet to whom the academy of the future would open its doors, though the jeers of the disapproving majority would continue to echo in his mind.

John Ashbery: the picture of little J. A. in a prospect of flowers

One should be an enigma not just to others but to oneself too. I study myself. When I tire of that I light a cigar to pass the time, and think: God only knows what the good Lord really meant with me, or what He meant to make of me.

—Søren Kierkegaard,
Either/Or

"Remarks aren't literature," Gertrude Stein wrote. And anecdotes aren't criticism. But remarks and anecdotes can assist in the practical task facing a poet's interpreter, just as slips of the tongue or pen can help the analyst to glimpse a true intention behind a misleading appearance. The implied analogy to psychoanalysis is misleading, and I wouldn't want to push it, though reading John Ashbery's poetry I do sometimes think of Wallace Stevens's remark: "It is often said of a man that his work is autobiographical in spite of every subterfuge."

Ashbery is certainly the least autobiographical of modern poets. No one's poems have less to do with the details of his life; in this regard his work is at the opposite end of the spectrum from Frank O'Hara's and James Schuyler's. "My own biography never interested me very much as a material for literature,"

Ashbery has said more than once. He has characterized one of his poems, the celebrated "Soonest Mended" (1970), as a sort of "one-size-fits-all" narrative that could fit anybody's biography.

> These then were some of the hazards of the course,
> Yet though we knew the course *was* hazards and nothing else
> It was still a shock when, almost a quarter of a century later,
> The clarity of the rules dawned on you for the first time.
> *They* were the players, and we who had struggled at the game
> Were merely spectators, though subject to its vicissitudes
> And moving with it out of the tearful stadium, borne on
> shoulders, at last.

This is autobiography raised to the abstract level of allegory. These arresting lines operate entirely in the realm of metaphor—that is, in the realm of the imagination. It is not the description of an experience but the experience itself: a moment of clarity, when "you" discover that you are a spectator, not a player, in the hazardous game, though it may be your destiny nevertheless to be "borne on shoulders," like the home-run-hitting hero, as the crowd is moved to tears. The lines suggest a dream narrative loaded with plot twists and complications, and the dreamer is anyone. As Ashbery writes in "More Pleasant Adventures" (1984), "Heck, it's anybody's story, / A sentimental journey— 'gonna take a sentimental journey,' / And we do, but you wake up under the table of a dream: / You are that dream, and it is the seventh layer of you. / You haven't moved an inch, and everything has changed."

Pressed by an importunate interviewer, Ashbery allows that he now knows what to say when asked about the content of his work. "As I have gotten older, it seems to me that time is what I have been writing about all these years during which I thought I wasn't writing about anything." (Growing old interests him because it is "something that I never thought I would do when I was young.") Time—"how it feels, not what it means"—is in a general sense the subject of Ashbery's long poems, such as "The System" and "A Wave," which chart out not the growth of a poet's mind (Wordsworth's project in *The Prelude*) but the serpentine gestures of a poet's mind in motion, a project as Romantic as Wordsworth's and as American as Emerson's notion that "To believe your own thought, to believe that what is true for you in your private heart is true for all men, —that is genius."

According to one of Ashbery's casual maxims, "the worse your art is the easier it is to talk about," but he refutes his own maxim; for a reticent man, Ashbery's table talk is memorable. Of the exotic poetic form known as the pantoum, he observes wryly that the form has the advantage of "providing you with twice as much poem for your effort, since every line has to be used twice." In another context he speaks of the "Cordelia syndrome," which encourages American poets to speak "varnished truths" for fear of the fate that befell the third daughter of King Lear, who was disinherited for her unvarnished truthtelling. For his part Ashbery tosses off complex truths about human behavior in a disarmingly offhanded way: "Ambiguity supposes an eventual resolution of itself, whereas certitude implies further ambiguity. I guess that's why so much 'depressing' modern art makes me feel so cheerful." "Someone once remarked about an obscene passage in one of my poems. I replied that it shocked him not because it was there, but because there were not more of them." "Very often people don't listen to you when you speak to them. It's only when you talk to yourself that they prick up their ears."

I can think of no better way to launch a discussion of Ashbery's poetry than with an odd pair of anecdotes that have stuck in my memory for upward of ten years. The first is from a crowded New York party following an art opening. The poet and art critic Peter Schjeldahl, known for his contentious spirit, had cornered Ashbery in what appeared to be an impromptu debate. Ashbery wriggled uncomfortably. "You can't argue with me," he finally said, "because I don't exist." I can date my second anecdote more exactly; it took place in October 1984 in Ashbery's Chelsea apartment in New York City. I had gone to interview him for an article I was writing for the *New York Times Magazine*. Over coffee we talked about the much-vexed issue of poetic influence. Ashbery said that he felt he had been influenced more by the German Romantics than by the French Symbolists. "How about the Surrealists?" I asked. "Not the actual Surrealists," he said, "but hybrid ones like Reverdy and Max Jacob." When I had a typist transcribe our interview, however, this is what the exchange looked like:

> Interviewer: How about Sir Realist?
> Ashbery: Not the actual Sir Realist, but hybrid ones like the Reverend D. and Max Jack Hoe.

I cite the first remark—"you can't argue with me, because I don't exist"—as an example of a certain conversational prowess, the way Ashbery can disarm an inquirer or inquisitor with a surprising non sequitur delivered with a poker-face in an accent he once characterized as "hick." But it is evidence, too, of a kind of irony that delights in uttering an outrageous paradox that turns out even more outrageously to be true. For in a crucial sense John Ashbery does not exist in his poems. A singular quality of his poetry is what I would call its egolessness: the absence of the self as the self is traditionally conceived. The speaker in an Ashbery poem has a curiously distant relation to the living man who types his poems on an old-fashioned Royal typewriter, revises them seldom, teaches one day a week at Bard College, travels widely, has won just about every available literary honor, and carries an American passport made out to John Lawrence Ashbery. It would be fairer to speak of the speakers, plural, in Ashbery's work. The "I" has a feckless habit of sliding into "you," "he," "she," "we," and sometimes "they," each pronoun representing a voice in the poet's mental choir, with the result that, as Kenneth Koch once jested, the paradigmatic Ashbery sentence might be, "It wants to go to bed with us." Just as all the characters in a dream may be understood as projections of the dreamer's self, so too with the voices populating Ashbery's poetry. But there is a further twist. Ashbery's capacity for egolessness endows him with a sort of negative capability—the ability to empty himself so thoroughly that he can lose himself amid the objects of his attention. As he writes in his poem "Wet Casements" (1977), he wants "to see, as though reflected / In streaming windowpanes, the look of others through / Their own eyes." It is as if, for Ashbery, the act of writing a poem involves an emptying of his mind, an escape from his personality, and a departure from the particulars of his daily and professional lives.

The poem improbably titled "And *Ut Pictura Poesis* Is Her Name" (1977) has a particularly rich description of the poet's state of mind in the act of writing. This is the way the poem ends:

> Something
> Ought to be written about how this affects
> You when you write poetry:
> The extreme austerity of an almost empty mind
> Colliding with the lush, Rousseau-like foliage of its desire
> to communicate
> Something between breaths, if only for the sake
> Of others and their desire to understand you and desert you
> For other centers of communication, so that understanding
> May begin, and in doing so be undone.

As in many Ashbery poems, the title of this one is not a descriptive label (as, say, "Mending Wall" is descriptive of Robert Frost's poem) but a supplemental element. *"Ut Pictura Poesis"*—"as with the painter's work, so with the poet's"—was a famous pronouncement in that seminal document of classical criticism, Horace's "Art of Poetry." In his title, "And *Ut Pictura Poesis* Is Her Name," Ashbery goes so far as to identify Horace's phrase as a synonym for poetry itself. And then, in the first line of his poem, he renders his verdict: "You can't say it that way anymore." This may be a restatement of Horace—a recognition that poetry must constantly renew itself. But it is also an emphatic rejection of past modes of seeing and saying. The old rules of poetic diction and decorum are hereby declared defunct. This was Ashbery's starting point: the astonishing revelation that poetry, for all its richness of heritage, stood in need of being invented anew.

Ashbery dislikes explaining his poems, he once told me, because he is afraid that his explanation will be permanently affixed to his work. "I learned my lesson from *The Tennis Court Oath*," he said. When that book was in production in 1962, the publisher, Wesleyan University Press, asked him for a statement that could be used as the basis for the book's jacket copy. Ashbery wrote that there were parallels between his work and Abstract Expressionism, and the statement "haunts me every week." Why "haunts"? Because in critical discourse all too often labels choke off thinking; Abstract Expressionism is part of what went into Ashbery's poetry, but it is only one part. Ashbery's evasiveness, which sometimes seems reflexive, reflects not only his conviction that he is bound to be misinterpreted but his resistance to being categorized, classified, and put away. There is something of this evasiveness but also considerable candor in Ashbery's casual comments on the title of "And *Ut Pictura Poesis* Is Her Name." At a poetry reading at the Morgan Library in New York City on November 10, 1997, Ashbery prefaced his reading of this poem with the observation that he "never understood why I chose this title." After explaining that the Latin refers to Horace's dictum, he noted that the phrase "is her name" evokes the titles of patriotic World War II movies on the order of "And Miss Liberty Is Her Name." But then he allowed that he wrote the poem shortly after he had begun his teaching career at Brooklyn College in 1974, when he was forty-seven. He had been, he said, "sheltered from teaching," but now that students were asking him what poetry was, he found himself obliged to think on the question and one outcome of his thinking was this poem.

If poetry was something that had to be rethought from scratch, what of the traditional conception of the poet himself? He remains "a center of communication," who desires nothing more than to requite the reader's desire for "understanding." This urge to "communicate / Something between breaths" is what makes him a poet. He is, however, enough of a realist to know that readers are fickle and that "understanding" is a doomed project, a lifelong delusion that we may name as such even as we allow ourselves to pursue it, like the phantom of happiness itself. The question is, If misunderstandings are inevitable, what is the poet to do?

The answer is given in my second anecdote. What could be more in keeping with the surrealistic principle of linguistic transformation—and with the idea of "misunderstanding" as a liberating aesthetic principle—than the typist's dilemma listening to a tape in which the sounds of coffee cups and fire engines vie for audibility with a conversation loaded with unfamiliar names? The French poet Pierre Reverdy becomes "the Reverend D." Max Jacob becomes the rapper Max Jack Hoe, and Surrealism acquires a knighthood, because misunderstandings, though sometimes lamentable in our daily lives, have a value like that of dreams or jokes for the artist bent on making a virtue out of a necessity.

The theme of misunderstanding—sometimes deliberate, sometimes inadvertent, but always implicit in the acts of creation and communication—is one to which Ashbery has long been drawn. In his play *The Heroes* (1950), in which Greek champions of antiquity disport themselves as if at a Hamptons beach weekend, Theseus has a speech about the moment of illumination he had on his way to the party. At the station where his train was delayed, Theseus happened to see a couple in the window of the next train. "For fifteen minutes I watched them," he says. "I had no idea what their relation was. I could form no idea of their conversation. They might have been speaking words of love, or planning a murder, or quarreling about their in-laws. Yet just from watching them talk, even though I could hear nothing, I feel I know those people better than anyone in the world."

In the same sense that necessity is the mother of invention, ignorance is the mother of poetry, and metaphor is a polite term for a species of misunderstanding. The imagination, which eschews scientific certainty, is nourished by philosophical skepticism and inspired by partial knowledge. And since time is the dimension that alters all the others, and tomorrow modifies the lessons of today, it follows that, as Ashbery puts it in "Soonest Mended," "the promise of learning" is at once a delusion and a continuing enterprise, "so that from this standpoint / None of us ever graduates from college, / For time is an emulsion, and probably thinking not to grow up / Is the brightest kind of maturity for us, right now at any rate."

A recent Ashbery poem, "A Poem of Unrest" in *Can You Hear, Bird* (1995), demonstrates the persistence of the theme of misunderstanding in his work. The poem begins on a rueful note: "Men duly understand the river of life, / misconstruing it." Writers tend to be careless in their use of adverbs, but *duly* here makes its subtle point: With our misunderstandings we take our place in the proper order of things. Then the paradox turns tragic: "But since I don't understand myself, only segments / of myself that misunderstand each other, there's no / reason for you to want to, no way you could // even if we both wanted it." Yet such is the nature of desire that the desire to communicate persists in the face of apparently insuperable obstacles.

Does Ashbery merit the reputation he has as a difficult poet? Or is this a false impression, though an understandable one, given his heightened awareness of the limitations of language and his devotion to avant-garde poetics? I do not think Ashbery is merely being coy (which he can be) or perverse (ditto) in insisting that his notorious difficulty is, if not a bum rap, a nonissue. "In a line from one of my poems, 'All the true fragments are here,' I may have been, unconsciously, making an estimate of my poetry," Ashbery told Bill Berkson in 1969. "From my point of view, I find my poetry simple and immediate. I believe Pasternak quoted Scriabin as saying, 'Whatever you do, write as simply as possible.' And Scriabin's music, of course, is fantastically complicated. So apparently he felt even greater complications than those he reproduced in his music and was trying to give one the simplest possible statements about things—which may be true in my case."

Wallace Stevens, in such poems as "Sunday Morning," demonstrated that poetry could conduct a philosophical argument elliptically, with poetic leaps and bounds. Ashbery built on this lead. He had also learned, from the prose styles of Henry James and Marcel Proust, that the subordinate elements in a sentence may steal the show. A dependent clause might subvert the whole. Or a simile may eclipse the idea it was meant to illustrate—in technical lit-crit terms, the situation that results when the "vehicle" replaces the "tenor." In an Ashbery poem, the poetic logic can become complicated indeed. But the argument *is* advanced, the logic is not merely circular. Thus, in his poem "My Philosophy of Life" (1995), Ashbery conducts an argument about the subject announced in the title—the viability of "living the way philosophers live, / according to a set of principles." The argument is marked by digressions. At a crucial moment in his meditation, the poet introduces a simile that all but obliterates the ostensible subject of the sentence, "the new moral climate" that would ensue from having a "philosophy of life." But what results is not an undermining of the argument but a deepening of it. The poet resolves to

> . . . sort of let things be what they are
> while injecting them with the serum of the new moral
>   climate
> I thought I'd stumbled into, as a stranger
> accidentally presses against a panel and a bookcase slides
>   back,
> revealing a winding staircase with greenish light
> somewhere down below, and he automatically steps inside
> and the bookcase slides shut, as is customary on such
>   occasions.
> At once a fragrance overwhelms him—not saffron, not
>   lavender,
> but something in between. He thinks of cushions, like the
>   one
> his uncle's Boston bull terrier used to lie on watching him
> quizzically, pointed ear-tips folded over. And then the great
>   rush
> is on. Not a single idea emerges from it.

This is what happens when ideas are translated into words and images; the words and images take over, the "great rush" is on.

Nevertheless the argument, though interrupted, does continue. It reaches its climax as the result of another interruption, something that is "blocking" the poet's "train of thought." The epiphany comes in the form of a rhetorical question: "What was the matter with how I acted before?" At this, the turning point in the poem, the poet resolves to be content with "a compromise."

He will continue to "let / things be what they are, sort of," though this time without the "serum" of a "new moral climate" to immunize him. Ideas are there to be entertained, picked up, examined, replaced. But the poetry is elsewhere, in the winding staircase behind the bookcase, a place to which books may lead, but where the air is heavy not with ideas but with a fragrance and a memory. The very logic of this poem, with its detours into hidden chambers (and, later, visits to the seashore), enforces the poem's idea about ideas. "Still," he writes, "there's a lot of fun to be had in the gaps between ideas. / That's what they're made for!" In a sense, "My Philosophy of Life" is an elaboration of the position Ashbery stated in "Self-Portrait in a Convex Mirror":

> Each person
> Has one big theory to explain the universe
> But it doesn't tell the whole story
> And in the end it is what is outside him
> That matters, to him and especially to us
> Who have been given no help whatever
> In decoding our own man-size quotient and must rely
> On second-hand knowledge. Yet I know
> That no one else's taste is going to be
> Any help, and might as well be ignored.

The proliferating number of readers drawn to Ashbery's work have been given no help whatever in "decoding [their] own man-size quotient." They learn to read him not by cracking a master code (there is none) but by their willingness to enter the bounds of his sensibility with all its complications. None of Ashbery's poems have made more instant converts than "Self-Portrait in a Convex Mirror." Not atypical is the ardor of the poet Karen Pepper on first reading this poem. "I am reminded of a scene in one of Woody Allen's movies in which Woody lies on a couch in a state of fake despair, listing the reasons to go on living," Pepper writes. "I remember that he included Mozart's *Jupiter* Symphony and Mariel Hemingway's face. On my own personal list (and I think everyone must have one, who has had occasion to draw up a list for reasons *not* to go on living) I would put 'Self-Portrait.' " Vocal critics, regarding "Self-Portrait" as an anomalous exception, continue to complain that his work is incomprehensible. "Purists Will Object," as the title of an Ashbery poem has it. It is possible, however, that these critics are trying too hard—or trying in the wrong way. Ashbery's poems defeat the analytic methods of the New Criticism. Like mysterious equations in which the terms take on multiple values, they cannot be easily reduced to syllogisms. The effort to make conventional sense of the poems would be wasted; rather the reader should approach Ashbery's poems without preconception, or with the willingness to allow expectation to be dashed. For Ashbery, it is important to remember, the poem is the performance of an experience rather than a commentary on experience. So radical a departure from the norm is this that critics today are still catching up with poems Ashbery composed nearly half a century ago.

Ashbery once described *Stanzas in Meditation*, one of Gertrude Stein's most uncompromisingly experimental works, as a "hymn to possibility," and the same may be said of his own poems, which are negotiations of desire rather than expressions of ideas or ideals. Several of his early poems conform to the pattern of the high Romantic ode. The transcendent vision comes, transporting the poet from a place "where men sit and hear each other groan," as Keats puts it in "Ode to a Nightingale." The experience is so powerful that it leaves the poet wondering whether he is awake or asleep. A daydream in a boring office might provide the vehicle of escape, as in the case of "The Instruction Manual," which Ashbery wrote in the offices of McGraw-Hill, the textbook publisher he worked for, in July 1955, after returning from a car trip to Mexico. In another poem in *Some Trees*, the underrated "And You Know," also from 1955, the same pattern establishes itself: The transcendent vision takes the form of a wished-for visit to a distant land. In this case, the globe spinning on the teacher's desk in school is what awakens the students' desire to "travel on, not to a better land, perhaps, / But to the England of the sonnets, Paris, Colombia, and Switzerland / And all the places with names, that we wish to visit." So the students must say farewell to their teacher, "carrying your lessons in our hearts," and at just this strategic point in the poem, to signal the departure of the visionary moment, the poet shifts his point of view and speaks with the abandoned teacher's sad voice:

> And so they have left us feeling tired and old.
> They never cared for school anyway.
> And they have left us with the things pinned on the bulletin
> board,
> And the night, the endless, muggy night that is invading our
> school.

As a textbook example of a metonymy—in this case, a single attribute representing grade school as a whole—it would be hard to better the "things pinned on the bulletin board."

Ashbery's poetry has far more to do with names than with ideas, though ideas are what "we" return to "as to a wife, leaving / The mistress we desire." This remarkable simile is from "What Is Poetry," a companion piece to "And *Ut Pictura Poesis* Is Her Name," which was written around the same time (the poems are printed on back-to-back pages of Ashbery's *Selected Poems*). The phrase "What Is Poetry," given without a question mark, is as much a statement as a question, but it makes other questions follow. The poem culminates in a line that Ashbery says he happened to overhear in a conversation in a bookstore: "It might give us—what?—some flowers soon?" That the overheard line uttered by a stranger in the store should have its place in poetry—should, despite its provenance, conclude a poem that asks "what is poetry" and answers that this is it—is something that Ashbery may have learned from the musical compositions of John Cage or the café poems of Guillaume Apollinaire. For Ashbery, poems are made of words and names, not ideas, and the immediate source of those words is immaterial. "I think that in the process of writing all kinds of unexpected things happen that shift the poet away from his plan, and that these accidents are really what we mean when we talk about poetry," he has said. Many critics have noted Ashbery's fondness for the clichés and infelicities of the American language, which he incorporates in his work as if between invisible quotation marks. Ashbery overhears a woman on West Twenty-second Street talking to her dog. "Come on, dear," she says, and he has the title of a new poem. The speaker in an Ashbery poem might lapse into lines lifted from Milton or Walter Pater but is just as happy to utter colloquialisms: "I thought I had died and gone to heaven" or "Nobody wants my two cents / anymore." The idiom of the streets is redeemed simply by being included in the poem of the mind, the poem that is going on at all times. What Mallarmé called "the dialect of the tribe" is "sacred for me, just because it's the way we all talk," Ashbery once told me, adding with irrefutable logic: "We must know what we're doing or we wouldn't talk as we do."

Ashbery's readiness to ignore the facts and circumstances of his life, his ability to forget who he is when he writes a poem, says something additional about the subject of his poetry and the conception of the self from which it issues. The subject of Ashbery's poetry is his consciousness, and what makes it exemplary—to use a word the poet is fond of—is that it is so inclusive of the world beyond his room. Ashbery's consciousness *is* his self, but a self that is inseparable from the rush of phenomena that bombards it on all sides, to which it is extraordinarily welcoming. There is no "ego" to get in the way. The "stoic pose, tinged with irony and self-mockery," as Ashbery puts it in his prose poem "The System" (1972), is not just a pose but a reflexive habit of mind. I call it irony for want of a more exact term, but the important point is that it is an enabling condition, permitting the poet to present his "sequence of fantastic reflections as they succeed each other at a pace and according to an inner necessity of their own." Ashbery does not so much reject the idea of mimesis, or representation, as he extends it to a new area: the recording of his own mind in motion, "examined from a point of view like the painter's: in the round, bathed in a sufficient flow of overhead light, with 'all its imperfections on its head' and yet without prejudice of the exaggerations either of the anathematist or the eulogist: quietly, in short, and I hope succinctly."

It was perhaps Ashbery's capacity for "egolessness" that made him an ideal collaborator. It is certainly a peculiarity of his collaborations with Koch that they sound tonally more like Koch than like Ashbery, who is as invisible as a professional translator. "A Postcard to Popeye," a characteristic performance, was written when Ashbery visited Koch in Florence for the holidays in December 1956. The two poets contrived a set of arbitrary rules for the occasion—in this case, the requirement that each line include the word *record*, followed preferably with a genitive *of*. For example,

> The record of Herbert Hoover eating corn-on-the-cob was
> a complete sell-out,
> As was the record of J. Edgar Hoover reading *Pendennis* to
> the Czech shoplifters.
> Here, in the little town square, they are playing a record of
> Marianne Moore reading tea leaves;
> It is tied on the popularity shelf with the record of the
> emptying of Bing Crosby's Christmas stocking.

Such a collaborative exercise made it possible for Koch to produce "You Were Wearing," one of his signature poems, which he wrote in Florence after Ashbery's return to Paris. Here, too, the names of American icons are appropriated jubilantly:

> Father came in wearing his Dick Tracy necktie: "How about
>   a drink, everyone?"
> I said, "Let's go outside a while." Then we went onto the
>   porch and sat on the Abraham Lincoln swing.

"You Were Wearing," which seemed funnily incongruous to its first readers, accurately predicted the designer-label craze that transformed American marketing; Calvin Klein jeans and Michael Jordan sneakers are both variants on a "Dick Tracy necktie."

For his part, collaborating with Koch prepared Ashbery to write "Into the Dusk-Charged Air," 150 lines long, every line of which includes the name of a river, with the effect that the poem itself resembles a river in its propulsion and flow:

> Far from the Rappahannock, the silent
> Danube moves along toward the sea.
> The brown and green Nile rolls slowly
> Like the Niagara's welling descent.
> Tractors stood on the green banks of the Loire
> Near where it joined the Cher.
> The St. Lawrence prods among black stones
> And mud. But the Arno is all stones.

Having collaborated with Koch on "A Postcard to Popeye," Ashbery went on to write a Popeye sestina—"Farm Implements and Rutabagas in a Landscape" (1970)—about Popeye, Wimpy, Olive, Swee'pea, and spinach.

In 1960 Koch excitedly made plans to publish a volume of

his collaborations with Ashbery. In a letter dated "Mayberry the 22nd," written from "69 Berry Street, Newberry 14, Newberry," and addressed to "Dear Johnberry," Koch ordered Ashbery to "reply at once." The question was, "What shall we call the book? A Postcard to Popeye? Gottlieb's Rainbow? Cleopatra's Last Class? New Year's Eve? New Year's Day? All radiant titles, to be sure, as is indeed A New Pension Plan (original title of Death Paints a Picture, as you no doubt remember from those glorious licorice Excelsior days) or The Inferno (a bit glum, perhaps), and The Young Collectors is not so bad either." The book didn't come off, but that wasn't for want of Koch's enthusiasm. "Guess what I just found? 'The Canary'! You have no doubt forgotten this little-known, totally unread masterpiece, as have I; huh, let me look at it, honest I haven't, and quote you a few lines; I think you'll remember the delicious 'device' (I guess Dainty Devices is out as a title?)." The poem begins:

> After enjoining the precious cassoary
> To build pine seeds grumpy January
> By pleasing the multiple statuary
> We are afraid to hit the Po with a raspberry.
> It is no longer stuffy nor is it airy
> Within the fire escape or beyond the dairy
> Those boarding the pine-seed ferry
> Agree. . . .

Six of the Ashbery/Koch collaborations were published in *Locus Solus* in 1961, two others in *Chelsea* magazine in 1994. When "A Postcard to Popeye" appeared in *Chelsea* twenty-eight years after it had been written, a line in the poem was inadvertently omitted when Koch's faded typescript was transcribed onto a computer disk. Since I had edited this issue of *Chelsea*, Ashbery phoned me to point out the error—and quoted the missing line from memory: "Popeye has many records. Among his favorites is that of T. S. Eliot singing to Bernard Berenson." This was "the high point in that poem for me," Ashbery said, adding that to the best of his recollection it was Koch's line.

Fairfield Porter characterized Ashbery as "lazy and quick," two adjectives that don't usually go together. Both apply. When Ashbery delivered the Charles Eliot Norton lectures at Harvard in 1989–90, he would drive to Cambridge from his house in Hudson, New York, on the morning of each lecture. There were six of them, scheduled months apart. Each dealt with a neglected figure, the poets of an "other tradition": John Clare, Thomas Lovell Beddoes, Raymond Roussel, John Wheelwright, David Schubert, and Laura Riding. On the morning of his lecture on Roussel, Ashbery phoned James Tate to say that he wouldn't be able to stop in Amherst, Massachusetts, to pick up Tate and bring him along as they had previously planned. Amherst, where Tate lives, is on the way to Boston from Hudson but would represent a detour from Ashbery's apartment in New York City, where Ashbery unexpectedly found himself. And there was another thing, Ashbery said. He hadn't yet written the lecture. Fortunately, this lazy man is quick: The lecture on Roussel—one of the highlights of Ashbery's Norton series—was written that day in the backseat of the car motoring from Manhattan to Cambridge.

There is a portrait of Ashbery by Larry Rivers showing the poet in a short-sleeved shirt, white jeans, and loafers, seated on a couch hunched over a typewriter table pecking at the keys. He gives the impression of utter concentration and casual ease. Poems are "going on all the time in my head and I occasionally spin off a length," Ashbery has said. The poems, as a result, are cool; no sweat has gone into them in the way that the gnarled lines of Robert Lowell's early poems are dripping with perspiration. Ashbery's element is cool intelligence saturated with an irony so powerful and complex that one has to go back to Kierkegaard for a comparable example of a writer who thinks naturally in paradoxes. Ashbery is particularly fascinated by the liar's paradox—that is, by the capacity of language to generate sentences that can logically be neither true or false, as when someone says, "I am a liar." Or as Ashbery writes in "Grand Galop" (1975),

> The lies fall like flaxen threads from the skies
> All over America, and the fact that some of them are true of
>   course
> Doesn't so much not matter as serve to justify
> The whole mad organizing force under the billows of correct
>   delight.

The effect here is heightened by the push-button phrases—"the fact that," "of course"—and by the strategic double negative. A second animating paradox in Ashbery's work is Zeno's proposition that the arrow can never reach the target if space is infinitely divisible. Zeno's Paradox informs the many Ashbery poems in which a journey is interrupted before it gets off the ground and the dénouement, "advancing slowly, never arrives," though it remains imminent.

It is sometimes said of the poets influenced by Ashbery that you can tell at what stage in his career he was when they discovered him. For poets who came of age in the 1960s, the Ashbery of *The Tennis Court Oath* (1962) and *Rivers and Mountains* (1966) was the initiating experience. The great poem in *The Tennis Court Oath* had the beguiling title "How Much Longer Will I Be Able to Inhabit the Divine Sepulcher . . ." The poem is a meditation on the themes of confinement, release, freedom, growth, and puzzlement. But the logic throughout is elliptical, allusive, resembling an argument whose terms are constantly morphing, as when the apparent subject of the poem turns into a plant, and the soil in which the plant grows turns as suddenly into a sea, and the author steps back from his creation in a burst of lacerating self-consciousness:

> For he needs something or will forever remain a dwarf,
> Though a perfect one, and possessing a normal-sized brain
> But he has got to be released by giants from things.
> And as the plant grows older it realizes it will never be a
>   tree,
>
> Will probably always be haunted by a bee
> And cultivates stupid impressions
> So as not to become part of the dirt. The dirt
> Is mounting like a sea. And we say goodbye
>
> Shaking hands in front of the crashing of the waves
> That give our words lonesomeness, and make these flabby
>   hands seem ours—
> Hands that are always writing things
> On mirrors for people to see later—
>
> Do you want them to water,
> Plant, tear listlessly among the exchangeable ivy—
> Carrying food to mouth, touching genitals—
> But no doubt you have understood
>
> It all now and I am a fool.

The "crashing of the waves" was a spectacular transition, as if the quiet simile in the previous line had been enough to conjure the sea into roaring existence. And the reflexive pulling back at the end of the passage—"but no doubt you have understood / It all now and I am a fool"—contributed to the reader's amazement. Reading Ashbery one felt one was on the edge of comprehension (or of incomprehension, which means the same thing). But the state of uncertainty to which his poetry transported one was as oddly intoxicating as it was perplexing. The bafflement itself produced a mental commotion not unlike that of the uncanny, in which a familiar image is suddenly bathed in a foreign light. By the conclusion of "How Much Longer . . ." one felt that one was reading something like a generalized autobiography—"everybody's autobiography," in Gertrude Stein's phrase—the details of which could be filled in by each reader:

> Meanwhile what am I going to do?
> I am growing up again, in school, the crisis will be very
>   soon.
> And you twist the darkness in your fingers, you
> Who are slightly older . . .
>
> Who are you, anyway?
> And it is the color of sand,
> The darkness, as it sifts through your hand
> Because what does anything mean,
>
> The ivy and the sand? That boat
> Pulled up on the shore? Am I wonder,
> Strategically, and in the light
> Of the long sepulcher that hid death and hides me?

Because of the popularity of Kenneth Koch's writing classes, Columbia University became a bastion of the New York School in the 1960s. As a sophomore in 1967, I was told by a former editor of the *Columbia Review* that "The Skaters"—the long poem in *Rivers and Mountains*—was a latter-day equivalent of T. S. Eliot's *Waste Land*. The analogy did not seem exaggerated to me. As in Eliot's great poem, "The Skaters" offers a vision of urban alien-

ation, a portrait of a "professional exile" (Ashbery wrote "The
Skaters" in Paris) to whom the news of the day ("crime or revolution? Take your pick") is irrelevant:

> None of this makes any difference to professional exiles like
> me, and that includes everybody in the place.
> We go on sipping our coffee, thinking dark or transparent
> thoughts . . .
> Excuse me, may I have the sugar. Why certainly—pardon me
> for not having passed it to you.
> A lot of bunk, none of them really care whether you get any
> sugar or not.
> Just try asking for something more complicated and see how
> far it gets you.

In Ashbery's poem, as in Eliot's, the poet does "the police in
different voices," now the voice of the Romantic poet transported
to a desert isle,

> The west wind grazes my cheek, the droplets come pattering
> down;
> What matter now whether I wake or sleep?
> The west wind grazes my cheek, the droplets come pattering
> down;
> A vast design shows in the meadow's parched and trampled
> grasses.
> Actually a game of "fox and geese" has been played there,
> but the real reality,
> Beyond truer imaginings, is that it is a mystical design full
> of a certain significance,
> Burning, sealing its way into my consciousness.

now that of the rueful city dweller who cannot quite realize his
dream of escape:

> In reality of course the middle-class apartment I live in is
>   nothing like a desert island.
> Cozy and warm it is, with a good library and record
>   collection.
> Yet I feel cut off from the life in the streets.
> Automobiles and trucks plow by, spattering me with filthy
>   slush.
> The man in the street turns his face away. Another island-
>   dweller, no doubt.

The questioning of "art" and "reality" in passages like these is intense. The poet keeps pulling down the curtain on his own performance, only to lift it again, depicting the same action as before, this time in modern dress. And in "the real reality, beyond truer imaginings," he achieves the ultimate aporia, a knot of meaning that can never be unraveled, an unsolvable conundrum yet one that seems to make perfect sense. As an undergraduate at Columbia, I was so taken with the ironic undercutting in "The Skaters" that I immediately aimed for the same effect in my own poems. When I met the poet, I told him I loved the moment in "The Skaters" when the poem, which has been dwelling on the difficulties of sailing to a desert isle, is interrupted with the poet's admission that "in reality of course" he lived in a "middle-class apartment" with a "good library and record collection." Ashbery replied, "Actually, I lived in a slum when I wrote those lines." Years later I reminded him of this conversation. He looked blank. "I never lived in a slum," he said.*

The reality that Ashbery wants to dwell in and depict bears little resemblance to reality as defined on the front page of newspapers (though Ashbery is himself an avid reader of newspa-

---

*Asked recently to clarify this mystery, Ashbery explained that he wrote the poem in his cold-water flat on the rue d'Assas, which was small and "slum-like, but in a very nice neighborhood," in Paris's Sixth Arrondissement.

pers). The news is not reality; the news is an aberration, and only when it ceases to be news—that, for example, there are women students at Princeton and women cadets at West Point—does it become an almost invisible aspect of reality. There is, indeed, a "real reality" out there, but it has little to do with "a revolution in Argentina" and everything to do with the consciousness of a poet capable of equanimity amid uncertainty—what Keats called "negative capability." Ashbery is not entirely kidding when he complains, in a new poem, that his "negative capability [is] acting up again." It is this that enables him to balance, in the continual oscillations of his mind, the escapist impulse, on the one hand, and the determination to "sort of let things be what they are," on the other.

The critical reaction to Ashbery in those years was almost reflexively hostile. In 1970 someone in the *Saturday Review* called him "the Doris Day of Modernism." No one was sure what this meant. In what way could Ashbery be said to resemble Doris Day, the singer and actress with the wholesome image, about whom Oscar Levant wittily said, "I knew her before she was a virgin"? No matter; something about Ashbery's poetry, its ironies, juxtapositions, and leaps of logic, seemed to license critics to take liberties. To this day Ashbery is vilified in extravagant terms. He is the most imitated poet in America, and also the one most often parodied. Some parodies are goofy. In 1992 Ashbery published a collection of poems entitled *Hôtel Lautréamont*, the title a nod to the French Surrealist writer who might have been defining Surrealism itself when he wrote of his hero that "he is as handsome . . . as the chance encounter of a sewing machine and an umbrella on a dissecting-table." The poet John Haines dashed off "Hotel Laundromat" in response to Ashbery's new book. Haines's poem opens:

My plane has landed . . . It must be Egypt,
and night has arrived in an ark

> of bullrushes. The doorman grimaces,
> announcing the name of a city
> sprinkled with shoddy crumbs—
> Why, it's Nashville, but I'll just
> pretend it's Vienna, Budapest,
> or Cairo—anywhere but America!

The poem goes steadily downhill from there. In a more recent poem entitled "John Ashbery," Jeffrey Skinner parodies the poet and his fans. Ashbery, Skinner writes,

> was from *New York*, he was a skyscraper!
> He wrote a sestina called "Daffy Duck in Hollywood"!
> He mumbled his readings!
> He wrote book-length poems, any section of which
> could have been lifted or dropped
> from his shorter poems!
> He won three awards for a book no one could explain!

The fact that "Daffy Duck in Hollywood" is not a sestina does not disqualify the poem as a parody, and when Skinner writes against the grain of his animus his poem rises to a muted eloquence. Ashbery, he writes, "*is* the definition / of avant garde, given by a Chinese // poet (oh memory!): an ant who, / when coming upon a line of marching ants, / turns and goes the opposite direction."

Though he is America's best-known poet, with a strong readership in Britain and a larger international following than any of his American contemporaries, Ashbery remains an issue and for some a litmus test. A respected editor declared that one cannot like both Ashbery and Philip Larkin, and though I feel that one can, I understand the logic of her position. Ashbery's poetic assumptions are the opposite of Larkin's. Larkin set store by his sincerity and his control; Ashbery, by his fancy and his abandon. If your sense of literary tradition extends from Keats and the Romantics to Emerson and Whitman and from there to Wallace Stevens, Ashbery's your man; if, on the other hand, you derive your sense of tradition from Thomas Hardy and William Butler Yeats, Ashbery will seem a renegade.

The redoubtable Harold Bloom, who played Clement Greenberg to Ashbery's Jackson Pollock in the 1970s, made a series of influential pronouncements identifying the poet as "the most legitimate of the sons of Wallace Stevens." Bloom was even more effusive in private than in his published writings, I learned while reading through Ashbery's archive at the Houghton Library at Harvard. In his correspondence Bloom addressed Ashbery as "Best of Poets," described himself as the "most adoring of your exegetes," and predicted that "1956–1996 will be remembered as: *THE AGE OF ASHBERY.*" On my way to the Houghton Library one day, I encountered Seamus Heaney in Harvard Square. I told Heaney what I'd been up to. He wished me well on the project and then produced his own nutshell version of Ashbery's poetics: "That's all very well in practice, but what's it like in theory?"

From the start, Ashbery's precocity was prodigal. He won school prizes and spelling bees, went on a national radio show as a "quiz kid" with an expertise in French painting, and in prep school wrote poems good enough to be published in *Poetry.* On an afternoon in 1950, while waiting for the perennially late Kenneth Koch to turn up, Ashbery finished reading Boris Pasternak's memoir, *Safe Conduct.* The book concludes with a valedictory to Vladimir Mayakovsky, the great Russian poet who was, in the end, devoured by the Bolshevik revolution he had served. "He was spoilt from childhood by the future, which he mastered rather early and apparently without great difficulty," Pasternak wrote. Ashbery liked the sentence so much that he lifted it for the epigraph of the poem he wrote while waiting for Koch that afternoon, "The Picture of Little J. A. in a Prospect of Flowers." This is how the poem concludes:

Yet I cannot escape the picture
Of my small self in that bank of flowers:
My head among the blazing phlox
Seemed a pale and gigantic fungus.
I had a hard stare, accepting

Everything, taking nothing,
As though the rolled-up future might stink
As loud as stood the sick moment
The shutter clicked. Though I was wrong,
Still, as the loveliest feelings

Must soon find words, and these, yes,
Displace them, so I am not wrong
In calling this comic version of myself
The true one. For as change is horror,
Virtue is really stubbornness

And only in the light of lost words
Can we imagine our rewards.

Born on July 28, 1927, in Rochester, New York, John Lawrence Ashbery grew up on his father's fruit farm on Maple Avenue in Sodus, thirty miles east of Rochester on the edge of Lake Ontario. Sodus is an Indian word meaning "moonlight on water," and its proximity to *Solus*, the Latin word for "alone," would not be lost on Ashbery's fellow editors of *Locus Solus*; in homage to Ashbery they nicknamed the magazine "Locus Sodus." Ashbery's mother and father were a marriage of opposites. Helen Lawrence Ashbery, a college graduate in an era when that distinction was uncommon, was a high school biology teacher when she married Chester Ashbery in her thirties. Chester, known as Chet, was as extroverted and athletic as his wife was shy and retiring. A Buffalo native, he had taken an agricultural degree at Cornell and for years afterward liked driving down to Ithaca to watch the Cornell football team in action. (That John was closer to his mother than to his father is instantly evident to one spending time with the Ashbery archive at Harvard's Houghton Library, in which there is but one postcard from Chet Ashbery to his son as opposed to the more than three dozen folders full of letters from Helen.) John spent summers working unenthusiastically in his father's orchards, picking cherries or canning them in a local factory. Growing up in the snowbelt—"I hear America snowing," he wrote—he learned to amuse himself with books and magazines telling of the great world outside. "One of my earliest memories," he wrote, reviewing a show of wallpaper at the Cooper-Hewitt Museum in New York, "is of trying to peel off the wallpaper in my room, not out of animosity but because it seemed there must be something fascinating beyond the surface pattern of galleons, globes and telescopes." *The Book of Knowledge,* a twenty-one-volume illustrated children's encyclopedia, answered his native curiosity. He liked its Edwardian tone—it dated to 1912—and was drawn to the section entitled "Things to Make and to Do," which included instructions for building a telephone, crafting a brush-and-comb bag, and designing a paper shade for a candle.

There is a secret to "The Skaters," which Ashbery wrote in Paris in 1963, and that is that this poem, with its medley of voices, its dreams of desert isles, its tales of journeys interrupted or postponed, is at its source an expression of homesickness for the lonely childhood of a clever lad seeking desperately to amuse himself on snowbound days. What triggered off the poem was Ashbery's purchase, on a Paris quay, of a book entitled *Three Hundred Things a Bright Boy Can Do,* which had been published in

England in 1911. The book reminded him strongly of the encyclopedia of his childhood. And indeed, the Edwardian *Book of Knowledge* is a little like the sled called "Rosebud" in *Citizen Kane*: a fitting aesthetic solution that leaves the initial problem—whether of Kane's character or the meaning of "The Skaters"—unsolved. Although Ashbery had never learned how to skate properly, he decided to base "The Skaters" on a collage from his new purchase.* He took his title from this passage: "Some sounds, of course, it is almost impossible to reduce to writing, as, for example, the hollow scam and murmur produced by a multitude of skaters, or the roar of an excited crowd."

The dominant figure in Ashbery's life as a young man was his maternal grandfather, Henry Lawrence. Lawrence was a professor of physics and long-standing chairman of the physics department at the University of Rochester, and in his grandson's eyes a great man. "I resemble him and I took after him," Ashbery remarked. His grandfather "kind of took over my education . . . displacing my father, which caused a certain amount of friction in the family." The boy preferred his grandfather's library to his father's farm; "I wasn't cut out to be a farm boy and Huck Finn type." Henry Lawrence knew Greek and Latin, had read the classics, and owned a library that his grandson loved. "I did a great deal of reading and lived in a sort of fantasy world with what I read," Ashbery said. "Also, my grandfather encouraged me to be whatever I wanted to be and he had a lot of books which I pored over, including Shakespeare and the Victorian novelists. Not that I got very much out of it, but even when I was ten years old I tried to read Shakespeare's plays." When Ashbery met with a setback at boarding school or college, he would turn to his grandfather. Henry Lawrence responded with the expected encouragement,

---

*More than a few Ashbery poems—the recent ". . . by an Earthquake" is another—have been inspired by, or collaged from, old, out-of-date books bought at used-book stores.

but more valuably with the moral instruction crucial to the development of the young man's character. "If you at times feel lonely I would not have it otherwise," Henry Lawrence advised his seventeen-year-old grandson at Deerfield Academy in 1944. "It is a malady from which one recovers."

It was thought that the Rochester schools were superior to the one in Sodus, so young John attended kindergarten and first grade in Rochester, living at his grandparents' house. In 1979, when the poet, a longtime apartment dweller in Manhattan, bought a house in Hudson, New York, he did so with an eye toward replicating his grandfather's house on Dartmouth Street in Rochester. The architecturally eclectic Hudson structure, which dates to 1894, "has the gloomy but somehow welcoming aspect ('a gloom one knows,' as I tried to describe it to a friend) of houses in the turn-of-the-century neighborhood in Rochester, New York, where my grandparents lived," Ashbery wrote in *Architectural Digest*. "I loved to visit their house as a child, and felt a sense of loss when it passed out of the family."

John greatly preferred spending summer days in Pultneyville—the little village on Lake Ontario to which his grandparents retired in 1934—than at the Sodus farm six miles away. In Pultneyville he met Mary Wellington, a pretty Rochester girl, whose grandmother owned a summer house on the lakeshore. The two played on the beach as children and later had an "idyllic" teenage relationship that lasted through Ashbery's years at Deerfield. "I had a crush on her," Ashbery remembers. "We had a place where we played called 'the Kingdom.' We each had a castle, which was usually a willow tree. I made a map of the whole place." In winters he would write his Rochester friend three or four times a week, illustrating the letters with drawings. The letters also contain to-be-continued stories—set in "Gruesome Gables, Nova Scotia"—in a manner suggestive of Ashbery's play *The Compromise*. The project was inspired by the movie *Topper Returns*, which

John and his friends saw on his fourteenth birthday. "I always thought of 1941 as the last time it was fun in my childhood," Ashbery says.

Ashbery wrote his first poem, "The Battle," at the age of eight:

> The trees are bent with their glittering load,
> The bushes are covered and so is the road.
> The fairies are riding upon their snowflakes,
> And the tall haystacks are great sugar mounds.
> These are the fairies' camping grounds.

The poem was read aloud at a Christmas party in the Fifth Avenue apartment of the popular novelist Mary Roberts Rinehart, a family relation. "The poem had rhyme and made sense, and I felt it was so good I couldn't go on from this pinnacle," Ashbery remembers thinking.

Also at eight, Ashbery began taking piano lessons and learned to read music. The conclusion of Grieg's *Peer Gynt Suite*—the same part Fritz Lang used in his movie *M*—was an early favorite. A taste for Wagner followed a few years later. The acquisition of the Overture to *Tannhäuser* and the Venusburg Music, a $5.25 purchase in 1942, was a big event, as was listening to Rachmaninoff's "To the Children" sung by Lawrence Tibbett on "The Bell Telephone Hour." Ashbery, who would continue to take lessons until he was fifteen, went on to develop a rare expertise in modern music. To this day he likes writing poetry to the accompaniment of one of New York City's all-classical radio stations, and a visitor invited for cocktails may be treated to the playing of a new compact disc of *Peer Gynt* by the Russian composer Alfred Schnittke (1985). John Cage seemed to formulate one of the poet's ambitions when he told Ashbery, who was interviewing him for the *International Herald Tribune*, that "he wanted to stretch people's ears a little so that they could hear a little bit more," in Ashbery's paraphrase. But Cage was scarcely the only composer who exerted an influence on Ashbery. He played Elliott Carter's *Concerto for Orchestra* while writing the first of his *Three Poems* (1972) and turned to Brahms's first sextet when working on later parts of the book. Luciano Berio, in whose *Sinfonia* the scherzo movement of Mahler's *Resurrection* Symphony is juxtaposed with a text of Samuel Beckett, was another musical model for Ashbery's "polyvocal" poems. Ashbery especially liked Berio's *Omaggio* to James Joyce, in which the composer transformed the words of a poem "until they were incomprehensible but still gave an idea of the original." Ashbery described the result approvingly as "one part shimmer, three parts shriek."

The boy was nine when he discovered Surrealism in the pages of *Life* magazine. *Life* was then brand-new. The issue dated December 14, 1936, with the Archbishop of Canterbury on the cover, was only the magazine's fourth appearance. There were two items that were bound to compel the interest of "little J. A." One was a photograph from Rochester, New York, of a propeller plane lodged in an apple tree while children dressed for snow look on. (Needing to make an emergency landing, the pilot had apparently headed for an empty playground, missed it by a hundred feet, and took refuge in the apple tree as the next best thing.) But what made a bigger impact on the Rochester native was *Life*'s coverage of Alfred Barr's "Fantastic Art, Dada, and Surrealism" show, which had opened at the Museum of Modern Art in New York City that December 9. The piece was lavishly illustrated with photographs of such Surrealistic standbys as Meret Oppenheim's fur-lined teacup and saucer, a René Magritte eye with clouds in the horizon, a Max Ernst elephant, and a haunting Giorgio de Chirico colonnade looking like the backdrop to a metaphysical thriller by Franz Kafka. Salvador Dali's vision of liquid timepieces, *The Persistence of Memory* (1931), was reproduced at two thirds its actual size. "I pored over that magazine for years," Ashbery has said. "I became a Surrealist at that moment." But by the time literary critics, catching up with Ashbery's poetry in the 1960s and '70s, called him a Surrealist, he no longer considered himself one. He had digested the influence and had moved on, and it annoys him to be considered "a late-blooming umbilical cord between the French Surrealists and Americans," as he once put it. One of the funniest moments in Ashbery's Paris correspondence with Kenneth Koch occurs in an undated letter from 1956 whose salutation is "Dear Montcalm." "I *hate* all modern French poetry, except for Raymond Roussel," Ashbery proclaims. "Molière, Racine, and La Fontaine are the only truly modern French poets. I do like my own wildly inaccurate translations of some of the 20th century ones, but not the originals." In the end what Ashbery learned from Surrealism was, he felt, an abstract lesson on a par with Henry James's advice, "Be one of those people on whom nothing is lost." What the Surrealists offered was, in Henri Michaux's phrase, *la grande permission*—"the big permission." And from Marcel Duchamp, the Papa of Dadaism, who notoriously installed a urinal in a museum and called it a work of art, Ashbery learned that an artist's hand and skill may count for less than his mind and will.

Ashbery took weekly painting lessons at the Memorial Art Gallery in Rochester until he was fifteen. Not until he entered Harvard would he identify himself as primarily a poet rather than a painter. Looking back half a century later, Ashbery liked recalling the example of William Carlos Williams, who had also given up painting in favor of poetry, saying it was easier to lug around a manuscript than a wet canvas.

In 1940 a network quiz show featuring bright children made its debut on the nation's airwaves. "Quiz Kids" was an immediate success. Listeners tuned in to hear how a precocious nine-year-old might answer the question: "What would a musical automobilist do if he approached highway signs that read a) *andante*,

b) *a tempo,* c) *finale?"* And someone like little Ruthie Duskin, a "Quiz Kids" prodigy from the age of seven, could be expected to pipe up that the answers were a) slow down, b) resume regular speed, c) stop—end of road. "Quiz Kids" was the inspiration for the radio program that J. D. Salinger calls "It's a Wise Child" in *Franny and Zooey.* All seven children in the fictional Glass family "had managed to answer over the air a prodigious number of alternately deadly-bookish and deadly-cute questions—sent in by listeners—with a freshness, an aplomb, that was considered unique in commercial radio," Salinger writes. "Public response to the children was often hot and never tepid. In general, listeners were divided into two, curiously restive camps: those who held that the Glasses were a bunch of unsufferably 'superior' little bastards that should have been drowned or gassed at birth, and those who held that they were bona-fide underage wits and savants, of an uncommon, if unenviable, order."

"Quiz Kids" had been on the air for a year when Ashbery, fourteen, entered a local competition for the honor of representing the Rochester area on the national program. On a Saturday morning that November, Ashbery and four other finalists assembled at the RKO Palace, the largest movie theater in Rochester, while parents, friends, and classmates watched. Three contestants had been eliminated when Ashbery and a Rochester lad named Charles McHale were asked to name the presidents whose first and last initials were the same. Sodus's representative was able to name two of the three, Woodrow Wilson, Calvin Coolidge, and Herbert Hoover, and was crowned champion. Ashbery had also correctly identified Liszt's Hungarian Rhapsody no. 2, defined homicide, patricide, matricide, and herbicide, and named the gents whose pictures appear on the one-, two-, five-, ten-, twenty-, and fifty-dollar bills. For his efforts, Ashbery was awarded a $100 war bond, a console radio, and a free trip to Chicago, where the national program was based.

In the first week of December 1941, Ashbery, accompanied

by his mother and grandmother, took the train to Chicago, where they stayed at the Palmer House. Three days before his scheduled appearance on the show, the Japanese bombed Pearl Harbor. "The first ten minutes of the hour were taken up with news bulletins, which annoyed me no end," Ashbery confessed. Ashbery's specialty was eighteenth-century French painting. On the show the quizmaster asked the contestants, "If you wanted somebody to draw you a cartoon, would you choose Fragonard, Corot, or Daumier?" Ashbery knew the answer was the nineteenth-century Daumier. "It was the only answer I got right," he told me, "though I knew the answers to some of the other questions. However I didn't get my hand up fast enough, unlike the permanent contestants on the program who had honed that to a fine art."

In 1943 Ashbery, nearing his sixteenth birthday, won a current-events competition sponsored by *Time* magazine. For his prize he chose Louis Untermeyer's anthology *Modern British and American Poetry*. At first his favorites were Robert Frost, Edna St. Vincent Millay, Elinor Wylie, Edwin Arlington Robinson, and Edgar Lee Masters, because they seemed easy. But he soon found himself drawn to W. H. Auden ("In Time of War") and Dylan Thomas ("The Force That Through the Green Fuse Drives the Flower"), precisely because these works baffled him. Ashbery now had a new ambition: to have the sonnets he was writing accepted by *Scholastic* magazine. Poems by a young student named Richard Avedon had appeared there, and Ashbery felt that his poems were as good as the future photographer's.

That same year a private grant from a Sodus neighbor enabled Ashbery to transfer from the local public high school to Deerfield Academy, an elite boarding school in western Massachusetts, where a poet's life was far from the romantic thing it is in *Dead Poets Society*. He was neither rich nor a good athlete at a time when these things were of the utmost importance, and felt as isolated as he had on the family farm, though he did make friends with the other "outcasts" and misfits at the school. He was at ease in the painting studio, where he learned how to paint a still life by making study after study of a copper jug. He found algebra rough going and needed pep talks from his grandfather to help him get through it. French was more fun; Ashbery got high marks when he gave an oral presentation analyzing his class-mates on the basis of the neckties they were sporting that day. And he made a name for himself in literary and dramatic circles. He wrote poems and at least one story for the Deerfield *Scroll,* and he joined the Deerfield Players, playing Miss Preen in *The Man Who Came to Dinner* in December 1943, and Martha Brew-ster, one of the two mad aunts in *Arsenic and Old Lace,* a year later. The latter "was a superb success as shown by the mirthful applause of the audience," the Deerfield *Scroll* reported in a front-page story. "The play is the story of two elderly aunts and a houseful of maniacs and other people generally lacking in human characteristics. Among the menagerie of 'queers' is a man who firmly believes that he is 'Teddy' Roosevelt, a murderer, and the two aunts whose avocation is mercifully removing old men from society." A photograph of actors from the play, including Ashbery in wig, dress, and necklace, appeared next to the article. That the Deerfield faithful were still talking about the play decades later is evident from the class mailing the school sent out for the class of 1945's fortieth reunion. The memory of "John Ashbury [*sic*], Ed Douglas and Doc Bell gaining critical acclaim for their per-formances in 'Arsenic & Old Lace' " was on a par with that of "the undefeated Tennis team (they beat Amherst Varsity) and the Lacrosse team beating the Williams Varsity 8–6 with Dixie Vaughan scoring 6 goals" and the "68 inches of snow in the win-ter of '45."

At Deerfield, Ashbery developed a surprisingly mature un-derstanding of what he was up to, or up against, in modern poetry. "Poetry today has the smallest audience of almost any period since the middle ages," he wrote in "Recent Tendencies in Poetry" in his senior year. "Yet, strangely enough, the poetry of today is good poetry, it shows an awareness and an intellectual responsibility which one might say has been rarely equalled in any era. Its high caliber and its extreme complexity may both be accounted for by the fact that the poet, neglected by a society of which he is a member whether he wishes it or not, turns from the outside world as inspiration for his poetry, and feeds on the processes and intricacies of his own mind. Poetry becomes then highly personal and highly original."

Two of the poems Ashbery wrote that year were published in *Poetry* magazine in November 1945. "Lost Cove" begins with this stanza:

Where the sun delved in trees and darkly
Faltered, we made our stopping place
And that day swam off the naked beaches,
Or pried in the swamp for specimens,
Or simply tanned or talked on the rocks.

And here is "Poem" in its entirety:

Though we seek always the known absolute
Of all our days together, love will not occur
For us. Love is a fact
Beyond the witches wood of facts that is
Our sorcery's domain. And though we may
Charm lion into squirrel, push back the sea,
Love is made outlaw, sat beyond all art,
The ultimate error of our reasoning.

But when I see you walk or catch your face
Edged with season's most erratic leaves

Love grows superfluous, and I look at you
As I would look at flowers. Our only need
The sympathy of darkness for the seed.

The same issue of *Poetry* featured three poems by a rifleman in the 96th Infantry Division named Kenneth Koch. But Ashbery's poems, unlike Koch's, were printed without his name or his knowledge. A Deerfield classmate named William Charlton Haddock, who had roomed with Ashbery for a semester and had acted with him in *The Man Who Came to Dinner* and *Arsenic and Old Lace,* copied the works, mixed them with his own, and brought them to the school's poet-in-residence, David Morton. Morton, a respected poet who wrote in a traditional idiom, liked the young man's poems. Morton's own collected poems appeared from Knopf that year, and he seized this favorable moment to send his student's work to *Poetry* with a cover letter praising the author's "mystical imagination" and "authentic eloquence." The editors snapped up two of the poems—the two Ashbery had written. The plagiarist chose the pseudonym Joel Michael Symington, perhaps because the son of Missouri senator Stuart Symington was a Deerfield classmate. Months passed, and when Ashbery sent the same poems to *Poetry*, they were rejected in a one-word note ("Sorry"). Still later, after the shock of seeing them in print and figuring out what had happened, Ashbery reasoned that the editors must have assumed that *he* was the plagiarist. He feared that he would be "permanently blackballed" from publishing in *Poetry*, which was "virtually the only outlet for poetry at the time," and wondered whether his career "had ended before it began." For Ashbery, whose work has occasioned so much misunderstanding, and in fact seems to thrive on misunderstanding, to the point that a careful reading of his poems could give rise to the view that "poetry is mistranslation"—how ironically apt it was that his "official" literary career began on such a bizarre and paradoxical note, with a mix-up in identities as profound as the celebrated enigmas and ambiguities in his work.

Ashbery had just turned eighteen when "Poem" and "Lost Cove" appeared under the name Joel Michael Symington in *Poetry*. He had completed his junior year at Harvard and was still a month shy of his twenty-first birthday when he wrote the earliest of the poems that he would retain for his first book, *Some Trees*. "The Painter," a sestina, was written on June 16, 1948. "Sestinas are easy to write," Ashbery advised Kenneth Koch two days later. "After the first stanza they practically write themselves, as if a bicycle, which was hard to pump at first, ended up by pushing your feet with the pedals. Also, the effects gotten by repetition are delightful, and suit my fun-making purposes." In August, Ashbery typed out a copy and on the back of the sheet wrote a letter to Koch in free verse. He was having a crisis of confidence, he said, because the magazines to which he was submitting his work were rejecting it "with furious regularity." Perhaps they were right; he was sure that his new sestina was "bad bad bad." In fact, however, "The Painter" is not only a brilliant handling of the sestina form but a kind of prescient parable about Ashbery's own career.

Paradoxically, the complicated rules of the sestina make it an easy form for a writer who is willing to trust his words to guide him on a direction seemingly of their own choosing. There are six end-words, technically known as teleutons, that must appear seven times each, in a predetermined order, in the thirty-nine lines of a sestina. Six stanzas containing six lines each are followed by a three-line envoi. If the end-words of the first stanza are designated 1-2-3-4-5-6, they recur in the pattern 6-1-5-2-4-3 in the second stanza, 3-6-4-1-2-5 in the third stanza, 5-3-2-6-1-4 in the fourth, 4-5-1-3-6-2 in the fifth, and 2-4-6-5-3-1 in the sixth; 1 and 2 return in the first line of the envoi, 3 and 4 in the second, and 5 and 6 in the third. The teleutons should be flexible enough to allow for variation of sense and at the same time focused enough to permit a coherent argument or narrative to emerge. The sestina's repetitions create a strange music of insistence. They are also opportunities for the poet to explore the various meanings of a given word. The form is surprisingly congenial to the rhetorical purposes of an argument or a narrative; there is a built-in transition from stanza to stanza, since the last word of any stanza must also recur as the last word of the first line of the next stanza.

In "The Painter," Ashbery chooses five teleutons from one paradigm and the sixth from another. The recurrent end-words are *buildings, portrait, prayer, subject, brush,* and *canvas:* five terms having to do with art, the sixth with religion. Ashbery derived this five:one ratio from Elizabeth Bishop's sestina "A Miracle for Breakfast" in *North & South* (1946), which he read with rapt interest that year. In Bishop's sestina, five of the end-words name tangible things *(coffee, crumb, balcony, sun,* and *river)* while the sixth, *miracle,* names a supernatural condition. In "The Painter" as in "A Miracle for Breakfast," the effect of the sixth word is to impose a kind of moral order on the narrative that the other words suggest. So impressed was Ashbery with Bishop's poetry—especially "her surreal combination of urban landscape and seascape" and the "patina" her poems had—that he sent her a fan letter and was overjoyed to receive a "very nice postcard from Maine" in return. Bishop would remain Ashbery's favorite American poet; "The Painter" was merely the first fruit of her salutary influence on him.

"Be sure to read Elizabeth Bishop's poem in the June PR [*Partisan Review*]," Ashbery told Koch in the letter accompanying "The Painter." "I have read it at least 20 times—I know this will prejudice you against it, but read it anyway." The Bishop poem in the *Partisan Review* that June is a great one: "Over 2000 Illustrations and a Complete Concordance." Reviewing Bishop's prematurely titled *Complete Poems* for the *New York Times Book Review* in 1969, Ashbery was still marveling at the poem's conclusion:

> Everything only connected by "and" and "and."
> Open the book. (The gilt rubs off the edges
> of the pages and pollinates the fingertips.)
> Open the heavy book. Why couldn't we have seen
> this old Nativity while we were at it?
> —the dark ajar, the rocks breaking with light,
> an undisturbed, unbreathing flame,
> colorless, sparkless, freely fed on straw,
> and, lulled within, a family with pets,
> —and looked and looked our infant sight away.

"I am unable to exhaust the meaning and mysteries of its concluding line: 'And looked and looked our infant sight away,'" Ashbery wrote, "and I suspect that its secret has very much to do with the nature of Miss Bishop's poetry. Looking, or attention, will absorb the object with its meaning." In March 1997, at a group reading from Jorie Graham's "Golden Ecco" anthology of great poems of the English language, Ashbery read "Over 2000 Illustrations and a Complete Concordance." When he reached the last stanza, he cried.

In "The Painter," the two end-words with the greatest resonance are *prayer* (for it casts the whole story in a religious light) and *subject* (a telling choice, since the crisis in subject matter was either the signal of, or a symptom of, the rise of abstract art). Ashbery's painter, whose search for subject matter has taken him to the sea, begins by backing off from the task. "Just as children imagine a prayer / Is merely silence, he expected his subject / To rush up the sand, and, seizing a brush, / Plaster its own portrait on the canvas." His "prayer / That nature, not art, might usurp the canvas" prompts catcalls and boos; the public instinctively scoffs. Next the restless artist seems to go through a de Kooning period ("He chose his wife for a new subject, / Making her vast, like ruined buildings"), but then returns to the sea for one last effort. Some greet it with "malicious mirth," while

> Others declared it a self-portrait.
> Finally all indications of a subject
> Began to fade, leaving the canvas
> Perfectly white. He put down the brush.
> At once a howl, that was also a prayer,
> Arose from the overcrowded buildings.
>
> They tossed him, the portrait, from the tallest of the
>   buildings;
> And the sea devoured the canvas and the brush
> As though his subject had decided to remain a prayer.

The ideas in this poem—to which we return "as to a wife, leaving / The mistress we desire"—are possibilities that Ashbery will work through in his poetry: that a seascape can be a "self-portrait," that the title of a poem or a picture may indicate a subject otherwise absent, that erasure may afford a method of composition, that subject matter may be eliminated altogether. The problem of what to include and what to omit became a central preoccupation for Ashbery between *Rivers and Mountains* (1966) and *Three Poems* (1972). In "The Skaters," Ashbery refers to "this leaving-out business," calling attention to his poetry's obliqueness but refusing to offer an explanation, "except to say that the carnivorous / Way of these lines is to devour their own nature, leaving / Nothing but a bitter impression of absence, which as we know involves presence, but still. / Nevertheless these are fundamental absences, struggling to get up and be off themselves."

It is curious that Ashbery should opt for the phrase "this leaving-out business" to describe an aspect of his poetic strategy. A version of this phrase appeared in Ashbery's diary when he was fifteen years old. In September 1942, Ashbery misplaced his diary and was obliged to use loose-leaf pages for his daily notations until the missing book turned up. These pages have survived. "Right here and now I want it said that nobody detests this business of leaving out days more than I," Ashbery wrote after allowing a weekend to go by unannotated.

On the level of desire, beneath the surface complexity of ideas, the most significant element in "The Painter" is the martyrdom of Ashbery's hero. When the angry crowd throws the painter, who like Dorian Gray is indistinguishable from his portrait, off the top of a tall building, it is clear that part of the modern artist's role is to play the scapegoat and that it is the fate of scapegoats to be lynched. The predicament is echoed in "Illustration," another early Ashbery poem, in which a "novice" (that is, a religious initiate) leaps off a "cornice." For Ashbery, art involves a vertiginous leap, possibly a suicidal one: It is this that painting, and by implication poetry, shares with religion. "He who leaps into the abyss owes no one an explanation," Ashbery once said to me, paraphrasing Nietzsche.

Ashbery was an indifferent student at Harvard. In his freshman year he earned a C in modern art and a C in French, and he always had more B's in his portfolio than A's. No one could have predicted from his performance at Harvard that he would go on to turn out translations of French writers, such as Max Jacob, Pierre Reverdy, and Raymond Roussel, that are among the best we have. Nor is there any hint that he would produce a body of art criticism as discerning and profound as the sum of the pieces he wrote regularly for *Art News*, *New York*, and *Newsweek* magazines for twenty years after his return to New York from Paris in 1965. On the other hand, Ashbery's senior thesis on the poetry of W. H. Auden was so sensitive to the nuances of the poetry and so well written that the Harvard English department voted to grant him his degree cum laude on the strength of this achievement alone. The influence of Auden is clearly discernible in the poems Ashbery published in the *Advocate* as a Harvard undergraduate. For example, "Point of Departure" (1947), which concludes:

> But all escape prefigures
> The choices and goodbyes
> And freedom like a statue
> Dominates the square:
> In classic Greek attire
> And formal in all weathers.

One evening Ashbery and Kenneth Koch were playing pinball at a Harvard café when Auden himself entered, had a cup of coffee, and left. Ashbery said he was miffed that the poet had not greeted them. "But we don't even know him and we haven't published anything," Koch said. "Well, you'd think that he would know," Ashbery replied glumly.

At Harvard Ashbery grew close to Koch and O'Hara but also maintained cordial relations with the other aspiring writers. *The Advocate* printed his work regularly. In the fall of his senior year he wrote the poem that would provide the title for his first book. When Ashbery submitted "Some Trees" to the *Advocate*, Robert Bly, then the magazine's "Pegasus," or literary editor, was bowled over. "I was amazed that someone my age could write that," Bly remembers thinking. Ashbery and Robert Creeley sat "almost side by side," in a course on the eighteenth-century English novel. "Creeley was much too forbidding looking" for the perennially shy Ashbery to break the ice. But though they never sat down together to compare notes on Richardson and Fielding,

Ashbery muses, "we may well have realized then that we were on the opposite sides of the poetic fence: me so European and maximalist, influenced by Auden and Stevens; he so American, with perhaps an Asian conciseness gleaned from the Pound-Williams tradition to which [Charles] Olson's presence would soon be added." In an interview, Ashbery told me that in college he found Alison Lurie and Barbara Zimmerman (who would later, as Barbara Epstein, become editor of *The New York Review of Books*) particularly "sophisticated." When I repeated this remark to Alison Lurie, she said she remembered thinking *he* was particularly sophisticated. "No one," she added, "is ever again as sophisticated as the people one knew and admired in college—especially the people who were slightly older than we were."

Ashbery was less interested in courses and grades than in poems and prizes. In 1949, the poet L. E. Sissman—who shared with Ashbery the distinction of having been a radio Quiz Kid—won Harvard's Garrison Prize. Ashbery sent Koch the news. "Since I heard, I have been under the constant supervision of a physician and a trained nurse," he wrote dryly. His letters to Koch are packed with his latest poems, his eagerness to have Koch's opinion of them, his own comments on Koch's works, and his reactions to the movies he has recently seen. (Ashbery's love of movies turned out to be far more enduring than his early interest in the stage.) On one occasion Ashbery summed up their differing approaches to poetic closure. You "put a simile in the last line as a sort of sculptor's last loving pat," Ashbery observed in the same letter in which he declared it was easy to write a sestina, "whereas I try to erect a smokescreen near the end of my poems so I can withdraw unperceived—I never like to be around for the last line."

Following his Harvard graduation, Ashbery lived in New York City for six years before his departure for Paris on a Fulbright Fellowship in 1955. Despite a bout of listlessness and self-doubt that afflicted him during much of 1950 and 1951, Ashbery was highly productive in New York. In addition to the poems of *Some Trees*, he began *A Nest of Ninnies* with Schuyler, wrote his first collaborations with Koch, acted in a Living Theater production of Picasso's *Desire Trapped by the Tail*, and wrote two plays, *The Heroes* and *The Compromise*. He did this all at night and on weekends; days were spent writing jacket copy for Oxford University Press and later writing press releases and circulars for the college textbook department at McGraw-Hill.

Ashbery's plays reveal the same ability to vanish into the form that mark his collaborations with Schuyler and Koch. "The theatre is not a suppressed passion of mine, something I wish I'd gone into," Ashbery told an interviewer in 1978, the year *Three Plays* was published. "Nevertheless, I have enjoyed writing plays, and I think this is because I tend to think in different voices, none of which ever seem to be my own. Perhaps I am able to write more easily when I imagine what another person might be thinking or saying than if I were to imagine what I might be thinking or saying. I think that in my poetry one can become aware of a number of different voices carrying on a dialogue or conversation in the poem even though it's not indicated, of course, as it is in a play. This I think kind of naturally led me to attempt writing plays."

Ashbery wrote *The Heroes*, a one-act play in prose, in 1950. The play could almost be considered an eclogue—that is, a poem in the form of a dialogue—on the model of W. H. Auden's *The Age of Anxiety* (1948). An eclogue depends on a deliberate incongruity between the setting and the diction, as between the shepherds' trade and their high-minded conversation in the classic pastoral eclogues of Theocritus. In Auden's *The Age of Anxiety* a Third Avenue bar in Manhattan is the setting, and a quartet of New Yorkers speak alliteratively in the style of Anglo-Saxon verse. In *The He-*

roes, a group of larger-than-life Greek characters, including Pa-
troclus, Theseus, Ulysses, Hebe, Circe, and a Greek Chorus out
of Aeschylus, gather in the "country house near the sea" belonging to one of them, Achilles. The atmosphere is that of a summer
weekend. "Well, what would anybody like to do? How about a
swim before tea?"

While the immediate inspiration for *The Heroes* was a short
novel by André Gide entitled *Thésée* ("Theseus"), the play is, in
part, a send-up of Gilbert Murray's translations of Greek trage-
dies. It also reflects, in its drawing-room ambiance, the currency
of T. S. Eliot's *The Cocktail Party*. The Chorus says Chorus-like
things: "I have seen many many people in every possible relation
to each other and I have never seen any good come of it." The
aesthete's enjoyment of theatrical conventions for their own
sake, rather than for the sake of a message, is to a large extent
the point of *The Heroes*. But there is a moment early in the play
when, with the air of one who has told the tale many times, Theseus describes his fabled encounter with the Minotaur in a way
that makes the myth seem ironically apt to Ashbery's own predicament as a poet in midcentury America.

The maze he had to penetrate to reach the Minotaur was
like "a vast fun-house in some deserted amusement park," Theseus says. Once inside for several days and nights, he began to
realize that he had changed several times and that as a result so
had the maze. "I realized that I now possessed the only weapon
with which the minotaur might be vanquished—the indifference
of a true aesthete. Drawing my sword with as much assurance as
you might deal a card, I kicked open the door to the little privy-
like enclosure where he lay. There was nothing there but a great
big doodle-bug made of wood and painted canvas." The Minotaur
itself "was the least important part of the whole scheme. I'd always supposed the world was full of fakes, but I was foolish
enough to believe that it was made interesting by the varying

degrees of skill with which they covered up their lack of integrity. It never occurred to me that the greatest fake of all would make not the slightest effort to convince me of its reality . . . not a pretense! But there it was—a stupid, unambitious piece of stage machinery."

This is a key revelation. It is the mark of Ashbery's poetry that with "the indifference of a true aesthete" he is able to undermine his own romantic gestures and visionary ambitions, to expose and critique the artifice of his work at the same time as he revels in it. In one other place in Ashbery's work does he opt for the same theatrical metaphor. "Yes, friends, these clouds pulled along on invisible ropes are, as you have guessed, merely stage machinery," he writes in "The Wrong Kind of Insurance" (1977). "And the funny thing is it knows we know / About it and still wants us to go on believing / In what it so unskillfully imitates and wants / To be loved not for that but for itself."

In 1953 *The Heroes* was produced by the Artists' Theater in New York City together with one-act plays by James Merrill and Barbara Guest. According to Merrill, Ashbery's play was "the hit of the evening." It was, however, missed by Arthur Miller and Dylan Thomas, who were in the audience when the evening began but left in the middle of Merrill's *The Bait*, Miller whispering to Thomas, "You know, this guy's got a secret, and he's gonna keep it."

Ashbery's next two plays were both inspired by old movies he had seen. *The Compromise*, a three-act comedy, was suggested by a silent Rin Tin Tin feature called *Where the North Begins* (1923). Ashbery simply lifted the plot from the movie, omitting the movie's center of interest—the dog. *The Compromise* is a deadpan parody of early Hollywood Westerns with their romantic clichés. All the stereotypes are present: the Mountie who always gets his man, the treacherous redskin, the dastardly villain, the damsel in distress, the dance-hall queen. Invoking the conventions of the Western and deviating from them at will, *The Compromise* is pre-postmodernist—a parody that communicates delight in the parodied thing; camp that transcends camp. The play was written in 1955. In June of that year Schuyler wrote to Kenneth Koch, then in Paris: "John's play, *The Compromise*, a satire on the Northwest and a romance of religion, or vice-versa, is the nuts. I was instantly converted into a follower of the Raven who lives in the sunset." In his own letter to Koch, O'Hara described the play accurately as "an hommage à Rin Tin Tin with Pirandello-esque touches," and with gusto: "It is full of something like fresh mountain air and has a simplicity like quicksand. You'll adore it." O'Hara was right about Koch's reaction. The latter read *The Compromise* to the students in his "comic writing workshop" at the New School in February 1959, and it was he who arranged for it to be published in Alfred Leslie's one-shot magazine, *The Hasty Papers* (1961).

As *The Compromise* begins, the Mountie is offstage on a crime-solving odyssey while his Penelope stays home a prey to the rogue suitor who dupes her into thinking her husband has run off with another woman. By the end of act three the hero has turned the tables and unmasked the criminal and is now ready to ride off into the sunset with his sweetheart in the bliss of mutual forgiveness. It turns out, however, that she is torn between our hero and another Mountie, who proved his devotion to her in the hero's absence. Whom shall she marry? "She loves us both! Can this be?" asks Harry. "If only I could die—that would solve every-thing and the play would end," Margaret says. At this climactic moment, the stage directions call for the Author to enter and confess that he has not yet made up his mind about how to end the play. Should "the man of action or the melancholy dreamer" be rewarded with the bride? The Author is a version of Hamlet, undecided to the last; he would like to work a compromise, and if that requires him to expose the elaborate stage machinery of his work, so be it. Ashbery had just seen the Living Theater's production of Pirandello's *Tonight We Improvise*, "and was," he told an interviewer, "affected by it on the stage to the point that I started being Pirandellian without probably realizing it."

An unsigned review of *The Compromise* that appeared locally in Cambridge, Massachusetts, where the play was performed in 1956, is enthusiastic about everything except this Pirandello-esque touch. "Ashbery's spoof of the glorious Westerns from the golden age of the silver screen rollicks along inventively, hilariously, often uproariously," the critic writing for *Audience* (who may have been John Simon) observes. But he complains that Ashbery all but ruins his "lusty parody" by inserting "the Author" into the final scene. I disagree. It seems to me that the Author's speech is the most resonant moment in the play. Like the hero of "The Painter," Ashbery the playwright is faced with a crisis in the mimetic ideal. Since he says he could find no patterns or rules for either human speech or human relationships, "there was nothing in life for my art to imitate." He decides that the solution to his quandary is to avoid solving it. "I would omit the final scene from my masterpiece," he says. In this way "my play would reflect the very uncertainty of life, where things are seldom carried through to a conclusion, let alone a satisfactory one."

The next time Ashbery wrote a play, he lived up to this speech. *The Philosopher* (1959), a parody of country-house murder-mystery plays, breaks off just as the second act is about to begin. The inspiration for *The Philosopher* came from Hollywood movies such as Paul Leni's silent *The Cat and the Canary* and a B-movie from the 1940s called *Who Killed Aunt Maggie?*, in which the heirs assemble to hear the reading of an eccentric millionaire's will. The play features an unexplained masked man, a jewel with magical powers, and an old mansion with many secret passages. As in *The Compromise*, the author's ironic obeisance to theatrical conventions is the primary thrust of the experience.

In an application for a Guggenheim Fellowship in 1957,

Ashbery discussed his plans to write *The Philosopher*. The play would resemble *The Compromise*, he wrote, in drawing from the mythology of Hollywood movies. He hoped to "build up a strange kind of poetry out of trite situations and commonplace dialogue." In Paris on his Fulbright Fellowship he had made a study of the French "well-made play" and he felt that an ironic appropriation of its characteristic devices was in order. "The currently popular 'mood play' is too often tiresome to watch and (worst of all) does not even succeed in establishing a mood," Ashbery wrote. "In order to keep an audience in a theater entertained, playwrights will at some point have to turn to the acceptance, even an ironic one, of the principles of sound construction, or give up writing for the theater. In my play I do not intend to neglect the poetry, the mystery even, that can arise from precise craftsmanship, and which so often lends the hopelessly corny and outdated plays of Scribe and Sardou an odd enchantment." Ashbery concluded this, his most considered statement on writing for the theater, by remarking that *The Philosopher* will be in prose, not verse: "I do not think that poetry has a place in the theater at the present time."

Again as in *The Compromise*, Ashbery had trouble ending the play. He had originally planned to write a second act that would astonish the viewer. The cardboard characters would begin talking seriously, "and the play would suddenly cease being a farce and become a sort of Ingmar Bergman drama." But the part of the second act that he wrote seemed unsuccessful to him, and he concluded by letting the first act stand unadorned. It had suddenly occurred to him that it was sufficient to set the stage machinery in motion; there was no need to follow it through to its implied conclusion. The lack of an ending is surprise enough. What could better dramatize the playwright's problem of closure? The gesture seems perfectly in line with Ashbery's habit of creating a smokescreen near the end of his poems so he can "withdraw unperceived." It is yet another example of "this leaving-out business" whose sole proprietor cannot shake his awareness of the artifice at the heart of his maze.

The year 1955 was the turning point in Ashbery's career. In addition to *The Compromise*, he wrote two new poems for *Some Trees*—"And You Know" and "The Instruction Manual"—and Auden chose the manuscript rather than O'Hara's *Meditations in an Emergency* for the Yale Younger Poets Prize. With four friends—Jane Freilicher, Joe Hazan, the painter Grace Hartigan, and her boyfriend, the photographer Walt Silver—he went on the three-week car trip to Mexico that inspired him to write "The Instruction Manual." It was the first time he had been out of the country, and it stirred his appetite for more exotic adventures. When he returned to New York in June, he was surprised to learn that he had won a Fulbright Fellowship to France and could expect to sail tourist class on the S.S. *Queen Mary* sailing from New York on the 21st of September. Although he had previously been notified that his application had been rejected, a vacancy had opened up when another recipient declined the award. Ashbery boarded ship on that September day knowing that his first book of poems was scheduled to be published in the most prestigious poetry series in America. He was leaving behind his friends, yes, but he had every reason to suppose that they would meet again, in Europe if not in New York. What he was really quitting was the desk and the office routine and the paper clips and the house organ. "But once more, office desks, radiators—No! That is behind me. / No more dullness, only movies and love and laughter, sex and fun," he would write in "The Skaters." What awaited him was "the unknown, the unknown that loves us, the great unknown." He was twenty-eight years old and was eager to go to "the places with names" that had enchanted him as a book-devouring boy. As a writer he was thirsty for a taste of the unutterable (but equivocal) glory that his new hero, Raymond Roussel, said he had felt while writing *La Doublure,* a novel in verse, which Roussel thought surpassed anything by Homer, Dante, and Shakespeare, but which was, alas, received with complete silence.

Ashbery's decision to go to France is not difficult to comprehend. France had fascinated him from the time when, as a teenager, he would pepper his diary entries with French phrases and sign off with an exuberant "bong soir." The question to ponder is why Ashbery stayed away so long. When he embarked, he had no idea that he was going for more than the one year stipulated in the Fulbright program. It took a combination of luck and resourcefulness to keep extending his stay to the ultimate length of a decade. Though his fellowship was for study at the University of Montpellier in the south of France, Ashbery soon tired of that provincial city. He concurred with the assessment of Montpellier that Henry James made in *A Little Tour in France.* "The place has neither the gaiety of a modern nor the solemnity of an ancient town," James wrote, "and it is agreeable as certain women are agreeable who are neither beautiful nor clever." In Montpellier, Ashbery made few friends and found himself going for days without speaking to anyone. He was overjoyed to be able to switch from Montpellier to Paris, where he arrived on Valentine's Day, 1956. He appears to have fallen in love with that city at first sight. "Most of the time I just walk around," he wrote to Fairfield Porter. "It's nice, for instance, that American Express is so far from the Left Bank—it takes me just about all day to get my mail and get back to my hotel, which is on the rue de Vaugirard near the Boulevard St. Michel, what with stopping and looking at things and buying tickets to other things." He had, he added, "no desire to leave Paris even overnight for the next 30 years or so." Contriving to renew his Fulbright for a second year, Ashbery was appointed *lecteur américain* at the University of Rennes, where he gave courses in American history, government, and literature, but he continued to spend most of his time in Paris. In 1957 he returned to New York, enrolled in a master's program in French literature at New York University, and promptly set his mind on going back to Paris.

Ashbery would live in Paris from 1958 until 1965, making do on a small allowance from his parents and on a variety of literary jobs, which included translating a pair of tawdry French thrillers under the pseudonym "Jonas Berry" (which approximates the French pronunciation of "John Ashbery"). It was not an experience he was eager to repeat. Ashbery was asked to invent some steamy scenes for the American market, and he did so. The two books, *Champagne obligatoire* by Noel Vexin (which the publisher retitled *Murder in Montmartre*) and *La Biche* by Geneviève Manceron (which became *The Deadlier Sex*), were duly issued by Dell in 1960 and '61. But the publisher had had qualms about Ashbery's translations and hired a writer named Lawrence G. Blochman to save the text. Some translators are hampered by an inadequate knowledge of the language from which they are translating, Blochman recalled thinking. But he felt that the translator he was bailing out here "just couldn't write English."

Ashbery thought of extending his academic career. "YOU can do me a favor," he wrote Kenneth Koch in June 1958. "All you have to do is write me a letter, of which you owe me one anyway, telling me what is a PhD thesis and how can I write one. How do I use the library in Paris? Is there a Reader's Guide to Periodical Literature? How does one get into the Bibliotheque de l'Arsenale? I'd appreciate a few tips from an old China hand, as I am leaving for France after all—the 25th—and must do my thesis."

Ashbery had settled on Raymond Roussel as his thesis subject. It was Koch who had introduced Ashbery to Roussel's work. In Paris in 1950 Koch had gone to a famous Paris bookshop—the *librairie* José Corti on the rue de Médicis across from the Luxembourg Gardens—and asked the owner to recommend an unusual

French writer, the stranger the better. "What's really exciting and crazy?" he asked. "I've read Surrealism." "Have you read Roussel?" The man handed him a faded yellow book containing *Nouvelles Impressions d'Afrique* (1928), a long poem in four cantos, each of which consists of a single sentence expanded to fantastic length by an accordion system of parentheses within parentheses. Koch brought the book back to America and lent it to Ashbery, who felt an immediate rapport with the eccentric genius whom Jean Cocteau had dubbed "the Proust of dreams." Roussel's method of writing a novel—such as *Locus Solus*—began with the composition of a sentence whose double-meanings allow it to be read in two completely different ways. It becomes the writer's task to construct a narrative leading seamlessly from the first sense of the sentence to the second. An example (not from Roussel): The sentence, *A dark horse has won the Triple Crown*, could refer to the feat of Seattle Slew in horse racing or to the election of an obscure cardinal to the papacy. A story written in the Roussel manner would begin at Belmont Park and end in the Holy See. While Ashbery never followed this particular narrative recipe, he subscribed to the general principle exemplified by Roussel—that any artificial stimulus to writing is valid and that poetry may as easily result from a complicated linguistic exercise as from any other means.

Roussel's peculiar methods of composition led him to extravagant inventions. In the most beautiful section of *Locus Solus*, Martial Canterel, the book's inventor hero, concocts a fluid that he calls "resurrectine." When injected into deceased characters who have been artificially preserved, they spring back to life and reperform the most memorable actions of their lives. "*Locus Solus* is the greatest thing I've read in years," Ashbery wrote to Koch. "It's like a bouquet of cast-iron forget-me-nots, a thing that may well turn up in the book yet. I especially like the story of the fashionable Englishwoman, who couldn't stand the sight of blood or the color red, and had had her fingernails silvered by a complicated process, who faints at seeing a red map of Europe on the lantern in front of a hotel reflected in the moon of her mirrored fingernail: 'Dans la lunule . . . l'Europe entière . . . rouge . . . tout entière . . ." she murmurs as she collapses. Her name is Ethelfleda; she has just emerged from the hotel in an elegant toilette de bain, carrying a letter in one hand and a tea-rose in the other."

In his first years in Paris, Ashbery proceeded with his research toward a dissertation on Roussel. Although he eventually set the project aside, his research yielded several articles that contributed mightily to the revitalization of Roussel's reputation in France (where he was neglected) and in the United States (where he was unknown). He wrote cogently about Roussel in *Art News* and again in the *New York Times Book Review*, and he chose Roussel as the subject of one of his Norton lectures at Harvard.

Pierre Reverdy was a second French poet whose work came as a revelation to Ashbery. Like Roussel, Reverdy is sometimes classified as a Surrealist. But Ashbery was quick to distinguish Reverdy from the Surrealists, who "insisted on automatic writing," which "as practiced by the Surrealists seems to have been merely a euphemism for extreme haste." For Ashbery, the Surrealists were "uninteresting from the standpoint of language" and too respectful of the rules of grammar and syntax. Reverdy was another matter. "He is not afraid to experiment with language and syntax, and it is often difficult to determine whether a particular line belongs with the preceding sentence or the one following it," Ashbery wrote in an essay for *Evergreen Review*. "The lines drift across the page as overheard human speech drifts across our hearing: fragments of conversation, dismembered advertising slogans or warning signs in the metro appear and remain preserved in the rock crystal of the poem." Reverdy is quoted approvingly: "One has said almost nothing about man's misfortunes after one has spoken only of the major ones, about which he thinks or feels only rarely. The worst are the small ones, which are constant, always present and tailored to his size." While Reverdy's poetry can have a "disconcerting" effect—"one can have the impression one moment of contemplating a drop of water on a blade of grass; the next moment one is swimming for one's life"—this is part of their enchantment. Reverdy's poems are "like novels compressed into a tiny space by some colossal force," Ashbery wrote. "We are left only with the mysterious essentials of a story: we see a man walking down a dark road, the reflections of a candle in a window; we have the feeling that something enormous has happened, but we will never know any more of the drama than this." Ashbery concluded that Reverdy "is with Proust one of the rare writers of our time in whose work despair seems beautiful."

Ashbery's incidental literary criticism adds more to our literary knowledge than any score of scholarly dissertations. But Ashbery never felt very comfortable in a university context, and the exigencies of an American academic career seemed more and more remote to one who was seeking, with every means at his disposal, to stay in Paris. Art criticism—which Ashbery did not write before he turned thirty—offered an alternative way of making a living. Three of Ashbery's closest friends, O'Hara, Schuyler, and Fairfield Porter, had written for *Art News*, so the opportunity was there for him to seize. In 1959 he wrote a long piece on the French painter Jean Hélion for *Art News*. In 1960 he happened to be on hand when Yvonne Hagen, the art critic for the European edition of the *New York Herald Tribune*, gave up her job and needed a replacement immediately. "A friend of mine once said that I had backed into a career as an art critic, which is absolutely true," Ashbery told an interviewer. And how had journalism affected him as a poet? "When I was writing at the *Herald-Tribune*, I had to produce an article every week, rain or shine, exhibitions or no exhibitions, and the mere fact of having to sit down at the typewriter once a week and grind out several pages of copy possibly helped in the sense that it eventually dawned on me that I could sit down the same way with a poem and type if I wanted to."

In Paris, Ashbery struck up a friendship with Harry Mathews, another American expatriate who had packed his literary ambitions in a valise marked for France. For Mathews, the friendship was crucial, confirming him in his vigorous commitment to an experimental ideal. Ashbery was a remarkable mentor. He had a "power," Mathews felt, "to exert an influence both great and beneficial, without trying, without seeming to, on those around" him. Mathews, who became the sole American member of the French group of experimentalists who call themselves the Oulipo, began writing his first novel, *The Conversions*, soon after coming under his friend's influence. *The Conversions*, a picaresque adventure triggered off by the reading of a rich man's capricious will, is like an inspired blend of Jules Verne and Raymond Roussel. It was serialized in *Locus Solus*, a magazine that would not have come into existence if Mathews had not offered to fund it. For him, the opportunity to work with Ashbery—and with Koch and Schuyler, whom he met on a visit to America—was irresistible.

If in the career of a major poet there is invariably a wilderness period, in Ashbery's case it was his long sojourn in Europe. The Paris years proved decisive to his emergence as a major poet with *Rivers and Mountains* in 1966 and *The Double Dream of Spring* in 1970. Living abroad, Ashbery obeyed the avant-garde imperative of nonconformism precisely by absenting himself from the avant-garde revolution going on at home. In America, he had always felt like an outsider, but he had friends and allies; in France his isolation was nearly complete. He could lose himself in French as in another sense he could dispense with his autobiographical ego when writing a poem. To speak French (which he was able to do by his second year abroad) was to abandon one identity and don another. ("French and English don't quite mix in a fruitful way," Ashbery said to Mathews. "It's as though French were like a violin and English, or American, were like a piano.") Ashbery would become sensitized to the American language as at the same time he would develop cravings for American products that had never delighted him in America: Coca-Cola, iced tea, pumpkin pie. As the French poet André du Bouchet told Mathews, "You have [a] great privilege [in] living in a country where your language is not spoken, because it obliges you to be conscious of your own language in a way that you never would be if you were living at home."

Paris, Mathews observed, offered "an atmosphere that enforces a rewardingly unique estrangement, free of the illusory comforts of Nordic gregariousness and Mediterranean ease. Years with one companion and half a friend: in no other city could one survive and thrive on such solitude." Although Ashbery and Mathews did not feel a special connection to the lost generation of the 1920s, a remark Gertrude Stein made in that earlier time enchanted them both. Paris, she said, is where "Americans can discover what it means to be American." Paris is where Ashbery discovered his true direction as an American poet. But to achieve this identity he first needed to shed it.

Toward the end of his time in Paris, Ashbery wrote an article about American expatriate artists in Paris that explains why he wished to live in Paris when all the action, in poetry as well as art, seemed to be going on in New York City. "The Americans in Paris are permanently out of fashion, first ahead of it and now behind it, without ever having gone through an intervening period of acceptance," Ashbery wrote. "This may account for a look that many of them have in common, even when they are working in entirely different ways. It is not so much a look perhaps as a quality. It is as though they had given up all efforts at trying to please a public, whether French or American, and had gone back to pleasing themselves. For once, you don't have the feeling that the artist is breathing down your neck in his work, or that you are catching the work in a split-second of its trajectory from easel to gallery to museum." It was liberating to be free of the world of approval and rejection. "The feeling of being a stranger even in moments of greatest rapport with one's adopted home is the opposite of the American 'acceptance world' which so often ends up by stifling an artist's originality through the efficacious means of overencouragement. If indifference and even hostility are not exactly beneficial for an artist, too much success is usually worse, for it corrupts subtly. What is especially moving in the world of the Americans abroad is a general resolution in the face of apathy and apartheid to determine their individuality, to create something independent of fashion." Perhaps "the calm and the isolation of exile" can best enable the American to understand what his American-ness consists of.

In a profile of the abstract painter Joan Mitchell, his friend and fellow expatriate, Ashbery wrote that American artists lived in Paris primarily for "personal reasons," which "can mean being in love or liking the food or the look of the roofs across the courtyard—or in some cases the art." All these reasons apply to Ashbery himself. There was the art he wrote about in *Art News* and the *Herald Tribune*, and there were the delights of French food. In France Ashbery developed expensive culinary tastes; he would cross Paris to sample a dish of kidneys in mustard that he had heard about. Then there was the look of the place. Walking around Paris without an agenda seemed stimulus enough for the imagination. "I found my poetry being more 'influenced' by the sight of the Paris phenomenon of clear water flowing in the street gutters, where it is (or was) diverted or dammed by burlap sandbags moved about by workmen, than it was by the French poetry I was learning to read at the time," Ashbery has written. There were literary enthusiasms: Roussel, Reverdy, the prose poems of Max Jacob, *Locus Solus*, and later *Art and Literature*, the foremost international avant-garde magazine of the mid-1960s, which Ashbery coedited. And there was love.

Ashbery and Pierre Martory met in 1956 at the Fiacre bar on the rue du Cherche Midi on the Left Bank. Born in Bayonne in southwest France, the son of a career military officer, Martory spent much of his childhood in Morocco. He studied at the School of Political Sciences in Paris and caught the last train to leave the city before the Germans took over in June 1940. During the occupation, he enlisted in the French army and took part in the Tunisian campaign. After the liberation, he returned to Paris, where he wrote a novel entitled *Phébus ou le beau Mariage*. Although it was received well, his next two novels were turned down by his publisher, the first because of its homosexual theme, the second because the publisher wanted Martory to change the ending of the book. Martory stubbornly refused and never wrote another novel, though he continued to write poems, a volume of which has been published in the United States (in Ashbery's translation). In the years he and Ashbery lived together in France Martory earned his living as a correspondent for *Le Monde diplomatique* and later as a reporter for the French weekly *Paris-Match*. During the last five of his twenty-five years at *Paris-Match*, he had his own page, which he devoted to the cultural life of Paris. Ashbery has likened Martory to the character of Alceste in Molière's *Le Misanthrope*. Martory "was the ideal guide to France and things French for an American," Ashbery wrote. "In addition, his take on them has something distinctly and irreverently American about it. He has always had more American friends (and Moroccan ones) than French, and says that he loves France but detests the French!" "I remember when I was living with him [Ashbery] in rue d'Assas," Martory told an interviewer. "He was spending days and days writing, writing, writing. I heard him on the typewriter in the other room and I admired his determination to write and write and write. I was just writing a poem every month, something like that, I didn't care. I was really like an amateur living with a professional, like if you live with a diva of the opera and you can just sing 'Au Clair de la Lune.' "

Although Ashbery would rather avoid the subject of homosexuality, his reticence has not deterred an industrious critic, John Shoptaw, from devoting an ingenious book to the thesis that Ashbery is writing incessantly about homosexual love, though always in code, with "crypt words" that require critical assistance to be understood. In his book *On the Outside Looking Out*, Shoptaw analyzes the "crypt words" in Ashbery's poetry—where "metal" can signify "mental," "borders" is concealed in "boarders," and "long piers of silence" leaves "periods" behind. The analysis is often brilliant, though the danger of the approach is obvious: It turns criticism into a form of outing. For Shoptaw it is a given that Ashbery's "cryptic" strategy reveals one story and one story only.

Take the example of "They Dream Only of America," which Ashbery wrote in Paris on his thirtieth birthday in 1957. It is one of the most admired poems in *The Tennis Court Oath* and was a particular favorite of Frank O'Hara's. Its absence from Ashbery's *Selected Poems* is a lamentable omission:

They dream only of America
To be lost among the thirteen million pillars of grass:
"This honey is delicious
Though it burns the throat."

And hiding from darkness in barns
They can be grownups now
And the murderer's ash tray is more easily—
The lake a lilac cube.

He holds a key in his right hand.
"Please," he asked willingly.
He is thirty years old.
That was before

We could drive hundreds of miles
At night through dandelions.
When his headache grew worse we
Stopped at a wire filling station.

Now he cared only about signs.
Was the cigar a sign?
And what about the key?
He went slowly into the bedroom.

"I would not have broken my leg if I had not fallen
Against the living room table. What is it to be back
Beside the bed? There is nothing to do
For our liberation, except wait in the horror of it.

And I am lost without you."

It is possible to read this haunting poem as an allegory about the poet's relationship to Pierre Martory. Shoptaw proposes just such a reading:

> The misrepresentations of "They Dream Only of America" are insistently homotextual. The "thirteen million pillars of grass" suggest not only Whitman's *Leaves of Grass*, but the "pillar of salt" to which Lot's wife, no pillar of the community, was reduced for looking back on the destruction of Sodom. "Was the cigar a sign? / And what about the key?" In this cluttered poem, in which every personal

pronoun except "she" is represented, the spermal "honey" and phallic props ("pillars," "key," "cigar," "leg") take on a parodic significance. The dismembered names of the perpetrators, "Ashbery" and "Martory," may be partially reconstructed from the line "And the *murder*er's *ash tray* is *more* easily—." The romantic secrecy of the fugitive gay lovers is parallel here to the French Resistance (Martory fought in its ranks, after his escape to Algeria) waiting for America's liberation. Though the term "gay liberation" had not yet been coined, this poem seems to wait for its minting. The utopian "American dream" here fantasizes a time and a place where gay lovers could come out of their lilac cubes.

In the spirit of this analysis, one might be moved to add that "thirteen million" may be unpacked further as a rough demographic count of gay people coded as an unlucky number.

It is incontestable that aspects of Ashbery's poetry, and in particular his irony and evasiveness, owe something to the culture of homosexuality, in which concealment and disguise—and their opposite, the occasional histrionic display—play a vital part. It is also possible to compare Ashbery on the whole question of subject matter to the Abstract Expressionists, who seemed to eliminate subject matter at the same time that several of them insisted that subject matter was the most important element in their work. In Ashbery's case, the apparent absence of subject matter may lead the critic to emphasize this very aspect of his writing. The avoidance of autobiographical elements—the fact that Ashbery's work appears sometimes to be a critique of the autobiographical impulse—may find the critic willing to counter, as Helen Vendler has done, that Ashbery's poetry is a form of "disguised autobiography." Shoptaw's book on Ashbery fleshes out this contention with scholarly zeal.

Ingenious or not, however, Shoptaw's allegorical interpretation of "They Dream Only of America" is a bit like the symbol-hunting of the New Criticism at its most exasperating. It is not that the interpretation is wrong; it is that the poem gives rise to any number of competing narratives, which the reader may be prompted to provide. The poem can be read less tendentiously and less fancifully as an allegory about growing up; as in a particularly eerie kind of fairy tale, there is an emphasis on clues and signs, only here the horror of imprisonment is matched by that of the promised liberation. But I prefer to read the poem as precisely a truncated narrative lacking a key, a dream that haunts the waking person because it exists only in fragments whose relation to one another remains mysterious. The strangeness of the adverb in the line,

"Please," he asked willingly,

is not easily explained, and that is one of its virtues. And if one notices that

"This honey is delicious
Though it burns the throat"

is metaphorically a taste of brandy, and if one learns that this was something Martory said in all innocence at breakfast one morning, one still has not explained the effect of trembling significance these lines achieve.

It is important to remember that all the New York poets, Ashbery most of all, were resolutely antiprogrammatic, mistrustful of labels and leery of political causes. John Shoptaw is committed to the idea of the Intentional Fallacy, that bedrock of the New Criticism, according to which the author's intentions are deemed critically irrelevant and may safely be disregarded. I am not so quick to dismiss the author's stated intentions. To connect

Ashbery's poetry narrowly to the specific circumstances of his life at the time he wrote the poems is to deny the poet one of his major premises—that poems are acts of imagination, not coded messages, or memories, or emotion recollected in tranquillity. There can exist no ideal key for Ashbery's works as there might be one for, say, *Finnegans Wake,* for Ashbery does not preside over his fictive universe in the way that a mathematical God is supposed to have reigned over the eighteenth century. On the contrary, no poet has committed himself more strenuously to the importance of chance in literary creation.

It is true that love is a subject to which Ashbery frequently returns. Of what poet could this not be said? But it is misleading as well as reductive to give the impression that his oeuvre is a monument to the love that dare not speak its name. It is as much as to say that Ashbery's poems would be easier to get if he didn't have something to hide. Say, rather, that Ashbery's love poems omit the name of the beloved out of a certain reticence, a reverence for mystery, which Mallarmé said was essential to any holy thing wishing to retain its holiness. The identity of Ashbery's "erotic double," to whom some of his love poems are addressed, is no more stable an entity than the shiftily indeterminate pronouns in his work. All are aspects of a consciousness that defines itself by what it apprehends. As he writes in "A Love Poem" (1979),

> The dripping is in the walls, within sleep
> Itself. I mean there is no escape
> From me, from it. The night is itself sleep
> And what goes on in it, the naming of the wind,
> Our notes to each other, always repeated, always the same.

The poems of *The Tennis Court Oath,* which Ashbery wrote in Paris, are largely the product of such avant-garde procedures as

the collage (in which lines culled from various sources are con-
joined) and the cutup (in which the lines of an existing work are
scrambled). He wrote about "America" and "Europe"—the titles
of two of the poems in the volume—but strictly by implication.
"Europe," a poem consisting of 111 fragments, began as a collage
and cutup of an Edwardian book for girls, *Beryl of the Bi-plane*,
which Ashbery bought on a Paris quay in the fall of 1958. The
poem was an attempt to achieve an equivalent in poetry for the
sort of erasures that Willem de Kooning had incorporated in his
paintings:

> Absolve me from the hatred I never
> she—all are wounded against
> Zeppelin—wounded carrying dying
> three colors over land
> thistles again closed around voice.
> She is dying—
> automatically—
> wanting to see you again, but the stone
> must be rebuilt. Time stepped

Although Ashbery's "Europe" seems to have as little to do with
that continent as with the Place de l'Europe in Paris, the poem
was nevertheless a response to the situation of being in a foreign
country and realizing that one's language and identity are in flux.
"There's a Métro station called Europe in Paris," Ashbery told an
interviewer. "The name is in bleak ceramic letters in the station.
I happened to notice this as I was passing through, and it seemed
sort of a funny way of summing up Europe, which it, in fact, did
in some peculiar way. But I guess from all this you might say that
I was intrigued by the relationship between the name of something and what it is." It is a perfect Ashbery parable: You go to
"Europe" and find it in an obscure Métro station.

When Allen Ginsberg wrote a brilliant, angry, funny poem entitled "America," the reader knew exactly where he stood: "America two dollars and twentyseven cents January 17, 1956." It was the America of *Time* magazine, the atom bomb and Cold War paranoia, against which the "nearsighted and psychopathic" poet protests, putting his "queer shoulder to the wheel." In contrast, Ashbery's "America," written in Paris, leaves the reader in a wholly disoriented state, where fragments seek other fragments to link with, stories are told piecemeal, and the names of things have drifted away from the things themselves:

Piling upward
the fact the stars
In America the office hid
archives in his
stall . . .
Enormous stars on them
The cold anarchist standing
in his hat.
Arms along the rail
We were parked
Millions of us
The accident was terrible.
The way the door swept out
The stones piled up—
The ribbon—books. miracle. with moon and the stars

Only after unleashing such verbal disintegrations was Ashbery ready to write the great works of his maturity, beginning with "The Skaters" and continuing for more than thirty years, as long a stretch of sustained creative productivity as any American poet has enjoyed. "The Skaters" ends on a note of rest, the per-

ception of a "perfect" order. At least that is the impression these
lines give on a first reading:

> The constellations are rising
> In perfect order: Taurus, Leo, Gemini.

But as with many of Ashbery's rhetorical gestures, the lines need
to be read a second time. For upon inspection, the zodiacal order
given here is incorrect. The correct order would read Taurus,
Gemini, Cancer, Leo. But Ashbery (a Leo himself, with Virgo rising) was not flaunting his astrological ignorance but making the
point that an incorrect order may be a "perfect" one, since any
order is finally arbitrary. The information following the colon in
the quoted lines contradicts the preceding assertion, and yet the
effect of the lines is one of calmness and serenity and rest rather
than of cosmic chaos—an important paradox in Ashbery's work,
though as far from the paradoxes dear to the hearts of New Critics
as one could get.

"Having lived in Paris unfits you for living anywhere, including Paris," Ashbery remarked. He had every wish to continue
his expatriate existence, but in December 1964 he was summoned home; his father had suddenly died. The Paris years were
over. Knowing that his mother needed him to look after her,
Ashbery returned to New York the following fall. He arrived on
the S.S. *France* on the November day after the big blackout
trapped subway riders in stationary trains and shut off the lights
in the metropolitan area. Despite this ambiguous portent, Ashbery's return to New York got off to an auspicious start. The problem of how he was to support himself was quickly solved. Upon
the death of Alfred Frankfurter, the longtime editor of *Art News*,
Thomas B. Hess was promoted to succeed him, and Hess appointed Ashbery to fill his former position; Ashbery would hold
the job of executive editor until 1972. There were signs, too, that

Ashbery's poetry had begun to attract an ardent following. His third book, *Rivers and Mountains*, appeared in 1966 and was promptly short-listed for the National Book Award in poetry. Now, for the first time in ten years, he and O'Hara, Koch, and Schuyler would all be living in the same city and could look forward to picking up where they had left off. Ashbery, Koch, and O'Hara immediately decided to continue a joint effort at a play that they had begun years earlier. They planned to work on it during the summer of 1966.

Frank O'Hara: you just go on your nerve

Some sunny days, it's great to try
to see the world
through Frank O'Hara's eyes

20 / 20
All the way

–JAMES SCHUYLER,
"SEPTEMBER 6, 1969"

Frank O'Hara, as the world saw him: Reading W. H. Auden's great poem "In Praise of Limestone" (1948), I sometimes think of O'Hara when I get to the part about "the nude young male who lounges / Against a rock displaying his dildo, never doubting / That for all his faults he is loved, whose works are but / Extensions of his power to charm." These lines could not have been based on O'Hara, whom Auden had not met in 1948. But they seem eerily apropos to the cocksure poet wearing cowboy boots and otherwise proudly nude in the full-length portrait of O'Hara that Larry Rivers painted in 1954. Then I turn to James Schuyler's elegy "To Frank O'Hara" (1974), where the shutter clicks on the poet in whirlwind motion, hurrying to cram everything into a single charged moment. In this multiple exposure he is dancing, smoking, talking, diving into breakers and swimming

in an electric storm
which is what you were
more lives than a cat

dancing, you had a feline
grace, poised on the balls
of your feet ready
to dive and

all of it, your poems,
compressed into twenty years.
How you charmed, fumed,
blew smoke from your nostrils

like a race horse that
just won the race
steaming, eager to run
only you used words.

Schuyler seized upon O'Hara's most prominent facial detail to characterize his poems: "So witty, so sad, / so you: even your lines have / a broken nose."

O'Hara's broken nose was the first thing you noticed about him. When he posed for the painter Alice Neel, she felt that his profile resembled a falcon's and she produced this effect in a striking painting (1960). The broken nose, John Ashbery commented, "gave him the look of a scrappy boxer." On the other hand, when Elaine de Kooning painted O'Hara in 1962, she found that she could capture O'Hara's presence while omitting his facial features altogether. His casual contrapposto was as recognizable as a face. "When I painted Frank O'Hara, Frank was standing there," she wrote. "First I painted the whole structure of his face; then I wiped out the face, and when the face was gone, it was more Frank than when the face was there."

The second thing you noticed about O'Hara was his distinctive way of walking. "He was thin and about five seven," Larry Rivers writes in his autobiography, *What Did I Do?* "He walked on his toes, stretched his neck, and angled his head, all to add an inch or two to his height. I never walked the same after I met him." "I remember Frank O'Hara's walk," Joe Brainard writes in *I Remember*. "Light and sassy. With a slight bounce and a slight twist. It was a beautiful walk. Confident. 'I don't care' and sometimes 'I know you are looking.' "

In Harold Brodkey's story "What Going Out Without Ora Is Like: Johnno: 1956," the poet Johnno Fynner is a dead ringer for O'Hara: Irish-American, a lapsed Catholic, possessed of a marvelous bitchy wit that was unmalicious until he was drunk, haunted by a drunken mother whom he detested but came to resemble, and given to saying things like "Oh I hate all that *Death in Venice* crap." Brodkey was a meticulous if misanthropic chronicler of his own impressions of the world. "The thing of being a poet, he used all his time that way," Brodkey writes. "He worked for a salary, ate, slept, telephoned, talked, looked, read, wrote as *a poet* and not as a man or human being or as a faun or boy, either. He led a professional life. It had been self-consciously embarked on, self-consciously announced, self-consciously and expensively carried out. It had a clear madness in it, what he did." The O'Hara figure in Brodkey's story "was good at friendship," "had a Harvardish resonating tin *brilliance*," and "was more martyred than saintly." He was "a poet of major presence," whose life was "autobiography in an ironic tone." Brodkey is a remarkable phrasemaker, and his prose sometimes breaks into an aria, as when he analyzes O'Hara's appearance, reading into it as he will:

He wore sneakers, always clean ones. He was short-legged. He walked and sat like a gothic strut or pier, phenomenally erect—that was the determining grotesquery by which you recognized him at a distance. His chest and shoulders and his hands and head were like spreading fans of skinny bone, thinly muscular. The velocity of his will was apparent as an elegant fluster in his voice. Sometimes in his eyes and lips. His movements which were self-conscious and carefully stylish and stylized both—they bordered on cuteness, on extreme miscalculation of effect. His face maintained a deadpan that yet sparked and buzzed with signals—a form of wit. His sensibility, increasingly famous downtown and derided or ignored uptown at that point, was being dulled and coarsened by his *position.* His fame increasingly slowed and dulled the operations of his face; and in fact, he grew coarse and tough (in a way) and *clever*—that is to say, dishonest. And the quick-semi-anguished face of his youth in its category of amazed and pained beauty, intelligent, luminous, vanished in the purposes of his being memorable and a star.

Frank O'Hara was a star, the natural center of attention in a room. Because he lived fast, died young, and left a handsome corpse, his life turned to legend on that early Sunday morning in July 1966 when the poet, barely forty, was hit by a jeep on the beach in Fire Island, where there isn't supposed to be any traffic. *The Killing Cycle*, a celebrated painting cycle by Al Leslie, mythologized the accident in which O'Hara lost his life. In these huge paintings O'Hara becomes the allegorical personification of the delicate but defiant artist victimized by a brutal society. In "The Accident," for example, the poet is hurled in the air by a Rambler American with its headlights menacingly on, while a pair of naked furies fly over the beach in the foreground. Leslie was mindful of the fact that car crashes had also claimed the lives of Jackson Pollock and David Smith; in the painting, the big American car bearing down on the poet has a license plate that reads "DE1208," which spells out *death* when you translate the numbers into letters. On the back of the picture Leslie wrote down these lines of O'Hara's: "I have the other idea about guilt. It's not in us it's in the situation. You don't say that the victim is responsible for a concentration camp or a Mack truck."

The artist as the heroic victim, whose flame burns too intensely to last very long in contaminated air, is a legend that grows out of O'Hara's life and work. The specter of an untimely death makes his happy-go-lucky persona seem witty and sad at the same time. In the first of his "I do this I do that" poems, "A Step Away from Them" (1956), the quotidian narrative is interrupted by death—the premature deaths of friends—and then is calmly continued, with the effect that the most ordinary of activities seems endowed with a nobility, for life, this life, is being led in the presence of mortality:

> First
> Bunny died, then John Latouche,
> then Jackson Pollock. But is the
> earth as full as life was full, of them?
> And one has eaten and one walks,
> past the magazines with nudes
> and the posters for BULLFIGHT and
> the Manhattan Storage Warehouse,
> which they'll soon tear down. I
> used to think they had the Armory
> Show there.
>   A glass of papaya juice
> and back to work. My heart is in my
> pocket, it is Poems by Pierre Reverdy.

The attention to urban detail is loving, and life-giving. The place names and the details are how O'Hara captures the feeling of

living, and it is as a disruption of the living day that death breaks
in. The incidental details add not only to the poem's accuracy but
to its resonance. That the Manhattan Storage Warehouse will soon
be torn down is a fact of urban life that subtly reinforces the
sense of impending doom that shadows the poet. A thesis could
be written on O'Hara's error ("I / used to think they had the
Armory / Show there") and how it connects to the errancy in the
poem, the poet as a kind of knight errant deviating, in his peripatetic postprandial way, from the straight and narrow path into the
lanes and back alleys of poetry.

O'Hara discovered a way to elevate the prose of everyday
life—the diary entries, bread-and-butter letters, memos, and
obituaries—into the stuff of lyric poetry. *Lunch Poems* (1964),
containing some of the poems he would dash off during his lunch
break at the Museum of Modern Art, recovers for poetry a singular part of the day in a place, midtown Manhattan, otherwise neglected in verse. O'Hara developed an elastic colloquial idiom in
tune with the rhythms of his city life. Able to write while friends
were present, he would put a Rachmaninoff piano concerto on
the record player, amble over to the typewriter, and bang out a
poem. He liked the whole idea of occasional poetry, the idea that
poems could be occasioned by circumstance. Anything could
qualify as an event: a friend's wedding, a national holiday, a favorite composer's birthday, a friend's dare. One morning in 1955
O'Hara was having his breakfast with James Schuyler and Joe Le-
Sueur when they began ribbing him about his "unquenchable inspiration," as Schuyler put it. "The cigarette smoke began jetting
from Frank's nostrils and he went into the next room and wrote
'Sleeping on the Wing' in a great clatter of keys." The poem, one
of O'Hara's most admired, concludes with this vaulting image:

> Curiosity, the passionate hand of desire. Dead,
> or sleeping? Is there speed enough? And, swooping,
> you relinquish all that you have made your own,

the kingdom of your self sailing, for you must awake
and breathe your warmth in this beloved image
whether it's dead or merely disappearing,
as space is disappearing and your singularity.

It appears to have been a more than usually productive breakfast.

O'Hara had no doubts about his talent and his originality, but it was part of his charm to transmute his self-confidence into witty self-deprecation, as in his poem "Mayakovsky," in which he declares that his "wounded beauty" is "only a talent for poetry" and adds with ironic grandeur worthy of the eponymous Russian poet: "I embraced a cloud, / but when I soared / it rained." O'Hara's distinctive tone—two parts melancholy, three parts joy—is necessarily absent from the myths that by monumentalizing O'Hara's death obscure his life. Brad Gooch's 1993 biography of O'Hara, *City Poet*, substitutes a 1990s narrative line for the old myth of the doomed artist who could not survive society's hostility and whose death was an indictment of that society. The hero of *City Poet* is a hopelessly alcoholic, prematurely washed-up, promiscuous homosexual, whose death accuses society of homophobia and O'Hara of not living a more moderate existence.

Gooch makes the end of O'Hara's life sound very sad indeed—as if he were reeling drunkenly from party to grave, his talent at an end. That O'Hara had a world-class drinking problem is indisputable. His "alcoholism was so far advanced, the last few times I saw him I couldn't believe it," Schuyler said. "He was red-eyed and looking awful. Frank used to be very handsome. And his health was deteriorating, which also had to do with his having been shot." (O'Hara had been shot years earlier in a mugging; the bullet was never removed.) The painter Grace Hartigan, an O'Hara muse whose relationship with him had ended badly, told Gooch she "always felt that Frank's death was at least part suicide." Gooch adds that the "ingredient of suicide was part of the general destructiveness of alcohol."

O'Hara spent the night of his death drinking with buddies, among them the composer Virgil Thomson, at the Fire Island Pines, a bar and discotheque. O'Hara and his friend J. J. Mitchell were returning to the Water Island house of Morris Golde, where they were weekend houseguests, when their beach taxi broke down with a flat tire. It was close to three in the morning. While the other passengers milled around waiting for a replacement vehicle, O'Hara wandered off tipsily in the dark to look at the ocean. The driver of a joyriding jeep, who said his eyes had been blinded by the lights of the disabled taxi, ran him down. The driver, a twenty-one-year old on a hot date, claimed that O'Hara stepped in his path; J. J. Mitchell vehemently denies this. According to Mitchell, the jeep had failed to slow down and was passing perilously close to the disabled vehicle, "causing at least nine of us to jump hastily aside." O'Hara was taken to a hospital, but his internal injuries were not correctly diagnosed until the following day. When he died, his liver was shot. There is a chance that he would have survived the accident if he hadn't begun so many mornings with vodka and grapefruit juice or bourbon and soda right after lighting up his first Camel, Gauloise, or Picyaune of the day. "That the liver was the organ responsible for O'Hara's death seemed apt," Gooch remarks.

The suggestion that O'Hara's death was a quasi-suicide doesn't quite fit the facts. Rather it exemplifies the misguided impulse to read an intention into every accident. The actual circumstances of O'Hara's death were not heroic or gothic but absurd; not an allegory of inevitability but one of tragic surprise. As Marjorie Perloff wrote in her excellent book *Frank O'Hara: Poet Among Painters*, "if he had wanted to commit suicide, if he had 'courted death' as the myth has it, there would have been a much surer way of doing it" than by being hit by a beach buggy coming at a speed of twenty miles per hour. The assumption that O'Hara was suicidally depressed is hotly contested by several friends and close intimates. Joe LeSueur, who lived with O'Hara for ten years, told me, "Frank O'Hara was not this sad person you read about in Gooch's book. He was not a miserable Hart Crane or Delmore Schwartz figure. He celebrated life constantly. He was fun to be with right up to the end." A few weeks before the freak accident that ended his life, O'Hara spent the weekend at Patsy Southgate's house in East Hampton. Southgate, who had married O'Hara's friend Mike Goldberg, was the fourth (and last) in a line of the poet's muses. (Her predecessors were the poet and playwright Bunny Lang, Jane Freilicher, and Grace Hartigan.) Southgate was beautiful; O'Hara liked to call her "the Grace Kelly of the New York School." She remembers how elated O'Hara was on that summer weekend. He was helping her with a carpentry chore, standing on the top rung of a ladder, when Willem de Kooning came by on his bicycle to give his long-withheld consent to a major retrospective that the MOMA would mount under O'Hara's direction. At the time, O'Hara was also preparing a large Jackson Pollock retrospective with the full cooperation of Pollock's widow, Lee Krasner. Far from suicidal, O'Hara seemed to Southgate to radiate the enthusiasm of a man getting ready to do the professional work of a lifetime.

The impulse to turn O'Hara's death into a parable or a cautionary tale may be an understandable one, but the result is that the man himself is lost, and that is a pity, because the real O'Hara was more complicated and more vital—more unpredictable, dashing, maddening, ambitious, and inspiring—than legend allows. Yes, he drank heavily and hard, found it difficult to sleep because he dreaded his dreams, and woke up hung over on too many mornings. But the remarkable thing is how well he functioned, and how amazingly productive he was, despite his excesses. He was a poet of great originality, a relentless instigator and inveterate collaborator, as well as a champion of the avant-garde in painting and sculpture, and he managed to combine these roles more effectively and with more imagination than anyone since Apollinaire hailed the virtues of Cubism and Surrealism in Paris. "Frank O'Hara was a catalyst for me, although I was much older," the poet and dance critic Edwin Denby said. "But then, he was everybody's catalyst." To Kenneth Koch, O'Hara's work represented "the last stage in the adaptation of twentieth-century avant-garde sensibility to poetry about contemporary American experience."

Everyone, it seemed, contributed to a remarkable volume entitled *Homage to Frank O'Hara*, which Bill Berkson and Joe LeSueur edited in 1978. There were drawings by Philip Guston, Alice Neel, Elaine de Kooning, Alex Katz, Larry Rivers, Grace Hartigan, Fairfield Porter, John Button, elegies by Allen Ginsberg, James Schuyler, Barbara Guest, Ted Berrigan, David Shapiro, reminiscences by John Ashbery and Kenneth Koch. "To us he seemed to dance from canvas to canvas, from party to party, from poem to poem—a Fred Astaire with the whole art community as his Ginger Rogers," the composer Morton Feldman said. He treated "the whole thing as if it were some big, frantic, glamorous movie set." At O'Hara's funeral, Larry Rivers said that sixty people in New York City thought of O'Hara as their "best friend," and the number has continued to climb in the three decades since the Museum of Modern Art issued a special memorial edition of O'Hara's poems with illustrations by de Kooning, Newman, Motherwell, Frankenthaler, Rauschenberg, Johns, Oldenburg, Rivers, and Joan Mitchell.

For a band of younger poets that led bohemian lives in the East Village and made St. Mark's Church in the Bowery their poetry headquarters—poets such as Ted Berrigan, Ron Padgett, Joe Brainard, Peter Schjeldahl, Anne Waldman, Bernadette Mayer, John Godfrey, Maureen Owen, Jim Brodey, Tom Clark,

Michael Brownstein, Lewis MacAdams, Tony Towle, John Giorno, Lewis Warsh, Alice Notley, and Andrei Codrescu—O'Hara was, to use a phrase from one of his poems, "the wings of an extraordinary liberty." Inspired by *Lunch Poems*, the younger poets turned out diurnal chronicles in the O'Hara manner. Berrigan made the "I do this I do that" style his own. Padgett wrote an homage to O'Hara's poem "Rhapsody," in which the portal of 515 Madison Avenue is identified as the "door to heaven":

> In front of a Dubuffet a circus that shines through
> A window in a bright all-yellow building
> The window is my eye
> And Frank O'Hara is the building
> I'm thinking about him like mad today
> (As anyone familiar with his poetry will tell)
> And about the way Madison Avenue really
> Does go to heaven
> And then turns around and comes back, disappointed.

O'Hara loved the city as much as he loved Hollywood movies, poems, novels, friends—passionately, unreservedly, and in a way that quickened the reader's interest in the persons, places, or things mentioned. The young painters he wrote about were interesting because he said so; they were on a level with the other things O'Hara endorsed, from Rachmaninoff to the aperitif Ricard, the Empire State Building and Elizabeth Taylor, Jean Dubuffet and Maria Tallchief. Many poets took their first taste of Strega, an orange-flavored Italian liqueur with a golden glow, simply because O'Hara bought a bottle of the stuff on the day Billie Holiday died.

For Brad Gooch, looking back nostalgically from the era of AIDS, the Village scene in the 1950s and '60s was the period just before the golden age of gay promiscuity set in. Gooch traces "a pattern of episodic promiscuity" in O'Hara's life. Always attracted to straight men, O'Hara had an appetite for "rough trade," and "cruising was a big part" of his life. For corroborating evidence, one may turn to Harold Brodkey's story, in which the O'Hara figure is said to have "*a kind* of erotic authority" and to use a "method of seduction [that] is a common one in New York among successful people; he is in love with everyone he likes or wants, he loves with varying degrees of sincerity; and then he talks." Brodkey could be describing the seductive manner of O'Hara's poems, which woo the reader with their vulnerability and their charm. But there is a danger in mistaking the metaphoric for the literal. *City Poet* conveys the impression that O'Hara was "a sex goddess of America," as Jane Freilicher put it. When John Ashbery encountered Lawrence Osgood, a Harvard friend and lover of O'Hara, he said, "Is it my memory that's going or was Frank the sexually obsessed person that he's made out to be in this book?" "Would he had been," Osgood replied. Ashbery said he thought that sex was about Frank's sixth favorite thing in life, and Osgood said, "Well, fourth."

Formerly the most prolific of poets, O'Hara drank more and wrote less during the last three years of his life. But there is another explanation for his thinning poetic output that goes beyond the inverse ratio of alcohol to poetry. What had changed was his position, his profile, in the greater world. At the Museum of Modern Art, O'Hara's curatorial responsibilities had grown with every promotion. In the museum's hierarchy he had gone from being an assistant curator in 1960 to an associate curator in 1965 and a full curator the year after that. In effect he had become the leading emissary between the Downtown world of the Cedar Tavern and the Club and the Uptown headquarters of the modern art establishment. Never one to observe a distinction between his personal life and his professional work, eager for company to avoid the pain of being alone, and with a true believer's sense of his own limitless obligation, O'Hara found himself overwhelmed with people and duties. "John [Ashbery] guarded his talent. He had sense enough to shield himself from the painters," Barbara Guest told me, "whereas Frank was getting more and more harried by all the work he had to do with the painters, who were essentially talking him to death."

Gregarious and seemingly indefatigable, O'Hara had what many artists lack—the capacity to enjoy the work of others—and he had it to the nth degree. His natural pace was faster than anyone else's, and he left nothing of himself in reserve. He was the boy who refused to shut his eyes in bed. "If I had my way I'd go on and on and on and never go to sleep," he said a fortnight before he died. He may have been exhausted but would not have admitted it.

O'Hara did everything to excess. As Joe Brainard wrote, O'Hara "went to extremes. Or perhaps he just found himself there." And as Barbara Guest observes, he left himself unprotected—he didn't shield himself from the demands of others. O'Hara, she said, "was a very great person and a great friend, and he expressed our emotions for us, and he lived dangerously, as some of us did, and he was so vastly knowledgable, about life and people, and he was willing to give it away. He burned with a temperature, and he had this wonderful gift of love which so many of us withheld. John Ashbery withheld it, Kenneth Koch withheld it, I withheld it, each of us in our own fashion. . . . Frank was more generous than we were, and he was that way with everyone." Guest and O'Hara lunched often, and he would punctuate some of their meetings with poems. At Larré's in midtown Manhattan, a favorite lunching spot because of its proximity to the Museum and because of its slightly faux-French cuisine (Schuyler once pointed out that the pâté at Larré's was another name for meatloaf), O'Hara wrote that he and Guest "pour Martinis in our ears, listening / for each other's silence." That was in

1955. In 1958 they spent time together in Paris: "Oh Barbara! do you think we'll ever / have anything named after us like / *rue Henri-Barbusse* or / *canard à l'Ouragan?*"

O'Hara's letters to other artists demonstrate his readiness to play the roles of catalyst, coach, fixer, and buddy. He campaigned vigorously, for example, to obtain an Ingram Merrill Foundation fellowship for the painter John Button in 1960. He wrote to Button with the details of the application process, how many recommendation letters would be needed, and so forth. "If this all seems like too much work, I will be delighted to do it," O'Hara wrote. He was sure that Tom Hess of *Art News* would serve as a recommender, and Bill de Kooning, too. "I could ask them for you so you wouldn't have to write a lot of letters, if you decide who you want when the time comes." Also, John Bernard Myers, who helped administer the Ingram Merrill awards, will "be happy to advise as to who he thinks might be most impressive to the judges or whoever handles getting the thing, though he can't guarantee anything, naturally. NOW YOU DO WANT TO APPLY, DON'T YOU?"

The letters O'Hara wrote in his last months do not support the hypothesis that his death was a passive form of suicide. There are few references to alcohol or depression. Rather there is fresh evidence of the born mentor and the staunch advocate. Joseph Ceravolo, a marvelously original younger poet who had studied with Kenneth Koch at the New School, had approached O'Hara timidly, saying he was fearful of being pushy or "using people" to further his career. "As for your thing about using people you know, that is ridiculous," O'Hara wrote in a letter notable for thoughtful encouragement and plain good sense. "Why do you think people know each other if they are not going to get any information from them? If I think you're one of the most important poets around, as I do, I don't see any sense in keeping it a secret, unless you are intent on keeping your poems a secret, in which case I should honor your intent. At any rate, it would be my moral problem, not yours. It is all part of my knowledge and taste and what I want to do with it. I can assure you that it is a rare case indeed, and an amusing and even funny one, when someone gets published because of knowing someone. But you are losing sight of the main objective, which is to make the poems available to be read by people. I doubt very much if John Myers would ever have published my first pamphlet, *A City Winter*, if one of his artists, Larry Rivers, hadn't wanted him to and wanted to do the drawings for it. So what? Am I supposed to dislike Larry for 'pushing' my work, or John for publishing it?"

One of the last letters O'Hara ever wrote was a tribute to Barnett Newman. "Suddenly last night (shades of Tennessee Williams) I realized how incredible it is, after so many conversations about them, that I never wrote to tell you how much I love and admire your *Stations of the Cross* and how awed I am by them," O'Hara wrote. "I think the reason I didn't do it before is because they are so moving, so eloquent, so right, that it's almost impossible to talk about them—the best way to express one's feelings is simply to burst into tears."

O'Hara felt that the painters were the heroes of a modern artistic revolution. "You do what I can only name," he wrote in a poem dedicated to Larry Rivers. As a critic, O'Hara was very much the poet as critic, who wrote with enthusiasm and spirit and employed lyric means rather than argumentation and analysis. To others he left the task of making critical discriminations and comparative judgments; he preferred inclusiveness to hierarchy. He was one of the few in the art world of the 1950s who refused to choose between Jackson Pollock and Willem de Kooning when everyone else had chosen sides as if at a stickball game in the street. O'Hara took up the rivalry in his monograph on Pollock, which was published in 1959. The years 1947 to 1950 were Pollock's "classical" period, O'Hara wrote, and the term itself seemed to spark the further observation that "Pollock is the Ingres, and de Kooning the Delacroix, of Action Painting. Their greatness is equal, but antithetical. Because of this, to deny one would be to deny the other." The classification of de Kooning as Romantic in the manner of Delacroix is somewhat arbitrarily made, as is the comparison of Pollock to Ingres, but to dwell on this is to miss the point. As with all his critical writings, the style of O'Hara's Pollock monograph is poetic rather than analytical, animated by ardor rather than cool detachment, and full of a phrasemaker's panache. O'Hara particularly favored what might be called the "duke of earl" construction: if Pollock was the Ingres of Action Painting, Salvador Dali was "the Marshall Rommel of Surrealism."

Unlike Clement Greenberg, who set store by making critical judgments and establishing the theoretical underpinnings of the work he admired, O'Hara wrote art criticism as if it were an extension of poetry by different means. Exuberant in praise and associative in logic, he subscribed to Baudelaire's opinion that the "best criticism is that which is entertaining and poetic," and that the "best account of a picture may well be a sonnet or an elegy." Although Baudelaire, the first in the line of great poets who doubled as art critics, would sour on revolutionary politics, he was still inflamed with fervor in 1846 when he issued his most famous critical proclamation. Criticism proper, criticism that wasn't itself a poem, "must be partial, passionate, political," Baudelaire wrote. Here O'Hara took leave of his French precursor. The critic is "the assassin of my orchards," O'Hara wrote in his poem "The Critic" (1951). The poem is Eden, and the satanic critic, who would cause Eve to confuse penises and snakes (as a Freudian critic might), is rebuffed. If criticism is to follow from poetry, it must transcend the structural enmity between critic and poet; it must be not partial, passionate, and political, but three very different things:

> Oh be droll, be jolly
> and be temperate! Do not
>
> frighten me more than you
> have to! I must live forever.

Most poets tend to fetishize their works, retaining multiple drafts of every poem. Not O'Hara. He would carelessly shelve his poems with his towels or give away the only copy of a work written that day. "Memorial Day 1950," one of O'Hara's great early poems, would have been lost if John Ashbery hadn't mailed a copy of it to Kenneth Koch and if Koch had failed to hold on to it until Donald Allen edited the posthumous volume of *Collected Poems* (1971) that assured O'Hara an audience wider than the self-selected New York elite for whom the poet had long been a hero. "Memorial Day 1950" reflects in its title the particular conception of occasional poetry—that is, poetry imbued with a sense of its occasion—that O'Hara favored. The information given in the title is found nowhere else in the poem, but it doesn't need to be; as in the case of paintings by Marcel Duchamp and Arshile Gorky, the title adds an additional dimension to the work. Full of war imagery and the theme of destruction at the service of creation, "Memorial Day 1950" commemorates the day of its composition, a national holiday of remembrance for the casualties of war. O'Hara wrote it five years after the end of World War II, at the exact midcentury point, a fitting moment for a retrospective look at the first half of the century. The poet himself was then on the verge of his graduation from Harvard, and the poem is also his valedictory address, his "good-bye to all that" at the commencement of a career that was not quite what his elders had predicted for him when he was growing up in the parochial schools of Grafton, Massachusetts, a blue-collar town forty miles west of Boston. The poem is a memorial for his childhood as well as for his recently deceased father. But it speaks not in mournful accents. Rather it announces, in the bold exclamations that marked O'Hara's early style, that the writer has sought and found an artistic paternity to replace his dead father.

"Memorial Day 1950" is a kind of generalized Bildungsroman in verse, a negotiating of the way between boyhood and manhood. It is also a crash course in modernism. The poem names some of the influences not only upon O'Hara directly but on a generation of self-consciously modern poets; the "I" in the poem widens to take on the attributes of both "you" and "we," as O'Hara with gleeful irony proclaims his own development as exemplary. As Joyce's Stephen Dedalus in *A Portrait of the Artist as a Young Man* (one of O'Hara's favorite books) chooses the "silence, exile, and cunning" of art, rejecting the labyrinthine world of turn-of-the-century Dublin, O'Hara rejects his biological father ("Now my father is dead and has found out you must look things / in the belly, not in the eye") in favor of the "Fathers of Dada" and other freely elected father-substitutes. Auden, Rimbaud, Picasso, Apollinaire, Gertrude Stein, Boris Pasternak, Max Ernst, and Paul Klee are named as teachers. Picasso is an ax-wielding construction worker turning plane trees into "rubbish," an activity that is also likened to "creation" and to "surgery":

> Through all that surgery I thought
> I had a lot to say, and named several last things
> Gertrude Stein hadn't had time for; but then
> the war was over, those things had survived
> and even when you're scared art is no dictionary.
> Max Ernst told us that.
>
> How many trees and frying pans
> I loved and lost! Guernica hollered look out!
> but we were all busy hoping our eyes were talking
> to Paul Klee. My mother and father asked me and

> I told them from my tight blue pants we should
> love only the stones, the sea, and heroic figures.
> Wasted child! I'll club you on the shins! I
> wasn't surprised when the older people entered
> my cheap hotel room and broke my guitar and my can
> of blue paint.

The connection between "my tight blue pants" and "my can of blue paint" is both visual (blue) and aural (pants and paint) and suggests the sexual component in O'Hara's artistic vocation, as he conceives it—one thing that young poets have always responded to in O'Hara is this confident sexiness. As in Arthur Rimbaud's *"Les Poètes de sept ans,"* the poet in "Memorial Day 1950" is a child playing with toys. If dolls (as he tells us) "meant death," so does any art that resembles the dollmaker's—it is a dangerous game that is bound to land one in trouble with disapproving elders. Poetry gives the permission that parents deny, and the poet aspires to the status of the man with the blue guitar as Picasso painted him and as Wallace Stevens wrote about him. The man with the blue guitar knows that a picture can be "a hoard of destructions" and that this can be true of a poem as well. And if destruction is a necessary accomplice of creation and "love is first of all / a lesson in utility," it is only fitting that the broken guitar strings reemerge to "hold up pictures" in the poet's room. "I don't need a piano to sing," says the erstwhile music major, who will henceforth play the typewriter to create symphonies and songs.

"Memorial Day 1950" is full of energy: exclamations, oracular utterances, contradictions, and false parallelisms ("trees and frying pans," "lovely as chewing gum or flowers"). Clever literary allusions are made with élan. Mindful that Tennyson had written, in "In Memoriam," that " 'tis better to have loved and lost than never to have loved at all," O'Hara exclaims that he "loved and lost!" (and a line break conveniently obscures the direct object of those verbs). "Our responsibilities did not begin / in dreams, though they began in bed," O'Hara writes, mindful of Delmore Schwartz's story "In Dreams Begin Responsibilities," in which the young narrator goes to the movies, sees his father courting his mother on the screen, stands up and shouts, "Don't do it! Nothing good will come of it, only remorse, hatred, scandal, and two children whose characters are monstrous."

The poem doesn't quite resolve the contradictions and paradoxes that it proposes. These fall into four categories. (1): In what sense can destructiveness be a creative activity? The Futurists' idealization of war and machinery survives in O'Hara's ironic image of airplanes as "perfect mobiles." "Crashing in flames they show us how to be prodigal," O'Hara writes. The intent is not to glorify war but to recommend that the artist appropriate the engines of destruction for his own life-affirming ends. (2): If poetry is the most gratuitous of activities, how can it also be "as useful as a machine"? This problem is related to (3): Although poetry isn't "crap," through its agency wreckage and rubbish can become aesthetic products. Whitman wrote, "I hear America singing." O'Hara hears sewage instead. The poet and unnamed cronies have been "throttled" for thinking that "poetry was crap," but then O'Hara decides to give this dead metaphor a shake:

> I hear the sewage singing
> underneath my bright white toilet seat and know
> that somewhere sometime it will reach the sea:
> gulls and swordfishes will find it richer than a river.

So, then, poetry *is* crap, after all? Or is the toilet in effect a catalytic converter, transforming excrement into the nourishment of gulls, the machine as useful as the poem? Finally, (4): If "naming" as an activity is inferior to "making," is poetry fated to be a lesser art than painting?

"Naming things is only the intention to make things," O'Hara writes toward the end of the poem, echoing his earlier assertion that "art is no dictionary." The distinction between *naming* and *making* is critical. Here, as elsewhere in his work, O'Hara associates poetry with the act of naming—following the view that Adam's first task in Genesis, the distribution of the names to the animals, was the initiating act of poetry. But the distinction implies a hierarchy between poetry and a higher aesthetic activity, making—and we know of O'Hara's deference to the visual artists of his time. It was as if, for O'Hara, the painter had a greater capacity for self-expression than the poet and therefore poetry needed to transcend its very nature to achieve true creation. What makes this line of reasoning so fascinating (and perplexing) is that O'Hara's poetry is very precisely a poetry of naming. No poet has done more to turn naming into a central activity and name-dropping into a fine art; no poet is more attentive to the names of things, places, persons, and streets. And this brings me to an animating paradox in O'Hara's work.

The surface of O'Hara's poems is so dazzling, with taste so fine and sensibility so rare and appealing, that it comes as a surprise to investigate and realize that there are depths of meaning in his offhanded poems that seem as disarmingly immediate and perishable as telephone calls. The prejudice against humor and lightheartedness in poetry has caused some readers to overlook not only the lyric pathos informing O'Hara's work but also the incisive way his work captures a world, a time, and a place. The names in O'Hara's poetry are not only autobiographical markers, chronicling his taste and sensibility, but also a form of news and cultural commentary.

The point may be illustrated by a close look at O'Hara's mock manifesto, "Personism," together with the poem O'Hara had in mind when he wrote it, "Personal Poem," which he had written a week earlier. "Personism" is a spoof of a manifesto that nevertheless achieves the effects of a manifesto—the announcement of a new style, the declaration of an antiprogrammatic program. It should be read as a prose poem more than anything else, a triumph of irony and wit, but the jokey manner should not blind us to its serious import. Not only does "Personism" name a specific strategy for poetry that O'Hara and later others of the New York School used, but it defines O'Hara's stance, in his life no less than in his poetry: "You just go on your nerve. If someone's chasing you down the street with a knife you just run, you don't turn around and shout, 'Give it up! I was a track star for Mineola Prep.'" "I'm not saying that I don't have practically the most lofty ideas of anyone writing today, but what difference does that make? They're just ideas. The only good thing about it is that when I get lofty enough I've stopped thinking and that's when refreshment arrives."

"Personism" was written at the request of Donald Allen, who wanted a prose statement for his *New American Poetry* anthology. O'Hara wrote it in about an hour, with a Rachmaninoff concerto blaring in the background, on September 3, 1959. It came in the middle of O'Hara's most fertile period. He had written some of the most memorable of his lunch poems that summer: "The Day Lady Died" on July 17, "Rhapsody" on July 30, and "Adieu to Norman, Bon Jour to Joan and Jean-Paul" on August 7. On August 27 he dashed off "Personal Poem," after lunching with LeRoi Jones (now Amiri Baraka), and it was this poem that O'Hara held up as representative of his methods in "Personism." Both Donald Allen and LeRoi Jones are, as it happens, mentioned in "Personal Poem," which lends an additional element of irony to the situation. Allen, thinking "Personism" too frivolous, rejected it, and it made its first appearance in Jones's magazine *Yugen.* Unfazed by Allen's rejection, O'Hara wrote another statement for *The New American Poetry*, not quite as high-spirited, not quite as good, though in its way equally accurate: "What is happening to me, allowing for lies and exaggerations which I try to avoid, goes into my poems. I don't think my experiences are clarified or made beautiful for myself or anyone else; they are just there in whatever form I can find them."

"Personism" is far more buoyant. In inflated accents befitting a literary manifesto, O'Hara makes great claims for "a movement which I recently founded and which nobody knows about," to which he has given the name Personism. "It's a very exciting movement which will undoubtedly have lots of adherents," O'Hara writes. "In all modesty, I confess that it may be the death of literature as we know it. While I have certain regrets, I am still glad I got there before Alain Robbe-Grillet did." And what can the world expect from this movement that so far exists only on paper, as either a hoax or a promissory note? "Everything, but we won't get it. It is too new, too vital a movement to promise anything. But it, like Africa, is on the way." As the piece swaggers to a close, the reader has to pinch himself to remember that it began on a down note. In the course of writing "Personism," refreshment has arrived. The poet who had pictured himself menaced by a knife-wielding thug has, through the act of writing, turned into a brash and confident man who considers himself a rather charming fellow.

O'Hara asserts that "Personism" was based on a discovery he had made when writing "Personal Poem" on the previous Thursday. He had wanted, after lunching with Jones, to write a poem for Vincent Warren, the young dancer who inspired some of O'Hara's most affecting love poems. "While I was writing it I was realizing that if I wanted to I could use the telephone instead of writing the poem, and so Personism was born," O'Hara writes. The jest conceals an important insight. To conceive of a poem as a substitute for a telephone call that nevertheless resembles a telephone call is to recognize that poetry—avant-garde poetry, at any rate—is conditioned by the most technologically advanced means of communication of the time. Once one has made this discovery for oneself, one's whole notion of writing poetry must change. I have long felt that a thoughtful study on the influence of the typewriter on modern poetry is overdue. Less apparent but surely as interesting is the effect that the telephone has had on poets. When Elizabethans addressed sonnets to each other, there was no faster means of communication available. In 1959, however, one has the telephone at one's fingertips. What does one do? One writes a poem that is consciously not a telephone call but something like a message left on an answering machine (which hadn't been invented in 1959). Here is the out-of-breath, unpunctuated message O'Hara left for Vincent Warren that August Thursday:

PERSONAL POEM

Now when I walk around at lunchtime
I have only two charms in my pocket
an old Roman coin Mike Kanemitsu gave me
and a bolt-head that broke off a packing case
when I was in Madrid the others never
brought me too much luck though they did
help keep me in New York against coercion
but now I'm happy for a time and interested

I walk through the luminous humidity
passing the House of Seagram with its wet
and its loungers and the construction to
the left that closed the sidewalk if
I ever get to be a construction worker
I'd like to have a silver hat please

and get to Moriarty's where I wait for
LeRoi and hear who wants to be a mover and
shaker the last five years my batting average
is .016 that's that, and LeRoi comes in
and tells me Miles Davis was clubbed 12
times last night outside BIRDLAND by a cop
a lady asks us for a nickel for a terrible
disease but we don't give her one we
don't like terrible diseases, then

we go eat some fish and some ale it's
cool but crowded we don't like Lionel Trilling
we decide, we like Don Allen we don't like
Henry James so much we like Herman Melville
we don't want to be in the poets' walk in
San Francisco even we just want to be rich
and walk on girders in our silver hats
I wonder if one person out of the 8,000,000 is
thinking of me as I shake hands with LeRoi
and buy a strap for my wristwatch and go
back to work happy at the thought possibly so

So casual and conversational and spontaneous is this poem, so
committed to the rhythms of speech, that the reader may not
even hear the closing rhyme. And that is as it should be: The
music is in the heart of noise, the poetry something subtle in the
midst of all that seems wildly antipoetic.

"Personal Poem" begins by mentioning amulets or charms,
and it is easy to regard the poem itself as another sort of good-
luck charm. For O'Hara, luck and nerve go hand in hand. As the
last line of the first stanza tells us, happiness for this wounded
narcissist is a temporary condition whose effect on the poet is to
keep him "interested." Several meanings of this seemingly bland

word come into play. The poet is romantically "interested" in one of his 8 million fellow New Yorkers. But he is also, when happy, interested in the sense of being alert and attentive. It is to this state that O'Hara aspires. As he puts it at the end of "Larry Rivers: A Memoir," generalizing from his friend's painting to all art, "what his work has always had to say to me, I guess, is to be more keenly interested while I'm still alive. And perhaps this is the most important thing art can say."

Just about all the names mentioned in "Personal Poem" refer to people and places associated with New York: LeRoi Jones, Miles Davis, Henry James, Herman Melville, Donald Allen, Lionel Trilling, the Seagram Building, Moriarty's, Birdland. At a rapid reading, the poem seems to be simply the notations of a city stroller, but the information given is not quite as haphazard as the rapid associative flow would suggest. Take that lady begging for a nickel. She has multiplied a hundredfold since 1959, and inflation has rendered her demand as quaint as the jukebox nickel in the song "One for My Baby (and One More for the Road)." Or consider the antitheses in the last stanza. The predilection for Melville over James was fraught with symbolic significance in postwar America. In the 1940s, *Partisan Review* had organized a symposium whose participants had to choose between Walt Whitman and Henry James, an either/or choice between two sensibilities: the raw versus the cooked or, in the terms proposed by *Partisan Review*'s editor Philip Rahv, the redskin versus the paleface. O'Hara's simple statement that he prefers Melville to James is symbolically a vote for the rough as opposed to the smooth, for the rebellious outsiders in the poetry wars rather than the academic elite, and would have been read as such by his readers.

Having worked as Lionel Trilling's research assistant at Columbia in the early 1970s, I was always curious about the lines opposing Trilling (whom "we don't like") to Don Allen (whom "we like"). The antithesis is comically one-sided—the Columbia eminence at the height of his influence versus the little-known Grove Press editor. The fact that Trilling cast his vote for James in the old *Partisan Review* James-versus-Whitman sweepstakes didn't go far enough to explain the animus. What had Trilling done, or what did he stand for, that made O'Hara register his dislike on August 27, 1959?

The first possibility I considered was the Robert Frost brouhaha of 1959. At a banquet celebrating Frost's eighty-fifth birthday that year, Trilling delivered a toast in which he argued that some of Frost's admirers loved his work for the wrong reason. Frost was not, Trilling said, a genial homespun Yankee sage but a "terrifying poet" uttering dark and tragic truths about our no less terrifying universe. "Read the poem called 'Design' and see if you sleep the better for it," Trilling said. Trilling's statement is one that ennobles Frost, and it has become the generally accepted view of the poet. Indeed the prevalence of this view is one reason that Frost's stock continues to make record highs in the stock market of literary valuation. Nevertheless there were many who took offense in 1959. J. Donald Adams, an editor of the *New York Times Book Review* best remembered today for having made a horse's ass of himself in the controversy, devoted an entire column to the affair. Interpreting Trilling's toast as an assault on the poet with the beloved shock of white hair, Adams cited the "terrifying" remark and replied with disbelief: "Holy mackerel! Frost simply sees the universe as it is and accepts it. He isn't terrified by what he sees, and neither should we be." Adams scolded Trilling: "Come out of the Freudian wood, Professor Trilling, and face the facts of life." The irony of Adams's outrage is that his chilled view of Frost—who has, Adams wrote, "a private air-conditioning system" permitting him to keep cool—is not only a less accurate reading of the poet but one that would, if taken to heart, seem to diminish Frost's accomplishment.

But it could not have been the Frost affair that accounted for O'Hara's disparaging reference to Trilling in "Personal Poem." O'Hara would not have sided with the middlebrow columnist; he had no vested interest in an iconic image of Frost on a par with the bald eagle (an identification Adams urged). However, another controversy involving a Trilling—not Lionel, this time, but his wife Diana—had also broken out in 1959, and since New York literati tended to view the Trillings as a joint entity, it is conceivable that what O'Hara had in mind when he said "we don't like Lionel Trilling" was Diana Trilling's essay "The Other Night at Columbia: A Report from the Academy."

Like Lionel's "Speech on Robert Frost," Diana's essay appeared that year in *Partisan Review*, which was as central to the intellectual culture of 1959 as *Life* was to the nonintellectual culture. "The Other Night at Columbia" was occasioned by a Beat poetry reading at Columbia featuring Allen Ginsberg, Gregory Corso, and Peter Orlovsky. The reading marked Allen Ginsberg's triumphant return to his alma mater, which had expelled him for assorted offenses (such as writing "fuck the Jews" in the dust of his dormitory windowsill) a decade earlier. Now he was reading his poems, as Mrs. Trilling observed, from the same stage where T. S. Eliot had read his. Ginsberg and company reveled in but also resented their image as (in Corso's words) "filthy beatnik sex commie dope fiends." But it wasn't so much what Mrs. Trilling said as the patronizing way she said it that angered the poets. Curiosity and a certain incipient sense of indignation had prompted her to attend the event. She registered her surprise and relief that Ginsberg, Corso, and Orlovsky didn't smell bad, but she made a point of withholding her approval from children—so they seemed to her—craving it. She felt that "these *were* children, miserable children trying desperately to manage, asking desperately to be taken out of it all, so that I kept asking myself, where had I had just such an experience before, and later it came to me: I had gone to see O'Neill's *Long Day's Journey into Night*, and the play had echoed with just such a child's cry for help . . ."

Diana Trilling's words were disliked. Robert Bly wrote an amusing parody. Ginsberg and Corso were still complaining about the piece twenty years later. Resentment of the Trillings, of her schoolmarm scolding and his grave tone, was widespread in 1959. Alfred Kazin in his memoir *New York Jew* etches a portrait of an unforgiving Diana, who was "a dogged woman, and looked it." In Kazin's tart account of his unhappy relations with the professor and his wife, Mrs. Trilling's favorite literary genre is said to have been the letter to the editor. "Sometimes she wrote in to criticize an unfavorable review of a book for not being unfavorable enough," Kazin wrote.

Granted that Diana Trilling's essay was not calculated to charm O'Hara. But would it have been sufficient to prompt O'Hara to "decide" that "we don't like Lionel Trilling"? Possibly not; O'Hara was perfectly capable of distinguishing one Trilling from the other, and besides, his own relations with the Beats had come under strain earlier that year when Kerouac was rude and Corso gauche at a reading O'Hara allowed himself to be talked into doing. No, it is in another work by Diana Trilling that one may discover the key to this literary mystery. In her book *The Beginning of the Journey*, a portrait of her marriage to Lionel, she brought up the issue of happiness.

For Lionel Trilling, his widow points out, seriousness, not happiness, was the goal worthy of an intellectual life. The gravity of his tone in his literary essays was consistent with a depressive personality. "Except when he was alone with me, he never allowed his depression to show," Diana Trilling writes. "But even apart from these shifts of mood, he was not to be described as a happy person. Indeed, he thought poorly of happiness and of people who claimed to be happy or desired happiness above other gratifications in life. He often repeated the question which Philip Rahv put to us with such gusto. Rahv had been in Russia and had trouble pronouncing the letter *h*. 'Oo's 'appy?' he would inquire with obvious relish. Lionel would have replied that it was not the serious people of the world. Seriousness was the desirable condition of man, especially literary man."

Here, in a nutshell, is the value system that O'Hara rebelled against. Not the stern Old Testament god of moral seriousness but the Greek goddesses of pleasure and beauty were his animating deities. What else is "Personism: A Manifesto" if not a blast against didacticism? "Too many poets act like a middle-aged mother trying to get her kids to eat too much cooked meat, and potatoes with drippings (tears)," O'Hara wrote in his mock-manifesto. "I don't give a damn whether they eat or not. Forced feeding leads to excessive thinness (effete). Nobody should experience anything they don't want to, if they don't need poetry bully for them, I like the movies too." It may be that in saying "we don't like Lionel Trilling," O'Hara is rejecting the whole point of view associated with that living metonymy of the New York Jewish intellectuals, *Partisan Review*.

The flip side of O'Hara's rejection of didacticism is his quiet but incessant pursuit of happiness. "Personal Poem" concludes with the expression of a fragile happiness or better yet the unextinguished possibility of happiness: not an unequivocal yes but a hedged bet, "possibly so." And at this second instance of the word *happy* in "Personal Poem," the reader would do well to recall that *happiness* has the same root as the word *perhaps*, and that both words are connected to *hap*, meaning chance or hazard. Happiness is a matter of luck; may this poem serve as an amulet to perpetuate the romance.

There is another moment in "Personal Poem" that widens out into a rich field of cultural implication, and that is the moment when LeRoi Jones tells O'Hara about the clubbing of Miles

Davis in front of the jazz club called Birdland on Fifty-second
Street the night before. The incident was a rank example of racial
harassment. The great trumpeter had accompanied a white
woman to her taxi in front of the club. Evidently this was incite-
ment enough for the policemen patrolling the street. Told to
"move on," Davis pointed to his name on the marquee. The cop
said, "I don't care where you work, I said move on! If you don't,
I'll have to lock you up." "Go ahead, lock me up," Davis replied;
he had mixed with boxers and was not easily intimidated. In the
ensuing melee, Davis was beaten with a blackjack. "They beat me
on the head like a tom-tom," he said. He needed five stitches in
his scalp. Adding insult to injury, he was taken to jail and kept
there overnight; he was charged with disorderly conduct and assault, and his cabaret license was revoked. When he was cleared
of the charges in October, the presiding judge commented that
"it would be a travesty of justice to adjudge the victim of an illegal
arrest guilty of the crime of assaulting the one who made the
arrest."

Born in 1926, and thus O'Hara's exact contemporary, Miles
Davis was the musician most responsible for the "cool" sound of
jazz in the 1950s. As a young man still in his teens he came to
New York from his native East St. Louis and played with Charlie
Parker and Coleman Hawkins. He grew up comfortably middle-
class—his father was a dentist—but his music was the music of
melancholy and it inspired flights of metaphors from listeners.
When you listen to Davis's playing on *Porgy and Bess*, particularly
in such songs as "Bess, You Is My Woman Now" and "I Loves
You, Porgy," you are struck by the near proximity of ecstatic joy
and deep, dark, irrevocable sorrow. It is there in the Gershwin,
is brought out sublimely by Davis, and is perfectly continuous
with the rapid mood shifts of O'Hara's poetry.

Birth of the Cool, Miles Ahead, and *Porgy and Bess* were "cool"
in the sense that the music was relaxed, even languid in places,

bittersweet, restrained, graceful. But Davis was also "cool" in the more familiar sense—in the sense just becoming popular in America on the eve of the 1960s. "To be *cool* was, in its most accessible meaning, to be calm, even unimpressed, by what horror the world might daily propose," LeRoi Jones wrote in 1963. To be cool enabled one to reverse the old "Steppinfechit" stereotype. "Given his constant position at the bottom of the American social hierarchy, there was not one reason for any Negro, ever, to hurry," Jones wrote.

Miles Davis perfected the "calm, unimpressed" look of cool detachment, in his person no less than in his music. He "was original, caustic, self-aware, and artistically demanding," the jazz commentator Jamie Katz observes. "He had style, in that special 50's/60's way: sharp Italian clothes, sexy women, sports cars. He epitomized cosmopolitan taste, and he helped give jazz musicians an urbane new persona that communicated a hip self-respect. A large part of his approach, I am convinced, had to do with positioning himself within the complex racial cosmos—he wanted to stay one elusive step ahead of those who would capture him and bottle him on their own terms, however innocently or appreciatively, even. These were usually white folks, with whom, just to complicate the picture, he was clearly capable of dealing individually. So at the height of his fame, lionized by sophisticated people the world over, a true artist and cool guy, he gets clubbed on the head as if to remind him of his real place in the world. He was Miles Davis, not some common sidewalk junkie. Would Stravinsky or Gershwin have been treated this way? Of course it blew his mind."

When O'Hara wrote "Personal Poem," the racial tension in New York was reaching ominous levels. All that summer the pressure mounted—it was as if a major race riot were waiting to erupt. If the Birdland incident made Davis, in his words, "more bitter and cynical than I might have been," over the next few years

LeRoi Jones would go through a personal revolution that led him to change his name to Amiri Baraka, sever ties with his white friends, and devote himself to a species of artistic guerrilla warfare determined (as he put it in a poem) "to smash / capitalism / to smash / to smash / capitalism / to smash / to smash / capitalism." The mention of Jones and Davis in O'Hara's poem is significant not only because it aligns the poet on the side of the protesters on the eve of the decade of the Civil Rights Movement, but also because by and large black people were invisible in the poetry of the 1950s. O'Hara was one of the first American poets to include them matter-of-factly in his vision of America. The harassment of a major jazz musician was one piece of front-page news that has stayed news through O'Hara's poetry.

It may be argued that O'Hara fetishized blacks in his poems. Yusef Komunyakaa was moved to write a poem based on "Personal Poem" because of his admiration for O'Hara's "inclusiveness," on the one hand, and because of his uneasiness with "the conspicuous exoticism in some of his poems (especially about blacks)." Komunyakaa added: "When the human body becomes mere object, this kind of voyeurism dehumanizes us." It is true that some of O'Hara's poems idealize the Negro as a cultural icon and jazz as a form of vanguard art. In doing so O'Hara participated in a tendency of which the supreme expression was Norman Mailer's essay "The White Negro: Superficial Reflections on the Hipster" (1957). The source of hip and hipsterism is the black man, Mailer wrote: "In such places as Greenwich Village, a ménage à trois was completed—the bohemian and the juvenile delinquent came face-to-face with the Negro, and the hipster was a fact in American life." As if deconstructing the binary opposition between white and black in their writing, white writers who would be hip tended to identify themselves with the black man; where blacks had often been portrayed by whites as the projection of their fears, they were now portrayed as the object of their envy.

Thus Jack Kerouac in *On The Road:* "At lilac evening I walked with every muscle aching among the lights of 27th and Wilton in the Denver colored section, wishing I were a Negro, feeling that the best the white world had offered was not enough ecstasy for me, not enough life, joy, kicks, darkness, music, not enough night." And thus O'Hara, hurling a tirade against the Russian poets Voznesensky and Yevtushenko: "I consider myself to be black and you not even part where you see death." O'Hara described "the strange black cock which has become ours despite your envy."

It is true that O'Hara's "Answer to Voznesensky & Evtushenko" falls in line with a tendency spoofed by his friend Larry Rivers in a provocative mixed-media construction he called *America's Number One Problem* (1969), which shows a pink penis and a burnt-umber penis and a ruler each measuring exactly nine inches. But I think the suggestion that blacks are "dehumanized" in O'Hara's poetry is too harsh. The handshake between LeRoi Jones and Frank O'Hara at the end of "Personal Poem" evokes not stereotypes but a vision of friendship across the racial divide; it calls to mind the pacts between Huck and Jim and between Ishmael and Queequeg in the great American novels of Mark Twain and Herman Melville. (O'Hara's personal disappointment when Jones rejected his erstwhile white friends was profound.) And O'Hara's poetic preoccupation with Miles Davis in "Personal Poem" and with Billie Holiday in "The Day Lady Died" is evidence less of white-negroism than of peerless aesthetic taste.

O'Hara's datebook for 1959 shows that he had a typically hectic second week of July. He lunched with the painter Norman Bluhm on Monday the thirteenth and with LeRoi Jones on Tuesday, Bastille Day. He also had an unscheduled drink that day with Jasper Johns, during the course of which the painter asked O'Hara whom he should be reading. O'Hara promptly wrote him a long letter bubbling over with literary enthusiasm. The next day he wrote a poem, "All that Gas" ("and the rainbow is slooping over the Chrysler Building / like a spineless trout, ugly and ephemeral / it is no sign of hope when things get ugly"). On Thursday O'Hara had drinks with Larry Rivers.

For Friday, O'Hara had made plans to take a late-afternoon train to East Hampton. He and Joe LeSueur were going to spend the weekend there as houseguests of Patsy Southgate and Mike Goldberg, and he decided to use his lunch hour to buy gifts for his host and hostess: books, cigarettes, brandy. Strolling back to his office at the Museum of Modern Art, he shelled out a dime for the early-afternoon edition of the *New York Post*. The headline was BILLIE HOLIDAY DIES. Together with a photograph of the singer, it took up the entire front page.

O'Hara had heard Lady Day sing the previous autumn at the Five Spot Cafe, where Thelonious Monk regularly played. It was a Monday night. Monday was Monk's night off, and on those nights Mal Waldron, who was Billie Holiday's piano accompanist, played with a trio consisting of Elvin Jones on drums, Julian Newell on bass, Pepper Adams on baritone sax. Others, too, joined in; Larry Rivers, whose first love was jazz, sometimes got in the action with his tenor sax. It was Rivers who persuaded the Five Spot's owner to let him conduct some experimental sessions in poetry and jazz—partly to spoof the new vogue of beat poetry and mournful saxophone sounds and partly to join in on the fun. One Monday Kenneth Koch came and read from the Manhattan telephone directory while Rivers played saxophone. Afterward Billie Holiday, who had wandered in to greet Waldron, told Koch, "Man, your poems are weird." Holiday, whose cabaret card had been revoked because of her heroin use, consented to break the law for one song while Waldron hit the keys. She sang in a husky whisper. O'Hara stood leaning against the bathroom door, listening.

Having digested the news of Lady Day's death, O'Hara went up to his office and typed out a poem, folded it, and put it into his jacket pocket. When he and Joe LeSueur arrived in East

Hampton, Mike Goldberg met them in his olive drab Bugatti, which he had bought the previous fall on his and Patsy's honeymoon in Italy. Goldberg had brought a Thermos of martinis along, and the friends passed it around as Goldberg drove them to Briar Patch Road, where Patsy was waiting. Mike put on a Billie Holiday record, Patsy brought out a tray of hors d'oeuvre, and the four of them sat on the screen porch, where O'Hara announced that he'd written a poem that afternoon. This is what he read:

THE DAY LADY DIED

It is 12:20 in New York a Friday
three days after Bastille day, yes
it is 1959 and I go get a shoeshine
because I will get off the 4:19 in Westhampton
at 7:15 and then go straight to dinner
and I don't know the people who will feed me

I walk up the muggy street beginning to sun
and have a hamburger and a malted and buy
an ugly NEW WORLD WRITING to see what the poets
in Ghana are doing these days
                              I go on to the bank
and Miss Stillwagon (first name Linda I once heard)
doesn't even look up my balance for once in her life
and in the GOLDEN GRIFFIN I get a little Verlaine
for Patsy with drawings by Bonnard although I do
think of Hesiod, trans. Richmond Lattimore or
Brendan Behan's new play or *Le Balcon* or *Les Nègres*
of Genet, but I don't, I stick with Verlaine
after practically going to sleep with quandariness

and for Mike I just stroll into the PARK LANE
Liquor Store and ask for a bottle of Strega and

then I go back where I came from to 6th Avenue
and the tobacconist in the Ziegfeld Theatre and
casually ask for a carton of Gauloises and a carton
of Picayunes, and a NEW YORK POST with her face on it

and I am sweating a lot by now and thinking of
leaning on the john door in the 5 SPOT
while she whispered a song along the keyboard
to Mal Waldron and everyone and I stopped breathing

"The Day Lady Died" is a classic instance of a poem chronicling its own coming into existence—you can trace the poet's footsteps up to the moment when he sat at his typewriter recapitulating the hour he had just spent. Part of the poem's charm lies in its mix of populist and elitist elements: a hamburger and a malted and "a little Verlaine," a trip to the bank to cash a check, the purchase of exotic cigarettes and liqueurs. Here again, as in "Personal Poem" and "Memorial Day 1950," the names mentioned in the poem are not merely gratuitous; from our distance we can see just how much they tell us about the world in 1959. Even the detail about the bank teller—"Miss Stillwagon (first name Linda I once heard) [who] / doesn't even look up my balance for once in her life"—has an interest beyond the sass in the speaker's voice; it helps evoke a once commonplace situation remote from us today, used as we have become to automatic teller machines and the universal American first-name basis. As a map of literary allusion, the poem is eclectic and heterodox: Brendan Behan and Jean Genet are given equal billing with Hesiod and Paul Verlaine. Then there is the reference to the June 1959 issue of *New World Writing* featuring the "voices of Ghana." It was the fifteenth and final issue of the eight-year-old magazine, which was published in the form of a Mentor paperback by New American Library. The issue contained a powerfully enigmatic story by

Boris Pasternak and an account by the French poet Henri Michaux of his experiences with mescaline, and it is more than likely that O'Hara picked up the "ugly" paperback (the adjective is apt—the cover is a graphic designer's nightmare) to read these two items rather than the voices of Ghana. But Africa, as O'Hara put it in "Personism," was "on its way," and surely there is a strong sense of negritude in "The Day Lady Died": it's there not only in the reference to the newly independent Ghana, which was celebrating its liberation from colonial status, but in the title of Genet's play (Les Nègres), in the sad demise of Billie Holiday, possibly even in the skin color of the shoeshine man, though this is not specified. Perhaps Yusef Komunyakaa is right, and the professed interest in "what the poets / in Ghana are doing these days" is a prime example of O'Hara's "exoticism" of blacks. Perhaps exoticism is the point: Cigarettes from France and New Orleans, liqueur from Italy, poets and painters from all over—the names in "The Day Lady Died" represent a whole way of life that would have seemed exotically bohemian to O'Hara's first readers. It was the same exoticism that young Americans, black and white, responded to in bebop jazz. Amiri Baraka, when he was still LeRoi Jones, understood that "the goatee, beret, and windowpane glasses were no accidents," that they signaled "the beginning of the Negro's fluency with some of the canons of Western nonconformity, which was an easy emotional analogy to the three hundred years of unintentional nonconformity his color constantly reaffirmed."

"The Day Lady Died" was an instant hit, though it provoked dismay from critics who wondered whether a poem that doesn't get around to mentioning the deceased until four lines from the end, and then in the most incidental way, could possibly be a sincere expression of grief. This reaction put the poem in the company of other great elegies. Milton's "Lycidas," the greatest elegy in the language, suffered a similar fate: There were readers—the great Samuel Johnson among them—who felt that the poem's pastoral conventions were artificial, that the poem therefore lacked sincerity, and that it was moreover unseemly of Milton to acknowledge, as he does, that one of his motives in writing this elegy for a drowned classmate was the hope that he, in turn, would be similarly memorialized. As the detractors of "Lycidas" were wrong, so the critics of "The Day Lady Died" misjudged the poet's conversational ease and seemingly self-centered stance. "The Day Lady Died" is a moving elegy not in spite of the poem's preoccupation with the poet's self but because of it; the death of the great singer at age forty-four occurs as an interruption, a shock that the reader is invited to share. The sharpness of the contrast between the vitality of the living man, attending to the errands and tasks of life, and the dead singer is like a last percussive note held in an expectant stillness. The poem's breathless ending virtually enacts the death of the "first lady of the blues" (as the *New York Post* put it) whose nickname, "Lady Day," is inverted in the poem's title, a gesture as witty as it is poignant. To the charge that O'Hara is too ironic to be sincere, I would borrow the distinction Lionel Trilling made between sincerity and authenticity: O'Hara's suspicion of sincerity as a rhetorical mode is paradoxically what makes his work more authentic.

A delicious irony about "The Day Lady Died" is that this most casual of utterances will, in becoming an anthology standard, someday require a whole battery of footnotes. But that is another way of saying that the poem opens out to include much more of the universe of 1959 than many another seemingly more ambitious poem. Indeed, to borrow a hyperbole from O'Hara's beloved Mayakovsky, it could be said that if all that survived of 1959 was "The Day Lady Died," then historians a century hence could piece together the New York of that moment in the same way that archaeologists can reconstruct a whole extinct species of dinosaur from a single fossil bone.

Kenneth Koch: the pleasures of peace

Kenny!
Kennebunkport! I see you standing there
assuaging everything with your smile
at the end of the world you are scratching your head
      wondering what is that funny French word Roussel
     was so fond of? oh "denouement"!
and it is good

                  —FRANK O'HARA,
                "ON A BIRTHDAY OF KENNETH'S"

Kenneth Koch is a recurring character in Frank O'Hara's poems. In one of his diurnal chronicles, "excitement-prone Kenneth Koch" is throwing a party. In a second, he is "our Hermes, the fastest literary figure of his time":

He never, Kenneth, did an effortless thing
in his life, but it pains us to send him into the world
in a hurry, he might stumble and commit a series!
Under the careful care of our admiration his greatness
appears like the French for 'gratuitous act' and we're proud
of our Hermes, the fastest literary figure of his time.

A third O'Hara poem is a perfect illustration of "Personism"—the poem on the model of a telephone call, quick, spontaneous, and immediate. "I am so nervous about my life the little I can get ahold of," O'Hara writes, "so I call up Kenneth in Southampton and presto / he is leaning on the shelf in the kitchen three hours away."

Koch pronounces his name "Coke," an apt pronunciation for a poet who wants his works to be as fizzy as soda, as American as pop. A bantering character in "The Pleasures of Peace," badgering the author, observes, "You're that famous COKE, aren't you, / That no one can drink?" When Edward Koch, whose name is pronounced "Kotch," was elected mayor of New York in 1977, the poet told him that people had begun to pronounce his last name Kotch. "And they're calling me Coke," the mayor quipped right back.

Koch's poetry remains an underrated treasure, arousing discipleship and high ardor wherever the spirit of the New York School is strong and ignored wherever not. He has won his share of prizes, the Bollingen among them, and the *New York Review of Books* has always treated him favorably, but none of his books has won, or contended seriously for, the annual Pulitzer and National Book Award sweepstakes. Prominent critics and kingmakers have shied away. While Koch has been championed in print by Tom Disch, Mark Halliday, John Hollander, and others for whom his poetry is, in Hollander's words, a "continuing celebration of the playful sublime," Koch remains miles away from the mainstream—his is "a sort of gaudy tent, pitched among the ruins of high seriousness," as Hollander put it. Why the critical neglect? Because Koch is a comic and narrative poet, and in academic America the bias against humor in poetry is matched only by the bias in favor of the short, sincere, autobiographical anecdote. This twin bias is easily exposed, and as easily refuted, but the problem has not gone away. Charles Simic sums it up. "If it's funny, then, obviously, it can't be serious, people will tell you," Simic has written. "I disagree. Comedy says as much about the world as does tragedy. In fact, if you seek true seriousness, you must make room for both comic and tragic vision. Still, almost everybody prefers to be pitied rather than to be laughed at. For every million poems lamenting the cruel fate of a much-misunderstood and endlessly suffering soul, we get one funny Russell Edson or Kenneth Koch poem." Simic concludes: "The dirtiest little secret around is that there are as many people without a sense of humor as there are people with no aesthetic sense."

Koch, our funniest poet, has had the misfortune to be a protean comic genius at a moment when the lyric poem is the be-all and end-all of verse and is mistakenly held to be incompatible with the spirit of comedy. He has uproariously mocked the poetry of humorless self-involvement, skewering what he calls " 'kiss-me-I'm-poetical' junk," and the antagonism has been mutual. To the offended he's puerile or sexist. The excessively somber regard him as the Phil Silvers of poetry, clever and silly and full of zany schemes; the righteously indignant read his "Art of Love"—

> The best way to conquer women in different cities is to
>   know the mayor or ruler of the particular city
> And have him introduce you to the women (perhaps while
>   they are under the influence of a strong love-making
>   drug)

—and complain about the objectified status of women in his work.

For a poet who has written an epic catalogue of his most entertaining misunderstandings (it's called "Taking a Walk With You"), it is a nasty irony that his own work has been so powerfully misconstrued. The truth is that Koch is a masterly innovator, not merely a comedian of the spirit, who has used his extravagant powers of wit and invention to enlarge the sphere of the poetic. In the development of the New York School, Koch campaigned tirelessly for his friends' work, proselytizing for it, making converts at the New School for Social Research (where his students in the early 1960s included Bill Berkson, Joseph Ceravolo, and Charles North) and Columbia (where he taught Ron Padgett, David Shapiro, Aaron Fogel, Gerrit Henry, Luc Sante, Darryl Pinckney, and Daphne Merkin, among many others). Koch may have been "our Hermes," but he was also the New York School's Horace, laying down the law on matters of style and diction. He summed up his doctrine in "The Art of Poetry," in which he speaks in propria persona as the nutty but wise professor offering instruction to the followers of mad Orpheus:

> Remember your obligation is to write,
> And, in writing, to be serious without being solemn, fresh
>   without being cold,
> To be inclusive without being asinine, particular
> Without being picky, feminine without being effeminate,
> Masculine without being brutish, human while keeping all
>   the animal graces
> You had inside the womb, and beast-like without being
>   inhuman.
> Let your language be delectable always, and fresh and true.

Even his detractors must admit that Koch's impact in pedagogical circles has been lasting, profound, and salutary. He revolutionized the teaching of poetry to children (in *Wishes, Lies, and Dreams* and *Rose, Where Did You Get That Red?*) and then did the same with elderly nursing-home residents (in *I Never Told Anybody*). What the detractors are not so quick to acknowledge is that his teaching is continuous with his own poetry, and indeed springs directly from it. A poet of the highest originality, however that term is defined, Koch has revived the epic and the drama as viable vehicles for verse and revealed an uncanny knack for marrying unusual forms to unconventional matter. He has written epics in ottava rima (*Ko, or, A Season on Earth* and *The Duplications*) and narratives about fairy-tale characters (Santa Claus is the hero and the Easter Bunny the villain of *The Red Robins*, which Koch wrote first as a novel and then as a play). Many of Koch's plays have been produced, and a book of 112 very short verse dramas with the beguiling title *One Thousand Avant-Garde Plays* (1988) is a brilliant example of conceptual drama that begs to be performed. In a variety of ways, Koch has stretched our ideas of what it is possible to do in poetry.

The comic element in Koch's poetry allows it to act as a corrective—to ward off the false poeticisms that mar many overly earnest poems. But it is his particular genius to celebrate what he implicitly critiques. *One Thousand Avant-Garde Plays*, for example, parodies the very avant-garde impulse that it exemplifies. The poet's irony takes in his own sacred rituals, yet the self-mockery coexists with sheer unbridled delight. Six plays illustrate six ways of turning Hamlet's "To be or not to be" soliloquy into an exemplary act of avant-garde theater; Koch presents the same speech with six different sets of stage directions. In one case, the hero interrupts himself after the "sea of troubles" sentence—he lights a cigarette, inhales, exhales, and walks offstage ("Smoking Hamlet"). In another, two actors go through the motions of the Little Red Riding Hood fairy tale while reciting Hamlet's speech ("Little Red Riding Hamlet"). In a third, a team of readers recites the speech one syllable at a time, changing their posture after every six syllables ("Team Hamlet"). The irreverence is not in regard to Hamlet but to the avant-garde strategies that are enacted in these miniature verse-dramas. The term *avant-garde* itself, so slippery and so often debased, gives rise to the wonderfully absurd exchange with which "After the Return of the

Avant-Garde" concludes: "Which is more avant-garde—a giraffe or an elephant?" "A giraffe is more avant-garde, but an elephant is more surreal."

Sure, Koch can be silly, but so, as Auden says, was Yeats. "I don't think being comic keeps one from being serious," Koch points out. "It keeps one from being solemn." The distinction has been eagerly embraced by younger writers. "The little I knew about literature, gathered from high school in West Virginia, was that I wanted it to be ransacked," Tom Andrews has written. "Koch's poems were among the first that showed me that poetry was, or could be, more than the dreadful solemnities I'd been taught to associate with it." And if the wince-provoking attitudes displayed in some of his poems are anachronistic, well, that's precisely the basis on which they can be defended. As Koch writes in "Artemis," one of the short-short stories in his *Hotel Lambosa* (1993), "We had to live sometime. It might as well have been in the fifties. There—look! It's fifties! Fifties wine. Still, you drink it and it makes you drunk. Whatever the epoch, I was drunk on and mystified by my wife."

It is usually a mistake to judge modern poetry on the basis of its political rectitude, or lack of same. There are, of course, exceptions. Where a poet's political motives are strong—as in the case of Brecht or, in a different way, Pound—the critic is invited, even urged, to consider the poems in the light of their hypothetical or actual consequences as political documents. But such a strategy seems particularly flawed in the case of a poet such as Koch, who eschews politics and commits himself instead to the possibilities of the art medium itself. One doesn't read Kenneth Koch for his politics any more than one travels to Casablanca for the waters. One reads Koch for his vision. His work is like an amusement park of the imagination, full of wild rides and spooky fun houses and a tunnel of love where the girl in braids with the cotton candy will be kissed by a handsome stranger. Politics in the conventional sense plays no role in his work, except as part of the American decor, a motive for metaphor, as in this recollection of a lunch with Frank O'Hara in the 1950s:

> Frank comes out of the doorway in his necktie and his coat
> It is a day on which it would be good to vote
> Autumn a crisp Republicanism is in the air tie and coat
> Soon to be trounced by the Democrats personified as a
>   slung-over-the-shoulder coat
> Fascism in the form of a bank
> Gives way to a shining restaurant that opens its door with a
>   clank

The true seriousness of Koch's endeavor becomes apparent only when you stop laughing long enough to realize that he takes spectacular risks, including the risk of being dismissed as a silly old ego-tripping white male chauvinist. The effect of this risk taking is that whole aspects of modern experience are recovered in his work—he gives back to us the parts of the day we had foolishly discarded. Consider "The Boiling Water" as a subject for poetry, a moment that makes it possible for the poet to interrogate the whole notion of seriousness:

> A serious moment for the water is when it boils
> And though one usually regards it merely as a convenience
> To have the boiling water available for bath or table
> Occasionally there is someone around who understands
> The importance of this moment for the water—maybe a
>   saint,
> Maybe a poet, maybe a crazy man, or just someone
>   temporarily disturbed
> With his mind "floating," in a sense, away from his deepest
> Personal concerns to more "unreal" things.

Koch's influence has been a liberation not only for the many students affected by his teaching but for his New York School colleagues, particularly O'Hara and John Ashbery. In a 1959 poem O'Hara called Koch "the backbone of a tremendous poetry nervous system" (O'Hara meant his own). On another occasion, Koch's latest "masterpiece" inspired an O'Hara epiphany: "where there's a W. C. Fields of lyricism there's a Mae West of psychological insight not far behind waiting to take a turn at the billiards." Ashbery, introducing Koch at a reading in New York in the 1960s, said that Koch's poetry "occupies my mind to the point where I might be said to live inside it." Koch's poetry, he added, "gives you the impression that you are leading an interesting life: going to parties and meeting interesting people, falling in love, going for rides in the country and to public swimming pools, eating in the best restaurants and going to movies and the theater in the afternoons. By comparison, most other modern poetry makes me feel as if I were living in a small midwestern university town."

Koch continues to threaten the people who expect poetry to be "ruled with the sceptre of the dumb, the deaf, and the creepy," as he wrote in his antiacademic tirade, "Fresh Air" (1955). In this hilarious poem, Koch unleashes "the Strangler" to eliminate some bad poets:

Here on the railroad train, one more time, is the Strangler.
He is going to get that one there, who is on his way to a
    poetry reading.
Agh! Biff! A body falls to the moving floor.

In the football stadium I also see him,
He leaps through the frosty air at the maker of comparisons
Between football and life and silently, silently strangles
    him!

Here is the Strangler dressed in a cowboy suit
Leaping from his horse to annihilate the students of myth!

The Strangler's ear is alert for the names of Orpheus,
Cuchulain, Gawain, and Odysseus,
And for poems addressed to Jane Austen, F. Scott
    Fitzgerald,
To Ezra Pound, and to personages no longer living
Even in anyone's thoughts—O Strangler the Strangler!

Perhaps the most remarkable thing about "Fresh Air" is the furious animus it displays, rare in a poet of such native sunniness. The tension between naked aggression and comic-book antics ("Agh! Biff!"), between moral indignation and a comic spirit, situates the poem in the tradition of verse satire whose greatest practitioners in English are Pope and Byron. Koch hates bad poetry—poetry that is dull, pious, ponderous, or sentimental—as if it were a wicked thing. "Bad poetry was like a crime against humanity," he has remarked. "Back then [in the 1950s] it was like poison." The poem he wrote in protest was like a manifesto by another name.

At first, Koch wasn't sure about "Fresh Air." Were parts of it, perhaps, too loud and boisterous? So he sent it to Ashbery, then in France on the first year of his Fulbright. Ashbery's reply illustrates how the dynamic of this literary friendship worked. "I have reread 'Fresh Air' several times; its searing beauty turns me into a charcoal whale," he wrote, with the high spirits characteristic of their correspondence. Then, more seriously: "I think you should leave all those parts in; the effect of profound quiet which the work induces depends so much on its necessary loudness and screechiness. The louder the better, says this reader." Ashbery was right. The poem is still fresh forty years later, a remarkable combination of anger and joy—and a vision of poetry transcending both. These questions are as compelling today as when Koch first asked them:

> Is there no voice to cry out from the wind and say what it is
>   like to be the wind,
> To be roughed up by the trees and to bring music from the
>   scattered houses
> And the stones, and to be in such intimate relationship with
>   the sea
> That you cannot understand it? Is there no one who feels
>   like a pair of pants?

Beyond the humor in Koch's poetry, beyond the polemic edge of "Fresh Air," there is the joyful immediacy of "one who feels like a pair of pants" flapping on a clothesline in the firm March wind; Koch has the rare ability to identify himself naïvely with the world of appearances and bring inanimate objects to poetic life. What seems at first like pure non sequitur is, then, loaded with implication, and we remember—and may consider as evidence of a shared aesthetic—that O'Hara, too, invoked "a pair of pants" in the course of a manifesto. Trousers are the measure of poetic form in "Personism": "As for measure and other technical apparatus, that's just common sense: if you're going to buy a pair of pants you want them to be tight enough so everyone will want to go to bed with you."

The reader imagines that the author of such poems as "To You" ("I love you as a sheriff searches for a walnut / That will solve a murder case unsolved for years / Because the murderer left it in the snow beside a window / Through which he saw her head, connecting with / Her shoulders by a neck, and laid a red / Roof in her heart") has a perennial cat-that-licked-the-cream look on his face. But as the example of "Fresh Air" implies, the psychological basis for Koch's humor was quite a bit more complicated than a sunny disposition. What gives his humor its particular edge is the sense that he has found a socially acceptable form of working out his aggressions. Koch's poetry transmutes outrageousness into an aesthetic stance and hostility into benign wackiness, as when, in "Thank You," he expresses gratefulness for things and opportunities that no reasonable person could want:

> Here is another letter, this one from a textbook advertiser;
> He wants me to advertise a book on chopping down trees.
> But how could I? I love trees! And I haven't the slightest
>   sympathy with chopping them down, even though I
>   know
> We need their products for wood-fires, some houses, and
>   maple syrup—
> Still I like trees better
> In their standing condition, when they sway at the
>   beginning of evening . . .
> And thank you for the pile of driftwood.
> Am I wanted at the sea?

Jay Kenneth Koch was born in Cincinnati in 1925. He grew up in Avondale, then a solidly middle-class neighborhood. In an autobiographical ramble he delivered at a gathering in New York in 1994, Koch said, "The first page of my notes has on top of it in big letters THE ESCAPE. I was brought up in Cincinnati, Ohio. My parents were very nice. The first time I wrote a poem, my mother gave me a big kiss and said, 'I love you.' The whole idea of writing poetry has a lot to do with escaping, escaping from the bourgeois society of Cincinnati, Ohio, escaping from any society of Cincinnati, Ohio, and escaping from any society anywhere." As a four-year-old, Koch started writing plays, and a year later he penned his first poem:

> I have a little pony,
> I ride him up and down;
> I ride him in the country,
> I ride him in the town.

"I did not have a pony," Koch reflected, "I did not want a pony, I don't know what I would have done with a pony in suburban Cincinnati; and I don't know why I wrote this poem, but it made me happy to write it."

Koch's escape into poetry was facilitated by his English teacher at Walnut Hills High School, Katherine Lappa, to whom *Wishes, Lies, and Dreams* is dedicated. In his junior and senior years, Koch turned in poems that seemed to him both "sexy and sadistic" and expected to be rapped on the knuckles; Lappa inspired him to a lifelong love of poetry when she told him it was okay to allow his antisocial impulses into his poetry. In his senior year Koch read John Dos Passos's *U.S.A.* and was taken with the stream-of-consciousness sections. The sensuality and violence that the boy felt he had to repress in his daily life found their way into the stream-of-consciousness writing he set himself to do. In one piece he wrote of the urge to "step on a baby's head because it is so big and round and soft like a balloon, and would go squash under my feet." Katherine Lappa remained unflappable. "That's very good," she said. "That's just what you should be feeling—part of what you're feeling. Keep doing it." Koch would come to regard this as an "instance of the benevolent influence that Freud has had on my life. I was able to enjoy the benefit of a teacher who in Cincinnati in 1942 had undergone psychoanalysis." Koch's parents belonged to an affluent country club, and it was there that young Kenneth played tennis, swam, flirted, understood the meaning of snobbery, and suffered all the pangs of adolescence. He played Dogberry in a high school production of *Much Ado About Nothing*. He also wrote radio plays, served as lit-

erary editor of the school's literary magazine, and wrote features
for the student newspaper.

Koch writes affectionately about Cincinnati, a city of parks
and hills, in *Ko, or, A Season on Earth*, an epic in the Byronic
manner of *Don Juan*, about a baseball player named Ko. Ko, a
Japanese pitcher with a mean fastball, is able to

> feel the buildings beating with a heart
> That knew you, knew you! and to watch the slow
> Movement of the streetcars, where, apart,
> They climbed upon the hill, and then to go
> With burning faces out to some park where art
> Has ordered nature—Eden Park, for example—
> And see Kentucky, where the gamblers trample;
>
> Then climb to Clifton, where the dazzling sun
> Beats down upon you 'mid the drugstores, and
> Past campus grasses till you come to one
> Of the streets which leads to Vine Street, which, with grand
> Bravura and agility, seems to run
> Irrespective of the way the town was planned,
> From in the center to bright Clifton hill—
> Plain German houses and a dark slum chill.

The first poet Koch loved was Shelley. When Koch was fifteen, his favorite uncle, Leo Loth, invited him to the family store.
(Koch's father, Stuart Koch, was an executive in the company.)
The retail furniture business held little interest for the boy, but
he perked up when his Uncle Leo unlocked the safe to show him
the poems he had written at the age of nineteen. They were all
sonnets, and they memorialized an unrequited love. In the vault
was a complete volume of Percy Bysshe Shelley's poems. "I remember the *Bysshe* was very important to me, as was the red

cover, as was the picture of the poet wearing an open-collared shirt and wild hair." Uncle Leo gave the volume to his nephew, "and that was it for me," Koch said. The dashing cameo of Shelley with his hair in the wind became, for Koch, the liberating image that poetry represented. T. S. Eliot once described Shelley as "an intelligent and enthusiastic schoolboy, but a schoolboy who knows how to write," and this (though Eliot did not mean the remark kindly) may have been true for Koch as well. Alison Lurie, who was an undergraduate at Radcliffe when Koch was at Harvard, theorizes that everyone has an ideal age and that in Koch's case the age is nineteen.

Koch was a brilliant adolescent. He earned a score of 800— then the highest possible score—on the verbal portion of the Scholastic Aptitude Test that high school seniors headed for college universally took. In the second semester of what would have been his senior year of high school, Koch enrolled at the University of Cincinnati and distinguished himself at his studies. "I was trained to be a meteorologist and a lieutenant," Koch recalled. "I studied Plato and I studied physics. But then they gave me a physical exam and decided my eyes weren't good enough to be a meteorologist. Then I was drafted." When he turned eighteen, he did his basic training at Camp Hood, Texas, then joined the Army Specialized Training Program (ASTP), in which soldiers were trained as interpreters and engineers. The translation program, which Koch preferred, was full, so he was sent to the Illinois Institute of Technology near the stockyards in Chicago for a course in army engineering. The linguist S. I. Hayakawa was teaching in Chicago when Koch was in ASTP. Hayakawa was the first professor to tell the young poet that his poems were good. "It quite turned my head that he liked my work," Koch told me.

The ASTP program was largely disbanded, perhaps because, Koch speculates, a lobbying group in Washington had spoken out against "cushy jobs for privileged college kids like me." Koch was sent to the 96th Infantry Division in California. "We did amphibious training, getting in and out of boats in the water with people shooting at us. An officer said: 'Men, some of you aren't going to come back.' I was as ill prepared then as I am now to shoot at people."

Koch saw action as a rifleman in the Philippines. He shipped out for Okinawa in March 1945 but was evacuated to a hospital on Guam when he contracted hepatitis. Upon recovering he was sent to a replacement depot on Saipan, where he worked as a clerk-typist and "was possibly the only two-finger typist and probably the only soldier in the Philippines with a subscription to *View*," a Surrealist magazine edited by Charles Henri Ford and Parker Tyler. (John Bernard Myers was the magazine's managing editor.) As a Columbia student in Koch's modern poetry course in 1968, I recall the time he referred to his army experiences. It was during one of our classes on T. S. Eliot. We had been assigned to read "The Hollow Men." The famous conclusion of that poem reminded Professor Koch of the time Pfc. Koch had tried to impress a beautiful girl with the magical language of poetry. Koch had grandly pointed to a scene of devastation and said, "This is the way the world ends." "Not with a bang but a whimper," the woman replied, taking the words out of his mouth but giving them a different intonation. The dialogue seemed almost like a use of Eliot's lines as code, so that "This is the way the world ends" meant "Do you want to go to bed with me?" and "Not with a bang" was a cool no.

Koch wrote his "Poem for My Twentieth Birthday" in the army:

> Passing the American graveyard, for my birthday
> the crosses stuttering, white on tropical green,
> the years' quick focus of faces I do not remember . . .

The palm trees stalking like deliberate giants
for my birthday, and all the hot adolescent memories
seen through a screen of water . . .

For my birthday thrust into the adult and actual:
expected to perform the action, not to ponder
the reality beyond the fact,
the man standing upright in the dream.

Koch sent the poem and two others to *Poetry* magazine, which accepted them for publication but not before the poet was called up to the company commander. It seems that the envelope was flagged by the censor. "What's this all about, Cock?" the lieutenant who was the company censor barked. He gravely warned the poet against revealing information that could conceivably fall into enemy hands. "I was so cocky," Koch recalled, happily punning on the mispronunciation of his name, "that I gave him a whole lecture about poetry. It was one of the first times I ever puzzled somebody with my poetry."

Discharged from the army at the rank of corporal in 1946, Koch set his sights on attending Harvard. His grades were good enough, but Harvard had a restriction against transfer students, and Koch had already done a semester's worth of work at the University of Cincinnati. Murray Seasongood, a wealthy Jewish philanthropist after whom the Seasongood Pavilion in the city's Eden Park is named, stepped in to help. Koch's father, who arranged for the boy to meet the great man, suggested that Kenneth send Seasongood tear sheets from the November 1945 issue of *Poetry* magazine with his three poems in them. In those days, more than one poem by more than one poet might appear on one of the magazine's pages. In his enthusiastic letter to Harvard, Seasongood singled out for especial praise a poem entitled "There's Margaret." It was the one poem printed in the tear sheets that Koch hadn't written—a poem by one Dorothy Alyea in a cloying style ("With hoarded lollipop and sticky dime") utterly unlike Koch's own.

When he came to Harvard for the interview that would make or break his application, Koch made a winning impression. Finding him to be "bright, affable, humorous" and with "a lot on the ball intellectually," the admissions officer recommended that the rule barring transfer students be waived in this one case. The admissions officer may have been struck by Koch's decisiveness, but he could not have realized the young man's predictive accuracy. "My reason for choosing Harvard is this: I plan to make creative writing my life work," Koch wrote in a preliminary letter to the Harvard admissions office.

At Harvard, Koch lived in Kirkland House, which had a reputation for beer parties, athletes, and cheers ("Ten Thousand Men of Kirkland" was the house fight song), but also boasted the largest library of any Harvard house. Koch's poetry had a galvanizing influence on his close friends. His recklessness was inspiring. In the fall of 1948, the semester following Koch's graduation, Ashbery, then in his senior year, wrote an homage aping the accents of a Koch poem entitled "Question in Red Ink":

THE KOCH

I come to you smelling mustily
Of wet cheese and salvias,
But your salience rings my fluency,
And I am left like a burnt match in somebody's pocket.
Together we parse the atom,
Tasting the minutes like ripe fruit.
And desire is a lost child
Behind the wheel of an unbelieving Buick.
But your hands soften me until

I am beautiful as a sleeping dog.
Phebe, in buskins, you bastard,
Who set our watches so
We could not tell time by them,
But found, instead of the incredible flowers,
Love, reckless and obtuse as a bad egg?

The letter also contained Ashbery's brand-new poem, "Some Trees." It was signed "Ashes."

Like Ashbery, Koch is a New York poet in the sense that a characteristic of New York is that it is, in Ashbery's phrase, "a logarithm / Of other cities." Koch's poetry bears out Delmore Schwartz's witticism that "Europe is still the biggest thing in North America." His poems are unthinkable without a meat-and-potatoes diet of Ovid, Ariosto, Lorca, Pasternak, Mayakovsky, and a dozen French poets. And though his poems are saturated with a pastoral vision of American innocence, he seems to have discovered his American theme in the act of immersing himself in the Europe of France and Italy.

Two years after graduating from Harvard, Koch went as a Fulbright student to France. Though he wanted to spend the year in Paris, he was assigned to Aix-en-Provence on the theory that he'd be more likely to speak French in Aix, where fewer Americans lived than in Paris. Koch customarily cut the classes in which elderly gentlemen taught traditional French *explication de texte*. He preferred walking along the road leading to Cézanne's favorite mountain, Mont Saint-Victoire, and frequenting the café called Les Deux Garçons on the rue Mirabeau. In Aix he read Virgil's Eclogues and Georgics translated into French, translations of Provençal poetry, and all sorts of things that might not have filled him with as much enthusiasm had he read them in English. One night he wrote a pitch-perfect parody of Ezra Pound's *Cantos*. He called it "Canto CXXIII." Here is the second half of the poem:

And you will grow up to be a high commercial
So that people of esteem will read your verses
Then you shall return to this valley and teach eating
    For who hath eaten phooey
    Returneth not unto paradise
Dem mudder fuckers doan unnerstan me
Said the Princess Toy Ling A.D. 1922
Dey doan unnerstan nuttin but smut
That was the year the doves fell at Livorgno
Six thousand of them and Caspia walking among them
From morning till night until finally there was nothing
But her feet and then nothing.
But her ankles as white as doves
    nothing but ankles moving
   I have brought these jewels to Mantua
   I have been fortunate in my choice of birds
  for this beak eateth phooey
      PING CHONG
for this beak eateth Ping Chong phooey.

Living in Aix, Koch found it inspiring to be surrounded by
a foreign language only imperfectly understood, and he began
trying to communicate this same buzz of incomprehensibility in
his poetry. "My poetry was very much like a foreign language to
me for about a year and a half," he noted. The deliberate mistranslation became a self-assigned exercise. Koch improvised an
example for an interviewer, Mark Hillringhouse. Say he were
reading a line of French verse: *"Comme c'était la veille du quatorze
juillet vers les quatres heures de l'après-midi, je descendi dans la rue
pour aller voir les acrobates"* ["At four in the afternoon on the day
before Bastille Day, I went down the street to see the acrobats"].
Koch said he might retain the English meaning of *descend*, capitalize on a confusion between *veille* (eve) and *vielle* (old), and
picture *les quatres heures de l'après-midi* as "the four hours of the

afternoon, since I wasn't familiar with the French way of saying things, and could almost envision the hours as four girls walking down the street."

Robert Frost had famously declared that poetry is what gets lost in translation. Now it appeared that the inversion of this rule was also true. Poetry was, or could be, a species of mistranslation:

Sweet are the uses of adversity
Became Sweetheart cabooses of diversity
And Sweet art cow papooses at the university
And Sea bar Calpurnia flower havens' re-noosed knees

Koch is describing here his working method in *When the Sun Tries to Go On*, which he wrote in 1953 but which was not published in book form until 1969, a delay that suggests just how unassimilable it must have seemed. Consisting of one hundred stanzas, each twenty-four lines long, the poem adamantly refuses to conform to the normative expectations of verse in the English language. Here is a chunk of a relatively intelligible stanza, in which a number of important New York School figures turn up:

Saith Bill de Kooning, "I turned my yoyo into a gun,
Bang Bank! Half of the war close pinstripes.
Timothy Tomato, Romulus Gun." "The magic of his
Cousse-cousse masterpiece," saith Pierre, "is apple
      blossoms'
Merchant marine gun." Ouch. The world is Ashbery
Tonight. "I am flooding you with catacombs,"
Saith Larry Rivers (more of him later on).
There is also some fools laying on their stomachs.
O show! Merchant marine of Venice!
At lilac wears a beetle on its chest!
These modern masters chew up moths. How many drawers

Are in your chest? Moon Mullins' Moon Mullins
Put his feet in my Cincinnati apple blossoms. Many
Dry cigarettes have fallen into work's colors. The shop
Of geniuses has closed. Jane Freilicher
Might walk through this air like a French lilac,
Her maiden name is Niederhoffer, she tends the stove.
"O shouting shop, my basement's apple blossoms!"

An attempt to present language at its most animated, liberated from the need to make ordinary sense, *When the Sun Tries to Go On* was Koch's most concerted effort to simulate in poetry the effects of Abstract Expressionism. Koch was intent on using words as an abstract painter uses paint, without regard for their meaning, knowing that new meaning may result. The rupture between language and sense—between "signifier" and "signified," as the French critics were starting to say—is neither deplored nor analyzed but enjoyed for the liberation it bestows. The author of *When the Sun Tries to Go On* was, in a radical sense, a poet of transgression and errancy, levity in defiance of gravity.

Koch, a proponent of psychoanalysis from his college days on, determined that errors could be as important a stimulus for poetry as for the talking cure. Misunderstandings were metaphors. The theme is given lavish treatment in Koch's "Taking a Walk with You": "I thought Axel's Castle was a garage; / And I had beautiful dreams about it, too—sensual, mysterious mechanisms; horns honking; wheels turning . . ." When Koch went into the public schools to teach poetry, he communicated his enjoyment of accidents and chance, and showed the students how to capitalize on errors in their work. A misspelling in a child's poem had turned the ordinary "swarm of bees" into "a swan of bees," and Koch, excited, told the third-graders to write poems in which each line contained a "sky of hand" or a "paper of dresses." What could have been dismissed as a mistake and forgotten had turned

out to point the way toward a sophisticated metaphorical construction. A "swan of bees," Koch explains in *Wishes, Lies, and
Dreams*, is "really the elementary idea of form and content: a
poem of words, a table of wood" transformed by the fantastic—by
what Koch unabashedly calls the magic of poetry. Koch never forgot the great lesson of the Surrealists—that in art, unlike ethics,
the ends justify the means. If one should achieve a vision of the
grail, it is immaterial whether intention or error, the conscious
mind or the unconscious self, thought or dream, had led to this
sublime end. All ways are valid; none are holy.

Koch's experimentalism counters the establishment view
that poems arise out of experience and express irreproachable
sentiments in an earnest manner. Many of Koch's works originate in a "poetry idea," something broadly resembling an old-
fashioned conceit. Reading from poem to poem in *Thank You and
Other Poems*, Koch's first collection (1962), you might have concluded that the poet felt he needed to invent a new style or form
each time he wrote a poem. "The Artist" took the form of the
journal of a conceptual artist who plans to paint the Pacific Ocean
and has, to this end, ordered sixteen million tons of blue paint.
"All of Pop Art is a trivial illustration of 'The Artist,' " John Hollander observed. Or there was a gathering of one-line poems,
each with a title of its own so that the relation of the titles to
the texts they head could be put into play. "Collected Poems"
inaugurated an entire genre of poems, as in this example:

SLEEP
The bantam hen frayed its passage through the soft clouds.

In the 1960s and '70s, it seemed as if everyone in New York were
writing one-line poems in the manner Koch introduced. The
most memorable issue of Bill Zavatsky's literary magazine, *Roy
Rogers*, which appeared irregularly in the 1970s, was wholly de-

voted to the new genre. For a time, each issue of *Janet Benderman*, a mimeographed daily published on the Columbia campus in various Aprils in the late 1960s and early 1970s, contained a one-line poem by Mitchell Sisskind. The first in the series was called "I Am the Toilet." The text was: "Dance on, you pigs! I will never get used to it." The second in the series was called "Cardinal Spellman's Big Day," but the editors had misplaced Sisskind's poem of that title, so they simply reprinted the original text ("Dance on, you pigs! I will never get used to it") under the new heading.

In such poems as "Lunch" and "Locks," Koch initiated a second genre that became a New York School staple: the list or catalogue poem, in which the inventory as a structural device serves an ideal of inclusiveness and a delight in humorous incongruity. These lines are from "Lunch":

> The dancing wagon has come! here is the dancing wagon!
> Come up and get lessons—here is lemonade and grammar!
> Here is drugstore and cowboy—all that is America—plus sex,
>   perfumes, and shimmers—all the Old World;
> Come and get it—and here is your reading matter
> For twenty-nine centuries, and here finally is lunch—
> To be served in the green defilade under the roaring tower
> Where Portugal meets Spain inside a flowered madeleine.

"Lunch" reaches its transcendent moment when—to use Martin Buber's categories—"the lunch" is no longer an "it" but a "thou":

> Let us give lunch to the lunch—
> But how shall we do it?
> The headwaiters expand and confer;

Will little pieces of cardboard box do it?
And what about silver and gold pellets?
The headwaiters expand and confer:
And what if the lunch should refuse to eat anything at all?
Why then we'd say be damned to it,
And the red doorway would open on a green railway
And the lunch would be put in a blue car
And it would go away to Whippoorwill Valley
Where it would meet and marry Samuel Dogfoot, and bring
      forth seven offspring,
All of whom would be half human, half lunch . . .

Koch is enamored of the list as an organizing principle for, I suspect, the same reasons that attracted Whitman: Lists record the simultaneity of experience, they are antihierarchical, and they enable the poet to be as all-inclusive as possible in his embrace of life on earth. Like Whitman, Koch celebrates himself in the confidence that everyone is implicated in the act, "for every atom belonging to me as good belongs to you."

"One Train May Hide Another," the keynote poem in *One Train* (1994), is another characteristic performance: a theme-and-variations poem, in which a given phrase recurs in ever-shifting contexts. The classic example in the Koch oeuvre is "Sleeping with Women." In both cases the title phrase is repeated like a mantra. "One Train May Hide Another," a phrase Koch encountered on a sign at a railway crossing in Africa, replicates itself like a benign virus, as if its linguistic structure itself defined the "hidden" relations linking widely disparate phenomena. The poem begins,

In a poem, one line may hide another line,
As at a crossing, one train may hide another train.

The applications are seemingly endless: "In a family one sister may conceal another, / So, when you are courting, it's best to have them all in view / Otherwise in coming to find one you may love another." And, "One bath may hide another bath / As when, after bathing, one walks out into the rain." And, "One friend may hide another, you sit at the foot of a tree / With one and when you get up to leave there is another / Whom you'd have preferred to talk to all along."

John Ashbery nicknamed Koch "Doctor Fun" when the erstwhile Harvard chums were new to New York in the early 1950s. Both halves of the sobriquet are accurate, the second half more obviously so. An inveterate prankster, Koch is determined to create merriment in his poems. He has written brilliant parodies of modern poets. For example, this one of D. H. Lawrence:

I Like Rats

I never saw a rat
Sorry for itself.
I never saw two rats
Consoling one another for being rats.

Rats live good full rat-lives with other rats.
Rat mind and rat heart plunge them into rat sex with other
    impassioned rats.
People say they are poison and ugly and cause disease.
I say people cause disease.
I never caught a cold or syphilis or gonorrhea or manic
    depression from a rat.

As in the best parodies, the fun-making is informed not by scorn but by an appreciation of the lampooned author. One of Koch's funniest and most beautiful tours de force, "Some South American Poets," combines a witty parody of Federico García Lorca's concept of *duende* with an inventive appropriation of Fernando Pessoa's device of the heteronym, that is, the creation of poems by an imaginary poet, who comes equipped with his or her own curriculum vitae.

Koch has never lost the power to make the reader laugh out loud. In this excerpt from "Passing Time in Skansen," one of several poems in *One Train* about visiting Sweden in 1950, the repetition is the masterstroke:

> The only thing that I could say in Swedish
> Was "Yog talar endast svenska"
> Which meant I speak only Swedish, whereas I thought it
>   meant
> I DON'T speak Swedish.
> So the young ladies, delighted, talked to me very fast
> At which I smiled and understood nothing,
> Though sometimes I would repeat
> Yog talar endast svenska.

While Koch and Frank O'Hara are equally enamored of the exclamation point, Koch's natural mood is as extravagantly euphoric as O'Hara's is self-mockingly rueful. In Koch's poetry the id is on parade. His poems are monuments to the pleasure principle. In 1957, when he wrote *Ko, or, A Season on Earth* (1959), Koch was thirty-two and living with his wife, Janice, and baby daughter in Florence, on the wings of the Fulbright Fellowship that Janice had received. Writing *Ko*, Koch said, he wanted to include in it all the pleasures he had known: "Happiness, / I thought, was what life came to, more or less."

It is sometimes overlooked or forgotten that the New York School carried out a rebellion, not an angry, noisy rebellion but a pointed literary attack on the poetics of the New Criticism and the values of T. S. Eliot. The fun and games in Koch's poetry play their part in smashing "the verbal icon" and "the well-wrought urn" as the exemplary models of a poem. In "Seasons on Earth," which tells about how *Ko* was written, Koch provides the context:

> It was the time, it was the nineteen fifties,
> When Eisenhower was President, I think,
> And the Cold War, like *Samson Agonistes,*
> Went roughly on, and we were at the brink.
> No time for Whitsuntides or Corpus Christis—
> Dread drafted all with its atomic clink.
> *The Waste Land* gave the time's most accurate data,
> It seemed, and Eliot was the Great Dictator
> Of literature. One hardly dared to wink
> Or fool around in any way in poems,
> And Critics poured out awful jereboams
> To *irony, ambiguity,* and *tension—*
> And other things I do not wish to mention.

In this climate of opinion, it was not enough to be serious; one also had to be a little depressed. Koch rebelled by insisting on the imagination as sufficient unto itself. "And then new lines arose, like snakes to Hindus, / That for *depressed* spelled out *exhilarated.*" The fun in Koch's poetry, the hysteria as well as the joy, was simultaneously affirmative and escapist. It completed "the Escape" from the dull orderly world of bourgeois Cincinnati. What it affirmed was pleasure, which in Koch's lexicon is linked closely with the state of peace and the possibility of personal happiness. Let Rimbaud and Baudelaire spend their seasons in hell. Koch chooses to celebrate his "Seasons on Earth."

Nowhere does he do so more memorably than in "The Pleasures of Peace," which honors a triple ideal of pleasure, peace, and the pursuit of happiness. Peace presents an unusual problem to a poet, since it is a condition defined by a negative: peace is the absence of war. It is easy to list some of the great poems and novels of war, from *The Iliad* to *The Charterhouse of Parma*, but where can one find a model for an epic of peace? This was the literary problem Koch faced as he set out to chart out "the geography of this age / Which has had fifty-seven good lovers and ninety-six wars." Koch solved the problem by foregrounding the writing of the poem. "The Pleasures of Peace" wittily anticipates the critics' verdicts:

> "A wonder!" "A rout!" "No neeed now for any further
>   poems!" "A Banzai for peace!" "He can speak to us
>   all!"
> And "Great, man!" "Impressive!" "Something new for you,
>   Ken" "Astounding!" "A real
> Epic!" "The worst poem I have ever read!" "Abominably
>   tasteless!" "Too funny!" "Dead, man!
> A cop-out! a real white man's poem! a folderol of honky
>   blank spitzenburger smugglerout Caucasian gyp
> Of phony bourgeois peace poetry, a total shrig!" "Terrific!"
>   "I will expect you at six!"

After the critics have their say, the poet invites the reader to conclude his peace plea, "if you think it needs more—I want to end it, / I want to see real Peace again!" What follows is the most beautifully musical passage in Koch's oeuvre, orchestrated by the incantatory repetition of *peace:*

> And the Mediterranean peach trees are fast asleep for peace
> With their pink arms akimbo and the blue plums of
>   Switzerland for peace
> And the monkeys are climbing for coconuts and peace
>   the Hawaiian palm

And serpents are writhing for peace—those are snakes—
And the Alps, Mount Vesuvius, all the really big important
    mountains
Are rising for peace, and they're filled with rocks—surely it
    won't be long;
And Leonardo da Vinci's *Last Supper* is moving across the
    monastery wall
A few micrometers for peace, and Paolo Uccello's red horses
Are turning a little redder for peace, and the Anglo-Saxon
    dining hall
Begins glowing like crazy, and Beowulf, Robert E. Lee, Sir
    Barbarossa, and Baron Jeep
Are sleeping on the railways for peace and darting around
    the harbor
And leaping into the sailboats and the sailboats will go on
And underneath the sailboats the sea will go on and we will
    go on
And the birds will go on and the snappy words will go on . . .

Nature is singing for peace, and so is art: The pleasures of peace are the plenty of creation, and "fun" is a simple, all-American word for the state of being blessed.

Koch's use of comic-book characters and boy's-adventure-book shenanigans expresses the radical innocence of his vision. In his catalogues and long lines, he celebrates an America of the imagination, whose pure products are more likely to make merry than to go crazy. In his great sonnet *"Voyelles,"* Rimbaud gave each of the vowels a color; building on that example, Koch creates an enchanted terrain in which the parts of speech have a secret life of their own, in "Permanently":

In the springtime the Sentences and the Nouns lay silently
    on the grass.

A lonely Conjunction here and there would call, "And! But!"
But the Adjective did not emerge.

The universe is conceived as a comic opera, in which the writing of a love letter can be depicted as if it were the signing of a historic document and a chance encounter between citizens can turn into a melodious duet. Wait, here comes the postman now:

"Hello, Jim." "Hello there, Bill."
"I've got this—can you take it?" "Sure, I will!"

The muse figure in Koch's poetry is not just the embodiment of concupiscence, though that's where she begins. In "Fresh Air," the wished-for wind of inspiration arrives in the shape of "a young art student who places her head on my shoulder," the poet kisses her fervently and we know he is saved from the plague of bad poetry infesting the land. In "The Pleasures of Peace," the unnamed professor who badgers the poet about his poem ("so hysterical, so—so transitory") turns out to be his muse in disguise:

"Professor!" I cried, "My darling! my dream!" And she
    stripped, and I saw there
Creamy female marble, the waist and thighs of which I had
    always dreamed.

The American girl as rendered in an Alex Katz painting—in cool colors, wearing sunglasses and scarf on a beach—is one way to visualize Koch's muse. Another is as one of the enthusiastically nude high school girls of Kansas in canto one of *Ko, or, A Season on Earth.* Why have these young women decided to shed their clothes? Because, they say, "life is dry" in Kansas—"economic prosperity" without "a corresponding esthetic interest" has left them bored. The manic excitement in Koch's poems, the mad pursuit of fun, is a function of just this sort of "esthetic interest," a byproduct of the liberation of poetry from the didactic realm of "the men with their eyes on the myth / And the Missus and the midterms."

So much for the "fun" part of "Doctor Fun." In what sense does the doctor part apply? In the literal sense, first: Koch, the holder of a doctorate in literature from Columbia, used his vivacious pedagogical methods to convert a generation of Columbia undergraduates into sorcerers' apprentices. David Shapiro had already come under Koch's spell in August 1962 when, as a fifteen-year-old high school student, he enrolled in a poetry conference that Koch directed at Wagner College in Staten Island. Koch quoted poems that Rimbaud wrote at the age of fifteen. "He said that Rimbaud may have been the greatest poet who ever lived," Shapiro recalled, "and I decided I like that man." Shapiro, a prodigally gifted violinist whose first book of poems was published by a major trade house when he was eighteen, was two years my senior at Columbia. He told me to read Koch's *Thank You.* The book, he said, was full of poems of such originality that any of a dozen could launch a literary movement.

I took Koch's writing course in my sophomore year. It was the only writing course I ever took, and it changed my life. Unlike standard-issue creative writing workshops, class time was not devoted to the analysis of students' work; rather Koch gave specific and highly detailed assignments and he spent the hour explaining what he wanted. Off the top of his head he would demonstrate blank verse ("Before I go to sleep I think of you . . .") or do an instant and pretty fair imitation of William Carlos Williams on the blackboard. The assignments he gave us were inventive and sometimes bizarre. Rewrite the first scene in *Hamlet* without re-reading it first. Purchase a comic book, do not read it, tape white paper over all the dialogue balloons, then fill in your own dialogue. Write a story about a sports event in which the contestants are the members of your own family disguised. Class would begin with his reading aloud the best of our efforts at the previous week's assignment.

Koch enlarged our sense of poetic tradition—Eliot and Pound were authorities, but so were Rimbaud, Mallarmé, Leopardi, Ungaretti, Ariosto, Pasternak, Apollinaire. I remember his roster of aphorisms: "As Mallarmé said to Degas, 'Poems are made with words, not ideas.' " "A poem shouldn't be a forty-seven-year-old baby." "According to Hemingway, there's no going backward in pleasure." "Paul Valéry said a poem is a communication from one who is not the poet to one who is not the reader." "Writing for the theater, you have to remember that the stage is the page." "Plays are like parties: You prepare for them, people come, and then they're over." "Reading poems in translation is like kissing someone through a shower curtain." "As T. S. Eliot once wrote, it's a characteristic of great poetry that you can enjoy it before you understand it." "When Pasternak wants you to get the feeling of riding in a train, he writes, 'the landscape lurched to a halt.' " Writing a term paper for Koch, you were instructed to avoid jargon, omit fuzzy phrases such as "in terms of," begin without preamble, and get right to the point—a set of directions that literature professors would be wise to employ.

Koch's reading lists were eye-openers. We read and imitated William Carlos Williams, Wallace Stevens, John Donne, Gertrude Stein, Jorge Luis Borges, Boris Pasternak, and the nineteenth-century Brazilian novelist Machado de Assis, whose groundbreaking novels, *Dom Casmurro* and *Epitaph for a Small Winner*, written in short numbered sections, have still not achieved the above-ground fame that is their due. We were required to translate poems. We also wrote verse plays and comic books and we were planning a campus Happening (it was to have featured a *son-et-lumière* show) when the student demonstrations of April 1968—

five buildings occupied by militant students protesting the war in Vietnam and the building of a gymnasium in Morningside Heights—beat us to the punch.

In class Koch's style was jubilantly histrionic. When a student wrote a story that had a big buildup and a lame ending, he didn't say that the ending was anticlimactic. He said, "It's like being at a party and somebody grabs you by the shirt and says with great urgency, 'Let me talk to you for just five minutes,' and finally he gets you aside and after all that buildup says, very slowly and dramatically, 'Mitch, it's nice weather we're having.' " "Koch made us feel it was great to be young and great to be young in your writing," Aaron Fogel said. "It wasn't something you needed to do penance for for the next thirty years while you found your true voice." When the assignment was to write a prose poem, Koch read us "The Beggar Woman of Naples" by Max Jacob as translated by John Ashbery:

> When I lived in Naples there was always a beggar woman at the gate of my palace, to whom I would toss some coins before climbing into my carriage. One day, surprised at never being thanked, I looked at the beggar woman. Now, as I looked at her, I saw that what I had taken for a beggar woman was a wooden case painted green which contained some red earth and a few half-rotten bananas. . . .

When the assignment was to write a collaboration, Koch read us "Sybilline" by Ern Malley, the Australian hoax poet whose complete works were written in a single afternoon in 1943 by a pair of soldiers bent on parodying modernism. Here's how it ends:

> The rabbit's foot of fur and claw
> Taps on the drain-pipe. In the alley
> The children throw a ball against

Their future walls. The evening
Settles down like a brooding bird
Over streets that divide our life like a trauma.
Would it be strange now to meet
The figure that strode hell swinging
His head by the hair
On Princess Street?

The achievement of the hoaxers transcended their intent, Koch said. He quoted their statement:

> We opened books at random choosing a word or phrase haphazardly. We made lists of these and wove them into nonsensical sentences.

> We misquoted and made false allusions. We deliberately perpetrated bad verse, and selected awkward rhymes from a Ripman's Rhyming Dictionary.

Here he interrupted the reading. "Hmm," he said. "It sounds like the formula for an avant-garde poem."

Koch was fiercely loyal to Ashbery and O'Hara. When he talked about O'Hara's comic techniques, he made it clear that the "comic" was "part of what is most serious for art to get to—ecstasy, unity, freedom, completeness, dionysiac things." He likened Ashbery to "a happy Sisyphus"—"get up, fall down, get up, fall down"—who keeps approaching though never reaching "the nonexistent *subject*, the mystery that will never be revealed." On another occasion, Koch likened the experience of reading an Ashbery poem to paying the poet an unexpected visit. You ring his doorbell and are invited into his apartment, where he graciously fixes you a drink and gives you a quick tour of the place, and then, just as you're ready to settle in for a long chat, you suddenly find yourself back at the front door, shaking his hand good-bye. A young poet reported that this was exactly what happened when she visited Ashbery.

"There was this tremendous sense of teamsmanship, this tremendous sense of shared taste," David Shapiro remembered. "When I was a freshman at Columbia, Kenneth handed me an envelope full of thin manuscript paper. It was Ashbery's 'The Skaters.' 'What is it about?' I asked. 'It's not about anything, it's a whole philosophy of life,' Kenneth answered. That was one of the ten greatest aesthetic experiences of my life: to read that poem in manuscript. Later Kenneth and I were talking about 'The Skaters' and he said, 'Don't you think that's one of the loneliest poems ever written?' Kenneth was a wonderful teacher. I used to memorize everything he said." Years later, Shapiro wrote a poem entitled "The Lost Golf Ball," because Koch had told him to consider carefully the relation of titles to the texts they head. " 'The Lost Golf Ball' would be a good title for an abstract painting," Koch said. "People will look for the lost golf ball in the painting. They won't find it, but they'll look more closely at the painting."

Apropos of Koch's legendary status as a teacher of poetry, James Schuyler employed a different golf ball conceit. "Kenneth Koch / could teach a golf ball / how to write pantoums," Schuyler wrote. As a Columbia professor, Koch wore his learning lightly— but his judgments on matters of literary taste were observed like doctor's orders. As a teacher of schoolchildren and of nursing-home residents Koch resembled another sort of doctor: a literary pediatrician or gerontologist with an uncanny knack for instigating fresh poems and a penchant for regarding the therapeutic advantages as incidental. Then, too, the anarchic comic surfaces of Koch's poems make one think of their author as a doctor in a different guise, a slightly demented laboratory scientist, mixing flasks of sound with beakers of sense, experimenting with what he calls "formulalessness."

As it happens, Koch wrote his master's thesis at Columbia

on the figure of the physician in dramatic literature. The thesis traced the development of the doctor as a type into the modern psychoanalyst, a progression that affirms the possibility of individual happiness. In medieval plays the doctor was a magical figure, sometimes a comic figure, associated with resurrection. "In the fact that the physician became, in the English dramatic development of the rejuvenation ritual, a comic figure, there is evidence of that instinct for the artistic combination of comedy and high tragedy which might be called the specific genius of the English drama," Koch wrote. The psychoanalyst in modern drama remains a resurrector, though with a secular purpose, Koch observed. He concluded his study by calling for "a new kind of formal drama, in which the physician once more plays the role of resurrector with the profound and beautiful dramatic effect that the earliest audiences sensed in the ceremonial drama out of which our own has come down to us."

The figure of the doctor turns up in a number of Koch's own poems. In "A New Guide" in *One Train*, the medical man plays his old role of resurrector in performing an open-heart surgery: "The new heart is beating! He asks for the wound to be closed. / He takes off his mask and goes into another room. / The woman stays in this room. She has a good chance of staying alive." The doctor is associated with sexual desire and male mastery in other poems. In "The Art of Love," the incorrigible poet recommends "traveling with a doctor / As a way to meet sick girls." In "Thank You," someone has offered the poet a chance to be "ship's doctor," but he declines, declaring that the most he knows of medicine "is orange flowers / Tilted in the evening light against a cashmere red / Inside which breasts invent the laws of light / And of night, where cashmere moors itself across the sea." The doctor in the fourth part of "Variations on a Theme by William Carlos Williams" is a more ambiguous figure, the happy genius of the wards:

Last evening we went dancing and I broke your leg.
Forgive me. I was clumsy, and
I wanted you here in the wards, where I am the doctor!

Koch is parodying "This Is Just to Say," in which Williams apolo-gizes to his wife for raiding the refrigerator and eating the plums that she had been saving for the next day. "Forgive me," he says, but offers as his excuse only that the plums were sweet, cold, and delicious. Slyly reminding us that Williams was a doctor, Koch demonstrates (1) the aggression latent in Williams's seemingly benign poem, where the speaker cannot really be said to be con-trite, and thus, (2) the attractions of what can be called the insin-cere apology as a rhetorical gesture or form.

My favorite doctor in Koch's poetry is the one who shows up in "The Circus" when Aileen, the trapeze artist, falls to the dusty floor: "She is not dead, / But the doctor tells her he does not know if she will ever be able to perform on the trapeze again, / And he sees the beautiful orange and red and white form shaken with sobs, / And he puts his hand on her forehead and tells her she must lie still." The doctor here is a messenger, the bearer of glad tidings, and what his presence, so grave and so reassuring, signifies above all is that there is no death in this universe of eternal spring:

What is death in the circus? That depends on if it is spring.
Then, if elephants are there, *mon père*, we are not completely
        lost.
Oh the sweet strong odor of beasts which laughs at decay!
Decay! decay! We are like the elements in a kaleidoscope
But such passions we feel! bigger than beaches and
Rustier than harpoons.

In a tragic universe, "death is the mother of beauty," as Wallace Stevens wrote in "Sunday Morning." But there is no "change of death" in "The Circus." There is non sequitur instead, as if it were the first obligation of the poet to provide a continual sense of surprise.

The comic vision in Koch's poetry, which is so powerful as to "laugh at decay," is a trait that distinguishes his work from that of his closest friends. Consider by contrast the theme of thanatopsis in Ashbery ("Only one thing is real: the fear of death"), O'Hara ("First / Bunny died, then John Latouche, / then Jackson Pollock") and Schuyler ("Beautiful Funerals"). The sadness in Koch's poetry results not from an intimation of mortality but from a keen sense of nostalgia for a period of joyous innocence that seems to have sustained the poet until he was well into middle age. Koch was in his late forties when he began to write poems of recollection and recapitulation, many of them devoted to his friends Jane Freilicher, Larry Rivers, Frank O'Hara, and John Ashbery in New York in the early 1950s:

> I was
> Never so happy with anyone
> As I was with those friends
> At that particular time on that day with
> That bottle of Irish whiskey the time
> Four in the afternoon or
> Three in the afternoon or two or five
> I don't know what and why do I think
> That my being so happy is so urgent
> And important?

When I lecture on Koch I ask the students to prepare by reading the two poems entitled "The Circus" in *On the Great Atlantic Rainway* and deciding which is the better poem. The first, the one with Aileen the trapeze artist, was written in Paris in 1955 or '56. The second dates from the early 1970s and is about the other—it is the first of Koch's poems to take as its subject the composition of an earlier poem:

> I remember when I wrote The Circus
> I was living in Paris, or rather we were living in Paris
> Janice, Frank was alive, the Whitney Museum
> Was still on 8th Street, or was it still something else?
> Fernand Léger lived in our building
> Well it wasn't really our building it was the building we lived
>   in
> Next to a Grand Guignol troupe that made a lot of noise . . .

The penultimate (and best) line in the later poem invites us to make a comparative ranking: "And this is not as good a poem as The Circus." Do the students agree?

The choice between the poems is loaded with implication. It is, in a sense, a choice between dream and memory, though some might phrase that as a choice between art and life. In terms derived from William Blake, the first "Circus" stands for innocence, the second for experience. In Schiller's terms, the first "Circus" is naïve, the second sentimental. ("The poet . . . either *is* nature or he will *seek* her. The former is the naïve, the latter the sentimental poet.") In Wallace Stevens's terms, the first represents the principle of the imagination, the second that of reality. The first gives us a vision, while the second is like Koch's version of Coleridge's "Dejection Ode," a mourning of lost joy. In a curious and perhaps inevitable way, the reader's preference may indicate something more vital about the reader's value system than about the poems. When I lectured on Koch at the University of Cincinnati, one professor said that "The Circus (II)" is the superior poem, because it is about life while the other is about art and artifice. But "The Circus (II)" is parasitic on "The Circus (I)," a graduate student countered, observing further that the later poem seemed indebted to Frank O'Hara. Although we did not settle the issue in Cincinnati, it seemed clear that reading the two poems comparatively, as they ask us to do, is not only a useful exercise in practical criticism. It is also an excellent introduction to the two dominant modes in Koch's poetry. Which, in the end, is better, the circus of invention or that of nostalgic desire? I know the right answer, but my lips are sealed.

6

James Schuyler: things as they are

How Schuyler manages to be absolutely truthful and an
obsessed romantic at the same time is his secret.

—HOWARD MOSS,
"WHATEVER IS MOVING"

For much of his life, James Schuyler was the best-kept secret in
American poetry. He was forty-six when *Freely Espousing*, his first
collection, was published in 1969. (In contrast Ashbery, O'Hara,
and Koch had their first books published in 1956, '57, and '59,
respectively.) *Freely Espousing* had little impact in poetry circles
outside of New York, but it cemented Schuyler's high reputation
among followers of the New York School, who had previously encountered his work in the right magazines (*Locus Solus*, *The Hasty
Papers*) and anthologies (Donald Allen's *New American Poetry*),
and who knew of the esteem in which Schuyler was held by Ashbery, Koch, and O'Hara. When Ted Berrigan came to New York in
the early 1960s and anointed himself the chief apostle of the New
York School, he promptly enlisted Schuyler for *C*, the mimeographed, legal-sized magazine he had launched to perpetuate his
enthusiasms. "It seems that your manuscripts circulate just like
Elizabethan court sonnets," Berrigan told Schuyler. O'Hara had
mentioned a Schuyler story "about two homosexuals named Clyde

and Henry," and the painter John Button had said he had a copy of a play by Schuyler called *February*. "Whenever your name comes up everyone has lots of things of yours in mind that they think are great and should be published immediately!" Berrigan exclaimed. "Your work makes up an 'underground movement' all by itself!"

Like O'Hara, Ashbery, and Koch, Schuyler had his poems published in a handsome limited-press edition by Tibor de Nagy Gallery. Unlike them, he had planned to become a novelist and did write and publish two novels in addition to the one on which he collaborated with Ashbery, *A Nest of Ninnies*. Among those in the know, Schuyler enjoyed a reputation for his flawless ear, his fastidious avoidance of false notes. The remarkable thing about his writing is how clean it is—not a word out of place—and how seemingly simple; only if you try to imitate Schuyler do you see that it is not simple at all.

Schuyler's poems heed Ezra Pound's injunction: They are at least as well written as his prose. His novels, *Alfred and Guinevere* (1958) and *What's for Dinner?* (1978), reveal a comic sensibility, an ability to mime the American suburban vernacular, and a gift for the exposition of a plot primarily through dialogue. *A Nest of Ninnies*, in which the same virtues are on display, was "destined to become a minor classic," W. H. Auden wrote in the *New York Times Book Review* when the book appeared in print in 1969. In the wider poetry world, however, Schuyler remained unsung, and he was usually the odd man out in critical appraisals of the New York School (as Barbara Guest remains the odd woman out). When Stephen Koch wrote an appreciative essay for the *New York Times Book Review* in 1968, all the attention went to O'Hara, Koch, and Ashbery. The omission was far from incomprehensible. Slower to develop than his slightly younger friends, he had not yet published a book, and his precarious psychiatric condition did not permit him to hold the sort of professional appointment

Frank O'Hara, left, and
John Ashbery in New York,
November 1953.
In their poems, these closest
of friends were a study in
contrasts, "John all prophecy
and the sublime, Frank all
excited conversation
and the streets"
(Koch).

James Schuyler and Ashbery listening to Kenneth Koch, August 1956. They were each other's first
audience. "We inspired each other, we envied each other, we emulated each other, we were very
critical of each other, we admired each other, we were almost entirely dependent on each other
for support. Each had to be better than the others, but if one flopped we all did" (Koch).
Courtesy John Ashbery.

Schuyler, left, with W. H. Auden in Florence in 1948. "With Wystan, by the Arno at high noon (which accounts for our squints). The buildings across the river were destroyed during the war" (Schuyler's note on the back of the photo). Schuyler wrote an affectionate elegy for Auden ("kind man and great poet"), but the rejection of Auden's influence was a fundamental point of departure for the younger poet. *Courtesy Hilde Ridenour.*

Ashbery and Jane Freilicher at the Tibor de Nagy Gallery, c. 1951. Everyone smoked and wore ties, and Jane reigned as queen. The poets celebrated her witty repartee. "When [John] and Jane Freilicher meet it's as if they'd both been thrown into a swimming pool / Afloat with ironies jokes sensitivities perceptions and sweet swift sophistications" (Koch). When Ashbery lived in Paris, he and Jane corresponded voluminously. "Every letter [from John] is signed with a different name, usually that of a third-rate movie actor or radio personality," she commented. "He signed 'Jeff Morrow' on the letter I just read. Jeff Morrow was the Troy Donahue of his day. A lot of unknown movie stars signed John's letters to me." *Photo by Walt Silver.*

Freilicher's "vertical" portrait of O'Hara, 1951.
"Jane had gone out to visit him in Ann Arbor
[where O'Hara spent a year before coming to New York]
and painted a memorable portrait of him, in which
Abstract Expressionism certainly inspired the wild
brushwork rolling around like so many loose cannon,
but which never loses sight of the fact that it is a
portrait, and an eerily exact one at that" (Ashbery).
The painting was done, Freilicher says,
"not from life—it was a made-up portrait."
Courtesy Jane Freilicher.

Freilicher's portrait of Ashbery,
c. 1950. The painting has been lost.
"Jane's show is very lovely—and in the
New York Times they spoke of the
'almost hallucinatory portrait of
John Ashbery, whose Foujita gaze
follows one about the room'"
(Ashbery to Koch, April 1955).
Courtesy Jane Freilicher.

Freilicher in action (1955).
In "A Sonnet for Jane," O'Hara
wrote, "bring me that breath more
dear than Fabergé / your secret puis-
sance Operator loan / to pretty Jane
whose paintings like a stone / are
massive true and silently risqué."
Photo by Rudy Burckhardt.

Fairfield Porter's portrait of
Larry Rivers with hands bandaged after
an aborted suicide attempt (1951 or '52).
Rivers slashed his wrists with a razor
after Freilicher broke off their affair.
He then phoned O'Hara, who took him
to Beth Israel Hospital and arranged
for Rivers to recuperate at the Porters'
house in Southampton. Rivers stayed
a month, reading Proust and admiring
the de Kooning in the living room.
Later, Rivers joined forces with
Freilicher to help persuade John
Bernard Myers to give Porter a show
at the Tibor de Nagy Gallery.
*Courtesy Anne Porter and
Hirschl & Adler Modern, New York.*

Rivers painted O'Hara, and O'Hara returned
the favor, writing poems for and about Rivers.
The two also collaborated on lithographs
(*Stones*, 1957) and on high-spirited literary
compositions ("How to Proceed in the Arts,"
Kenneth Koch: A Tragedy). "When you feel
irritated with me you might think of the nice
things about me such as my hatred for so
many people and my prose and my leopard
look, and I in turn will temper my temper by
reflecting on your nervous stomach, your love
of mankind and your sublime baritone,"
O'Hara wrote to Rivers during a quarrel.
"I'm not an infant in swaddling clothes after
all and you're not the Blessed Virgin Mary."
Courtesy Larry Rivers.

Porter, *Male Nude* (1954).
A rare nude in the Porter
oeuvre, this drawing of O'Hara
must have been made at
Larry Rivers's studio while
Rivers worked on his portrait of
O'Hara wearing army boots.
"I am posing for Larry avec
la nudité in great big boots
for a canvas to be called
'The Truth About Christine'
and the drawings are going
along with wonderful
candor and verve" (O'Hara to
Freilicher, January 1954).
*Courtesy Anne Porter and
Hirschl & Adler Modern, New York.*

Ashbery and Nell Blaine at a costume party Blaine gave. The woman in clown-face, smoking, is Barbara Epstein, who went on to become a founding editor of the *New York Review of Books*. "I maintain that the whole New York School started in Nell's white loft. That was the Big Bang—the place where everybody met" (Arnold Weinstein). Nell "was our Joan of Arc" (Freilicher).

Ashbery and Rivers squaring off for the love of Ann Aikman (right) while Freilicher watches in this still from Rudy Burckhardt's fifteeen-minute movie, *Mounting Tension* (1950), a "silent-type comedy, spoofing psychoanalysis and the Museum of Modern Art" (Burckhardt). Freilicher played the psychiatrist. Freud, on the wall, looks on. *Courtesy Rudy Burckhardt.*

Left to right: Koch, Rivers (holding sign), Ashbery, Freilicher, Leila Talberg, and Blaine (1951). "Clement's refers to the name of the people who rented us this bungalow in East Hampton one summer" (Rivers). "East Hampton glaringest of Hamptons Hampton of sea shine of de Kooning and of leaves" (Koch). *Courtesy Larry Rivers.*

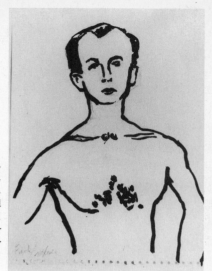

Blaine's *Frank III* (1952 or '53).
"Frank was the cock of the walk.
He was somewhat vain.
He didn't mind stripping and
posing for us" (Blaine).
*Photo by David Allison, courtesy
Tibor de Nagy Gallery
and Carolyn Harris.*

O'Hara with the painter Grace Hartigan, who succeeded Freilicher as his
major muse. O'Hara punned on her name when he extolled "Grace / to be born
and live as variously as possible" in "In Memory of My Feelings," which
he dedicated to Hartigan. In 1952 O'Hara wrote a "Portrait of Grace":
"Now / celebrate her, for that light which is anguish will / again and again
illumine her our shores." *Courtesy Joe LeSueur.*

Nell Blaine's
Jane Freilicher on 21st Street,
oil on paper, 1953. "For as the
war, art, dissipation, / led me on
and made me sane, / I find a
world of sweet sensation / leading
me now, and it is Jane," O'Hara
wrote in 1954. "Just as Grace
Hartigan put me in mind of
Ann Sheridan, Jane made me
think of Jeanne Moreau,"
Joe LeSueur recalled.
*Photo by David Allison,
courtesy Tibor de Nagy Gallery
and Carolyn Harris.*

Blaine, *Larry Sleeping*, 1950, Paris. "A ballsy older Nell, twenty-six and a graduate
of Hofmann's school, told us what Art was all about, impressionist art and
expressionist art and Giotto art. I still remember her attempts to show the
relationship between the art of the past and the art of now, between new jazz and
modern art. She introduced me to artists like Robert De Niro (the actor's father)
and de Kooning, and critics like—well, there's nobody *like* Clement Greenberg,
not that any of us liked him except Helen Frankenthaler, who had to love him
to like him" (Rivers). *Photo by Carolyn Harris, courtesy Tibor de Nagy Gallery.*

Fairfield Porter working on
Katie in an Armchair (1954),
the basis of Frank O'Hara's
article "Porter Paints a Picture"
in *Art News* (1955). Porter joshed
O'Hara about the piece, pointing
out that the references to
Henry James reflected what
O'Hara was reading but were
otherwise of dubious relevance.
"Well," O'Hara replied, "when
the cow's been in the garlic . . ."
Photo by Rudy Burckhardt.

Anne Porter reading to her daughter, aged five, while Fairfield painted. "I think it's impossible
not to get some sort of form if you don't think about it. If you do think about it you can get chaos.
But if you don't think about it you get form" (Porter). *Photo by Rudy Burckhardt.*

An American in Paris. "I found my poetry being more 'influenced' by the sight of the Paris phenomenon of clear water flowing in the street gutters, where it is (or was) diverted or dammed by burlap sandbags moved about by workmen, than it was by the French poetry I was learning to read at the time" (Ashbery). *Courtesy Larry Rivers.*

Ashbery on vacation at Cabourg, the real-life model for Proust's Balbec, in 1956. "Once when I was working at McGraw-Hill Book Company I produced a circular enumerating the virtues of the definitive textbook on feedbacks which moved some of the other employees to tears, although to this day I have never known what a feedback is. This of course did not make any difference—in writing advertising copy, literary criticism or poetry it is best to approach the subject with an open mind and preferably complete ignorance" (Ashbery). *Photo courtesy Rodney Phillips, Berg Collection, The New York Public Library. Photographer unknown.*

O'Hara visited Alice Neel in Spanish Harlem, where she lived, and she painted this profile of him (1960). "I thought he looked like a falcon" (Neel). "Having determined that Frank's somewhat intimidating punk-angel look was an anomaly, partly the result of a broken nose which gave him the look of a scrappy boxer, I decided to try to spend as much time as possible in his company during the few weeks that remained before my graduation from Harvard," Ashbery recalled. "Not since I had met Kenneth Koch a couple of years before had I encountered anyone so stimulating, with such a powerfully personal way of looking at art and poetry and at the world." *Reproduced courtesy Robert Miller Gallery and the National Portrait Gallery, Smithsonian Institution.*

"Something Frank had that none of the other writers and artists I know had to the same degree was a way of feeling and acting as though being an artist were the most natural thing in the world. Compared to him everyone else seemed a little self-conscious, abashed, or megalomaniacal" (Koch). *Photo by Harry Redl (1958).*

Fairfield Porter painted
*John Ashbery and James Schuyler
Writing "A Nest of Ninnies"* in 1967.
"We started out alternating almost
sentence by sentence, or a couple of
sentences, and then it got so we would
write longer, but not really very long,
parts, unless one of us had a real
donnée and took off" (Schuyler).
Ashbery on the advantages of the
collaboration process: "One can
get away with things more easily
if one is not the sole perpetrator."
*Courtesy Anne Porter and
Betty Cunningham,
Hirschl & Adler Modern, New York.*

Rivers and Koch posing with their collaboration "New York in the '50s" (c. 1960). "Larry would
put some color on the paper or canvas, then I'd write some words, and this went on until we got
something which looked like a billboard. It was like having the muse in the room with you." Wah
Kee was the name of a Cantonese restaurant that "our whole gang liked to frequent.
They had a table in the kitchen. Somehow it seemed distingué to eat in the kitchen" (Koch).
Photo by Rudy Burckhardt.

Koch flanked by the composer Morton Feldman and the playwright LeRoi Jones (later Amiri Baraka). "Some readers think of a poem as a sort of ceremony—a funeral, a wedding—where anything comic is out of order," whereas in truth "the comic . . . is part of what is most serious for art to get to—ecstasy, unity, freedom, completeness, dionysiac things" (Koch).

The painter John Button snapped this picture of O'Hara and Schuyler in Fairfield Porter's side yard in Southampton in the summer of 1956. Earlier that year, when Barney Rosset of Grove Press showed an interest in publishing his poems, O'Hara enlisted Schuyler to help with the manuscript. "I shall try not to send it off until you see it with your clippers, pruners and (I hope) grafting equipment. How would you like to take a couple of weeks off and rewrite the whole mess for me?" (O'Hara to Schuyler, February 1956). *Courtesy Alvin Novak.*

Burt Glinn, *A Back Table at the Five Spot* (1957). O'Hara, Rivers, and Hartigan "breaking the world's record for loquaciousness" (Koch) at the jazz bar. The sculptor David Smith is at left, talking to Helen Frankenthaler, whose face is turned away. Rivers organized evenings of poetry and jazz on Monday nights, Thelonious Monk's night off. On a night when Koch read his poems to jazz accompaniment, the painter Mark Rothko came in, and Rivers asked Rothko whether he liked the poems, and Rothko said, "Why can't these poets make more sense?"
Photo reproduced by permission of the Worcester Art Museum.

Porter painted
Jimmy in a Black Rocker
in 1960. Of Schuyler's poetry,
Porter wrote, "You see the poet's
inventions, rather than
the poet, whose art is in the
degree of disinterested attention
with which he follows them.
He tends toward a deceptively
simple Chinese visibility, like
transparent windows on
a complex view."
*Courtesy Anne Porter
and Betty Cunningham,
Hirschl & Adler Modern, New York.*

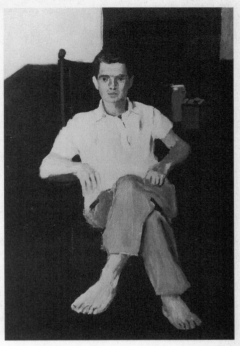

Porter's *Portrait of Kenneth Koch*
was done on Great Spruce Head
Island, Maine, in 1970.
Of Koch's poetry, Porter wrote,
"His irony recognizes the
childishness or ordinary
feelings which he shares with
the reader, and this irony
washes away conventional
sentimentality, until you are
left with the emotions of
childhood again, seen now
with an innocence of maturity."
*Courtesy Anne Porter
and Betty Cunningham,
Hirschl & Adler Modern,
New York.*

Water Mill, 1961. Group photo used on the jacket of *The Party's Over Now* by John Gruen. *Back row (left to right):* Lisa de Kooning, Frank Perry, Eleanor Perry, John Myers, Anne Porter, Fairfield Porter, Angelo Torricini, Arthur Gold, Jane Wilson, Kenward Elmslie, Paul Brach, Jerry Porter, Nancy Ward, Katherine Porter, friend of Jerry Porter. *Second row (left to right):* Joe Hazan, Clarice Rivers, Kenneth Koch, Larry Rivers. *Seated on couch:* Miriam Shapiro, Robert Fizdale, Jane Freilicher, Joan Ward, John Kacere, Sylvia Maizell. *Front row:* Stephen Rivers, Bill Berkson, Frank O'Hara, Herbert Machiz. *Kneeling on right, front to back:* Jim Tommaney, Willem de Kooning, Alvin Novak. *Photo by John Gruen.*

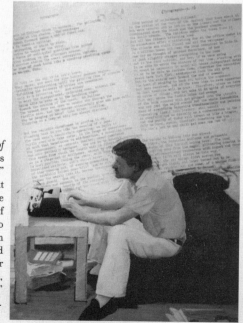

Rivers, *Pyrography: Poem and Portrait of John Ashbery*, 1977. "Larry Rivers paints whatever comes within his reach," Ashbery wrote in 1962. "This is what Lautréamont was thinking of when he wrote about the sublime logic of making love to the first person who comes along." Ashbery's poem "Pyrography" was commissioned by the U.S. Department of the Interior for its Bicentennial exhibition, "America 1976." *Courtesy Larry Rivers.*

that helped the others establish constituencies for themselves and their work.

"Freely Espousing," the title poem of Schuyler's first collection, was a brief statement of his poetics. It achieves the distinctive Schuyler tone immediately with its title, a striking phrase that describes what poets do when they write—or what this poet is doing right here and what he means to do in the future. Freely, without constraint or reservation, he will *espouse* in the full sense of that unusual word, which means not only to "embrace as a cause" but to marry. And what will the poet espouse? Language, first of all:

> The sinuous beauty of words like allergy
> the tonic resonance of
> pill when used as in
> "she is a pill"
> on the other hand I am not going to espouse any short
> stories in which lawn mowers clack.

Language is the agent of the imagination and is to be loved as a thing in itself. But for Schuyler, the love of language was always also the means to a further end: the embrace of the physical world. He rejects onomatopoeia ("it is absolutely forbidden / for words to echo the act described; or try to"), but an exception to this rule ("Oh it is inescapable kiss") prompts him to move from verbal espousals to "Marriages of the atmosphere." Light and air merge and unite "where Tudor City / catches the sky or the glass side / of a building lit up at night in fog." From there the poem moves to the level of blessedly ordinary human love, "a medium-size couple who / when they fold each other up /well, thrill."

In "Freely Espousing," as in the best of his early work, Schuyler weds the dialect of the tribe to the bride of descriptive exactness. He stands in relation to poetry as Fairfield Porter and

Jane Freilicher stand in relation to painting: committed to a vision of things as they are rather than as they might be in some idealized or reconfigured state. "I have always been / more interested in truth than in imagination," Schuyler writes in "A Few Days," adding the qualifier that clinches it: "I / wonder if that's / true?" This preference distinguishes Schuyler from Ashbery and Koch, who subscribed to the gospel of the imagination according to Wallace Stevens. Nevertheless it was clear from the start that Schuyler had more than personal friendship in common with his New York School buddies. His poems with their inviting surface, deadpan delivery, frequent use of quotation marks, and embrace of the quotidian paralleled the efforts of the others. Yet his poems were formally quite distinctive: He used skinny lines in some of his shorter poems and very long lines in his long poems, and the line breaks in his poems, made with what always seemed like casual disregard, can offer a primer on how a purely formal decision can yield powerful poetic effects. Even his punctuation holds lessons: Only A. R. Ammons among contemporary poets has relied so heavily on the colon as a means of emphasizing the connections between clauses in a constant postponement of closure. Above all, Schuyler possessed a quiet originality of tone and a flair for "a calm secret exultation / of the spirit," as in his poem "December":

> Each December! I always think I hate "the over-
> commercialized event"
> and then bells ring, or tiny light bulbs wink above the
> entrance
> to Bonwit Teller or Katherine going on five wants to look at
> all
> the empty sample gift-wrapped boxes up Fifth Avenue in
> swank shops
> and how can I help falling in love? A calm secret exultation

of the spirit that tastes like Sealtest eggnog, made from milk
    solids,
Vanillin, artificial rum flavoring; a milky impulse to kiss
    and be friends.

The use of names—brand names, place names, names of
shops—is another New York School trait that Schuyler makes entirely his own.

    Schuyler's lyric poems, sweet and pungent, offer observa-
tions too understated to be called epiphanies and too subtle to be
appreciated on one reading. The poem "Korean Mums" is a supreme example. It is set in a garden "in October, more than /
half gone over," amid flowers both beautiful (like the mums
"shrubby and thick-stalked, / the leaves pointing up / the stems
from which / the flowers burst in / sunbursts") and exotic ("aconite"). With the mention of aconite—a species of monkshood that
is poisonous but can be used for medicinal purposes—the mood
of the poem changes, as if the very word could toll the bell on
the edenic scene. The poet, who is roughly in the situation of
Coleridge in "This Lime Tree Bower My Prison," is in some distress, because of the violent events of the morning:

    This morning
one of the dogs killed
a barn owl. Bob saw
it happen, tried to
intervene. The airedale
snapped its neck and left
it lying. Now the bird
lies buried by an apple
tree. Last evening
from the table we saw
the owl, huge in the dusk,

circling the field
on owl-silent wings.
The first one ever seen
here: now it's gone,
a dream you just remember.

With the word *remember* the poem's first stanza ends.

In true Romantic fashion, the second and final stanza of the poem must resolve this crisis, and it does, by concentrating on the isolated lyric moment illumined by light and then by envisaging a future moment in which the poet may look back on this one. In an inversion of the characteristic Romantic memory poem, in which the poet imagines a future time in which the present memory will be most dear, Schuyler imagines a kind of divine forgetfulness. What gives him balm is the sure knowledge that he will forget the killing of the owl. But this reassurance is short-lived, since it implies an ultimate oblivion, the annihilation of consciousness. The symmetry is fearful; as the first stanza ends in memory, the second concludes in forgetfulness:

There is a
dull book with me,
an apple core, cigarettes,
an ashtray. Behind me
the rue I gave Bob
flourishes. Light on leaves,
so much to see, and
all I really see is that
owl, its bulk troubling
the twilight. I'll
soon forget it: what
have I not forgot?
Or one day will forget:

this garden, the breeze
in stillness, even
the words, Korean mums.

What is wondrous is that the poem is completely true to its moment and rises to eloquence without any verbal inflation. The literal particulars make metaphors superfluous. "Behind me / the rue I gave Bob / flourishes," Schuyler writes, insisting that *rue* is first a woodland plant that can "flourish" and is only secondarily a verbal emblem for regret. And the unembellished "apple core" is sufficient to suggest the mythic dimensions of another lost garden paradise. Or consider "I'll / soon forget it," where the line break would tempt a less exigent poet to write "never," not "soon." "It seems so simple but isn't," the poet Rae Armantrout has commented, knowing that this is the chief charge made by readers resistant to Schuyler's charms. "It isn't simple emotionally or in its handling of time: remembering something disturbing, then imagining a future in which he'll forget, which is comforting but also brings with it the fear of death."

Schuyler's prose is a vehicle for his powers of ventriloquism. One of the highlights of the first issue of *Locus Solus* (1961) was Schuyler's "Current Events," the story of an eighth-grade class trip to the state capital. The story achieves a high level of comedy simply from the accuracy with which Schuyler mimes the voice of the precocious cub reporter. Here, for example, is his thumbnail sketch of "our capable" bus driver:

> Mr. Olson, of Swedish descent on both sides, migrated to this country at the early age of two where he grew up attending Vocational High in this city. After gaining experience around Army trucks during the Great War in which he did not go overseas he subsequently became a driver for Inter-State Bus Lines not missing a day's work since for

which higher-ups singled him out for an award. His specialty is driving charter buses including pilgrimages gotten up by civic groups for which he is well acquainted with historic sights all over our land, such as Monticello, historic home of Thomas Jefferson.

Schuyler had an affection for children who talked like adults—as the children of Fairfield Porter did—and the reporter in "Current Events" is a marvelous example of naïveté and precocity combined. The reporter segues easily from polysyllabic words ("remuneration," "endeavor") to idiomatic constructions ("a high pressure job," "got a raise"). Nowhere is the effect funnier than when the earnest lad tries to make sense of "democracy in action":

> Some observers noted with surprise how senators talked and got up and walked around while one of their number was speaking. Being a senator is a high pressure job and the remuneration is not as great as in other lines of endeavor. People should think about this at the polls. Perhaps if senators got a raise they could concentrate more.

The story is utterly uneventful in one sense, lacking anything resembling a moral crisis, yet in another sense it is full of incident and drama. When the students convene "at 2:45 sharp" to board the bus going home, it is discovered that two of them are missing. The reporter, a diplomatist to the end, observes that "Speculations were rife and energetic plans afoot for a search party when the two in question appeared out of a drugstore down the street. It developed half the couple finds cherry cobbler indigestible and the other gallantly squired her in a sundae. As democracy was the order of the day the incident passed without reprimand although the self-conscious pair did not escape jocular thrusts and some good natured ribbing."

Alfred and Guinevere tells the story of a pair of precocious siblings, a girl and her brother, she on the verge of her teenage years, he a couple of years younger, who rib and tease each other mercilessly. Like the narrator of "Current Events," they are children who talk like adults without ever being anything other than children. The plot is advanced almost entirely by their dialogue with excerpts from Guinevere's diary interspersed. The book begins with the boy's appendicitis. After a brief convalescence, he and his sister travel by Pullman train to their grandmother and uncle Saul, with whom they will stay while their mother goes to New York City. She will be seeing off their father, who needs to go to Europe on a "business trip." That, at any rate, is the official story, but we begin to suspect that it's a cover. "Granny came home and told about Mother and her trip to the mountains," Guinevere writes in her diary. "She is entitled to a much needed rest and married people should have vacations from each other. It is the modern up to date way." Because of such hints of marital discord, there is a certain pathos in reading about the precocious girl and boy, clever beyond their years, whose repartee can be bitchy-witty in the Fire Island manner. Thus Alfred: "Mother's mad because Daddy didn't take her to Europe." To which Guinevere replies: "Of course you would take the obvious explanation at its face value." When Guinevere mischievously lets on to her friend Betty, possessor of a big mouth, that her parents have quarreled and are considering getting divorced, the cat is out of the bag. "Hello, daughter of divorce," Betty greets Guinevere, precipitating a fight between the two. But the book's twist is that the rumor of divorce has been wildly exaggerated; in this case, the obvious explanation for the events is indeed to be taken at face value. Guinevere's imagination has simply gotten the better of her. She is, after all, capable of reading *"Madame Bovary* by

Flaubert" and remarking that "the part where she buys the poison and dies is very true to life." And she is quite sophisticated
in her grasp of the distinctions between falsehoods and fictions:

"One time (this was a long time ago) I was telling a
dear friend a true-to-life story."

"I bet it was that Jeanne."

"Maybe and maybe not. Anyway, I told this story about
true people that was possible. I mean I thought about what
people said was happening but I also thought about how if
something different was happening they might tell you the
first thing instead of the truth. Do you know what I mean?"

"No."

"It's like if you tell a stranger you have a Shetland pony
when you're being conversational, it's a lie but it could possibly come true if Uncle Saul or somebody gave you one
sometime. But if you say you have magical powers, that's a
bare-faced whopper."

"You better watch out or I'll turn you into a toad. How
would you like to go hopping around on the ice?"

Full of travel and the promise of further travels, the book concludes with the siblings, their mother, uncle, and grandmother—
the whole kit and kaboodle—on board a ship taking them to
Europe, where they will reunite with the missing Papa. Naturally,
only Alfred and Guinevere are enjoying themselves on ship. The
rest of the party are in their cabins below, seasick.

When *Alfred and Guinevere* was published, the *New York Times
Book Review* treated it as a children's book. Kenneth Koch spoofed
this decision in his own review of the novel, which appeared in
Poetry. "*Alfred and Guinevere* does, in fact, tell the story of a few
months in the lives of two children, a brother and sister," Koch

wrote. "*Pride and Prejudice* is about a dance, a carriage ride, some rural marriage arrangements; and *Moby Dick* is about a whale." Koch went on to point out how much of the novel's "joy and shock" arise from language. Schuyler discovered humor as well as beauty in American clichés ("What did I find everybody hunting high and low for Alfred and our poor dear old Grandmother who deserves a better fate more dead than alive in the kitchen a total wreck") and foregrounded language itself as one of the subjects of his book.

Alfred and Guinevere is most remarkable for its refusal of all the options tempting the modern novelist. There is no sex in the book, no major upheaval, no violent change, no moral decision; it is not a parable, and there is no moral to the tale. Yet its contours suggest the shape of the traditional novel. We begin with disease, surgery, and recuperation, as in Thomas Mann's *The Magic Mountain* or Lionel Trilling's *The Middle of the Journey*. Next comes that familiar quest motif, the train ride to the country. Finally there is the family reconciliation and the promise of a new voyage and further adventures to come. It is not quite true that nothing really happens in the book; rather, it may be said that the book chronicles life at its most ordinary but with a healthy respect for the confusions, mystery, surprise, and humor of daily events. If from John O'Hara's novella *The Farmers Hotel* (1951), say, you were to delete the denouement, in which two of the travelers who meet by chance in a rural hotel are killed by a third, you would be removing the story's whole raison d'être. That no such denouement exists in *Alfred and Guinevere* attests to how radical a novel it is in its quiet, unpretentious way. Above all, there is the pleasure of characters who define themselves by their speech. Guinevere: "It was Alfred's turn to clear so I was settling down to the funnies when there was an ensuing crash like the last days of Pompeii. By a stroke of luck today is not Sunday and it was the willow ware that went and not the English bone. Granny gave me a rude shock as it seems she thinks men and boys should never clear just girls and women, like the dark ages. I was on the point of locking myself in my room but thought better of it. You have to respect the old no matter how horrible they are to you." Alfred: "I got appendicitis on the same day I saw him [i.e., a dead man in the park]. It will probably always be the day the most things happened to me on."

Whereas Schuyler scrupulously left himself out of his fiction, he is definitively a lyric poet in that his poems are communings between the self and the cosmos. But until the later autobiographical works ("The Morning of the Poem," "A Few Days"), in which the poet devised a means for enclosing narrative recollections within the arc of a chronicle of days, Schuyler entered his poetry mainly as an observer enjoying—as he puts it in "Hymn to Life"—flowers and trees that exist without explanation: "In the / Garden now daffodils stand full enfolded and to see them is enough." Where O'Hara's "I do this I do that" poems are full of frantic activity, parties, meetings, and phone calls, Schuyler's occasional poems are calm and mild, pastoral even when situated in an urban scape; a change in the weather or the light supplies all the drama that he requires. The notation of the weather turns into a sublime activity in Schuyler's diaries. This passage is dated December 3, 1970:

> Some days, like this one, not cold but cool, not so sunny but far from cloudy, are at once a kind of respite from all the other sorts of weather we might have had and yet not so special as to be called unseasonably anything. They refuse to be noticed, even in their ending, all things seen are so merged in a kind of undramatic softness—a gray beech against a gray house are taken into the night in which a slim moon is already high, and has been, for a long time— all going into the night as readily and unthinkingly as some-

one who comes back from a walk on the beach goes into his house. And shuts the door.

Among younger poets attracted to the New York School the response to Schuyler's debut volume was sensational. "Not only is *Freely Espousing* a collection of extremely good poems, but it also embodies the sort of vision that periodically reawakens us to the infinite range of possibilities open to the poet," John Koethe announced in *Poetry* magazine in 1970. Koethe proposed an analogy to Elizabeth Bishop; like her, Schuyler was "able to treat his own feelings and ideas as objects." Bishop herself became a fan. "I am going to write to James Schuyler, too," she wrote to Ashbery in 1973. "I like his poetry so much, & I have never told him so, nor seen him, & know next to nothing about him." (Two years later she told Charles North that Schuyler is "one of the few poets who writes good love-poems these days.") The analogy to Bishop was taken up by Howard Moss in an essay he wrote for *American Poetry Review* in 1981. In the intervening years Schuyler had published three full-sized collections, each better than the last, plus a miscellany of poems and prose (*The Home Book*, 1977) and his second and last novel (*What's for Dinner?*). Schuyler resembled Bishop, Moss wrote, in his "precision of detail" and his "knack of making the lyrical dramatic." Coming from Moss, the long-ensconced poetry editor of *The New Yorker*, where Bishop's poems exclusively appeared, this was high praise. Of the title piece in *The Morning of the Poem*, Moss wrote that it was "the work of a persistent romantic, and as American as apple pie; in fact, it sometimes reads like a perverse underground commentary on *Our Town*."

The volume Moss hailed won the Pulitzer Prize in 1981 and with it the wider recognition Schuyler had longed for. His ascending reputation was bolstered by the publication of *A Few Days* in 1985 and *Selected Poems* three years later. Each was an occasion for tributes to Schuyler from some of the younger poets who had taken his work to heart. In *The Nation*, Douglas Crase wrote, "Just as Porter became the central figure for painters who believed in an art outside the expressionist mainstream, so Schuyler is for younger poets an eminent example of instruction outside the workshop, of a poetry to fit what he has called 'the pure pleasure of / Simply looking.' "

Schuyler was the least prolific of the New York poets, the only one who did not have an Ivy League education, and was susceptible to feelings of resentment and deep insecurity about being overlooked and excluded. The painter Alex Katz delighted Schuyler by refusing to believe him when he said he had attended Bethany College in West Virginia. "Nah, you're Harvard," Katz said. "Wish I / were, but I'm a lot more panhandle than I am Cambridge, / Mass," Schuyler ruefully noted. Born in Chicago in 1923, the son of Marcus James Schuyler, a newspaperman whom everyone called "Sky," and Margaret Daisy Connor, James Marcus Schuyler was the product of a broken home. His parents divorced when he was six, and he was brought up by his mother and her second husband in Washington, D.C., and East Aurora, New York, a suburb of Buffalo famous for its crafts school founded by Elbert Hubbard. Schuyler seldom saw his father and became increasingly alienated from his stepfather, "a very hunting-and-shooting, outdoors sort of person," who "became quite crazy during the Depression—he had been very successful and then gradually was left less successful as he ran out of money." As a boy Schuyler had a tent behind his house in the summer, where he would read books. In *Unforgotten Years* by Logan Pearsall Smith, he read that Walt Whitman had visited the author in Philadelphia. "Knowing Whitman and reading him gave Smith the feeling that maybe someday he, too, would be a writer," Schuyler recollected. "And I looked up and the whole landscape shimmered, and I said, 'Yes, that's it.' "

Schuyler studied English at Bethany College ("an attractive group of buildings on a small, steep hill") in West Virginia. Florence Hoagland, the head of the English department, encouraged his literary aspirations. But he left without taking a degree. "I just played bridge all the time," he told an interviewer. Following his navy service, Schuyler worked for two years in "network traffic" for the Voice of America. With the proceeds from the small farm in Arkansas he inherited from his paternal grandmother, he financed a trip to Italy. He took classes at the University of Florence for a year and worked for a time as secretary to W. H. Auden in Forio d'Ischia in the Bay of Naples. Having formed a close friendship with Chester Kallman, Auden's lover, he lived in Auden's house.

While he was indebted to the older poet for many favors and kindnesses, including funds generously loaned, Schuyler grew to dislike Auden's poetry and to resent his authority. "I think you ought to lay the book out like a split cod," Schuyler told Koch, urging him to pan a volume of Auden's poetry in 1957. Schuyler mounted his case against Auden with shrewd insight and surprising bile: "Now, you like his early work. [Christopher] Isherwood had a great deal to do with it: he criticized his poems, cut them to pieces and so on. It's all in *Lions and Shadows.** But, as the boy grew older, there wasn't anybody bright enough to keep up with him (and don't forget how long his collaboration with Isherwood lasted: they went to China together, they came to America together). And he has little faculty for self-criticism (which is a quality—if it is worth anything—one might expect a poet, an artist, to develop rather than possess innately)." Auden's conversion from a psychoanalytical to a theological world view was another thing that aroused Schuyler's ire: "He has always talked and

*Isherwood wrote that Auden revised his early poems radically on the basis of Isherwood's opinion. The revised poems were, in effect, anthologies of Isherwood's favorite lines.

thought from the point of view of a lay analyst; but one who has
not himself been analyzed: a tricky business. His conversion—or
rather, reversion—to the Anglican church dates from his mother's
death, during the war (they used to sing Tristan and Isolde together at the piano). Since then he has become increasingly a
lay-preacher (I mean real sermons in real churches), an apologist
for Anglicanism and quite willing to attack psychoanalysis . . ."
Schuyler also attacked Auden's "periodic self-disgust" that
caused him to suppress or renounce certain of his early works,
such as *The Orators*, a remarkable book of prose poetry that Auden
wrote in the early 1930s and later did his best to disown.

Why such animus? In part, one suspects, because Auden's
example stifled Schuyler's growth as a poet; he found Auden's
formal elegance "inhibiting," his diction forbidding, and it was
only when he discarded Auden as an influence that he began to
come into his own as a poet. Affection replaces animus in Schuyler's elegy "Wystan Auden" but not at the expense of truthtelling:

> On Ischia he claimed to take
> St. Restituta seriously, and
> sat at Maria's café in the cobbled
> square saying, "Poets should
> dress like businessmen," while
> he wore an incredible peach-
> colored nylon shirt.

Lured by Auden's presence, Truman Capote, Tennessee Williams,
and other "disreputable American ticket-of-leave men" visited
Ischia. "One day, before lunch, Wystan and I went down to have
an aperitif on the piazza, and Truman was there. I asked him what
he'd been reading, and he said Stendhal's *The Red and the Black*.
And I asked, 'Well, how do you like it?' and he said, 'Well, I'm
really quite disappointed. The transitions are so clumsy.' And all

the way back to the house, Wystan, just white with rage, kept saying, 'The cheek! The cheek!' "

Schuyler's duties included typing up Auden's poems:

> And
> when he learned that in Florence
> I and my friend Bill Aalto had
> fished his drafts of poems
> out of the wastepaper basket,
> he took to burning them, saying,
> "I feel like an ambassador burning
> secret papers."

"I would type something of Wystan's and think, 'Well, if this is poetry, I'm certainly never going to write any myself,' " Schuyler recalled.

The flowering of Schuyler's poetry took place in the decade of gay liberation, the 1970s, and the steadily climbing rise in his readership has something to do with his unflinching portrayal of homosexuality. He tells us, for example, that his camp name was "Dorabella," and he casually peppers his long poems with anecdotes situated in gay bars. A friend named Brian "told / an American officer / that he was a clandestine homosexual. The officer knocked / him to the barroom floor. / Brian looked up and said, 'That proves it.' " Bill Aalto, who was one of Schuyler's first lovers, is recollected not only in the Auden elegy but in the terrific poem entitled "Dining Out with Doug and Frank." The poet's tumultuous affair with Aalto, who had been "a hero, a major in the / Abraham Lincoln Brigade," ended badly, with "Bill chasing me around / the kitchen table—in Wystan Auden's / house in Forio d'Ischia—with / a carving knife."

In 1950, Schuyler returned from Europe to the United States, taking a job in a New York bookstore. In 1951 he met

D a v i d   L e h m a n

O'Hara and later Ashbery, and in 1952 he and Ashbery began work on *A Nest of Ninnies.* "John had come out [to East Hampton] for a weekend," Schuyler recalled. "We were walking along the beach at sunset, heading for a cocktail party. The sun was casting those extraordinary Technicolor effects on the sea and sky. John turned to me and said, 'I always feel so embarrassed by these gaudy displays of nature.' I didn't feel embarrassed at all." Schuyler lived with O'Hara for a time in a cold-water flat five flights up on East Forty-ninth Street, and when Ashbery interrupted his ten-year Paris sojourn with a year in New York he and Schuyler shared the space, O'Hara having moved with Joe Le-Sueur in the interim into a loft on University Place.

Of the four leading first-generation New York School poets, Schuyler, so attentive to flowers and trees, had the most pastoral and least urban sensibility. Yet only O'Hara wrote more affectingly of New York City. Consider this passage from "Dining Out with Doug and Frank":

> It would
> have been so nice after dinner
> to take a ferryboat with Frank
> across the Hudson (or West River,
> if you prefer). To be on
> the water in the dark and
> the wonder of electricity—
> the real beauty of Manhattan.
> Oh well. When they tore down
> the Singer Building,
> and when I saw the Bogardus Building
> rusty and coming unstitched in
> a battlefield of rubble I deliberately
> withdrew my emotional investments
> in loving old New York. Except
> you can't.

And not even O'Hara, in whom the autobiographical impulse is so strong, was as committed as Schuyler was to the revelations of a self observed with the candor, tact, and lack of sentimentality of Montaigne.

All his adult life Schuyler was plagued with psychiatric problems and financial anxieties. He was lucky in his friends. They helped find him jobs and free-lance writing assignments, and when it became clear that he could not meet the demands of full-time work they rallied to get him the medical care he needed and provide for his housing and living expenses. In the 1950s he wrote for *Art News* and was employed by the Museum of Modern Art, thanks in both cases to O'Hara's sponsorship. In the 1960s he lived with Fairfield Porter's family in Southampton and spent vast periods of time as a house guest of Kenward Elmslie in Calais, Vermont. One of the worst of Schuyler's breakdowns occurred in the summer of 1971. Schuyler was staying at the Porter house with Ron Padgett, Padgett's wife, Pat, and their young son Wayne, in the absence of the Porters. For the Padgett family, it was a shattering and terrifying experience. Under the delusion that he was Jesus Christ, Schuyler washed dollar bills in the bathtub, hanging them out on the clothesline to dry. He also threw money away; Padgett discovered a wad of bills—roughly "eighty [or] a hundred dollars"—that Schuyler had tossed in the wastebasket. "I asked him why he was throwing it away," Padgett recalls. "He looked me right in the eye. 'Because money is shit,' he said with disdain." Not knowing what to do, and beside themselves with anxiety, the Padgetts called the police. Schuyler gave an account of his state of mind in a letter to Ashbery:

"Can you imagine how I blush, when I think of the things I said and did, while deluded? Why does it have to be loveable old J.C. we nuts pick on? If only I could have chosen someone a little more remarkable, less commonplace, like Max Reger. 'John, I'm in the midst of a great work for ocarina, Jaw Harp, and massed strings. I'm calling it, "Creation." ' Oh well. Oh: I was washing

D a v i d   L e h m a n

the money not because I thought (or think) money is in itself
dirty, but because I thought the airy predictions that bring the
Good Book to a weird climax were happening, literally, and that
this is both the earthly paradise and is, or was becoming, the
heavenly one. In the hospital I found a booklet on Revelations
which agreed with my mood, and listed various historical events
as the counterpart of the seven-horsemen, woman clothed with
the sun, etc. So I was washing money out of respect for it, and
love of all creation. That was how I felt anyway."

It may easily be imagined how vital it was for a man with
such a fragile psyche to be part of an intimate community of
writers and artists. His poem "June 30, 1974," which Douglas
Crase has aptly described as an "American ode, to happiness,"
depicts the quiet morning hours when the poet, a houseguest at
the country house of dear friends, fixes himself breakfast waiting
for his friends—John Ashbery, Jane Freilicher and Jane's husband Joe Hazan—to arise:

> I'd like to go out
> for a swim but
> it's a little cool
> for that. Enough to
> sit here drinking coffee,
> writing, watching the clear
> day ripen (such
> a rainy June we had)
> while Jane and Joe
> sleep in their room
> and John in his. I
> think I'll make more toast.

The deaths of friends hang heavily over Schuyler's work. With
elegiac tenderness he wrote about O'Hara's penchant for swimming in "the heaviest surf on the south shore of Long Island,

often to the alarm of his friends, and even at night when he was drunk and would turn waspish."

As a young man Schuyler had been handsome, witty, and charming. In later years he was, partially as a result of heavy doses of antipsychotic medication, a sedentary and stocky figure, seemingly immovable, who was sometimes silent for unnerving stretches. (At one dinner party given by friends in his honor, the poet left during dessert without having spoken a single word all evening.) The 1970s were particularly difficult for Schuyler. He lived in nursing homes and fleabag hotels and burned down an apartment when he fell asleep with a lit cigarette in his hand. Schuyler knew some stability only after he moved into the Chelsea Hotel in New York City in 1979. He lived at the Chelsea for the rest of his life, and a plaque in front of the hotel's entrance informs guests and visitors of Schuyler's place among the writers—like Arthur Miller and Dylan Thomas—who made this their New York headquarters. The Chelsea, a hotel with a history, was notoriously the place where Sid Vicious of the Sex Pistols killed his girlfriend. It was also the sort of hotel where you might see a policeman chasing a naked bearded man down the stairs and you couldn't be sure if this were really happening or if you had stumbled into the set of an underground movie. "This old hotel is / well built: if / you hold your breath and make a wish you'll meet Virgil / Thomson in the elevator / or a member of a punk rock band," Schuyler wrote in "A Few Days." The *Village Voice* once asked him for a statement about why he lived where he did. "When I was twenty I came to New York," he wrote. "Because it was the center, I guess. I was coming from west New York State, a place called East Aurora. It's still the center. I stay because I have friends here. I suppose I'd really rather live in the country, but I can't afford a house, so I live in the Chelsea. It's comfortable here and I have a balcony and it's convenient. Convenient to what? To John Ashbery."

Shy and reclusive, Schuyler gave his first public reading in the fall of 1988 at the DIA Center for the Arts, then on Mercer Street in downtown New York City. For many in the audience it felt like a historic occasion. The line of people waiting to get in, many poets, writers, and artists among them, snaked around the corner. Ashbery, introducing Schuyler, said he felt "jealous" because Schuyler had "somehow managed to draw on the whole arsenal of modernism, from the minimalism of Dr. Williams to the gorgeous aberrations of Wallace Stevens and the French Surrealists and still write in what Marianne Moore calls 'plain American which cats and dogs can read.' He makes sense, dammit, and he manages to do so without falsifying or simplifying the daunting complexity of life as we are living it today." The size of Schuyler's audience has grown steadily since that memorable evening. His reputation is particularly high among poets. In a recent issue of *Verse*, Donna Brook has an affecting poem entitled "I Have My James Schuyler Too." The Chelsea Hotel, she writes, is "the only reason I ever seem to think about 23rd Street, / just as James Schuyler is the only reason / I ever think about flowers."

That Schuyler should be a poet of warm benediction and praise is one of the splendid anomalies of his work. "Haze," the final poem in his *Collected*, is like an addendum to the theme robustly announced in the title of Schuyler's 1974 book *Hymn to Life*. It concludes:

> the endless city
> builds on and on
> thinning out, here and there,
> for the wet green velvet towels
> ("slight imperfections")
> of summer
> ("moderately priced")
> and a hazy morning
> in August,

even that
we may grow to love.

When "Haze" was selected for inclusion in *The Best American Poetry 1990*, the poet was asked to write a few words on the poem's composition. His note was revealing: " 'Haze' was written one humid August afternoon in the guest house at Little Portion, an Episcopal Franciscan Friary on the North Shore of Long Island, not far from Port Jefferson. Like many other of my poems, this is about what can be seen out the window: except here, though nothing is said about it, the poem combines the views from two windows, and several times of day. I do not usually take such license." The severe restriction Schuyler placed on himself, the disciplined refusal to "take such license" as poets customarily seize, the resolute determination to praise what is tangibly present and only that, is connected to the sense one has of the tremendous psychic repression that Schuyler endured in order to write so convincingly about happiness, which is to be found not in grand flights but in the celebration of ordinary pleasures. Probably no other poet of our time has written so convincingly of the pleasures of rain, snow, a shampoo, the application of aftershave lotion, flowers of all kinds, a smoke in the backseat of a cab. A cup of coffee was a lyric occasion. The Academy of American Poets has inscribed these lines of Schuyler's on the ceramic mug the organization gives to donors: "Lucky who have to eat / and drink, such as stimulating coffee, / slower than water, / that coats the cup if good and strong."

Schuyler was personally closer to Ashbery, his erstwhile collaborator, than to O'Hara, with whom he had a falling-out, or to Koch, who was initially reluctant to welcome him as an equal partner in the fledgling New York School. Nevertheless the contrast between Schuyler and Ashbery in their poetry seems, at first glance, complete to the point of antithesis. "I would say that the distinction between fiction writers and poets is becoming obsolete, that it might be more useful to think of authors as mirror-writers or window-writers," Howard Moss once wrote. "In America the two schools stem from two major figures, both poets, who may be viewed as their source: Emily Dickinson, the mirror, and Walt Whitman, the window." Moss's dichotomy seems fleshed out in the poetry of Ashbery and Schuyler. Schuyler, observing the dahlias and garbage trucks in the haze, is to the window of perception what Ashbery, the author of "Self-Portrait in a Convex Mirror," is to the mirror of speculation. Quietly Whitmanic, a planetary celebrator, Schuyler may be a shut-in, but his windows are open to the finite world of actuality. As he writes in an elegy for a friend named Mike, reality is an activity going on outside the window. What is there to be seen is as real as the smell of mortality in one's own hand:

> Look out
> the win-
> dow
> cluck:
> it's real,
> it's there,
> it's life.
> Look
> at
> your hand.
> It's real
> and so
> is death.
> Mike,
> so long!

Schuyler's poetic practice is far closer to O'Hara's than to Ashbery's or Koch's. It is conceivable that O'Hara's untimely death acted as a sort of imaginative liberation for Schuyler, who began, in a way, to take over O'Hara's poetic project and adapt it to his own sensibility. (It is certain that Schuyler would have deplored this formulation.) In any event, his poetry grew more and more to resemble O'Hara's ceaseless self-chronicling. Like O'Hara, Schuyler achieved a certain intimacy of tone, which, like a matinee idol's steadfast gaze, flatters each reader into thinking that the poem was meant for his or her ears alone. Just as many of O'Hara's poems illustrate the notion that a poem can be written in lieu of a telephone call, Schuyler's long poems, particularly "The Morning of the Poem" and "A Few Days," are informal epistles, letters to a composite or variable "you." "When you read this poem you will have to decide / Which of the 'yous' are 'you,' " Schuyler comments in "The Morning of the Poem." (Schuyler's work furnishes textbook lessons on the ironic advantages of quote marks in poetry.) O'Hara's poems were as speedy as phone calls; it was as if the whole contents of a day had been poured into any ten-minute stretch in his poems. The paradigmatic O'Hara line is, "you were there I was here you were here I was there where are you I miss you / (that was an example of the 'sonnet' 'form')." Schuyler slowed down the tempo. Nothing happens suddenly; the poet is hurrying nowhere. "The morning / passes like an elephant in no stampede," he writes in "A Few Days." Time, the way it passes, the way it feels while it is passing, becomes one of Schuyler's transcendent themes:

> Tomorrow is another day, but no better than today if you
>   only realize it.
> Let's love today, the what we have now, this day, not today
>   or tomorrow or
> yesterday, but this passing moment, that will not come
>   again.
> Now tomorrow is today, the day before Labor Day, 1979, I
>   want to

> live to see the new century come in: but perhaps it's bad
> luck to
> say so . . .

The wish was denied Schuyler, who died shy of his sixty-eighth birthday in April 1991.

Schuyler could write with a sourness that one seldom finds in O'Hara. In "My Heart," O'Hara describes an imagined fan of his work as an "aficionado of my mess," a phrase that is characteristically self-deprecating and simultaneously flattering to the fan, who is assigned the romantic term Hemingway made popular for connoisseurs of the bullfight. For O'Hara, the reader is someone to charm, woo, seduce, and delight. For Schuyler, on the contrary, the imagined future reader is as likely to be "some creep" who will uncover a certain discarded poem of his, "a stinker," and "publish it in a thin / volume called *Uncollected Verse*." O'Hara in "My Heart" had proudly proclaimed that his poetry, the "better part" of his heart, is "open." It could be said that this is a virtue of Schuyler's work, too, though he disdains the adjective. In "Dec. 28, 1974," one of the best of Schuyler's "daily" poems, he states his poetic credo in the form of a rebuke to "a clunkhead" who thought he was complimenting him:

> "Your poems,"
> a clunkhead said, "have grown
> more open." I don't want to be open,
> merely to say, to see and say, things
> as they are.

In April 1956, O'Hara and Schuyler collaborated on a poem they called "Ode." It is not an ode "to" anything; O'Hara just liked the idea of an ode. Stripped of the formal requirements that Horace or Pindar heeded, an ode simply meant a poem of a certain gravity and ambition. "Ode" scores off the critic John Simon; O'Hara was spending the season in Cambridge, where he acted in the Poets' Theatre production of Ashbery's *The Compromise*, which Simon may have attended. But the best lines in the "Ode" have nothing to do with Simon and everything to do with the harmonious workings of two "quite singular" sensibilities:

> if I did go out on the fire escape and piss on myself in the
> rain
> which is, I suppose, the male equivalent of having a good
> cry
> I might not want ever to come in again
> I would be emptying myself forever like a masthead for love
> longing for the scalding coffee and salt beer of your kisses
> but I would not come in, you would have to sail me away
> some people just never get over having heard "mon coeur
> mis a nu"
>
> The only word I like is crystal
> Debussy has sneezed his way into the Augean stables of my
> heart
> not a silence has been left
> I am blown into your heart while you stand around me
> watching
> and the tributaries of our sweat
> are launching two quite singular ships which seem to be the
> same ship
> on whose sail it says I LOVE YOU

O'Hara and Schuyler had a major falling-out in 1961. It happened shortly before the latter was institutionalized with a nervous breakdown that May, and it was the result, O'Hara maintained, of Schuyler's paranoia and persecution complex. "I don't mean that I blame or dislike Jimmy for what's happened— anyone's actions can be interpreted as amiable or hostile depending on your point of view and perhaps mine more than most—but I don't see any use in either of us going through the strain of pretending we like each other as much as we once did," O'Hara wrote to Ashbery. "I don't know why, for instance, he has singled me out for the accusation that I've put him in the shade as a writer, or whatever he said, except that I have been more handy than you or Kenneth, but that's the way it is. It's none of our fault, nor is it Allen or Gregory's that Jimmy has not written more and that he couldn't bring himself to let John Myers publish his poems, etc., but he apparently wants to blame it on me for allegedly damaging his self-confidence, so that's the way it is."

Schuyler's friendship with Kenneth Koch was less intense and less troubled. On the surface Schuyler and Koch had little enough in common. But they were astute readers of one another's work; each could count on the other's complete candor. And each could rely on the other's good taste. When Koch traveled to northern Italy in 1957, Schuyler guided him by letter, conjuring up this art-and-food outing in Bologna: "After drinking in the della Quercias you will look over your shoulder at an elaboration of Giambologna's, a fountain full of ladies with water squirting out of their tits and, behind that, the palazzo communale in which there is a superb staircase by Bramante which is little more than a ridged ramp. It's a great deal of fun to walk up and down it. It's quite nice to go to Bologna by bus, through Prato of the silk mills (and an outdoor pulpit by Donatello) and Pistoia, up and over a singularly steep mountain (four-star view of the Val d'Arno) down into Bologna! city of arcades! Of leaning towers! Famed for its veal! City of beautiful church facades! (do not miss the one in stucco) how fat all the people are! they eat too much! who can blame them! see them all piling into Caesarina's! Hear Caesarina shouting at them all! She is bringing out the lasagna! smell it? Uhmmmm. Can we really eat a veal steak à la Bolognese on top of all that lasagna? Well, we are damn well going to try." When Koch's "The Pleasures of Peace" appeared in *The Paris Review* in 1968, Schuyler paid him the compliment of writing this "Epistle to Dr. Koch," less in parody than in homage:

EPISTLE TO DR. KOCH

"Drinking a morning cup of coffee is one of the pleasures
    of peace,"
I thought as I drank my morning cup of coffee while reading
    "The Pleasures of Peace."
"It is also one of the pleasures of war," hinted a still small
    voice.
"A *what* kind of voice?" "Oh all right a small voice from a
    still.
(In truth, a white coffee biggin in which I infuse morning
    coffee essence.)
"You evade the issue," kindly stated S. A. Schoenbrunn &
    Co. of Palisades, N.J. 07650.
"A morning cup of coffee is a pleasure of peace
which will also prove savorful in time of war."
"In other words what you are saying," clattered Miss (1 lb.)
    Yuban, peering yellowly into her cup,
"is that there are also pleasures of war."
"By no means," affirmed the Marzo Maggio Medal on the
    Gold Medal coffee can.
"Coffee—black Italian roast by preference—is all things:
    stimulus, anodyone, palliative.
It drives the husbandman to work and mends the homely
    housewife's busted TV set in time for "Edge of Night."

It speeds the Avon Representative with a kindly word.

It irons the cat's pajamas.

It collects old labels which it sends to friends and other
    shut-ins.

In one cup of it lie all the colors that ever were, blending in
    searing heat.

It gives the soldier strength to fight—"

"Ha!" and "Alack," I cried, and started from my wooden
    chair.

"Off fancies, off! Vain imaginings, begone!

No more to the biggin will I hie

but take these fluttered pence—see, there's this, & this, &
    this—e'en with them buy

a samovar, whereof the amber fluent flux, though it cheers
    not, nor yet inebriates,

Nights' phantasms—may chance begot of the gorgonzola-
    faced and fruitless moon—in the dawn fluent. Yet

stay. I'll once more to the liquorice spring and sip, or,
    haply—

should the god-lurched and enspric'd nix so deem—gulp

a cup o' the morning, its blackness lightened to a passing
    tan

by a little something out of this gallon carton (Covered by
    One Or More U.S. Patents 3, 116, 002, 1, 120, 333, 3,
    120, 335 Other Patents Protection Pending)

of Wight's Dairy pasteurized homogenized vitamin D milk
    400 U.S.P. UNITS VITAMIN D PER QUART

Bucksport, Maine   Tel. 469-3239

and lace it liberally and well with Sailor's Warning.

The poem remained unknown until an archivist rummaging in
Kenneth Koch's filing cabinets turned it up in 1995.

    Schuyler resembled, and was conscious of resembling, a

painter surveying the picture that he means to record. This is from "February":

> The green leaves of the tulips on my desk
> like grass light on flesh,
> and a green-copper steeple
> and streaks of cloud beginning to glow.
> I can't get over
> how it all works in together
> like a woman who just came to her window
> and stands there filling it
> jogging her baby in her arms.
> She's so far off. Is it the light
> that makes the baby pink?

Asked whether he had ever written poems about Fairfield Porter's paintings, Schuyler said no but added that he "tried to write poems that were like his paintings." They are. Light is an implicit subject—and sometimes the explicit one—of many of Schuyler's poems and Porter's paintings.

Like Porter, Schuyler operated on the principle that the best criticism is simply the best description. Like few other poets, he committed himself to the task of painting what's there and only what's there. In his poems accuracy of observation is raised to a high form of praise. The natural or manmade particulars of the world are celebrated not so much for their utility as for their virtue in merely being. Consider "A Stone Knife," a poem written to acknowledge a Christmas present from Kenward Elmslie in 1969. The knife is presented first as a motive for simile and metaphor, then for its use, and finally, triumphantly, as a thing-in-itself. Notice the mileage Schuyler gets from turning over the phrase "just the thing":

Sleek as an ax, bare
and elegant as a tarn,
manly as a lingam,
November weather petrified,
it is just the thing
to do what with? To
open letters? No, it
is just the thing, an
object, dark, fierce
and beautiful in which
the surprise is that
the surprise, once
past, is always there:
which to enjoy is
not to consume.

The lining here hammers home the point. "It is just the thing" stands as a line by itself; the emphasis is on the object, not what it can do. There is a quiet insistence in all of Schuyler's work on things in themselves, not the reasons for things or what they might mean. The austerity of some of his short poems says no less. For Schuyler, who is quite sparing with figurative language, the literal description suffices more often than not, making similes seem supererogatory.

Wallace Stevens in his poem "The Man With the Blue Guitar," in which he contemplates a Picasso portrait of a guitar player, states the categorical imperative of the modern imagination: "Things as they are / Are changed upon the blue guitar." The imagination is transformative; it has the power not only to redeem a fallen world but to substitute itself for that world. The trope of the blue guitar is taken up by Frank O'Hara in his poem "Memorial Day 1950," in which a spilled can of blue paint and a broken guitar stand for the life of the artist—wounded, bruised, but determined to create something exemplary out of the wreckage.

Schuyler, in contrast, insists on affirming "things as they are."* The phrase appears more than once in Schuyler's work. In the opening pages of "The Morning of the Poem," for example, Schuyler casually, unobtrusively defines the ambition of his poem, its geographical compass, and his artistic credo. Writing from his family home in western New York State, he fastens his gaze on the image of "Baudelaire's skull," wondering what the image portends and why it came to him while thinking of his painter friend, Darragh Park, in his Chelsea studio in New York City. The poem means to account for the distance between Schuyler's origins and his present identity—between the broken home of his childhood and the bohemian life as he was living it—as between East Aurora and Chelsea. It is as he visualizes Baudelaire's skull that he articulates his poetic credo. He aspires "to see things as they are too fierce and yet / not too much":

> The jays are fatter than any jays I ever saw
> before and hanging
> In a parlor floor in far-off Chelsea I'm
> glad there is a
> Watercolor of me in blue shorts, sitting
> beside a black Britannica
> And a green-glass-shaded student lamp and
> a glass of deep red wine
> Ruby wine the throat of a hummingbird
> hanging on speeding
> Wings in fierce blue delphinium depths I think

*When he and Charles North edited the anthologies they called *Broadway* and *Broadway 2*, they took submissions "as they were," passing no judgment unless asked.

About those two blue jays, like me, too
    chubby, and Baudelaire's skull,
That sees in the tattered morning the passing of
The lost and indigent, the lost, the way
    the day when I arose
Seemed lost and trash-picking for a merciless morsel,
    a stinking
Bone, such as in this green unlovely village
    one need never
Seek or fear and you descend to your studio
    leaving on your roof
The exhalation of Baudelaire's image of
    terror which is
Not terror but the artist's (your) determination
    to be strong
To see things as they are too fierce and yet
    not too much: in
Western New York, why Baudelaire? In Chelsea,
    why not?

Not so much the dandy in Baudelaire as that poet's "determination to be strong / To see things as they are too fierce and yet / not too much" is what makes him exemplary for Schuyler.

Schuyler's readers have joined him in wondering why he, who distrusted symbols in favor of literal things, introduced Baudelaire's skull into "The Morning of the Poem." The literary detective's first resort is to Baudelaire's poetry. "Spleen (IV)" in *Les Fleurs du mal* concludes with the image of a skull ("Hope, vanquished, cries, and Anguish, the cruel despot, / Plants his black flag on my assenting skull"), but it is unlikely that Schuyler had these lines in mind. Darragh Park told me that he had asked Schuyler about the provenance of Baudelaire's skull when he was first shown the poem. It was "an image of determination" for

Schuyler, Park said. Schuyler may have seen a drawing or etching of Baudelaire, perhaps by Manet, "that makes him look nearly bald with a huge brainy forehead." Had Park worked on a picture of Baudelaire's skull at the time "The Morning of the Poem" was written? No, "I was working on a painting of cars charging down Ninth Avenue right at the viewer, as Jimmy points out in 'The Morning of the Poem.' "

In a piece on Jane Freilicher he wrote for *Art News* in 1966, Schuyler refers again to "things as they are," summing up what he perceives to be the distinguishing trait of Freilicher's work (and his own). "The scale of objects goes unadjusted (mediocrity in painting is often merely an inability to leave things as they are)," Schuyler writes. "If a bowl is too big, that is how big it is; if stems are floppy, then let them slump. It is as they are that they caught her attention, so why fiddle?" It is no accident that Ashbery makes the same point in his own essay on Jane Freilicher, written twenty years later: "Lesser artists correct nature in a misguided attempt at heightened realism, forgetting that the real is not only what one sees but also a result of how one sees it—inattentively, inaccurately perhaps, but nevertheless that is how it is coming through to us, and to deny this is to kill the life of the picture. It seems that Jane's long career has been one attempt to correct this misguided, even blasphemous, state of affairs; to let things, finally, be."

Helen Vendler contends that notwithstanding "superficial resemblances of form," Schuyler is essentially different from the other New York School poets. "Schuyler is not radically allegorical, like Ashbery, but literal; he is not a social poet, like O'Hara, but a poet of loneliness; he is not comical and narrative, like Koch, but wistful and atmospheric." Good though this is, it is also an object lesson in the difficulties of formulating critical dichotomies. Is Schuyler not a social poet? For all the loneliness in his poems, are they not populated with memorable characters, friends and lovers? Doesn't Schuyler's reader gain an intimate footing with Auden, Ashbery, O'Hara, Jane and Joe Hazan, Fairfield and Anne Porter, Kenward Elmslie, Ruth Kligman, Herbert Machiz, Bill Berkson, Tom Carey, Helena Hughes, and on and on? Moreover, does Schuyler's emphasis on the literal preclude the possibility that his poems might be "radically allegorical"? The ending of "Korean Mums" seems to me a notable example of an allegory emerging from literal truth, a case of exact identity between "the words" and what they mean. Finally, while Schuyler may be less comical than Koch, of whom can this not be said? But is it really true that Schuyler's work lacks narrative? It seems to me that his long poems are full of stories—and full, too, of humor. "The Morning of the Poem," which begins and ends with the poet needing "to go piss," is bawdily comic: "and who was it / who in the Café Montana told, / In all seriousness, that the triumph of Mrs. S., / future Duchess of W., was that / 'They say she's a circus in bed.' I like to / dwell on that, the caged lions / And the whips, ball-balancing seals, 'And now, / without a net . . .' " For his part, isn't Koch, like Schuyler, wistful, often given to contemplating the passage of time, and good at producing "atmospheric" effects?

Like Ashbery, Schuyler found his own way to capture the interior monologue of a mind in motion. Like O'Hara, he figured out how to convert an autobiography-in-progress into poetry. And while his reverence for untrammeled nature distinguishes him from his friends, what is most singular about Schuyler's poetry is his Keatsian conviction that true things truly observed will provide all the beauty one needs in a world however fallen. There is a great passage in "Hymn to Life" in which the list of things worth saving becomes a "dirty laundry" list, but then, in a fine twist, the washing machine emerges as precisely one of the things "worth the price of admission to the horrors of civilization":

I hate fussing with nature and would like the world to be
All weeds. I see it from the train, citybound, how the yuccas
    and chicory
Thrive. So much messing about, why not leave the world
    alone? Then
There would be no books, which is not to be borne. Willa
    Cather alone is worth
The price of admission to the horrors of civilization. Let's
    make a list.
The greatest paintings. Preferred orchestral conductors.
    Nostalgia singers.
The best, the very best, roses. After learning all their
    names—Rose
de Rescht, Cornelia, Pax—it is important to forget them. All
    these
Lists are so much dirty laundry. Sort it out fast and send to
    laundry
Or hurl into washing machine, add soap and let 'er spin.
    The truth is
That all these household tasks and daily work—up the street
    two men
Install an air conditioner—are beautiful.

On the surface it might seem that Schuyler's poetic practice
pits him against the avant-garde avatars of the New York School of
painting. His best poetry was as far from abstraction, and as wedded
to minute particulars, as the poetry of William Carlos Williams, who
made "no ideas but in things" a rallying cry. Still it is a superficial
view of the avant-garde that would limit it to abstract art. There
were, as Schuyler and his fellow poets demonstrated, other ways to
absorb the lessons of Abstract Expressionism, other ways of partici-
pating in the avant-garde phenomenon that hit New York with the
force of a typhoon in the aftermath of World War II.

part

two

the ordeal

of the

avant-garde

the avant-garde rides to the rescue

It is no longer possible, or it seems no longer possible, for an important avant-garde artist to go unrecognized. And, sadly enough, his creative life expectancy has dwindled correspondingly, since artists are no fun once they have been discovered.

—JOHN ASHBERY,
"THE INVISIBLE AVANT-GARDE" (1968)

(I)

It is the fate of words, particularly words bound up with changes in taste and fashion, to detach themselves from their original kernel of meaning. *Avant-garde*, like *existentialism* or *postmodernism*, is bedeviled by imprecise use and has been debased to the precise extent of its popularity. Applied to the arts, *avant-garde* refers loosely to artists or works in the forefront of change: Avant-garde art is advanced art, breakthrough art, art that anticipates the future. A more precise definition, however, would restrict *avant-garde* to a movement or group activity. "An individual can be an innovator, but there is no such thing as an avant-garde individual, except as follower or leader," Harold Rosenberg observed. "Cézanne is not avant-garde, Cubism is." Rosenberg meant not to disparage Cézanne but to treat *avant-garde* as a term with a history and a tradition, "the tradition of the new," in Rosenberg's phrase.

If one were to list the necessary conditions for an avant-garde art movement, one would begin by postulating the existence of a group. It could be an organized cadre issuing proclamations, as was the case with the Surrealists in Paris in the 1920s, or an informal clique of friends bound by elective affinities, as was true of the New York School of poets in the 1950s and early '60s. It will locate itself in an art capital: Paris in the first half of this century, New York in the postwar era. The artists must have a taste for adventure, and their art must in some sense be "advanced," new, innovative in its means and sometimes its ends. The movement will have a name, whether chosen by the artists themselves or imposed on them by a friendly or unfriendly observer. At its center will be a charismatic figure; on its periphery, somebody skillful at spreading the word. The movement must have an adversarial character. Conceived in opposition to the status quo, avant-garde art must be able to deliver a shock, though the shock value of any of its gestures will be only as great as the amount of resistance the artists must overcome. Historically, avant-garde movements have exhibited a strong sense of impatience for the future. As the Italian writer Umberto Saba put it, "The twentieth century seems to have one desire only, to get to the twenty-first as soon as possible."

Four distinct but related concepts are like tributaries feeding the larger currents of avant-garde art:

—The importance attached to the new, as in the years before the Great War, when Ezra Pound in London urged the modern poet to "make it new" and Guillaume Apollinaire in Paris hailed the "Spirit of the New," whose chief weapon, he wrote, is surprise. The disintegration of newness into novelty—as fame declines into celebrity—remains a constant danger. Rosenberg's phrase, the "tradition of the new," suggests another problem. Not only must avant-garde art define itself in relation to tradition; it is moreover always on the verge of becoming a tradition itself, with adherents and disciples and with the potential for ossification.

—The tremendous value placed on originality, which is not always the same thing as innovation. The prophet of artistic originality was Ralph Waldo Emerson. "Our age is retrospective," Emerson wrote in his essay "Nature." "It builds the sepulchres of the fathers. It writes biographies, histories, and criticism. The fore-going generations beheld God and nature face to face; we, through their eyes. Why should not we also enjoy an original relation to the universe? Why should not we have a poetry and philosophy of insight and not of tradition, and a religion by revelation to us, and not the history of theirs?" Emerson summed up an avant-garde precept when he warned in "Self-Reliance," his nonconformist tract, that "Imitation is suicide." The abstract turn in modern American painting was a rejection of imitation in a double sense: the rejection of mimesis (or the imitation of nature) as the goal of art, and the rejection of imitation in the sense Emerson intends here—imitation as copying or counterfeiting or patterning oneself after another. What the avant-garde artist wanted was what Emerson prescribed: an immediate relation to experience. This required the overthrow of the prevailing influences. Harold Bloom, the most Emersonian of literary critics, maintains that every truly original poet is in the position of the biblical Jacob wrestling overnight with the angel. The encounter leaves the patriarch with a limp but also with a new and blessed name, Israel.

—The idea that change is ameliorative, rapid change especially so, that destruction is essential for creation, and that the future is going to be an advance on the past. Hence the cult of the tabula rasa: the illusion of starting from scratch, which permits the artist to break rules and violate decorum, as if the art form itself had reached a supreme crisis and now had to be reinvented. The great antitext here is Ecclesiastes 1:9: "The thing that hath been, it is that which shall be; and that which is done is that which shall be done; and there is no new thing under the sun." Emerson in "Self-Reliance" has the answer: "Greatness appeals to the future," he wrote. "Power ceases in the instant of repose; it resides in the moment of transition from a past to a new state, in the shooting of the gulf, in the darting to an aim."

—The artist's adversarial instinct. "Avant-gardes are by nature combative," Harold Rosenberg wrote. The uneasy relation between artists and society is sometimes replicated in the relation between artists and their audience. The objective may be to shock the establishment, to shame it, to express outrage, or simply to exempt oneself from its strictures. By such measures, it may be argued, the avant-garde artist keeps the conscience of the time.

The odds are that a successful avant-garde movement will be as short-lived as it is rare. How could it be otherwise? Any would-be avant-garde enterprise faces three built-in contradictions. An avant-garde movement needs to embody an adversarial thrust, yet when politics is given dominance, the result is often fatal for art. It must be a collective movement, though acting collectively goes against the grain of that insubordinate individual, the modern artist. Finally, it must overcome resistance, but if it does so, it must also necessarily remove an enabling condition for its own existence. This is, after all, the historical pattern of avant-garde movements, which tend to decline in artistic vitality at the exact moment that they succeed as fashion statements, so that, as Renato Poggioli pointed out in his authoritative study, *The Theory of the Avant-Garde*, "the whole history of avant-garde art seems reducible to an uninterrupted series of fads."

The poet and anarchist Paul Goodman captured an aspect of the avant-garde ordeal. "As a style, *avant-garde* is an hypothesis that something is very wrong in society," Goodman wrote. However, "in a confused society, *avant-garde* does not flourish very well. What is done in order to be idiotic can easily be co-opted as the idiotic standard." The avant-garde artist seeks to make an event out of art, but an event when repeated tends not to shock the respectable but merely to amuse those in the know, who are also those in a position to indulge such amusements. "No work of art in our time is so extreme in the outrage it offers to society as to prevent its being given social canonization," Lionel Trilling wrote in 1973, summarizing an argument that Harold Rosenberg made at greater length in his book *The De-Definition of Art*. "Almost to the degree that art expresses its contempt of all that is established and official, it is sought and paid for—which is to say: taken into camp and deprived of its antagonistic force. The readiness of capitalist society to accept the art that avows its antagonism to capitalist society is therefore anything but the evidence of art's power; it is exactly the means by which art is made impotent. The expectation that art will supply the principle by which society can be redeemed is little more than a self-congratulatory fantasy. No redemption has occurred; all that has happened is that the highest achievement of the free subversive spirit has been co-opted to lend the color of spirituality to the capitalist enterprise."

The survival of *avant-garde* as a vague term of approbation confirms the suspicion that avant-garde art—the real embattled underground thing—has lost the force it formerly had in our cultural life. The avant-garde is dead, we're told, because there is no longer any significant resistance to artistic innovation.* Ev-

---

*Thus Michael Kimmelman, reviewing a pair of exhibitions in the *New York Times* (January 30, 1998): "Together, the shows neatly underscore just how anachronistic the idea of an avant-garde has become. Courbet needed Bouguereau, after

erything is instantly accepted, absorbed, glorified, bought, sold, copied, recycled, trashed. Such is the fate of artifacts in an age of mechanical reproduction and electronic transmission. The time-honored bohemian battle cry, "Shock the bourgeoisie," requires the existence of a middle-class capable of being shocked and shamed, but Court TV and supermarket tabloids have rendered that impossible. The old forms and formulas of the avant-garde are now in constant use but are often denuded of meaning or content; the effect is a species of parody, whether witting or inadvertent. The moustache on the Mona Lisa, once a superior *blague* (or jest), has turned into a ubiquitous cliché, and the sight of that famous head in curlers on postcards hawked in Greenwich Village will not raise an eyebrow. There is a degree to which success, especially early success or success attained without obstacles, must terminate the vanguard pretensions of any artist. It is all but inevitable. Janet Malcolm sums up "the common perception" in an article on David Salle, who made a fabulous amount of money as a thirty-something postmodernist painter in the 1980s. "The spectacle of young millionaires who made their bundle not from business or crime but from avant-garde art is particularly offensive," she writes. "The avant-garde is supposed to be the conscience of the culture, not its id."

How different from the conditions confronting the Abstract Expressionists fifty years ago. What they faced was open hostility, not indifference; ridicule, not grants from the government and major foundations; cafeteria meals and park benches, not champagne brunches and celebrity status. The abstract painters hanging out at such cafeterias as the Waldorf or Riker's, or in Washington Square Park, had every reason to suppose that public acceptance of their art was not a realistic possibility. While the

all, because there is no avant-garde without a rear guard, an academy to scandalize. Today everyone is simply on guard."

painters' ultimate success eased the way for the poets of the New York School, they, too, encountered heavy resistance—the critical response to the first published efforts of Ashbery and Koch bordered on outrage.

It was this resistance that made the idea of the avant-garde such a compelling one in the postwar era. The strength of the resistance, and the urgent need to overcome it, gave Abstract Expressionism both its impetus and its characteristic seriousness, which distinguished it so dramatically from the whimsicality of Pop Art, the movement that succeeded it as the art world's fashion statement in the 1960s. There is a world of difference—not only in degree of quality but in kind, in temper, and in aspiration—between Jackson Pollock's *Cathedral* (1947) and an Andy Warhol brand-name soap pad or soup can twenty years later. White-hot, the Pollock radiates the ferocity of defiance; laid-back, the Warhol is content to be a copy of a mass-produced copy, an icon of consumer culture. Pollock's is the art of refusal, Warhol's that of acceptance. Warhol coolly mimed the monuments of kitsch; Pollock fought them all the way.

Is, then, the avant-garde, with its dedication to the art of the future, a thing of the past, hopelessly obsolete in an era of postmodernist eclecticism and parody? Not necessarily, though it has a lot going against it. Once avant-garde has been identified publicly as a good and rewarding thing to be, there is no stopping the hordes from invoking the gods of vanguardism to justify their productions. In an application of Gresham's Law, the bad art committed in the name of the avant-garde will chase out the good. So it has happened. The fact that something advertises itself as avant-garde art is no guarantee that it is either art or avant-garde. In the best of times, the distinction between true artistic innovation on the one side and meretricious novelty on the other is difficult to discern and impossible to enforce. Today the task is complicated by the relentless hype that seems to accompany every new exhibition, with the effect that the intrepid gallery-goer is constantly on guard for fear of being had.

At such a moment, it is difficult to regard the term *avant-garde* as anything but an honorific, and a hollow one at that. The whole concept is therefore in bad odor, though that is subject to change—or to redefinition. I tend to Fairfield Porter's view that there will always be an avant-garde "if we define the avant-garde as those people with the most energy." Porter himself, a magnificent realist, who specialized in landscapes and still lifes and portraits at a time when pure abstraction was the height of fashion, illustrates that a contrarian impulse, a maverick strain of American independence, is a more valuable avant-garde quality than an ability to recognize and pursue the route of perceived correctness. The avant-garde artist, from this point of view, is the artist who is hidden among us, the exception. Avant-garde art has not disappeared; it has merely ducked into a subterranean cave and stayed there, waiting to be discovered. In the meanwhile, however, there is no denying the detrimental effect that indiscriminate acceptance can have on new art. The absence of cultural resistance gives rise to the seemingly unquenchable thirst for novelty, which leads in turn to Andy Warhol's conception of fame as an erasable interval lasting fifteen minutes. The Abstract Expressionists had a grander sense of fame and a loftier notion of time, and this is true of the New York School of poets as well.

The poets fulfilled the requirements of an avant-garde art movement without half trying. They were dedicated to the original and new, and implacably opposed to the poetry of the academy. But they did not confuse the new with the ephemeral. They never forgot that the aim of a poem was to live forever. They were interested in the eternal, as opposed to the merely permanent, to paraphrase an Ashbery poem. Nor did they blind themselves to the self-contradictions bedeviling their (or any) avant-garde movement as the 1960s neared their end. "Today one must fight acceptance which is much harder [than fighting neglect or hostility] because it seems that one is fighting oneself," Ashbery wrote in 1968. "If people like what I do, am I to assume that what I do is bad, since public opinion has always begun by rejecting what is original and new?" He found no easy way out of this dilemma, except to recommend "an attitude which neither accepts nor rejects acceptance but is independent of it." From now on it was, so far as he could see, every artist for himself or herself. Today's young artist, he wrote, "must now bear in mind that *he*, not *it*, is the avant-garde."

(II)

The idea of the avant-garde was invented by French utopian socialists in the aftermath of the French Revolution. In their vision of radical social progress, a forward-looking art was to serve the ideals of revolutionary politics as, in military terms, the soldiers in the vanguard of an army prepare the way for the invasion to follow. In 1825, Saint-Simon, the idealistic Count of French socialism, saw the arts "marching forcefully in the van" toward a better society. Three years before the 1848 revolution, a follower of the socialist visionary Charles Fourier reaffirmed the alliance of political and artistic radicalism: "Art, the expression of society, manifests, in its highest soaring, the most advanced social tendencies; it is the forerunner and the revealer." According to Renato Poggioli, this union of artistic and political radicals lasted until the 1880s when "what might be called the divorce of the two avant-gardes" took place. "What had up to then been a second-

David Lehman

ary, figurative meaning became instead the primary, in fact the only, meaning: the isolated image and the abbreviated term avant-garde became, without qualification, another synonym for the artistic avant-garde, while the political notion functioned almost solely as rhetoric and was no longer used exclusively by those faithful to the revolutionary and subversive ideal."

In the end, the definitive characteristic of the avant-garde artist in nineteenth century France was not his political commitment but his sense of social isolation—what everyone in the 1960s called alienation—and how this manifested itself in his work. Edouard Manet was the exemplar in painting with the haughty insolence of his nude *Olympia* and the bored barmaid amid the glitter of his *Bar at the Folies-Bergère* (1881–82). Charles Baudelaire embodied the type in poetry with the verse poems in *Les Fleurs du mal*, his "flowers of evil," and with the prose poems in the book he sometimes called *Spleen de Paris* and sometimes *Petits Poèmes en prose*. The prose poem, a rebellious form that has proved irresistible to avant-garde writers from Gertrude Stein and William Carlos Williams to the present, was invented by Baudelaire as the detective story was invented by Poe. In "The Stranger," the keynote poem in *Spleen de Paris*, Baudelaire depicts the alienated artist in the splendor of his despair. The poem's protagonist is an "enigmatic fellow" who has rejected family, religion, nation. He claims that he has no father, mother, sister, or brother, that *friend* is a word without meaning for him, and that he does not know where his country is located. He says he hates gold "as you hate God," though he is prepared to worship beauty as an immortal goddess. What does he love? "The clouds," he answers. "The clouds passing by . . . over there . . . over there . . . the marvelous clouds!" The clouds are fit objects for adulation because they are ethereal, fleeting, are constantly changing shape and hue, and are therefore symbols of the imagination—but also because of their remoteness from social concerns. The cloud-gazing artist could be a bohemian cellar-dweller or an aristocratic dandy like Manet; the ghetto and the ivory tower were twin sides of a single state of mind. In either locale, the artist had slipped outside the usual system of class differences and stood aloof, an outcast. Art was his declaration of independence—a way to complete his alienation (as a social fact) and transcend it at the same time (in art).

It began to be understood that a painting or a poem without explicit political content could make a radical gesture. The artist could transmute his adversarial impulses into a struggle with artistic tradition or with the formal limitations of his medium. From here it was a small step to the notion that freedom for an artist meant precisely freedom from politics. Baudelaire, whose prose poems advised the reader to "get drunk all the time" [*toujours être ivre*] and to "beat up beggars," condemned didacticism outright. He had witnessed the cataclysmic failure of the French Revolution of 1848 and now saw the danger and futility of subordinating art to politics. The aim of poetry, he wrote in 1857, the year of *Les Fleurs du mal*, is not to teach a lesson, to fortify conscience, to criticize social behavior, or even to demonstrate something that is useful. "No poem will be as great, as noble, so truly worthy of the name 'poem' as the one written for no purpose other than the pleasure of writing a poem." By midcentury, art for art's sake had become a more advanced position than art at the barricades.

The art historian Linda Nochlin has argued that if politics were decisive, Gustave Courbet's magnificent allegory *The Painter's Studio* (1855) would by rights make him the exemplary avant-garde painter. But if alienation were the key factor, it would (and does) make better sense to start with Manet, the urbane dandy. Nochlin calls Courbet's *Studio* "a pictorial paradigm of the most adventurous attitudes of its era." A huge composition, it is an allegory of social and artistic progress going hand in hand, with the artist in the center and the whole right side of the picture populated by fellow forward-thinkers. The little boy drawing in the foreground is the painter of the future learning by imitating the master, Courbet himself, in line with the advanced doctrine of the time regarding the educational development of children. Courbet, the master of realism, puts these allegorical ideas on a solid footing instead of leaving them up in the air of abstract formulations. The picture thus represents an advance in technique as well as in thought, though not in shock-delivering artistic innovation.

Manet, on the other hand, is the more advanced artist—if *advanced* implies originality, shock power, and adversarial force—though his work lacks an overt political aim. Like Courbet's *Studio*, Manet's *Déjeuner sur l'herbe* (1863) has a naked woman in it. But in the former the nude is the flesh-and-blood semblance of an allegorical ideal, Beauty or possibly Love; in the latter, she just *is. Déjeuner sur l'herbe*, in which two men in elegant evening clothes and the nude nonchalantly sit down to their picnic amid "the decor of Giorgione's venerated pastoral idyll," reveled in its incongruities. The picture was a deliberate affront to orthodox sensibilities and had a powerful effect on the first audiences to see it. It offended Napoleon III, who took steps to prevent future exhibitions. Nochlin calls it a "monumental and ironic put-on," a *blague* that "must have seemed as full of protest and constituted as destructive and vicious a gesture as that of Marcel Duchamp when he painted a mustache on the Mona Lisa."

The *blague* was the avant-garde gesture par excellence. It denoted a deadpan jest or prank with a thick layer of irony added: mockery mingled with self-mockery, doubt with defiance. The *blague*, writes the historian Noel Annan, was "the joke which threw doubt on everything, poisoned faith and murdered respect." It took the form of "the spoof, the lark, the snigger and the knowing smile, grotesque mirth and hilarious laughter," and its intent was to "send up reality." Baudelaire provided the critical rationale for the savage irony in modern art. "Laughter is Satanic, and is therefore profoundly human," he wrote. "It is in man the consequence of the idea of his own superiority; and, in truth, since laughter is essentially human it is essentially contradictory, that is to say, it is both the sign of infinite greatness and infinite wretchedness, infinite wretchedness in relation to the absolute Being of whom he possesses the conception, infinite greatness in relation to animals." The impulse to turn rage into outrage informs Baudelaire's prose poem "Le Mauvais vitrier" ("The Unfortunate Glazier") in which the hero has the spontaneous impulse to abuse a maker of window-glass, dropping a pot of flowers on his head and then shouting furiously at him: "Life is beautiful! Life is beautiful!" The poem blasphemously concludes, "What's an eternity of damnation to one who found in a moment an infinity of orgasmic pleasure [jouissance]?" Baudelaire's vented Spleen set a precedent for the bitter irony and black humor favored by avant-garde writers ever since.

In what could serve as a curious instance of a blague, or perhaps as an example of a deconstructive aporia, a self-contradictory proposition that leads you to the knot of indeterminacy, one of the points Linda Nochlin makes in "The Invention of the Avant-Garde: France, 1830–80" is subverted by the cover of the book in which her essay appears. Nochlin writes that Delacroix's Liberty Leading the People, in which Liberty personified as a bare-breasted woman holds a bayonet in one hand and waves the tricolor banner with the other, was supposedly an allegory of the revolutionary ideals of 1830. Looking at it, you would think it was an appeal to revolutionary fervor and the spirit of 1789. The woman embodying Liberty is youthful, vital, daring enough to expose her bosom. We see the French flag and we jump to the conclusion that Liberty is leading "the people." Yet, Nochlin writes, the picture was actually "conservative in both the political and the esthetic sense," nostalgically Bonapartist in its ideology and dependent on the iconography of Delacroix's neoclassical teacher, Guérin. Nevertheless a reproduction of that famous painting adorns the paperback edition of *Avant-Garde Art* (1968), in which Nochlin's essay is the lead piece. Whatever the fine points of her argument, those who judge a book by its cover—the majority of us—may come away with the distinct impression that Delacroix had been defiantly avant-garde and that *Liberty Leading the People* was a militant vision of revolution. And this irony, too, is in keeping with avant-garde practice, since the exact requirements of the avant-garde ideal have been fiercely contested, and the term itself has been in constant flux, and irony is the avant-garde order of the day.

Must avant-garde art manifest a radical aim? Does it require a collective identity? Is it the product of an "ideological community"? To each of these questions, Harold Rosenberg answered yes. He took stock of the avant-garde in the politically charged climate of 1968, the year Robert Kennedy and Martin Luther King, Jr., were assassinated, students seized five buildings at Columbia, and protesters had their heads bashed in at the Democratic National Convention in Chicago. "No matter how radical its effects, an action is not avant-garde without an ideology to characterize it," Rosenberg argued. Art that lacks "the will to change the world" is a "parody of vanguardism." Rosenberg conceded, however, that the radical will in a work of art may make itself felt in an almost purely aesthetic way. He could think of no better way to illustrate his "combative" position than with respect to the Fauves and their love of vibrant color in the early years of the twentieth century: "The politics of an avant-garde art movement might consist of nothing more rebellious than overthrowing the conviction of the middle class that color in a painting ought to correspond to that of appearances."

For Rosenberg, the term *avant-garde* conjured up the image

of an elite phalanx advancing on an enemy. For that stalwart champion of avant-garde causes, Richard Kostelanetz, the term evokes the image of shock troops on the front lines of cultural battle. But a more persuasive reading of the military metaphor buried in the term *avant-garde* casts the vanguard artist in the role of the spy on an advance reconnaissance mission, a foray into unknown territory. And the spy has always been a morally and politically ambiguous character, mistrustful of authority and prone to insubordination. So, too, the rebellious artist. Jealous of his independence, he may not want to heed the dictates of a cultural tsar. According to Rosenberg, art follows from ideology. History, however, seldom conforms to expectations based on "historical necessity" as revealed by an ideological crystal ball.

The dream of a political art has always been elusive, simply because art forms tend to obey their own imperatives and would be wise to rely on their own resources. Governments are fickle and political revolutions have unhappy endings. Although there are honorable exceptions, the melancholy truth is that political art is usually weak art to the extent that it subordinates its energy to the purpose of making an overt statement. Democratic ideals do not guarantee artistic originality. They don't even guarantee political wisdom. The dismal history of politicized avant-garde art movements stands as a warning. There was never anything to prevent a group of artists, even or especially vanguard artists, from hitching its wagon to the wrong star.

Italian Futurism, which celebrated speed and motion and modern machinery, glorified war ("our only hope, our justification for existence, our will," Marinetti wrote in 1912) at the catastrophic moment when Europe talked itself into World War I. In the twenties, the Futurists pinned their hopes on Fascism and Mussolini. On the other hand, when French Surrealism put itself in the service of the Marxist-Leninist revolution in 1930, disillusionment soon followed. Some Surrealists went down with the ship: Louis Aragon renounced the movement to join the Communist Party after André Breton criticized his "Front Rouge"—a screeching polemic written in Moscow—as "poetically regressive." But Surrealism achieved its revolutionary importance not because but in spite of such efforts to link artistic innovation to a political cause. The most fruitful Surrealist experiments involved methods of composition designed to liberate the unconscious, and the greatness of Surrealist works (the paintings of de Chirico, Miro, Ernst, and Magritte, the films of Buñuel, the writings of Raymond Roussel, and the prose collaborations of Breton and Eluard) has little to do with their politics but much with the way they assimilate chance, accident, humor, the anarchic id, and the irrational. As Charles Simic has put it, the Surrealists and Dadaists accomplished a revision of the poet from "a maker" to "someone able to detect the presence of poetry in the accidental."

Of the avant-garde revolution in poetry instigated by Ezra Pound and T. S. Eliot in the years of the Great War and just after, what lasted was the literary breakthrough, not the incidental political thrust of the two poets. Some would argue that Pound and Eliot, who brought modernism into American poetry, then turned around and arrested its development, by becoming an apologist for Mussolini in the case of Pound and a high-church monarchist in the case of Eliot. But what was truly avant-garde in their poetics had nothing to do with the politics they espoused. Eliot in *Prufrock and Other Observations* and Pound in *Personae* had accomplished a sort of surgical strike: They had removed the poetry from all that was merely decorative in the inherited tradition of Victorian verse. Pound and Eliot emancipated verse from a variety of outmoded exigencies; they insisted that poetry must be at least as well written as prose (as Pound put it) and that traditions were meant to be altered by the individual talent (as Eliot maintained). These were literary developments and they are to be judged for their artistic value, which was great, not their social consequence, which was minimal. This is not to excuse or deny Pound's treason or Eliot's anti-Semitism; nothing can condone these things. It is just to insist that the revolutionary gestures in their strongest work—Eliot's collagelike appropriation of the literary past in *The Waste Land*, for example—are not infected by the poisonous political virus that led the poet, on one occasion, to opine that "any large number of free-thinking Jews" was unhealthy for society. Indeed, what was most valuable in Eliot's poetry, from "The Love Song of J. Alfred Prufrock" (with its utter indifference to the Great War going on outside) through *The Waste Land*, was precisely that which resisted a political formulation: the speaker's ironic self-consciousness of "Prufrock," the juxtaposition of resonant fragments in *The Waste Land*.

In the same way, the European avant-garde in the first half of the century created a revolution in art, not politics. The Cubists shattered the object, the Expressionists tortured the model, and the masters of pure abstraction such as Mondrian pretty much discarded whatever was left of the principle of representation as the proper goal or function of painting. The abstract revolution hit New York hard in 1948 when Jackson Pollock produced the first of his "drip" paintings. *Number One* had no center, no perspectival depth, no illusion of mirror or window, but had such fierce energy and motion that it needed no subject other than itself. In the aftermath of *Number One*, all the rules of decorum came tumbling down. Henceforth a work of art needed to be less concerned with the task of communicating to others than with the expression of the artist's self. It didn't depict anything; it *was* something. No longer did the artist feel bound to give voice to a message, political or otherwise. Messages were irrelevant; the experience of art could not be paraphrased.

The abstract revolution was an admission that modern technology could more accurately reproduce nature than the artist can. In this sense, it was the camera that transformed the art of painting. But abstraction also signaled something else: a turning inward, a repudiation of nature, a disgust with the external world, including the social and political realms. "The artist must cultivate his own garden as the only secure field in the violence and uncertainties of our time," Meyer Schapiro wrote. "The poet must stand or fall by poetry," Wallace Stevens argued in a *Partisan Review* symposium in 1948. "In the conflict between the poet and the politician the chief honor the poet can hope for is that of remaining himself."

Politics had failed on both the left and the right. Under Stalin the Soviet experiment had regressed rapidly from tragic idealism to totalitarian terror. For its part, the American experiment in democracy had taken a wrong turn somewhere between the loyalty oaths of the Truman administration and the pieces of paper waved menacingly by Senator Joseph McCarthy. The artist's salvation lay neither in politics, by now decisively discredited, nor in religion, which had been edging toward obsolescence from the moment Nietzsche announced the death of God, but in art itself. And art stood in need of reinvention—it was ripe for the avant-garde gesture of erasure. Something drastic was needed to combat the complacent drift of the culture toward ersatz experience: a drift that has brought us, over the years, plastic flowers, vinyl siding, the institution of public relations, canned laughter, photo opportunities, and instant spin control.

It was Clement Greenberg who made the case for American avant-gardism. "Avant-Garde and Kitsch," Greenberg's first major essay, ran in the fall 1939 issue of *Partisan Review*. The critic had just turned thirty, but he'd already had the seminal experience of taking painting classes with Hans Hofmann. As Greenberg framed the terms, the avant-garde had to do battle with kitsch, or "ersatz culture," which was everywhere in America, where the "debased and academicized simulacra of genuine culture" were on sale. "Kitsch is vicarious experience and faked sensations," Greenberg wrote. "Kitsch is the epitome of all that is spurious in the life of our times. Kitsch pretends to demand nothing of its customers except their money—not even their time." The task of the avant-garde artist was to oppose this "rear-guard" action—"to find a path along which it would be possible to keep culture *moving* in the midst of ideological confusion and violence."

Greenberg identified the avant-garde artist as a painter, and necessarily an abstract painter, for the subject of an abstract painting is implicitly itself. This was a good thing, since it would help liberate art from the traditional task of slavishly reflecting the world of appearances. In the act of encompassing a world, the artist would have to renounce the world. Art itself would have to take the place of religion in our spiritual lives: "It has been in search of the absolute that the avant-garde has arrived at 'abstract' or 'nonobjective' art—and poetry, too. The avant-garde poet or artist tries in effect to imitate God by creating something valid solely on its own terms, in the way nature itself is valid, in the way a landscape—not its picture—is aesthetically valid; something *given*, increate, independent of meanings, similars or originals. Content is to be dissolved so completely into form that the work of art or literature cannot be reduced in whole or in part to anything not itself."

This barrage of pronouncements can be read as uncannily accurate prophecies—or as imperatives with prescriptive force, heeded by artists or disobeyed at their presumed peril. What Greenberg formulated is one of the fundamental paradoxes of Abstract Expressionism, which does away with subject matter, rejecting the idea that the artist must communicate something, yet proclaims the spiritual and even religious value of the statements it makes "on its own terms," as if it did have subject matter after all, only it happens to be invisible. The paradox enlivens the work of Mark Rothko, Adolph Gottlieb, and Barnett Newman, who issued statements insisting on the primacy of subject matter in their abstract paintings. In a sense they were rethinking the whole concept of subject matter; they also elevated the importance of titles and altered our understanding of the relation between the title and the work it names. Newman has a series of paintings called *Stations of the Cross*, though nothing that meets the eye would necessarily make a spectator think of Christ's ordeal.

The American avant-garde succeeded beyond Greenberg's wildest predictions—though it could not have done so without them. Greenberg, the Bronx-born son of Jewish Lithuanian immigrants, was not only a fearlessly opinionated critic but a highly persuasive rhetorician who made his boldest claims with blunt self-assurance. Between October 1947 and March 1948 he wrote a series of articles announcing the coming supremacy, the coming global supremacy, of American abstract painting. He aired his maverick views in highbrow journals of opinion, such as *The Nation* (whose art critic he was), *Partisan Review* (to which he contributed regularly), and the British *Horizon*. *Time* and *Life* rebuked him, but this worked to his advantage, since it had the effect of circulating his views to a much wider audience. Americans, he wrote in January 1948, were "the most advanced people on earth, if only because we are the most industrialized." And the best, the "most advanced" American painting was abstract—and was better of its kind than anything turned out in France or England.

Grasping the importance of the sea change taking place, Greenberg became part and parcel of the change. The future of Western art "depends on what is done in this country," he wrote, and the future of American art depended in turn on a small group of "advanced" artists. He was quite specific about the makeup of that small group: It consisted of Pollock and the sculptor David Smith—the only two American artists Greenberg considered major—and approximately "fifty people" who had studied painting with Hans Hofmann in New York City. They painted, these fifty, in Bohemian isolation, in cold-water flats on the upper floors of seedy walk-ups in Greenwich Village west of Seventh Avenue. They suffered from "the neurosis of alienation." The "ferocious struggle to be a genius" together with the "frantic scrabbling for money" made it difficult to get along with them. Their paintings went unsold and they were often broke, but they were serious, very serious, about art. And they possessed a capacity for "rigor and correctness" unmatched in Paris or London. In a word, they were the American avant-garde. They were eccentric, isolated, desperate individuals. "What," asked Greenberg plaintively, "can fifty do against a hundred and forty million?"

Quite a lot, evidently. In Greenberg's analysis, Cubism, the dominant European art movement, was in a state of irreversible decline. The disarray in Paris afforded an unmistakable opportunity for the American artist. What was more, the terrible "isolation" of the avant-garde artist in New York was a blessing in disguise, for isolation (wrote Greenberg) was "the truth"—"the natural condition of high art in America"—"the condition under which the true reality of our age is experienced." In degrees of isolation, America was miles ahead. "The alienation of Bohemia was only an anticipation in nineteenth-century Paris," Greenberg wrote. "It is in New York that it has been completely fulfilled." He wrote that in January 1948; by March he was willing to up the ante. "The main premises of Western art have at last migrated to the United States, along with the center of gravity of industrial production and political power."

Greenberg thought he was writing criticism. It turned out that he was writing history.

the last avant-garde

Summer in the trees!
"It is time to strangle several bad poets."

—KENNETH KOCH,
"FRESH AIR"

(I)

The Abstract Expressionists were the unquestionable leaders of the avant-garde. "Artists in any genre are of course drawn to the dominant art movement in the place where they live," Schuyler observed. "In New York," he added matter-of-factly, "it is painting." The painters were, as Koch put it, "the upper classes" of metropolitan bohemian life. Reading at the Painters' Club on Eighth Street and hanging out at the Cedar Tavern was "a way we baby poets got to be part of the grown-up tough-guy Abstract Expressionist world." It was easy to romanticize the generic life of the painter. "Painters had lives that were exciting," Koch said. "They painted in the daytime, so they got exercise, which put them in a good mood, and they had pleasant evenings. In an essay, Virgil Thomson depicts each artist as a different kind of citizen. The best citizens are the painters, because they work hard in the daytime." The poets went to the San Remo, O'Hara wrote, to "argue and gossip," while in the Cedar they "often wrote poems while listening to the painters argue and gossip. So far as I know nobody painted in the San Remo while they listened to the writers argue."

O'Hara saw the "powers and personality" of Abstract Expressionism clearly at work in the poems he and his friends were writing. Ashbery was less sure. He felt that the poets were linked to the painters mainly by proximity. But he conceded the larger point: that the painters exemplified the idea of the artist as an adventuresome nonconformist and thus set an inspiring precedent. The connections between the poets and the painters developed, Ashbery said at a symposium on poetry sponsored by the National Book Awards in 1968, "not entirely because we wanted to be 'influenced' by painting, as has been incorrectly stated, but because the artists liked us and bought us drinks and we, on the other hand, felt that they—and I am speaking of artists like de Kooning, Franz Kline, Motherwell, Pollock—were free to be free in their painting in a way that most people felt was impossible for poetry. So I think we learned a lot from them at that time, and also from composers like John Cage and Morton Feldman, but the lessons were merely an abstract truth—something like Be yourself—rather than a practical one—in other words, nobody ever thought he would scatter words over a page the way Pollock scattered his drips, but the reason for doing so might have been the same in both cases."

Disciplined nonconformism meant turning a deaf ear to the siren songs of politics. Just as the Abstract Expressionists liberated painting from the tyranny of subject matter, so the New York poets were intent on freeing their work from the burdens of a political consciousness. At a moment of intense global angst, when it sometimes seemed as if every responsible poem had to have a mushroom cloud in it, they felt that the pursuit of an artistic vocation imposed a different imperative. The artist's vocation required a struggle to attain "the state of spiritual clarity," O'Hara wrote in his monograph on Jackson Pollock. "Only when he is in this state is the artist's 'action' significant purely and simply of itself." It was in this sense that O'Hara's own work is the closest thing in poetry to Action Painting. O'Hara's cult of the artist is a Romantic notion taken to an extreme: the idea that the most crucial element in a poem is not the isolated text, nor its relation to either the world it describes or the reader it addresses, but rather the figure of the poet as creator, who has made a "monumental and agonizing" effort to achieve spiritual grace. The effort, and not the poem it yields, is what is "monumental." It is "not surprising," O'Hara wrote grandly, "that faced with universal destruction, as we are told, our art should at last speak with unimpeded force and unveiled honesty to a future which well may be nonexistent." Spiritual grace meant that one could embrace the material world and exempt oneself from the political world at the same time. The imagination was a transcendent realm in which one could dwell in moments of rare refreshment, whispers out of time.

When it isn't ignored in the work of the New York poets, politics is neutralized and transformed, as if it were one more crude element in the discourse of the tribe that needed to be captured in art and thus redeemed "with unimpeded force and unveiled honesty." The poets' collective attitude toward politics may be inferred from such a poem as Kenward Elmslie's "Melodramas" (1960), which is dedicated to Kenneth Koch. Notice how one of the angst-drenched symbols of the Cold War is rendered as part of the decor, a purely aesthetic experience, in this stanza:

> Mai Lung in the new communal kitchen
> With the black-hammer-striped-and-red-sickle-striped
> wallpaper

> Plunks down the evening cereal. "Winded from your annual
>   march to
> Protest the dirty sex practices of American priests, eat, o
>   old orphans!"

Politics has turned benignly into wallpaper. Or consider O'Hara's untitled poem beginning "Khrushchev is coming on the right day!" The poem is not about the bellicose Soviet leader famous for banging his shoe at the United Nations. In this example of O'Hara's diurnal style, Khrushchev has the weight of a name on the radio news on September 17, 1959; his imminent arrival in New York figures as one element in a collagelike composition whose other parts include blueberry blintzes, the comment of a Puerto Rican cab driver, a painting by O'Hara's friend Grace Hartigan, and the poetry of François Villon. The composition as a whole is meant to suggest an hour in the poet's crowded metropolitan life. The main theme of the poem sneaks in secretly in the poem's second line when "the cool graced light / is pushed off the enormous glass piers by hard wind / and everything is tossing, hurrying on up." Khrushchev returns at the poem's conclusion, but clearly the wind and the light of this September day have stolen the show: "New York seems blinding and my tie is blowing up the street / I wish it would blow off / though it is cold and somewhat warms my neck / as the train bears Khrushchev on to Pennsylvania Station / and the light seems to be eternal / and joy seems to be inexorable / I am foolish enough always to find it in wind."

In 1967, with the nation polarized by the escalation of the Vietnam war, a controversy broke out in *The Nation* between Ashbery and the combative Louis Simpson on the question of politics and poetry, and it is here that Ashbery gives the definitive statement of O'Hara's (and his own) position on politics. In the previous September Ashbery had eulogized the recently deceased

O'Hara in *Book Week*, then the Sunday book supplement of the *New York Herald Tribune*. Ashbery praised O'Hara as a go-your-own-way individualist unconcerned with whether or not his views were deemed correct by others. "Frank O'Hara's poetry has no program and therefore it cannot be joined," Ashbery wrote. "It does not advocate sex and dope as a panacea for the ills of modern society; it does not speak out against the war in Viet Nam or in favor of civil rights; it does not paint gothic vignettes of the post-atomic age; in a word, it does not attack the establishment. It merely ignores its right to exist, and is thus a source of annoyance to partisans of every stripe." Ashbery continued: "It is not surprising that critics have found him self-indulgent: his *culte de moi* is overpowering; the poems are all about him and the people and images who wheel through his consciousness, and they seek no further justification: 'This is me and I'm poetry, baby,' seems to be their message, and unlike the message of committed poetry, it incites one to all the programs of commitment as well as to every other form of self-realization: interpersonal, dionysian, occult or abstract."

Louis Simpson waited until the following April to take Ashbery to task for these sentiments. Simpson is a poet and critic with a fierce sense of moral rectitude, and he was writing at a time when the great example held up to American poets for emulation was that of the conscience-stricken Robert Lowell. Because of his opposition to the war in Vietnam, Lowell had turned down an invitation to accept a medal from President Lyndon Johnson at the White House in 1965. "We are in danger of imperceptibly becoming an explosive and suddenly chauvinistic nation, and may even be drifting in our way to the last nuclear ruin," Lowell wrote. Lowell's letter to President Johnson, duly printed on the front page of the *New York Times*, made him a hero of the literary wing of the antiwar movement. In 1967 *Time* put him on its cover, and Norman Mailer, marching beside him at a major rally at the

Pentagon, gave him an honored place in his Pulitzer Prize—winning account of the event, *The Armies of the Night*. Lowell represented, in short, the ideal of the poet as a public figure, politically enlightened, passionately serious, and always aware of his role in History. Lowell has sometimes "had a bad press for silly reasons" and sometimes a good press "for reasons scarcely less silly," Josephine Jacobsen observed in 1964. "At the moment, it would appear that he can scarcely do wrong."

In this climate, Ashbery's defense of antiprogrammatic poetry was heresy. Ashbery, Simpson wrote in *The Nation*, had "complimented [O'Hara] on not having written poetry about the war. This struck me as a new concept of merit—praising a man for things he has not written. But it is not amusing to see a poet sneering at the conscience of others." Ashbery fired off a letter to the editor in response. "I was not 'sneering at the conscience of other poets,' but praising Frank O'Hara for giving a unique voice to his own conscience, far more effective than most of the protest 'poetry' being written today," he wrote. "All poetry is against war and in favor of life, or else it isn't poetry, and it stops being poetry when it is forced into the mold of a particular program. Poetry is poetry. Protest is protest." This is an argument that we might test with inconclusive results. Is *The Iliad* an example of poetry that is "against war and in favor of life"? Possibly. Are all protest poems nonpoetry, or are we free to exempt such poets as Pablo Neruda and Bertolt Brecht from this charge? Ashbery is unlikely to be a hard-liner on this point. After all, for him and for the New York School collectively any establishment has the right to exist and they have the right to ignore it. As Ashbery wrote in 1968, when Yippie demonstrators outside the Museum of Modern Art punctuated the opening of a Dada and Surrealist show, "while it is perfectly OK to heckle the swells descending from their rainy taxis to sip MOMA champagne from fur-lined teacups, it is also OK to be them."

Ashbery has spoken of his own low morale in the early 1950s and cited political factors, such as the Korean War and "the loyalty-oath mentality," as he called it. It was, he told Harry Mathews, "sort of a low point in America." He has told me more than once that the only time in his life that he ever suffered from writer's block was in 1950 and 1951 and that in his mind it was connected with the politics of intimidation in Washington. When Ashbery wrote to *The Nation* to rebut Louis Simpson in 1967, he took the time to make it clear that he had in fact participated in antiwar protests. But the absence of any overt political intent in Ashbery's poetry is conspicuous. He has a poem entitled "The One Thing That Can Save America" (1975), which doesn't divulge the answer to the query implicit in the title but compounds it with other questions ("Is anything central?") having to do with civic pride and public lives. "These are connected to my version of America / But the juice is elsewhere," Ashbery writes. He acknowledges the private nature of his poetry: "I know that I braid too much my own / Snapped off perceptions of things as they come to me. / They are private and always will be." But this concession to an invisible debating partner turns into another question: What about the possibility that the poet's private experience may make him exemplary? The last stanza of the poem is a brilliant example of what Ashbery elsewhere calls "fence-sitting raised to an esthetic ideal." A poem that is nominally about the private self in the public sphere concludes in the wait for a letter that never comes, warning of danger:

> It is the lumps and trials
> That tell us whether we shall be known
> And whether our fate can be exemplary, like a star.
> All the rest is waiting
> For a letter that never arrives,
> Day after day, the exasperation

Until finally you have ripped it open not knowing what it is,
The two envelope halves lying on a plate.

This is a prophetic poem—and, in some attenuated sense, a political one. But it is far from political in the sense intended by poets such as Bertolt Brecht and Adrienne Rich who believe that poetry should protest injustice.

I am familiar with the argument that Ashbery is politically radical on the deep syntactical level—the level of form, which precedes content. The wildly experimental poems in *The Tennis Court Oath*, written and assembled in the city where the guillotine dispensed Jacobin justice, could be described as revolutionary and apolitical at once. The book's title refers to a signal event in the French Revolution. On a handball court in Versailles, rebellious members of the Third Estate convened to take their revolutionary pledge on June 20, 1789. Three weeks later the Bastille was stormed, and the revolution was on. But if Ashbery's title announces a connection to the world historical events of 1789, one looks in vain for any reference to political upheaval in the pages themselves. The book's revolutionary gestures are entirely in the realm of form—Ashbery does to conventional syntax what Robespierre did to the monarchy. Here is an excerpt from the title poem:

> the water beetle head
> why of course reflecting all
> then you redid you were breathing
> I thought going down to mail this
> of the kettle you jabbered as easily in the yard
> you come through but
> are incomparable the lovely tent
> mystery you don't want surrounded the real
> you dance
> in the spring there was clouds

The odd excitement in these lines would be lost in a more conventional, less truncated telling. All semblance of a narrative has been eliminated but some ghostly idea of a narrative hovers; the drama rests in the interruptions and the leaps. Perhaps part of the point is that "The Tennis Court Oath," that phrase familiar to legions of high school history students, is founded on a mistranslation of the French *jeu de paume*, literally "game of palm," which refers not to tennis but to handball. Ashbery's appropriation of the phrase can be seen as furthering the linguistic processes whereby meaning disintegrates. But it can also be seen as Ashbery's disloyalty oath: a violent rebellion against the rules of language itself.

There are those who contend that Ashbery's poetry in the years since *The Tennis Court Oath* has continued to mount an assault on what poststructuralist critics call the hegemonic discourse. Perhaps it does. Ashbery's irony, his belief that misunderstandings are inevitable and his further belief in the power of misunderstanding as another name for the transformative work of creative intelligence—these are central to his poetry. And his jubilant use of clichés, as in these lines from "Getting Back In" (1995), argues a skepticism that is just short of subversive:

What is this "today" you speak of so incessantly?

It's where the rubber meets the road and they discuss
in one long fawning kiss. It's the posse's
new poster child. It's . . . My system was downloaded
but bogus retorts are still coming out of it.
It's pleasures and palaces. A commitment.

But the question is whether these are fundamentally political gestures or whether it wouldn't be wiser to take Ashbery at his word when he maintains that poetry and protest are in two separate categories and that the former is life itself for him while the latter is an occasional extraliterary duty. At a question-and-answer session at the University of Iowa's Writers' Workshop in the fall of 1996, an enterprising graduate student asked the poet to describe the theoretical political dimensions of his poetry. "Well," Ashbery replied, "I'm a Democrat."

The poet Stephen Paul Miller has advanced the delightfully flaky thesis that Ashbery's "Self-Portrait in a Convex Mirror" has a covert political agenda. The poem, he argues, is allegorically about the Watergate scandal. Making much of the fact that "Self-Portrait" initially appeared in *Poetry* in August 1974, the month President Nixon resigned from office, Miller contends that the correspondences between "the Nixon White House and Ashbery's poetic creation of self-containment" are "as rife as they are obvious," which will come as a surprise to most readers, who think the poem is the record of a romantic vision, a soulful meditation on Parmigianino's *Self-Portrait in a Convex Mirror*, without topical reference or political intent. Miller urges an identification of the disgraced president with the painter of the self-portrait that Ashbery evokes in his most famous poem. "Richard Nixon, like Parmigianino, bugged himself in an 'Oval Office,'" Miller writes. The analogy is so inventive that I feel like applauding, though I am duty-bound to observe that Ashbery's poem never mentions or adverts in any way to Watergate or Richard Nixon, and that the allegory Miller spins out could not have been part of Ashbery's intent, since he wrote the poem before anyone learned that Nixon had "bugged himself."

In "Self-Portrait in a Convex Mirror," Ashbery turns an exercise in art criticism into so profound a meditation on Art and Time that it transcends its source. "As Parmigianino did it, the right hand / Bigger than the head, thrust at the viewer / And swerving easily away, as though to protect / What it advertises," Ashbery's poem begins. As the poet ponders the effects of the

convex mirror's distortion of the painter's face and hand held up
to it, it becomes clear that he is writing about all art, his own at
any rate, and that his face has gradually replaced Parmigianino's
in the poem-picture he has held up to examine. The picture suggests that Parmigianino is left-handed, as Ashbery is, but there
is a more urgent point of identification between the twentieth-
century American poet and the sixteenth-century Italian mannerist painter. In Ashbery's poetry, too, the hand is metaphorically bigger than the head, "as though to protect what it
advertises." The hand thrust out at the viewer is either "shield or
greeting," or perhaps it is both in one, "the shield of a greeting,"
a serene gesture "which is neither embrace nor warning / But
which holds something of both in pure / Affirmation that doesn't
affirm anything." Ashbery's poem is rich in metaphorical translations of the pose in Parmigianino's *Self-Portrait*:

> Francesco, your hand is big enough
> To wreck the sphere, and too big,
> One would think, to weave delicate meshes
> That only argue its further detention.
> (Big, but not coarse, merely on another scale,
> Like a dozing whale on the sea bottom
> In relation to the tiny, self-important ship
> On the surface.)

When the poet remarks at one point that we—he and his readers
or he and Parmigianino—"have been given no help whatever / In
decoding our own man-size quotient and must rely / On second-
hand knowledge," the *hand* in that phrase vibrates with meaning,
like the sound of one hand clapping.

The beguilingly ironic gestures in Ashbery's poetry—the
self-contradictions, blind alleys, and false scents—enable him to
include the world without necessarily endorsing it. He can find

serenity in situations of maximum uncertainty, as these lines
from his poem "Decoy" suggest:

> There is every reason to rejoice with those self-styled
>> prophets of commercial disaster,
>> those harbingers of gloom,
> Over the imminent lateness of the denouement that,
>> advancing slowly, never arrives.

Where the prefabricated discourse of the day would have termi-
nated this utterance with "the lateness of the hour," Ashbery substitutes his dramatic sense of time's paradox: Poised between the
past and the future, the present, our present, is "the denouement
that, advancing slowly, never arrives." The effect of such a remarkable rhetorical gesture—and Ashbery's poetry is loaded with
them—is that of a sudden jolt or rapid dip in an amusement
park ride. Though not at all autobiographical in the ordinary
sense, Ashbery's poems are like "epistemological snapshots" (his
phrase) of a mind capable of emptying itself out to the point that
it becomes a speculative mirror reflecting and distorting the rush
of external phenomena. As he points out in "Self-Portrait in a
Convex Mirror," the words *speculation* and *mirror* are etymologi-
cally linked in the Latin word *speculum*. All mirrors distort; all
art is speculative. The shadow of cities hangs over Ashbery's
poem: Rome, where Parmigianino "was at work during the Sack";
Vienna, where Ashbery saw the painting "with Pierre in the summer of 1959"; and New York, "where I am now, which is a
logarithm / Of other cities." Yet in the end when we "have seen
the city," we know it to be yet another convex glass: "the
gibbous / Mirrored eye of an insect."

Ashbery's own account of the origin of "Self-Portrait in a
Convex Mirror" is a little like Coleridge's account of the composition of "Kubla Khan"—an almost mystical experience having ev-

erything to do with the private life of the writer and nothing with events in the public world. "I was spending a winter in Provincetown, without much to do, not feeling very inspired because I was away from home, where I do most of my writing (wherever home at the time happens to be)," Ashbery told an interviewer. "I came upon a little bookstore on a narrow back street, and a book of reproductions with Parmigianino's *Self-Portrait in a Convex Mirror* on it was in the window. I went in and bought the book and kept it around a while and began writing about the painting. I felt at a very low level of inspiration then, and was inclined not to finish it. But I did later, when I got home. The funny thing is, when I went to find that bookstore, it had completely disappeared. There was no trace of its ever having been there. It was like De Quincey looking in vain for the store where he first bought opium. Being kind of susceptible to all kinds of mystical, superstitious ideas, I felt that this bookstore had just materialized for a few moments to allow me to buy this book, and then vanished."

Ashbery is a visionary poet in the sense that he can transport himself into a transcendent realm of the imagination, like Coleridge building his stately pleasure-dome in air or Keats communing with his nightingale. Bereft but stoic at the inevitable moment when his "waking dream" departs, the poet knows that his poem will when it is completed be lodged, together with Parmigianino's painting, in the museum of the past. By then Ashbery himself will have joined the public "pushing through the museum now so as to / Be out by closing time. You can't live there." You can't live in a work of art any more than you can inhabit the past. Yet the poet knows his visionary experience "was real, though troubled, and the ache / Of this waking dream can never drown out / The diagram still sketched on the wind, / Chosen, meant for me and materialized / In the disguising radiance of my room." Just as the little bookstore in Provincetown had "materialized for a few moments to allow me to buy this book, and then vanished," so too the "diagram still sketched on the wind"—the living hand in Parmigianino's painting and Ashbery's poem.

(II)

It is a paradox worth savoring that the painters closest in mood and temperament to the New York poets were not the makers of the abstract revolution but such "second generation" figures as Larry Rivers, Jane Freilicher, and Fairfield Porter, not one of them an abstract artist. To understand how the New York School of poets assimilated the influence of their painterly namesakes, we might linger for a moment over the differing ways in which a Rivers or a Porter responded to the avant-garde imperatives of the day. The example of Rivers was particularly crucial for O'Hara and Koch. Porter's example had a corresponding importance for Schuyler and Ashbery.

Born Yitzroch Grossberg in the Bronx, Rivers was an uninhibited, grass-smoking, sex-obsessed jazz saxophonist in his early twenties when he took up painting in 1945. His Bonnard-inspired early works made Clement Greenberg sit up and take notice. Though he would later modify his praise and then withdraw it altogether, Greenberg declared in 1949 that Rivers was already "a better composer of pictures than was Bonnard himself in many instances"—and this on the basis of Rivers's first one-man show. Rivers—who can, as I write this, still be heard playing the saxophone at the Knickerbocker Bar in New York City some Sunday nights—always retained the improvisatory ideal of jazz. The make-it-up-as-you-go-along approach is evident in even his

most monumental constructions—such as *The History of the Russian Revolution* (1965) in Washington's Hirshhorn Museum—
which have a fresh air of spontaneity about them, as if they had
just been assembled a few minutes ago.

Rivers relied on "charcoal drawing and rag wiping" for the
deliberately unfinished look of his pictures. Also distinctive was
his prankish sense of humor. In 1964 he painted a spoof of
Jacques-Louis David's famous *Napoleon in His Study* (1812), the
portrait of the emperor in the classic hand-in-jacket pose. Rivers's version, full of smudges and erasures, manages to be icono-
clastic and idolatrous at once. The finishing touch is the
painting's title: Rivers called it *The Greatest Homosexual*. A visitor
to Rivers's Fourteenth Street studio in 1994, seeing a picture on
the wall with the Napoleon motif in it, asked him why he had
given the original painting its unusual title. "In those days I was
carrying on with people in the gay bathhouse world," Rivers said.
"Napoleon's pose was like, 'Get *her!*' Also, it was a kind of joke,
since the art world at the time was primarily homosexual. And I
had just read that Napoleon was a little peculiar. In St. Helena he
used to be surrounded by an entourage of officers and he would
take a bath in front of them, nude."

There is a strand of Rivers's work that can only be understood if you take into account the homosexual aestheticism that
he found embodied in the poems and person of O'Hara. In the
early 1950s, "queerdom was a country in which there was more
fun," Rivers has said. "There was something about homosexuality
that seemed too much, too gorgeous, too ripe. I later came to
realize that there was something marvelous about it because it
seemed to be pushing everything to its fullest point."

If one condition of avant-garde art is that it is ahead of its
time, and another is that it proceeds from a maverick impulse
and a contrary disposition, Rivers's vanguard status was assured
from the moment when, in open apostasy, he audaciously made

representational paintings, glorifying nostalgia and sentiment while undercutting them with metropolitan irony. His paintings of brand labels, found objects, and pop icons—Camel cigarettes, Dutch Masters cigars, the menu at the Cedar Tavern in 1959, a French hundred-franc note—preceded Pop Art but eluded the limitations of that movement. And his pastiches of famous paintings of the past—such as his irreverent rendition of Emmanuel Leutze's *Washington Crossing the Delaware* (1953)—anticipated the breezy ironies of postmodernism without forfeiting the painterly touches of Abstract Expressionism. The painting, Rivers told O'Hara, "was just a way for me to stick my thumb out at other people. I suddenly carved a little corner for myself. Luckily for me I didn't give a crap about what was going on at the time in New York painting. In fact, I was energetic and egomaniacal and, what is even more important, cocky and angry enough to want to do something that no one in the New York art world could doubt was *disgusting, dead,* and *absurd.* So, what could be dopier than a painting dedicated to a national cliché?"

Rivers denied that his *Washington Crossing the Delaware* was specifically a parody of Emmanuel Leutze's painting at the Metropolitan Museum of Art. He maintained that his true inspiration derived from the patriotic grade school plays he had acted in or watched as a boy. This explanation made the picture no less heretical in an art world that had given up on representation and was bound to consider a patriotic theme as either hopelessly corny or retrograde. But for Rivers's poet friends, the painting—which the Museum of Modern Art purchased in 1955—was an electric charge. Kenneth Koch wrote a play, *George Washington Crossing the Delaware,* in which the father of our country is glorified with ironic hyperbole. And Frank O'Hara, in his poem "On Seeing Larry Rivers's *Washington Crossing the Delaware* at the Museum of Modern Art," used the opportunity to state a "revolutionary" credo:

> To be more revolutionary than a nun
> is our desire, to be secular and intimate
> as, when sighting a redcoat, you smile
> and pull the trigger.

It is conceivable that the "redcoat" O'Hara envisioned here was a coat of red paint. The gun in Rivers's hands, or in his own, held the promise of freedom from dogma or domination:

> Don't shoot until, the white of freedom glinting
> on your gun barrel, you see the general fear.

Rivers's work seems continuous with the spirit of O'Hara and Koch. "Someone who didn't like me could say, 'Sure, all you have to do is show him Larry Rivers or the sea, and out comes a poem,' " O'Hara wrote to Rivers in 1953. "But really, I don't see why one shouldn't enjoy something in life if one can stand not enjoying so much else." The admiration went both ways. "Kenneth, read the next sentence with your glasses off," Rivers wrote to Koch that same year. "No matter how you digress from the inner circles of affection and thoughts of being loved I think your poetry is marvelous. Whenever I work myself into a boil over the earth of your inspiration thinking that perhaps it lies in a different continent and is foreign all I need to do besides picking up one of your delights is think about the mud and hot air being pushed into the stream of Art and I'm glad you are alive and at it. Remember this for there must come a day when our collective madness will separate us."

In 1967 and again in 1968 Rivers went to Nigeria to work on a film with Pierre Gaisseau, the French filmmaker who had won an Academy Award six years earlier for his documentary about New Guinea, *The Sky Above, The Mud Below*. The two men were arrested and jailed several times. In Africa, however, "that's nothing," Rivers said. "It's like going to the grocery store." Then Rivers and Gaisseau ran into a Nigerian army major convinced that they were mercenaries paid to intervene in Nigeria's civil war. The major gave orders to have the two men shot, and three soldiers led them out of a Benin hotel with their hands raised. "I knew we shouldn't have come," Rivers said as if on cue. The men's lives were spared when Gaisseau succeeded in drawing the enraged (and probably intoxicated) major into a conversation in which they happily reminisced about their favorite Paris cafés. Recalling the episode later, Rivers was not sure whether it more nearly resembled a spy story or "a farce by Kenneth Koch."

In "Larry Rivers Paints a Picture," Fairfield Porter watched as Rivers painted his mother-in-law in May 1953. "Art gives him psychological power," Porter wrote. "It serves as a way of finding those distinctions that appear to be the true ones in the search for his life. His self-control stems from conscious spontaneity and constant awareness." Unlike Rivers, Porter did not actively seek out experience or "search for his life." On the contrary, he felt that all experience was valid and that "even the most ordinary things are quite as full of significance as the most dramatic." But he shared with Rivers and Jane Freilicher the desire to absorb the technical lessons of the abstract revolution without renouncing figuration. It is perhaps in the light of this shared aim that one can best understand Porter's cryptic remark that "the important thing for critics to remember is the 'subject matter' in abstract painting and the abstraction in representational work." That is, the important thing for critics to consider is the way in which certain abstract principles condition a Rivers pastiche, a Freilicher landscape, or a Porter view of the harbor at Great Spruce Head Island.

With quiet tenacity Porter revitalized figurative painting as a legitimate—and modern—enterprise in the teeth of the pressure (and it was fierce) to regard it as outmoded and passé. Nor did

Porter paint in ignorance of contemporary trends. On the contrary, the record he left as an art critic for *Art News* in the 1950s and *The Nation* in the 1960s shows him to be one of the most astute—and sympathetic—observers of the period. He immersed himself in the new art and found in Willem de Kooning, in particular, a master whose lessons he would endeavor to apply in his own works; he wrote penetratingly on de Kooning and became good friends of the painter and his wife Elaine. But for all his exposure to Mark Rothko's rectangles ("A whole Mondrian equals the sum of its parts, but a whole Rothko is greater than the sum of its parts," Porter wrote) and Robert Motherwell's abstract "formalities" (which can "make mess into an organism"), Porter's whole painterly career affirmed an old-fashioned mimetic ideal: the idea of depicting things as they are, not as we might will them to be; the idea that reality resides neither in Platonic forms nor in the dark recesses of the artist's unconscious but in the actual way things appear to an attentive observer.

Porter was born on an unseasonably cold June day in Winnetka, just north of Chicago, in 1907. "It was snowing on the day I was born and I've had a cold ever since," he liked to say. The Porter family came from patrician origins; T. S. Eliot was a distant relation. Fairfield, the fourth of five children, studied art history at Harvard (class of '28) and at the Art Students League, where he took instruction from Thomas Hart Benton. He visited Russia in 1927, his junior year at Harvard, and took leftist politics to heart. But he grew disenchanted with the Soviet experiment, and his letters from the 1930s chronicle a continual quarrel with Marxism. In 1931 he went to Italy, where he met Bernard Berenson. The paintings of the Italian Renaissance proved to be a more durable source of inspiration than socialist politics for the young painter. A substantial family trust supported Porter in an apprenticeship in painting that lasted twenty years.

In 1932 Porter married Anne Channing, whom he had met

at Harvard, and the couple settled in New York City. They would have five children. John, the first of their sons, was born with a serious mental illness, and it is possible that Porter's slow development as a painter was attributable to his preoccupation with the boy's malaise. "No psychiatrists or doctors seemed to know anything definite about him, and the result on me was that I really did nothing for about the first ten years of his life but try to somehow help him," Porter wrote in 1958. "This was a most frustrating experience, because I was trying to solve something for which there was no solution." Only after sending John to a foster home in Vermont did Porter feel he could have a career of his own. "It wasn't until after the war that I could concentrate on painting, that means paint without thinking of my supposed failure as a father in this one case."

A late bloomer, Porter developed his distinctive style of realism in the last twenty-five years of his life, a period coinciding exactly with the triumph of Abstract Expressionism. Content with conventional brush and easel at a time when Pollock was dripping his paint from the can onto a massive canvas stretched on the floor, Porter specialized in landscapes, still lifes, interiors, and portraits. He painted what he saw in a life lived with a large family and constant houseguests in Southampton, Long Island (where the Porters moved in 1949, before the Hamptons became posh) and in their summer home in Great Spruce Head Island in Maine. In a Porter still life, you may have a bouquet of flowers at the center, but you also have the artist's daughter and the remnants of breakfast on the table, the plates in the disarray in which they were left, and a copy of Wallace Stevens's *Collected Poems* beside the sugar bowl and a jar of jam. In such a work as *Lizzie at the Table* (1958) nothing has been arranged. Porter felt that the artist who imposes his own order on things kills the life of the painting. "Often in still lifes—almost always in still lifes—I don't arrange them," he commented. "Usually it's just that the way the dishes are on the table at the end of the meal strikes me suddenly. And so I paint it. Part of my idea or my feeling about form that's interesting is that it is discovered—that it's the effect of something unconscious like, you know, the dishes are in a certain arrangement at the end of a meal because people without thinking have moved things and then have gone away. And I think it's impossible not to get some sort of form if you don't think about it. If you do think about it you can get chaos. But if you don't think about it you get form."

An opinionated and impulsive man, Porter fired off letters to magazine editors with the gusto of an autodidact. He dissented from Clement Greenberg's major pronouncements in *Partisan Review* in 1940 and again fifteen years later. What he particularly objected to in Greenberg's criticism was its heavy emphasis on historical reasoning: Greenberg argued for the new art on the basis of its historical inevitability. The logic of Greenberg's position obliged him to claim, in Porter's words, that "it was impossible to paint the figure any more," since "it had already been so thoroughly done that nothing new could be added—an important consideration to a critic allied to the principle of social progress."

Porter saw the dangers of a position that would subordinate aesthetics to art history and would confuse the descriptive role of the critic with the prognosticative role of a dictator or seer. "To say that you cannot paint the figure today, is like an architectural critic saying that you must not use ornament, or as if a literary critic proscribed reminiscence," Porter wrote in 1962. "In each case the critical remark is less descriptive of what is going on than it is a call for a following—a slogan demanding allegiance. In this case criticism is so much influenced by politics that it imitates the technique of a totalitarian party on the way to power."

Through his friendship with Rivers and Freilicher, Porter

met Ashbery, Koch, O'Hara, and Schuyler, and became a cherished member of their set. For the pages of *Art News*, Porter wrote "Larry Rivers Paints a Picture" and "Jane Freilicher Paints a Picture," and O'Hara reciprocated with "Fairfield Porter Paints a Picture." Porter also put his friends into his paintings. His 1951 portrait *Larry Rivers*, his double portrait of Schuyler and Ashbery (*Jimmy and John*, 1957–1958), his 1967 picture of Freilicher with her daughter Elizabeth (*Jane and Elizabeth*), and his rendering the same year of *John Ashbery and James Schuyler Writing "A Nest of Ninnies"* are particularly fine.

Perhaps inevitably Porter took to writing poems and often attached his latest efforts to letters sent to friends. He learned the rules of the sestina from Kenneth Koch, and this became his favorite form; he and Koch even corresponded in sestinas for several years. Some of these are charming. In a sestina that Koch and Porter wrote collaboratively, the end-words include *Jimmy*, *John*, and *Frank*. But my favorite Porter poem is "I Wonder What They Think of My Verses":

> If Jimmy likes them, I believe him
> Because Jimmy is kind
> And he does not pretend
> If Larry dislikes them, I do not believe him
> Because his ambition distracts him
> If John dislikes them, I believe him
> Because he is lazy and quick
> If Frank likes them or dislikes them, I do not believe him
> Because Frank is considerate
> And he is led by his imagination
> Far beyond the ability to forgive
> If Jane likes them, I believe her
> Because her feelings guide her
> And if Anne is critical I believe her

Because she desires my credit
If Rudy is impressed
It is because he did not know I had it in me
If Walter dislikes them
He does so to prove his affection
If Edwin understands them
It is to reciprocate my trust
And Kenneth is pedantic
And filial and fatherly
But Jerry is contemptuous and sarcastic
Because he wants me to love him
And Laurence admires them
Because he wants to admire his father

The poem names, in order, Jimmy Schuyler, Larry Rivers, John Ashbery, Frank O'Hara, Jane Freilicher, Anne Porter, the photographer Rudy Burckhardt, the photographer Walter Auerbach, the dance critic and poet Edwin Denby, Kenneth Koch, and two of Porter's sons, Jerry and Laurence.

Porter proved himself to be an able polemicist in favor of the poetry his friends were writing. Ashbery's first book, *Some Trees*, baffled many readers in 1956. William Arrowsmith aired his misgivings in the pages of the *Hudson Review*. "I have no idea most of the time what Mr. Ashbery is talking about or being, beyond the communication of an intolerable vagueness that looks as if it was meant for precision," Arrowsmith complained. "What does come through is an impression of an impossibly fractured brittle private world, depersonalized and discontinuous, whose characteristic emotional gesture is an effete and cerebral whimsy." Porter defended Ashbery at length. "In Ashbery's poetry there is a kind of music new to poetry," he argued. "Ashbery's verbal phrases are to me ideas in the way that musical phrases may be so considered."

In 1961 Porter's essay, "Poets and Painters in Collaboration," was the first serious critical effort to come to terms with the New York School of poetry. Characteristically Porter considered the four poets less as a unified movement than as a quartet of highly distinctive individuals. He was especially eloquent in putting the case for Ashbery, who of all the poets came the nearest in his verbal practice to the methods of Abstract Expressionism. "Ashbery's language is opaque; you cannot see through it any more than you can look through a fresco," Porter observed. "And as the most interesting thing about abstract painting is its subject matter, so one is held by the sibylline clarity of Ashbery's simple sentences." Porter was moved to an epiphany: Ashbery, he wrote in a lovely sentence, "has retained the clear but incommunicable knowledge of the child who was surrounded by heaven in his infancy, when a sense of wonder precluded judgment." It is a sentence that Ashbery himself would echo in an essay he wrote for *Art News* in 1967 on the constructions and collages of Joseph Cornell. "The genius of Cornell," he wrote, "is that he sees and enables us to see with the eyes of childhood, before our vision got clouded by experience, when objects like a rubber ball or a pocket mirror seemed charged with meaning, and a marble rolling across a wooden floor could be as portentous as a passing comet." What these sentences have in common—indeed, what confirms Porter and Ashbery as kindred spirits—is a radical innocence whose most sublime expression may be found in Thomas Traherne's poem "Wonder":

> How like an angel came I down!
>   How bright are all things here!
> When first among his works I did appear,
> O how their glory did me crown!
> The world resembled his eternity,
>   In which my soul did walk,

> And everything that I did see
>   Did with me talk.

Following a visit to the Porters at Great Spruce Head Island in Penobscot Bay in the summer of 1955, Ashbery wrote a set of acrostic verses "strictly for domestic consumption on Great Rose Pebble Island." The initial letters of the lines in "French Poetry" spell out the name of Ashbery's host:

> Famous is the island
> And famous its residents, and
> In the winter, around a
> Roaring fire, we like to talk about the
> Famous island, and our regret at not being there
> In the winter.
> Even Lassie would have
> Liked it; it's too bad she had to
> Die.
>
> Perhaps she is enjoying herself more
> On some other island.
> Regrets, anyway, will not do on
> This island, which is
> Endlessly reticent, but without
> Resentment.

It is a paradox in keeping with Ashbery's art of ironic paradox that he should conceive himself to be more in tune with representational painters—from the mannerist Parmigianino to the Surrealist de Chirico to the luminous realist Fairfield Porter—than with the Abstract Expressionists who seemed to furnish a more immediate precedent for his labors.

Of the poets in the New York School, Porter was closest to

Schuyler personally and in artistic temperament. There is a sense in which Porter's paintings and Schuyler's poems amount to a largely unconscious collaboration of kindred sensibilities. Porter could have been describing his own art when he wrote of Schuyler's verse that it "tends toward a deceptively simple Chinese visibility, like transparent windows on a complex view." Some of the most touching lines in Schuyler's long poem "A Few Days" are about the years he lived at 49 South Main Street in Southampton. "That one back room in the ell was / *my* room. I could / lie in the four-poster on the horsehair mattress and stare / at Fairfield's color / lithograph of Sixth Avenue and the Waverly Theater en- / tranced by its magic," Schuyler recalled. The Porter adorning the cover of Schuyler's book *Hymn to Life* "is Fairfield's version of the view from my / south window: the wondrous pear tree in white bloom."

In an age when to be avant-garde seemed the highest good, Porter took the terrible risk of being dismissed as eccentric, reactionary, or worst of all, academic. The irony is that Porter managed to be a figurative painter without turning his back on modern art; he reconciled his deep steeping in the art of the past with the liberating sense of the medium that he found in the big powerful brushstrokes of de Kooning's paintings. The further irony is that Porter's stubborn nonconformism makes him seem, from our vantage point today, nothing if not an avant-garde hero. "I want to do everything that avant-garde theoreticians say you can't do," he remarked. "When someone says you can't disregard the past fifty years of art history, it makes me want to prove you can—the avant-garde implies a protocol which is more a challenge than a guide. Not that the academicians aren't even more ignorant." Porter's contrariness was exemplary. "When a critic suggests that something is not worth doing because it has been done before," Porter noted in a 1960 article, "he is in effect urging an artist toward one of the more exciting aspects of art, the attempt to achieve the impossible." This statement echoes a claim that Ashbery made three years earlier in a review of Gertrude Stein's radically experimental book *Stanzas in Meditation.* This posthumous volume of previously unpublished poems is full of departures from the conventions of syntax and punctuation; in one poem, for example, Stein places periods in the middle of sentences—an experimental move that still seems fresh today. *"Stanzas in Meditation* is no doubt the most successful of [Stein's] attempts to do what can't be done, to create a counterfeit of reality more real than reality," Ashbery wrote. "And if, on laying the book aside, we feel that it is still impossible to accomplish the impossible, we are also left with the conviction that it is the only thing worth trying to do."

(III)

No one could accuse the New York poets of giving in to the hobgoblin of little minds and overvaluing a foolish consistency. They embraced popular culture but not at the expense of the high end of the cultural scale; to them it was not an either/or proposition. There was no need to choose between Thomas Hardy and Laurel and Hardy; you could enjoy both, you could derive inspiration from both, and if Hardy's poems and novels were a more sophisticated pleasure than the slapstick duo's films, the important thing was that they could coexist in the same discourse. You could like opera and ballet as much as movies and comic books; you could as easily turn to Rachmaninov and Poulenc, Parmigianino and de Kooning as to a Jack Benny movie or a Bob & Ray radio show. (Commenting on his deadpan conversational delivery,

Ashbery likes to say that Jack Benny is his "role model.") From W. H. Auden, the New York poets learned that it was possible to freshen up a traditional verse form by using unconventional subject matter: Ashbery wrote a sestina about Popeye, and Koch weighed in with an epic poem in ottava rima about a Japanese baseball player. The variety of verse forms in the works of the New York poets helps give the lie to the assumption that an avant-garde movement necessarily rejects the whole past, when the truth is that the past can never be abolished, can only be modified, and that true poetic originality has more to do with the renewal of a tradition than with the rejection of one.

The poets of the New York School would command less attention if their relation to their predecessors were not as complicated and fruitful as it is. Critics have argued exhaustively that Ashbery's poetry can be understood in the visionary company of Wordsworth, Emerson, and Wallace Stevens. Koch's poetry, which critics tend to overlook, demands to be read in the context of comic literature, whose canonical authors include Rabelais, Lord Byron, Lewis Carroll, and Oscar Wilde. For their part, O'Hara and Schuyler revised the lyric model of the poem as found in Walt Whitman, Hart Crane, and William Carlos Williams. All four poets were at least somewhat receptive to Auden's influence and somewhat resistant to Eliot's. All four poets embraced foreign influences, O'Hara perhaps most emphatically. The voice in O'Hara's poems sometimes resembles Vladimir Mayakovsky's ("Mama! / I can't sing! / In the chapel of my heart the choir's on fire!") and sometimes Guillaume Apollinaire's ("O Eiffel Tower, shepherdess, today your bridges are a bleating flock").

A point worth reiterating: When I say that the New York poets were antiacademic, I do not mean to imply that they were anti-intellectual. On the contrary, this was a highly intellectual movement—and indeed the most overtly antiacademic of the poets, Koch, has been a tenured professor on the Columbia University faculty for more than thirty years. In his classes Koch made it clear that the inspiration he found in popular media implied no prejudice against high culture or indeed against the idea of a hierarchy of aesthetic values. In one class a student, arguing that the only difference is in the size of the audience, maintained that all art is equal and that therefore *The Lone Ranger* is as good as *Hamlet.* Koch's reply was a classic. "In that case, why do you write like *Hamlet?*" By antiacademic I mean that Koch and his confreres opposed the specific mood and mind-set, and the critical dispensation, prevailing in the English departments of America in the postwar era: the era of the New Criticism, when the canon of poetry as defined by T. S. Eliot was in place and poets were taught to regard a poem as a verbal icon, a taut web of tensions in balance, in the manner of a paradox-centered seventeenth-century work by John Donne or George Herbert. Antiacademic in this case means not a prejudice against the literary; it means an upheaval in canons of taste and judgment—a shattering of the well-wrought urn of midcentury verse.

The New Criticism was committed to the idea that poetry at its most compelling honored complexity, difficulty, ambiguity, and paradox as cardinal virtues. "An ambiguity in ordinary speech means something very pronounced, and as a rule witty or deceitful," William Empson wrote in *Seven Types of Ambiguity,* a central text in the evolution of the New Criticism. He proposed to use *ambiguity* "in an extended sense" embracing "any verbal nuance, however slight, which gives room for alternative reactions to the same piece of language." The examples of textual ambiguity Empson offers imply a scale of values in which multiple meanings enrich the experience of poetry and intellectual complication is preferable to direct statement. As Cleanth Brooks overstated the case in *The Well-Wrought Urn,* "the language of poetry is the language of paradox," and the touchstone by which modern poetry was to be judged was the "well-wrought urn" of John Donne's "The Canonization," from which the poem's lovers will rise from their ashes in the manner of the legendary phoenix bird. The urn "is the poem itself," Brooks wrote, containing Truth and Beauty as did Keats's Grecian urn.

By the canons of the New Criticism, the metaphysical poems of the seventeenth century—poems such as Donne's "The Canonization," Andrew Marvell's "To His Coy Mistress," and George Herbert's "The Sacrifice"—were interpretatively richer than the poems of subsequent centuries. Not that the New Critics' preference for metaphysical poetry was absolute. It was possible to apply New Critical methods to a Romantic poem as seemingly remote from the ideals of paradox and ambiguity as Coleridge's "Dejection: An Ode," in which that poet contemplates the decay of his creative powers, the loss of his "joy." Joy, Coleridge writes in a crucial passage in the ode, "is the spirit and the power, / Which wedding Nature to us gives in dower / A new Earth and new Heaven." The first impression of these lines is that Joy is the parent, Nature the spouse, of the poet. A New Critic could point out, however, that the syntax allows for a different interpretation, according to which Nature is the parent who weds us to Joy. This double sense of Nature is in fact implicit throughout Coleridge's poem, in which it is deliberately left unclear whether Joy, the agency of the imagination, is something external to humanity or is innately present in the human being. I cite this one example to suggest that New Critical methods do have a considerable sphere of application and do render much of the poetry of the past accessible to a modern sensibility. Unfortunately, however, the immediate effect of the New Criticism on practicing poets was not altogether salutary. Robert Lowell is a prime example. As the critic Joseph Epstein put it, "In his early poems, written as if for New Critical analysis, Lowell supplied enough ambiguity to plaster Mona Lisa's smile permanently on the *punim* of William Empson." But the poetic idiom seems worn out, the syntax clotted, the diction artificially inflated.

The conflict between academic and antiacademic poetry that

broke out in America in the late 1950s took the form of a bally-hooed battle of influential anthologies. In 1957, *The New Poets of Britain and America* was published. It was jointly edited by Donald Hall, Robert Pack, and Louis Simpson, and it boasted an introduction by Robert Frost. Devoted to poets under the age of forty, the book defined the academic canon of the day. Among the poets included were Donald Davie, Thom Gunn, Geoffrey Hill, and Philip Larkin from Britain, and Anthony Hecht, Donald Justice, Robert Lowell, James Merrill, W. S. Merwin, Howard Nemerov, Adrienne Rich, May Swenson, Richard Wilbur, and James Wright from the United States. Formal elegance, technical prowess, and literary wit were the virtues on prominent display. The academic cast of the undertaking was implicit from the start. "As I often say a thousand, two thousand, colleges, town and gown together in the little town they make, give us the best audiences for poetry ever had in all this world," Frost wrote in his introduction.

Three years after the appearance of *The New Poets*, Donald Allen's *The New American Poetry* delivered the counterestablishment's counterpunch. Allen's anthology accommodated the exclusions, at least some of them. It embraced the wild beasts of American poetry, which Allen divided into five rough categories: the Beats (such as Allen Ginsberg, Gregory Corso, Jack Kerouac), the Black Mountain poets (Charles Olson, Robert Duncan, Robert Creeley, Denise Levertov), the poets of the San Francisco Renaissance (Lawrence Ferlinghetti, Philip Lamantia), the New York poets (Ashbery, Koch, O'Hara, Schuyler, Barbara Guest), and assorted others who did not fit easily into a ready-made category (LeRoi Jones, Gary Snyder, Philip Whalen, John Wieners). It was a diverse gathering with, Allen observed, "one common characteristic: a total rejection of all those qualities typical of academic verse." The poems didn't rhyme, didn't scan; it wasn't a literary tradition they appealed to but the traditions of the blues, jazz, East Asian mysticism, Judaic chant, and French Surrealism. The poets were, Allen argued, following in the footsteps of Ezra Pound and William Carlos Williams toward the making of poetry in the spoken American idiom. "These poets have already created their own tradition, their own press, and their public," Allen wrote. "They are our avant-garde, the true continuers of the modern movement in American poetry."

The inclusion of Ashbery, Koch, O'Hara, Schuyler, and Barbara Guest in this counterestablishment context cemented their reputations as literary outsiders. To the extent that you are known by the company you keep, the anthology situated the New York poets squarely on the side of protest. What did the poets in Donald Allen's anthology have in common? "I thought the common element was interest in [William Carlos] Williams and the vernacular and idiom," Allen Ginsberg remarked in a recorded conversation with Kenneth Koch. "That's what Frank [O'Hara] said, and that's what was the common element between the Beat school, the Projected Verse people, Black Mountain and the New York school and the Northwest's Snyder and Whalen. Everybody had some reference to the transformation of the diction and the rhythms into vernacular rhythms and/or spoken cadences and idiomatic diction."

The alliance between the Beats and the New York School was always somewhat shaky. As Koch noted, the Beats were inclined to think the New Yorkers silly and effete. And as Ginsberg replied, the New York poets felt that the Beats were too provincial, unsophisticated, narcissistic, self-mythologizing, "and maybe a little too vulgar in the handling of fuck, shit, piss, motherfucker, and all that." O'Hara bridged the two groups by the sheer force of his personality, though there were times he felt ill used by his Beat buddies. In 1959 Gregory Corso invited O'Hara to give a poetry reading at the Living Theater and for weeks leading up to the event Corso personified O'Hara's devoted pal. But when the night of March 9 came "it was quite a disaster," O'Hara wrote, re-creating the episode for Ashbery and his companion Pierre Martory in Paris. "After my recent friendly relations with Gregory Corso, which had led into all sorts of effusive protestations of mutual devotion-in-poesy, etc., ad infinitum, he suddenly decided drunkenly during the reading that he really wanted to butter up Jack Kerouac who alas was there and is by now an openly avowed object of my dislike (which is mutual)." Corso read first, introducing his poem "Marriage," O'Hara wrote, "in the style of a beat Richard Eberhart by a prefatory speech about how he had fucked Jack's girlfriend when he came out of prison but Jack shouldn't have been so mad at him because he had never had a girl before and it was noble of him to take her. Then he read. Then he turned to me and said, 'You see, you have it so easy because you're a faggot. Why don't you get married, you'd make a much better father than I would.' "

> *Allen Ginsberg* (from the audience): Shut up and let him read.
> *Gregory:* And you're a fucking faggot, too, Allen Ginsberg.
> *Willard Maas* (from audience): Why don't you marry Frank, if you want to so much, Gregory.
> *Jack Kerouac:* Let me read. I want to read from *Doctor Sax* (his new novel).
> *Gregory:* No, it's our reading, you stay out of it.

Intent on disrupting O'Hara's reading, Kerouac heckled, "You're ruining American poetry, O'Hara." O'Hara had the aplomb to fire back, "That's more than you ever did for it." Bill de Kooning was also in attendance that evening. Corso kept addressing him from the lectern. "Now wasn't that beautiful, de Kooning? Aren't you going to give me a painting? [Mike] Goldberg and [Larry] Rivers did." De Kooning replied: "I'll give you a reproduction." As O'Hara concluded, "It really was quite a witty evening all in all."

The fact is that O'Hara and his friends were stylistically so at odds with the Beats that clashes were inevitable. Yet O'Hara's fraternal sympathy for his fellow bohemians survived the contretemps, and the feeling was mutual. Days after O'Hara's untimely death in 1966, Ginsberg wrote "City Midnight Junk Strains," one of the most affecting of the many elegies written for O'Hara. The poem begins with the "gaudy poet dead" and ends by saluting O'Hara's "common ear for our deep gossip."

The influence of Donald Allen's anthology on poets coming of age in the 1960s was tremendous. For them it was clear enough what the Beat poets and the New York School had in common. The two groups formed, as Ginsberg put it, "a united front against the academic poets to promote a vernacular revolution in American poetry beginning with spoken idiom against academic official complicated metaphor that has a logical structure derived from the study of Dante." Here was poetry of a certain intelligence that you didn't need a graduate degree to understand and enjoy. It was wild, rough, and definitely on the side of Walt Whitman in the perennial *Partisan Review* symposia pitting Whitman in the streets versus Henry James in the library as rival exemplars of the literary life. The book had Allen Ginsberg acting stoned in the "neon fruit supermarket," where Whitman lurked amid the bananas and the tomatoes, "poking among the meats in the refrigerator and eyeing the grocery boys." Here, too, were the opening parts of "Howl" and most of "Kaddish," Ginsberg's elegy for his mother, poems that took Whitman's long verse line and fitted it to the "vernacular revolution" ("the voices in the ceiling shrieking out her ugly early lays for 30 years").

Elsewhere in the volume Kenneth Koch stood Robert Frost on his head. "Something there is that doesn't love a wall," Frost had written in "Mending Wall." "Hiram, I think the sump is backing up," says a character in Koch's "Mending Sump." "The bathroom floor boards for above two weeks / Have seemed soaked through. A little bird, I think / Has wandered in the pipes, and all's gone wrong." "Something there is that doesn't hump a sump," Hiram answers. O'Hara memorialized the day Khrushchev came to town, and Kerouac played the saxophone in verse ("Glenn Miller and I were heroes / When it was discovered / That I was the most beautiful / Boy of my generation") when he wasn't touting the "Universal Mind" of the Buddha and the realization that "there is nothing / Whatever to be attained." The entire book was a dissent from the poetic pieties of the period. The enemy, in James Schuyler's words, were "the campus dry-heads who wishfully descend tum-ti-tumming from Yeats out of Graves with a big kiss for Mother England."

The orthodox poem of the 1950s had heightened diction, tight logic, and a sense of moral earnestness. The poetry of the concerned citizen was in vogue. There was subgenre of poems about dead animals. Looking back on the period years later, Hayden Carruth recalled "So many poems about the deaths of animals. / Wilbur's toad, Kinnell's porcupine, Eberhart's squirrel / and that poem by someone—Hecht? Merrill? / about cremating a woodchuck." Carruth can now provide the moral: "This / has been the time of the finishing off of the animals." But while the proliferation of dead-animal poems was going on, he couldn't help feeling irritated: "Mostly / I remember the outrageous number of them, / as if *every* poet, I too, had written at least / one animal elegy." In 1967 Koch quipped in one of his Columbia classes about the sort of poem in which "the poet in his car runs over a deer and feels like a rat, or maybe he runs over a rat and feels like a deer."

Where much of the mainstream poetry of the era was singularly joyless, the New York poets were animated by delight as well as by self-delight and by their commitment to the cadences of idioms of the American vernacular. Their own sense of seriousness demanded that they not appear to take themselves too seriously, and they felt that the comic spirit and the prankish *blague* had their place in poetry. Poetry for them was not testimony, not therapy, not an assertion of the will to change, but was itself a way of life, a way of confronting experience and giving it value. On New Year's Day 1952 O'Hara and Ashbery attended a concert of John Cage's "Music of Changes," which turned out to be a pivotal event. Cage made them realize that chance could be the determining element in a work of art. You could capitalize on what life threw your way and incorporate the inevitable interruptions—a phone call, a news bulletin—into your tableau, since that after all was the way life happens. Life was full of incongruities and charmed coincidences, and poetry could be the same; poetry was not a criticism of life, not a record of experieince but the experience itself, and if they succeeded the poets could rescue poetry from the powers that be: the stuffed shirts "with their eyes on the myth / And the Missus and the midterms," as Koch put it in "Fresh Air," a rant that had the force of a poetic manifesto in 1955.

The 1950s are perhaps too easily caricatured as an era of crew cuts and ponytails, "I Like Ike" and *Father Knows Best*, goldfish swallowing and *Peyton Place*—an age of conformity, consumerism, apathy, and repressed sexuality. The standard view of the period is that the nuclear threat had succeeded in hushing everyone except a few unruly beatniks at the end of the decade. The Russians were coming. They had the bomb and we had the bomb and doomsday could be near. "Allen Ginsberg thinks of those years as a liberating time," Gore Vidal observed. "I don't. I remember only conformity and fear and silence." President Truman had instituted loyalty oaths and a peacetime draft, and inevitably there was war in Korea and intimidation back home. Political dissent was limited to the fringes of society; it was dangerous to be a Marxist in a university. The silent generation was in control. The most exotic food to reach New York was the pizza pie. Everyone looked alike and dressed alike. The Dow-Jones Average hit 400 and cars sprouted tailfins. The "organization man" in the gray flannel suit came home faithfully to his split-level suburban house, where his wife baked Betty Crocker recipes, the kids wore Davy Crockett coonskin caps, and the grown-ups worried that the Soviet Union had the lead in space since they had launched Sputnik while our rockets self-destructed upon takeoff. "The great problem of America today," President Eisenhower told the nation, "is to take that straight road down the middle." He also said, "Things are more like they are now than they ever were."

These flashbacks make their point about the dominant social order in the 1950s. But precisely because it was a social order that strictly enforced its normative codes of behavior, the artistic act gathered a tremendous urgency. "Idealism retreated from the public sector; each man was an island," John Updike wrote about the 1950s, but he couldn't help thinking that the "silence" of his generation, "after all the vain and murderous noise of recent history," may not have been such a bad thing. The inward turn was certainly fruitful, not only for the production of cultural icons—Marilyn Monroe, Elvis Presley, James Dean—but for Willem de Kooning and Franz Kline, Action Painting, cool jazz, Miles Davis at Birdland and Thelonious Monk at the Five Spot, the poetry of the New York School, the Jewish-American novel of Bellow and Malamud and Roth, and the ferocious argumentation of the "New York intellectuals." Art was action—it was the imagination pressing back against "the pressure of reality," in Wallace Stevens's phrase—at a time when it meant something to be avant-garde. "In 1950 there was no sure proof of the existence of the avant-garde," Ashbery wrote years later. "To experiment was to have the feeling that one was poised on some outermost brink."

If it is true that the 1950s were a scary time because of the paranoia pervading American politics and the rabid anti-intellectualism that came with it, it is also true that the vocation of the artist still offered a way to elude the laws of conformism, while the city with its ferment furnished a more or less safe, more or less exotic refuge, and a steady source of adrenaline. The New York poets may have looked like everyone else, clean cut in sweaters and khaki trousers. In this they were unlike the bewhiskered Beats, who brought sunglasses and pot and Zen Buddhism and bongo drums into the living room. In 1959, the Beats were given a huge assist by *Life* magazine, which ran an article of such unremitting hostility that it made the magazine's earlier put-downs of Jackson Pollock seem like Valentines. The New York poets made a much smaller splash. They were leaders not in social attitude but in artistic innovation. It was in their poetry that they conducted their rebellion and overthrew the prevailing gods.

Aggressively modernist, eager to import the latest advances from Europe, the New York poets were wholly committed to experimentation as a literary ideal. "All poetry is experimental poetry," Wallace Stevens had written. "Not only is all poetry experimental, but all that is *truly* experimental is poetry," Koch chimed in when he was still a Harvard undergraduate. The spirit of avant-garde art gave Koch and Ashbery, O'Hara and Schuyler, something to believe, or at least a reason to suspend their disbelief. Experimentation could define and give meaning to experience. The aesthete's irony—the irony that informs Kierkegaard's *Either/Or*, for example—made it possible to sample and even exult in the cultural products of America while keeping aloof from its political institutions, "ignoring the establishment's right to exist," as Ashbery put it. Aesthetic pleasure rather than moral earnestness would serve as the poets' touchstone. Stevens had spoken for them when he wrote: "The morality of the poet's radiant and productive atmosphere is the morality of the right sensation."

I read *The New American Poetry* as an eighteen-year-old freshman at Columbia University in 1966. I had made up my

mind to become a poet, and one of the things that helped this
decision along was Frank O'Hara's poem "Why I Am Not a
Painter." I liked it so much in Donald Allen's anthology that I
copied it out in my notebook and read it aloud to my friends:

I am not a painter, I am a poet.
Why? I think I would rather be
a painter, but I am not. Well,

For instance, Mike Goldberg
is starting a painting. I drop in.
"Sit down and have a drink" he
says. I drink; we drink. I look
up. "You have SARDINES in it."
"Yes, it needed something there."
"Oh." I go and the days go by
and I drop in again. The painting
is going on, and I go, and the days
go by. I drop in. The painting is
finished. "Where's SARDINES?"
All that's left is just
letters, "It was too much," Mike says.

But me? One day I am thinking of
a color: orange. I write a line
about orange. Pretty soon it is a
whole page of words, not lines.
Then another page. There should be
so much more, not of orange, of
words, of how terrible orange is
and life. Days go by. It is even in
prose, I am a real poet. My poem
is finished and I haven't mentioned

orange yet. It's twelve poems, I call
it ORANGES. And one day in a gallery
I see Mike's painting, called SARDINES.

"Why I Am Not a Painter" made poetry seem as natural as breathing, as casual as the American idiom, and so imbued with metropolitan irony and bohemian glamour as to be irresistible. As a freshman in college I hadn't yet developed the critical vocabulary to describe the effects of O'Hara's line breaks, but it was impossible to miss the surprises enacted in the space between lines: "how terrible orange is / and life."

Only after many rereadings did I understand that the poem proposes, in its off-the-cuff way, a serious parable about the relations between poetry and painting. "Why I Am Not a Painter" begins by communicating the painter-envy to which poets in New York were susceptible during the reign of Abstract Expressionism: "I think I would rather be / a painter, but I am not." In a turnaround characteristic of O'Hara's poetry, however, wry resignation is transformed into nervy self-celebration. The seemingly inconsequential anecdote in the poem is actually a restatement of another, more celebrated anecdote illustrating that the medium is the difference between the painter and the poet. A century ago in Paris, the painter Degas had lamented that his poems weren't any good though his ideas were wonderful, and the poet Mallarmé responded, "But my dear Degas, poems are made of words, not ideas." The parable of *Sardines* and "Oranges" makes this point deftly but insistently. The rhetorical figure of the *chiasmus*—a crossing over, as in the shape of the X—is enacted in the inversions of the poet (who begins with a color and ends in "pages of words, not lines") and the painter (who begins with a word and ends with an abstract painting in which random letters remain as a purely visual element without verbal signification). The original inspiration for the painting ultimately called *Sar-*

dines is preserved only in the title of Mike Goldberg's work, because paintings are made of paint, not words, and the process of painting may erase any of the artist's preconceptions. And since poems are made of words, not ideas or colors, the orange that incited O'Hara exists only as the title of his work. The symmetry is complete. "It is even in prose, I am a real poet," O'Hara wrote in his patented tone of jubilant wonderment, and in the reader's mind the French tradition of the prose poem—from Baudelaire's *Spleen de Paris* and Rimbaud's *Illuminations* to Max Jacob's *Le Cornet à dés* and Henri Michaux's *Plume*—established itself as a form invested in modernity. For Barbara Guest, "Why I Am Not a Painter" was also an exact statement of an Abstract Expressionist principle. " 'Why I Am Not a Painter' is about the importance of not having a subject. The subject doesn't matter. That's straight out of Abstract Expressionism."

With its use of the present tense and its offhanded delivery, "Why I Am Not a Painter" seems, at first glance, to tell a "true" story. One thinks, reading it, that O'Hara wrote a prose poem called "Oranges" at the same time that Goldberg painted *Sardines*, and that the conjunction is an accident. It turns out, however, that "Oranges" was written in 1949, when O'Hara was still a Harvard undergraduate, many years before he met Goldberg. And this is another lesson that "Why I Am Not a Painter" teaches: What looks spontaneous may really be the product of a calculation, a fabrication, in the same way that Franz Kline's calligraphic black-and-white compositions, which seem like homages to an improvisatory ideal, were preceded by careful studies and sketches. Like a crime, true innovation in art requires premeditation, means, motive, and opportunity.

"Why I Am Not a Painter," so full of reversals and sly surprises, was, I came to see, a characteristic example of the New York School's aesthetic of irony. Irony was either "the citadel of intelligence," as Ezra Pound called it, or "the test of a first-rate mind," as Scott Fitzgerald maintained: the mind's ability to hold contradictory ideas at the same time and continue to function. In any case, it was the supreme expression of modernity, the trope of ambivalence and hedged bets. It involved a reflexive uncertainty, as in the poignant conclusion of Ashbery's "Decoy":

> There was never any excuse for this and perhaps there need
>   be none,
> For kicking out into the morning, on the wide bed,
> Waking far apart on the bed, the two of them:
> Husband and wife
> Man and wife

Deadpan wit was required. Irony could take a self-lacerating form, as when O'Hara announces that he is "waiting for / the catastrophe of my personality / to seem beautiful again, / and interesting, and modern." Irony also meant arched eyebrows, an effect that the poets obtained by the strategic use of quotation marks. Thus Schuyler delights in "the tonic resonance of / pill when used as in / 'she is a pill' " and O'Hara confides that "sometimes I think I'm 'in love' with painting." The quotation marks allow the speaker to use the language without necessarily subscribing to it. It was one way of redeeming the idioms of the day and achieving what Ashbery in "Self-Portrait in a Convex Mirror" calls "pure / Affirmation that doesn't affirm anything."

The New York poets directed much of their characteristic irony and comic energy against the poetry of the time that struck them as either freighted down with moral earnestness or marred by what Koch called " 'kiss-me-I'm-poetical' junk." Pomp and sanctimony were what the poets found particularly offensive in the mainstream poetry of the 1950s and early 1960s. The poet, newly in residence on a college campus, was at this moment supposed to be an agonized and agonizing "figure" who drank too much and wrote with the full burden of the world's suffering and injustice on his shoulders. With his tone like "that of a Jeremiah, reluctantly versed in Freud," as Josephine Jacobsen put it, Robert Lowell epitomized the type. Frank O'Hara couldn't stand his work. He objected to Lowell's "confessional manner which [lets him] get away with things that are really just plain bad but you're supposed to be interested because he's supposed to be so upset." Here is the second half—the last four stanzas—of that celebrated instance of confessional poetry, Lowell's "Skunk Hour":

> One dark night,
> my Tudor Ford climbed the hill's skull,
> I watched for love-cars. Lights turned down,
> they lay together, hull to hull,
> where the graveyard shelves on the town. . . .
> My mind's not right.
>
> A car radio bleats,
> "Love, O careless Love . . ." I hear
> my ill-spirit sob in each blood cell,
> as if my hand were at its throat. . . .
> I myself am hell,
> nobody's here—
>
> only skunks, that search
> in the moonlight for a bite to eat.
> They march in their soles up Main Street:
> white stripes, moonstruck eyes' red fire
> under the chalk-dry and spar spire
> of the Trinitarian Church.
>
> I stand on top
> of our back steps and breathe the rich air—

a mother skunk with her column of kittens swills the
    garbage pail.
She jabs her wedge-head in a cup
of sour cream, drops her ostrich tail,
and will not scare.

And here is O'Hara's put-down: "I don't think that anyone has
to get themselves to go and watch lovers in a parking lot necking
in order to write a poem, and I don't see why it's admirable if
they feel guilty about it. They should feel guilty. Why are they
snooping? What's so wonderful about a Peeping Tom? And then
if you liken them to skunks putting their noses into garbage pails,
you've just done something perfectly revolting. No matter what
the metrics are. And the metrics aren't all that unusual. Every
other person in any university in the United States could put that
thing into metrics."

At the time Lowell's eminence was taken for granted. "Robert Lowell is, by something like a critical consensus, the greatest
American poet of the midcentury, probably the greatest poet now
writing in English," the critic Richard Poirier had pronounced.
Such fanfare may have aroused a bit of *Schadenfreude* in O'Hara,
but I don't think that goes far enough to account for O'Hara's
animus. After all, O'Hara was usually the most generous of readers, lavish in his praise, and loath to condemn. About bad poetry
his attitude was, "It'll slip into oblivion without my help." He
bent over backward, sometimes comically, in defense of work he
had no real passion for. When Jasper Johns asked him for some
poetry recommendations, for example, O'Hara replied with a
two-page, single-spaced letter raving about the writers who truly
excited him and trying to do justice to those who didn't. John
Wieners was "wonderful" and Gary Snyder and Philip Whalen
were "both marvelous" and at the least Charles Olson was "interesting if sometimes rather cold and echoey of Ezra Pound." When

it came to Denise Levertov, O'Hara's gallantry failed him. "If you don't like Denise Levertov, you don't like Denise Levertov, but she does have something, though frankly not a great deal," he wrote. Even here, however, he was determined to rescue the situation. "That is not as damning as it sounds, I mean that she is very very good in a certain thing but can't do good when she's up to something else; but all it takes is one poem to keep you in history (if that's your idea of a good time, and it is most poets' idea)."

Lowell's poetry, however, offended O'Hara's sense of honor. Just as the skunk in Lowell's poem is symbolic and not merely a concrete particular, so for O'Hara "Skunk Hour" stood for everything that he detested in American poetry: didacticism, symbolism, and the grandiose egoism of a speaker who likens the welfare of the body politic to the state of his psyche and quotes Milton's Satan, "Myself am Hell," without a saving irony. For O'Hara, Lowell's declarations of agony were transparently confessions of his own moral superiority. O'Hara would have none of this. Self-pity was the enemy; ironic self-consciousness a defense. (As Schuyler put it in the title of a poem, "Self-Pity Is a Kind of Lying, Too.") Yes, the stink of filth was real, but it was not the only real thing. Where Lowell was animated by the impulse to preach and to mourn, O'Hara understood that poetry was meant to praise the things of the world that reward one's regard, and he felt this as a moral imperative. "It's my duty to be attentive," he wrote in his prose poem "Meditations in an Emergency." "I am needed by things as the sky must be above the earth." The point is reiterated in "A True Account of Talking to the Sun at Fire Island," the poem in which O'Hara declares himself to be the second coming of Vladimir Mayakovsky. Waking him up, the sun chides O'Hara for not being "more attentive." Not Jeremiah but Apollo is to be his model. "And / always embrace things, people earth / sky stars, as I do, freely and with / the appropriate sense of space," the sun advises the poet. "That / is your inclination, known in the heavens / and you should follow it to hell, if / necessary, which I doubt."

O'Hara got the chance to tweak Lowell's nose in public at Wagner College on Staten Island, where the two poets were scheduled to read on the same program. O'Hara regarded the event as something of a grudge match; his close friend Bill Berkson remembers it as a "mano/mano" duel. February 9, 1962, was a cold, snowy day in the city. On the way to the Staten Island Ferry, O'Hara bought the *New York Post* and on the choppy half-hour ride he wrote an instant meditation on the tabloid revelation that Hollywood actress Lana Turner had collapsed. This is the untitled poem that he wrote:

> Lana Turner has collapsed!
> I was trotting along and suddenly
> it started raining and snowing
> and you said it was hailing
> but hailing hits you on the head
> hard so it was really snowing and
> raining and I was in such a hurry
> to meet you but the traffic
> was acting exactly like the sky
> and suddenly I see a headline
> LANA TURNER HAS COLLAPSED!
> There is no snow in Hollywood
> There is no rain in California
> I have been to lots of parties
> and acted perfectly disgraceful
> but I never actually collapsed
> oh Lana Turner we love you get up

O'Hara read the poem that afternoon, making it clear that he had written it in transit. The audience loved it; Lowell looked put out.

D a v i d   L e h m a n

John Updike, an aficionado of Lana Turner, says he thinks the poem is O'Hara at his "silliest and emptiest," but it has always been a real crowd pleaser, a good example of a *blague* in verse. It is, moreover, possible to read the poem as an antithetical response to "Skunk Hour." Where Lowell proposed a correspondence between his own psychic condition ("My mind's not right") and a cosmic malaise ("The season's ill"), thus exemplifying the tendency that John Ruskin had labeled the "pathetic fallacy," O'Hara makes a point of calling attention to a correspondence in things as they are, a correspondence that is not simply the product of agonized self-projection. "The traffic was acting exactly like the sky" is a wonderful New York line, and if it serves as a metaphor for O'Hara's mental condition that is a bonus unavailable to the solipsist. To the moral agony animating Lowell's poem, O'Hara opposes the fighting spirit of his concluding injunction: "oh Lana Turner we love you get up." And of course the tone of O'Hara's poem is a precise deflation of Lowell's high accents. The poem, as Rudy Kikel has observed, is an instance of "a familiar O'Hara persona, the old-fashioned, mercurial, and sometimes bitchy camp," who addresses the star "as one *queen* addressing another."

This was not the only time that O'Hara put Lana Turner in a poem. She makes a spot appearance—along with Greta Garbo, Ginger Rogers, the Pittsburgh Pirates, and the Seagram Building—in O'Hara's "Steps," a love poem with a memorable ending:

> oh god it's wonderful
> to get out of bed
> and drink too much coffee
> and smoke too many cigarettes
> and love you so much

Why this loving attention to Lana Turner? The answer can be given in two key words. One is Hollywood, and the other is camp.

350

O'Hara loved the movies unreservedly, preferring the "big, over-produced first-run" products of Hollywood to self-consciously artistic films. As he put it in "To the Film Industry in Crisis," the best known of his odes to Hollywood, O'Hara loved the whole "Motion Picture Industry"—"glorious Silver Screen, tragic Technicolor, amorous Cinemascope, / stretching Vistavision and startling Stereophonic Sound." His taste was wide-ranging and happily vulgar, from the urbane detective romances of William Powell and Myrna Loy to Marx Brothers farce, "peach-melba-voiced Fred Astaire of the feet" and "Ginger Rogers with her pageboy bob like a sausage / on her shuffling shoulders," Marilyn Monroe in *Niagara*, Tarzan, and Mae West. O'Hara seems to have grasped instinctively that the movies constituted an entirely new category of aesthetic experience, not just a new branch of literature, and that literary standards of excellence were beside the point for the same reason that mediocre novels often make the best movies. "Only Whitman and Crane and Williams, of the American poets, are better than the movies," O'Hara declared.

O'Hara's passion for the movies consorted well with that form of cross-cultural reference that was not yet widely known as "camp" when O'Hara wrote his odes to Hollywood and Lana Turner. Camp, as Susan Sontag defined it in the 1964 essay that gave the word its general currency, is "a mode of aestheticism" that sees the world "not in terms of beauty, but in terms of the degree of artifice, of stylization." Camp "sees everything in quotation marks," Sontag wrote. It "incarnates a victory of 'style' over 'content,' 'aesthetics' over 'morality,' of irony over tragedy." It "is playful, anti-serious. More precisely, Camp involves a new, more complex relation to 'the serious.' One can be serious about the frivolous, frivolous about the serious." "Homosexuals, by and large, constitute the vanguard—and the most articulate audience—of Camp." "And movie criticism (like lists of 'The 10 Best Bad Movies I Have Seen') is probably the greatest popularizer of

Camp taste today, because most people still go to the movies in a high-spirited and unpretentious way."

Lana Turner, the sweater girl, famous for having been discovered drinking a nickel Coke at Schwab's Drugstore, was a natural for O'Hara's camp sensibility. She led a movie star's life—it could be monitored in the tabloids. In April 1958 Turner's fourteen-year-old daughter, Cheryl Crane, fatally stabbed her mother's gangster lover, Johnny Stompanato, in the actress's Beverly Hills bedroom. "One doesn't have to be old enough for Medicare to remember when 'Lana' elided into 'glamour' and she and Hedy Lamarr were considered the two most beautiful women in the movies—that is to say, in all America," Updike has written appreciatively. "Turner was M-G-M's female answer to Clark Gable, a fair-sex hunk," and she was also "one of the great screen kissers, her small-nosed profile expectant, her round chin lifted to give her throat a swan's curve." Turner was capable of stunning self-dramatization and the true movie star's unfeigned narcissism. When she fell in love with Tyrone Power she pursued him to his movie location in Mexico on New Year's Eve, 1947. Turner wrote in her memoirs, "In my memory, we will always be an especially beautiful couple. I say this, I think, without vanity. Tyrone, so stunningly handsome, was majestic, and I wanted so to be his equal—I like to think that on that night I succeeded. I wore white satin brocade, cut in the Chinese fashion, with a high mandarin collar and slits up the long, tight skirt. The sides and the sleeves of my gown were heavily beaded with seed pearls and rhinestones that gleamed like the stars in the Mexican skies. I'd even brought jewels with me. I like to think of that Mexican night glittering off the jewels I wore in my hair. Oh, I think we *were* beautiful. But more than that, there was such an aura of love about us that we would have shone just as brightly even without the diamonds and the pearls." The passage could stand as the epigraph to a disquisition on the camp sensibility.

The New York poets welcomed into their work all the pure and impure products of modernity that weren't thought to belong in poems. "Pie, tomatoes, eggs, coffee, spaghetti, / meat balls, dishes, shoes, cups, and punches / settled soft as airplanes to the kitchen floor," O'Hara wrote in an early poem. Building on O'Hara's lead, Schuyler made poetry out of quotidian details faithfully recorded. He saw the poetic possibilities of the laundry list. His "Things to Do" was the model for a genre that became a staple of second-generation New York School poets; in the 1960s and '70s, everyone wrote one.* "Things to Do" is quintessential Schuyler—unglib, fresh, and free of fake language:

> Give
> old clothes away, "such as you
> yourself would willingly wear."
> Impasse. Walk three miles
> a day beginning tomorrow.
> Alphabetize.
> Purchase nose-hair shears.
> Answer letters.
> Elicit others.
> Write Maxine.
> Move to Maine.
> Give up NoCal.
> See more movies.
> Practice long-distance dialing.

*The "things to do" poem appears to have been the simultaneous invention of two poets working separately and without knowledge of one another. Gary Snyder's "Three Worlds, Three Realms, Six Roads," in his *Mountains and Rivers Without End*, consists of six poems with the part titles "Things to Do Around Seattle," "Things to Do Around Portland," "Things to Do Around a Lookout," "Things to Do Around San Francisco," "Things to Do Around a Ship at Sea," and "Things to Do Around Kyoto."

With their witty appreciation of the detritus of modern life, it could be said that the New York poets transmuted camp into a viable literary idiom a full decade before Susan Sontag made the idea (or the attitude) intellectually respectable. Much of postmodernism—the most valuable part—is anticipated in their writing, as is Pop Art, and disapproving critics have judged the New York poets harshly as the harbingers of change. "Against the concept of seriousness, Camp invokes an alternative standard—the facetious," Hilton Kramer writes, citing Andy Warhol in the visual arts, John Cage in music, John Ashbery in poetry, Donald Barthelme in prose fiction, and the later work of Philip Johnson in architecture as outstanding examples. Kramer is right to connect Ashbery with Cage, a lifelong influence and inspiration, and right to discern in them all "an attitude of blithe impiety and insouciance." And he is irrefutable in his charge that camp, as Sontag summed it up, was a "wholly esthetic" point of view, a rejection of the "basically moralistic" tilt of high culture, and that poets like O'Hara and Ashbery were playfully serious aesthetes. But Kramer is too dour. He does not allow the possibility that camp, like any other style, can furnish the technical means to ends that are serious and complex. The wholesale rejection of camp defined broadly papers over the distinctions among the various manifestations of the impulse, and distinctions need to be made. The association of Ashbery as an aesthetic force with Andy Warhol is to my mind as tendentious an interpretation of Ashbery's poetry as that which alleges that he is secretly a political poet, undermining the foundation of our society, or that he is to poetry what deconstruction is to literary criticism. But then it is Ashbery's singular fate to come to seem so much the poet of his age that his poetry appears to illustrate all the popular shibboleths of the zeitgeist.

There is a difference between irony and paradox as found in the writings of Kierkegaard on the one hand and postmodernist parody on the other. And it seems to me that Ashbery—

perhaps especially in his book *Three Poems* (1972), which is entirely in prose—resembles Kierkegaard in the quality of his irony. I am not the first to sense the resemblance. In 1973, Elizabeth Bishop wrote to Ashbery saying she had been reading *Three Poems*, at first "completely baffled," now with greater enjoyment, and "when I do enjoy passages or pages most, they remind me very oddly of Kierkegaard (whose name I don't remember how to spell right, I think). Although no theologian, probably no Christian, I've always been able to read him with the greatest pleasure—and your *Three Poems* have now begun to give me the same sort of pleasure. I hope you don't mind my saying this—that I shd. be saying something like they remind me of Yeats!" There is a marvelous moment in "The System," the centerpiece of the book, when the poet distinguishes the travelers on life's journey who are saved by their "open-mindedness" from the self-righteous zealots "whose faces are turned toward eternity and who therefore can see nothing." What is most remarkable about this passage is the way the coils of syntax and the deliberately fustian prose capture the poet's extreme and almost reflexive brand of philosophical skepticism. The pious are so eager to achieve "a state of permanent grace," Ashbery writes, that they apprehend it where it does not exist:

> Hence the air of joyful resignation, the beatific upturned eyelids, the paralyzed stance of those castaways of the eternal voyage, who imagine they have reached the promised land when in reality the ship is sinking under them. The great fright has turned their gaze upward, to the stars, to the heavens; they see nothing of the disarray around them, their ears are closed to the cries of their fellow passengers; they can think only of themselves when all the time they believe they are thinking of nothing but God. Yet in their innermost minds they know too that all is not well; that if they were there would not be this rigidity, with the eye and the mind

focused on a nonexistent center, a fixed point, when the common sense of even an idiot would be enough to make him realize that nothing has stopped, that we and everything around us are moving forward continually, and that we are being modified constantly by the speed at which we travel and the regions through which we pass, so that merely to think of ourselves as having arrived at some final resting place is a contradiction of fundamental logic, since even the dullest of us knows enough to realize that he is ignorant of everything, including the basic issue of whether we are really moving at all or whether the concept of motion is something that can even be spoken of in connection with such ignorant beings as we, for whom the term ignorant is indeed perhaps an overstatement, implying as it does that something is known somewhere, whereas in reality we are not even sure of this: we in fact cannot aver with any degree of certainty that we *are* ignorant. Yet this is not so bad; we have at any rate kept our open-mindedness—*that*, at least, we may be sure that we have—and are not in any danger, or so it seems, of freezing into the pious attitudes of those true spiritual bigots whose faces are turned toward eternity and who therefore can see nothing.

The passage is framed by the image of faces turned upward in fright. Like the astronomer in the fable loved by satirists from Chaucer to Swift, who is so busy gazing at the stars that he doesn't see the ditch before him, Ashbery's "true spiritual bigots" cannot see things as they are; the longing for certainties has blinded them. "We," on the other hand, who doubt everything, including our doubting selves, have retained the "open-mindedness" that is our saving grace because it is the prerequisite for spiritual experience as well as every other kind. Ashbery's paradoxes, which approach the status of conundrums, and his logic, which proceeds by the baroque elaboration of a metaphor, are two qualities that might be called postmodernist. In Ashbery, however, these modes of irony are put at the service of a spiritual quest and an imaginative aspiration. The questions Ashbery raises are not the questions of postmodernism. What is heaven, and how am I to achieve it? What is the difference between the merely permanent and the possibly eternal? What can we know?

Kierkegaard in *Either/Or* has a parable about a man who has been summoned to heaven, where the gods allow him to make a wish. Does he want a fortune in gold? Fame? The love of a beautiful woman? He must choose: He has just one wish. Which will it be? "I wish," he says, "to have the laugh always on my side." And now the gods begin to laugh, which is how the man knows his wish has been granted, for it would not have been in keeping with the spirit of the occasion for the gods to have intoned solemnly, "It is granted thee." The celebration of laughter in this parable, the lone human wish for it and the celestial eruption of it in reply, make it seem peculiarly apposite to the poets of the New York School. Interested in the metaphysical dimensions of a joke, they recognized the comic as part of the lyrical impulse, not its antithesis. The echo of an infinite laugh reverberates in their work. "That was a good joke you played on the other guests," Ashbery writes enigmatically in "The Skaters." "A joke of silence."

The poets who were drawn to the Club and the Cedar Tavern wanted to expand the possibilities for poetry in much the same way that the Abstract Expressionists had done for painting. The poems O'Hara, Ashbery, and Koch wrote in their radical early phase approximate the experiments of the Abstract Expressionists most overtly in establishing that medium and message are mutually inextricable. As Schuyler wrote in "The Morning of the Poem," his masterpiece,

So many lousy poets
So few good ones

What's the problem?
No innate love of
Words, no sense of
How the thing said
Is in the words, how
The words are themselves
The thing said: love,
Mistake, promise, auto
Crack-up, color, petal,
The color of the petal
Is merely light
And that's refraction:
A word, that's the poem.

Preferring heterodoxy to orthodoxy, wit to solemnity, joy to melancholy, the experience or enactment of our moment in time rather than the moral castigation of it, the New York poets were aesthetes in revolt against a moralist's universe. They opposed the ancien régime, the Anglo-American literary tradition as embodied in the works of T. S. Eliot and the New Critics, and they were equally against the politically committed didacticism of the Beats and the poets of political protest. They believed that the road of experimentation leads to the pleasure-dome of poetry, and in pursuit of this goal they went, identifying the reader's pleasure with the author's happiness. They figured out how to do it, how to write modern poetry in America in works so much in advance of the sensibility of the age that they seem freshly minted today. In short, they were the avant-garde—the last avant-garde in American poetry.

A sequel to this book, picking up where this one leaves off, would begin with the Second Generation of New York School poets in the 1960s. The group's focal point was the Poetry Project at St. Mark's Church in the Bowery, where readings were held, magazines published, and workshops organized. Ashbery jokingly dubbed the Second Generation poets "the soidisant Tulsa School," because three leading figures grew up in Tulsa, Oklahoma (Ron Padgett, Joe Brainard, and Dick Gallup), while a galvanizing fourth (Ted Berrigan) came into their orbit while studying at the University of Tulsa on the G.I. Bill.

An exact measure of the Second Generation's achievement is not yet available, in part because so much of the best work of these poets remains uncollected. The reason is not difficult to fathom. One way these poets celebrated their freedom was to write in an astonishing array of styles and forms. Much of what they produced eludes classification. They mixed genres, collaborated with one another, and turned out works—they called them "works," not poems—in the form of letters from imaginary or real places, prose poems, plays, stories, one-liners, chronicles, mock-interviews. They could afford to be indifferent to whether their work found acceptance in the culture at large. All the validation they needed was available in the form of the literary magazines they produced, *C* and *Angel Hair* and *The World*, *Mother* and *Kulchur*, *Telephone* and *Adventures in Poetry*. It was a time when anyone with access to a mimeograph machine could, with a little help from his friends, put out a magazine. Doing so was nearly always a group endeavor. An artist such as Joe Brainard or George Schneeman would contribute the cover, and the poets would gather to collate and staple—and then celebrate with a party or a poker game.

Ted Berrigan's work is itself a manual of New York School devices. Some of his poems consist of one word per line, and in others—such as "Tambourine Life" (1966)—the words are sprinkled all over the page. In *The Sonnets* (1963), Berrigan used the cutup and collage techniques to great effect; he borrowed lines from Ashbery, O'Hara, Arthur Rimbaud, Henri Michaux, and a host of other writers, repeated the lines in different contexts, and sometimes scrambled them so that strange juxtapositions resulted. Occasionally, to get himself started, Berrigan would type out one of Ashbery's poems double-spaced, then write his own lines in the space between Ashbery's, then remove Ashbery's lines. "What I had wasn't very good, but I was able to take some of it and put it in some other poems [and] some of it did come out very good," Berrigan noted. "What I'm saying is that there are a lot of ways to write terrific poems, but there's only one way essentially to write poems that are no good. And that's to be not very amusing. And so don't do that, don't be unamusing. Don't write poems about how much you love your dog. Unless you can make a terrific poem."

In a recent poem entitled "April Not an Inventory but a Blizzard," Alice Notley recalls the effect Berrigan had on her when they first met:

I like him because he's funny he talks more like
me than like books or words: he likes my knowledge and
accepts its sources. I know that there are Channel swimmers
and that they keep warm with grease because of
an Esther Williams movie. We differ as to what kind
of grease it is I suggest bacon he says it's bear

really in the movie it was dark brown like grease from a car
Who's ever greased a car? Not him I find he prefers to white
  out
all the speech balloons in a Tarzan comic
and print in new words for the characters. Do you want
to do some? He says—No—We go to a movie where Raquel
  Welch
and Jim Brown are Mexican revolutionaries I make him
laugh he says something about a turning point in the plot
Do you mean, I say, when she said We shood have keeled
  him long ago?
Finally a man knows that I'm being funny

He's eleven years older than me and takes pills
I take some a few months later and write
I think it's eighty-three poems I forget about Plath and
  James Wright
he warns me about pills in a slantwise way See this
nose? he says. It's the ruins of civilization

I have quoted Notley's poem at such length not only for its (accurate) portrayal of Berrigan but because the poem exemplifies some of the strengths of the New York School influence in contemporary poetry: the unusual or absent punctuation, the ease of transition from dialogue to narration, the logic by association, the humor, the charm, the speed and intensity.

Ad hoc forms that the older poets adopted were turned into genres by the prolific Berrigan. If Schuyler demonstrated the witty possibilities of the "things to do" poem, Berrigan made it his own in "Things to Do in Anne's Room" and "Things to Do in Providence." If O'Hara created the "I do this I do that" chronicle of his daily round, Berrigan showed that O'Hara's jubilant whimsy and ironic lyricism could serve writers in circumstances far different from those of the author of *Lunch Poems*. O'Hara wrote "Personal Poem" and Berrigan wrote a whole series of them: "I think I was thinking / when I was ahead I'd be somewhere like Perry Street / erudite dazzling slim and badly-loved / contemplating my new book of poetry / to be printed in simple type on old brown paper / feminine marvelous and tough."

From Koch, Berigan took the idea of the one-line poem, as in these examples from "Rusty Nails" (1963):

MY BEST FRIEND

That was about you in my story.

BAD NEWS

The man in bed—staring at me appraisingly—was enormous.

THE DOORS OF PERCEPTION

There were seven to choose from, all putty.

I AM A MAN OF CONSTANT SORROW

"I know from my own experience that telepathy is a fact."

Berrigan's distinctive use of quotation marks was another New York School trademark. Putting quote marks around a word or phrase was as much as to say three things: (1) Somebody else is talking; I'm just mouthing, or (2) to quote T. S. Eliot in "Sweeney Agonistes," "here again that don't apply, but I've gotta use words when I talk to you," or (3) this is the dialect of the tribe, and I'm out to preserve it.

In 1965 Berrigan fabricated an interview with John Cage, in which the composer makes oracular utterances on cue:

Sex is a biologic weapon, insofar as I can see it. I feel that sex, like every other human manifestation, has been degraded for anti-human purposes. I had a dream recently in which I returned to the family home and found a different father and mother in the bed, though they were still somehow *my* father and mother. What I would like, in the way of theatre, is that somehow a method be devised, a new form, that would allow each member of the audience at a play to watch his own parents, young again, make love. Fuck, that is, not court.

"How does love come into all this?" the interviewer pluckily asks. "Cage" replies:

It doesn't. It comes later. Love is memory. In the immediate present we don't love; life is too much with us. We lust, wilt, snort, swallow, gobble, hustle, nuzzle, etc. Later, memory flashes images swathed in nostalgia and yearning. We call that Love. Ha! Better to call it Madness.

The made-up interview, as Berrigan fashioned it here, helps prove the point that Oscar Wilde, that consummate aesthete, first propounded: Given a mask, we will speak the truth.

How did the real John Cage feel about Berrigan's stunt? The usually imperturbable composer found himself greatly distressed by one passage in the interview, the one in which "he" describes his mother as "crazy": "She lay on top of me when I was tied to the bed." Ron Padgett recalls that this fictitious passage "struck the wrong note with Cage. He got a little steamed up. Someone who knew both Cage and Ted told Cage that Ted was a good guy and meant no harm. Then Cage cooled down. But for a moment it was hairy." The interview appeared in *Mother* magazine, which Peter Schjeldahl and Lewis MacAdams published on a shoestring budget. Appearing in the issue dated "Mother's Day 1966," the piece was selected to be anthologized and was given a cash award. "The judges didn't know it was a total hoax," Padgett says. "There was a lot of stirring and rumbling about that, too." Berrigan was vastly amused. It never occurred to him that anyone would be taken in, especially given the fake music that Joe Brainard drew to illustrate the piece in *Mother*—Brainard didn't know the first thing about reading or writing music.

Living in cheap apartments in the East Village long before that was a fashionable quarter, Berrigan and his friends translated the idiom of the New York School across class lines. In the 1950s the movement was predominantly shorthaired, Harvard-educated, and well dressed in an Ivy League way (tweed jackets and pleated khaki trousers). The poetry project at St. Mark's Church disseminated the gospel among the drug-taking, jeans-wearing, longhaired, antiwar children of rebellion. In the 1950s, alcohol was the intoxicant of choice; for the Second Generation, marijuana and "pills" were other ways that poets could attempt what Rimbaud had commended as the task of the would-be seer: "a willful derangement [*dérèglement*] of all the senses." Berrigan fancied himself the boss bard. Alice Notley, who married Berrigan, says he told people kiddingly that for five dollars he would certify them as members of the New York School.

The Second Generation got its start on the day in 1959 that Berrigan, an army veteran majoring in English at the University of Tulsa, walked into the bookstore where Ron Padgett, then still a high school student, worked part-time. Berrigan was accompanied by a girlfriend, Pat Mitchell; Padgett told them about the literary magazine he and his pals had launched, *The White Dove Review*. Berrigan bought a copy and was soon submitting his own poems. The friendships thus formed bloomed in unexpected ways; a few years later, Pat Mitchell married Padgett. Padgett could look back and marvel that he had met his future wife and his closest literary friend on the same day.

It is highly doubtful that Berrigan, Brainard, and Gallup would have gravitated to New York City had Padgett not enrolled there as a Columbia College freshman in 1959. Once there they could think of nowhere else they'd rather be. For Padgett and his chums, poetry held the promise of relief and escape from a place they considered terminally philistine. Tulsa, with its oil money, its gun culture, and its suppressed memory of the horrific race riot of 1921, was a dead end. Poetry, the poetry they admired, was as hip as Tulsa and high school were square. In Tulsa, Berrigan, Padgett, and their friends had been beatniks in a redneck town. In New York, they felt right at home amid the fruitful chaos they apprehended around them. "One minute in New York," Berrigan told his thesis adviser in 1961, "sufficed to convince me that five years in Tulsa had been much too long." (Though he completed his thesis—on George Bernard Shaw—Berrigan turned down the offer of a degree, saying, "I am by no means a master of arts," and adding his opinion that "the University of Tulsa hindered my development in the arts rather than forwarding it.") Berrigan, who grew up in Providence, Rhode Island, told an interviewer that he considered himself "a real New Yorker," which he defined as "somebody who was born and raised somewhere else and who came here by choice because it was best for my career. In almost no other city of America can an artist who doesn't really have a product that has much commercial value support him- or herself as well as in New York." Berrigan was determined to live the life of a poet twenty-four hours a day. He felt that poetry wasn't something you did at some appointed hour. It was something that could be done at any time, under any circumstances, day or night, while eating dinner or watching television or playing poker with friends. Berrigan stayed up late, sometimes talking all night with whoever would listen. When he felt like it he would sit at the typewriter and peck away, his beard full of ashes from the Chesterfields he chain-smoked. He never held a regular job and did not have a bank account; if he received a grant or an award, he would take it to the nearest check-cashing store, though he would forfeit 10 percent of the proceeds this way. Living from hand to mouth, he made the nickels and dimes he lived on by such methods as bumming or lifting books and selling them to the Phoenix Bookstore. Ashbery, aware of this habit, once gave Berrigan a copy of his latest book, signing his name on the title page and adding the words "not for resale purposes." He was not surprised to find the book at the Phoenix a few weeks later.

"There was a tremendous camaraderie among us," Padgett writes in an affecting memoir of Berrigan. "It went without saying that we were all buddies working to make some interesting and new art, together and separately. We disagreed all the time, we were fundamentally quite different, but we were in it together, we had escaped the Philistine vacuum of Tulsa, we had gone to the most energetic and insane city in the country, we were on some kind of edge, it was exciting, and we didn't care about being successful or making money or getting a safe job. Because we were together, we had a momentum and impudent confidence we could never have mustered alone. And we had mentors who, in everything they published or exhibited, inspired and challenged us." The first such mentor was Koch, whose classes Padgett attended at Columbia from his freshman year on.

One of the more spectacular literary accomplishments of the New York School's Second Generation began without fanfare in the summer of 1969. Joe Brainard had gone to Calais, Vermont, to spend the summer there at Kenward Elmslie's house. Brainard wanted mainly to paint. "If I had any sense in my head I would just paint and forget everything else," he told James Schuyler. "But I enjoy 'everything else' so much that I find this hard to do." In this case, "everything else" included completing a manuscript of poems and creating an issue of "C" comics for Berrigan's "C" Press to publish. Brainard hadn't expected to do much new writing, but one chilly early morning, he found himself composing sentences and short passages beginning with the words "I Remember." The first entry was "I remember the first time I got a letter that said 'After Five Days Return To' on the envelope, and I thought that since I had kept the letter for five days I was supposed to return it to the sender." That morning Brainard invented a literary form and simultaneously commenced writing the perfect example of that form.

"I Remember" is a device of seemingly utter simplicity, and therein lies part of its charm: It is merely a specialized instance of the rhetorical figure known as anaphora, or the systematic repetition of a word or phrase. But the effect Brainard obtains is anything but simple: *I Remember* turns out to be a subtle form of memoir, an autobiography by accretion (and on the installment plan), with a sort of discontinuous narrative implied throughout. The writing seems effortless. In fact, though, Brainard worked hard at it. (The last clause of the first entry, for example, was originally "and I thought that I was supposed to return the letter to the sender after I had kept it for five days," before Brainard strengthened it.) It took him five years to complete *I Remember*, which he wrote in three separate installments.*

Remembering did not come easily to Brainard, who felt that he didn't have a very good memory. It was like pulling teeth to come up with these three passages about a childhood friend and her family:

> I remember Bunny Van Valkenburg. She had a little nose. A low hairline. And two big front teeth. She was my girl friend for several years when we were very young. Later on, in high school, she turned into quite a sex-pot.

*The edition of *I Remember* now in print originally appeared in three separate parts: *I Remember* in 1970, *More I Remember* in 1972, and *More I Remember More* (1973) by Angel Hair Books, a small press operated by Lewis Warsh and Anne Waldman.

I remember Bunny Van Valkenburg's mother Betty. She was short and dumpy and bubbly and she wore giant earrings. Once she wallpapered her kitchen floor with wallpaper. Then shellacked it.

I remember Bunny Van Valkenburg's father Doc. He was our family doctor. I remember him telling of a patient he had who got poison ivy inside his body. The man was in total misery but it healed very fast because there was no way that he could scratch it.

Precisely because memory was something that required effort, the *I Remember* formula worked so well for Brainard. The fresh innocence of the writing, its appearance of utter naïveté, is the book's crowning virtue.

I have already mentioned, as hallmarks of the New York School, a flair for comedy (as opposed to satire), the habit of irony, and the conviction that the comic and the serious are far from mutually exclusive. The New York poet relies on the language as it is spoken rather than on a more literary argot (which may have its uses, too). The emphasis is on the imagination rather than on experience as the source of poetry. Poetry comes through the agency of language, not feelings. To this list Eileen Myles would have me add the hybrid quality of "chatty abstraction." Writing about a posthumous book by Tim Dlugos, a terrific New York School poet, Myles comes up with this succinct statement: "New York School poetry means chatty abstraction. John Ashbery heard John Cage's randomness of composition and was a fan of abstract expressionist paintings and John Ashbery decided we could do that in literature too. Abstraction. Let the sentences stop and start like one's attention. In Frank O'Hara's poetry the abstraction took a vivid human form, in James Schuyler's it's the friendly and frightening face of nature. But talk is the throughline in all this work, and Tim is virtually the son of these men, he did it too. The talk narrated the New York pace of life, the talk walked you through the party, the hangover." Poetry could be a species of talk—fluid, immediate, associative, direct. It could be talk heightened to the point that "the poet is performing himself." How true this is of such a poem as Dlugos's "Healing the World from Battery Park": "There's a quantity / of tenderness I feel sometimes / that drops into my chest precipitous / and golden as the sun into Fort Lee. / I couldn't tell you where it comes from, but / I'm learning where it hides."

Just as the old New York School was overshadowed in the public eye by the Beats, more recent representatives of the New York aesthetic have not received the attention that has gone to a group that has laid claim to avant-garde status: the poets of the Language School. From its start in the 1970s, Language poetry was self-consciously an experiment and an adventure. It was sparked by an insight into the nature of language and the instability of meaning—an insight derived from the most advanced linguistic theories of the day. If the relation between the word and the world, or between the word and the concept, was ever and always arbitrary, one's whole attitude toward language had to change and one's whole idea of poetry had to be rethought. Charles Bernstein, one of the Language School's chief theorists, speaks of his "preoccupation / with the radical morphogenerativeness of language / and its related instability and ambiguity, its / unsettling and polydictory logics, which constitute, / rather than impede, our mutual grounding in language / as a grounding in each other and form the basis not / of nations or ethnicities or races but of polis."

Impressive works have been produced under the Language School banner by poets as diverse as Michael Palmer, Lyn Hejinian, Bob Perelman, Carla Harryman, Rae Armantrout, Clark Coolidge, Ron Silliman, Nathaniel Mackey, Rosmarie Waldrop, Bernstein himself, and others. (Many of Bernstein's recent poems, which are very funny, make me think he's a New York School poet in disguise, and something similar might be said about other Language stalwarts.) In its rippling circles of influence, the Language School has some of the classic traits of an avant-garde movement: It is exclusionary and exclusive; manifestos are issued (Bernstein's *A Poetics*, for instance), magazines published; there is an implicit contempt for rival points of view or traditions deemed outmoded. But as Gertrude Stein said of Hemingway, the Language School looks modern but smells of the museums. It could not exist outside of the university. It is academic not only in the practical sense that its practitioners hold teaching appointments but equally because the noble experiment on language turns out sometimes to resemble an autopsy performed on a cadaver.

What *is* a Language poem? There are many varieties, and it is not easy to come up with a definition elastic enough to fit them all. In general, however, the intention of such poetry is neither to mean nor to be but to interrogate the language and our assumptions about it—to explore language "as a material and social medium for the staging of meaning or the construction of a social ideal." A theoretically political, deliberately "subversive" agenda is pursued. Poetry is a way of dismantling the structure of bourgeois discourse; a way of protesting kitsch, ersatz experience, and the corporate culture. Bernstein recommends absorption "in one's own immediate language practices / & specialized lingo" as a strategy of dissent, a declaration of otherness in a conformist society:

> the ideological strategy of mass entertainment,
> from bestsellers to TV to "common voice" poetry
> is to contradict this everpresent "other" reality through
> insulation into a fabricated "lowest" common
> denominator that, among its many guises, goes under
> the Romantic formula "irreducible human values."

The danger is that the poems issuing from such a poetics might resemble offshoots, or illustrations, of academic critical discourse—with the result that poetry becomes a subsidiary branch of literary theory.

An unwitting parody of a Language poem is produced by the demented character played by Jack Nicholson in Stanley Kubrick's *The Shining* (1980). The Nicholson character in the movie is a prime example of the way Hollywood treats the writer's profession. If the writer doesn't end up dead face down in a swimming pool (William Holden's fate in *Sunset Boulevard*), he may wind up crazier than a loon. In *The Shining*, Nicholson holes out in what looks like the ideal place to write a book—an out-of-season Colorado resort with amenities that venerable art colonies do not provide, plenty of solitude, plus the loving presence of his wife and child. Nicholson struggles on his magnum opus, working feverishly day after day. In the end, however, all he has to show for his effort are pages and pages consisting of the sentence "All work and no play make Jack a dull boy" repeated hundreds of times. This may be the greatest ironic homage to avant-garde writing in the history of the cinema.

There is, to be sure, some overlap between the Language movement and the New York School. Ashbery is the connecting link. Anthologies of Language poetry are like monumental footnotes to Ashbery's most radically disjunctive volume, *The Tennis Court Oath*, with its bizarre truncations and syntactical breakdowns. It was the work of a poet who was intent on dissecting language and interrogating the means of communication and expression. The fact that Ashbery long ago moved from this position, considering it a dead end, has not deterred others from picking up where he had left off.

When he received the Frost Medal from the Poetry Society of America in 1995, Ashbery summed up one difference between his own work and that of the Language School: "I wanted to stretch, not sever, the relation between language and communication." A second major difference between the Language poets and those of the New York School is that the latter are not theory-driven or politically preoccupied. Barbara Guest, whose recent work suggests affinities with Language poetry, is more properly to be understood in the context of Cubism and Gertrude Stein. Consider these lines from her poem "Words":

> . . . a newly laid table where related objects might gather
> to enjoy the interplay of gravity upon facetious hints,
> the chocolate dish presuming an endowment, the ladle
> of galactic rhythm primed as a relish dish, curved
> knives, finger bowls, morsel carriages words might
> choose and savor before swallowing so much was the
> sumptuousness and substance of a rented house where
>   words
> placed dressing gowns as rosemary entered their scent
> percipient as elder branches in the night where words
> gathered, warped, the straightened, marking new wands.

James Schuyler's characterization of Guest's poetry is apt: He likened one of her poems to a still life of tropical fruit that reminded him of a Kurt Schwitters collage. Guest identifies herself as a New York School poet for reasons that resonate. "The Language people are big on Marx, and I'm not a Marxist, and on French philosophy, and I'm not a philosopher," she told me. "They fell in love with poetics." The New York School's emphasis on humor and wit reflects not only a stylistic predilection but a vision of reality. As Guest put it, "It's not that I'm putting humor into that position of importance. It's that irony is so much a part of life."

Stripped of the ideological, Marxist, or deconstructive obsessions of the Language School, some of their strategies are not inconsistent with the practice of New York poets. Harry Mathews provides ample proof that linguistic gamesmanship may generate true poetry. Mathews's "Histoire" is a madcap sestina organized around a system of noun substitutions. "Histoire" is French for both *history* and *story*, or truth and fiction, and the poem is determined to conflate these categories. *Marxism-Leninism, fascism, sexism, Maoism, racism,* and *militarism* are the poem's six recurring end-words, but they are used without regard for their conventional meaning. Here is the final stanza:

> Biting his lips, he plunged his militarism into the popular
>   context of her Marxism-Leninism,
> Easing one thumb into her fascism, with his free hand
>   coddling the tip of her Maoism,
> Until, gasping with appreciative racism, both together sink
>   into the revealed glory of sexism.

In Mathews's poem the refreshment and the relief rest in the liberation of words from their dogmatic, ideological meanings. The advanced irony of "Histoire" is that it satirizes the way words lose their meaning when mindlessly repeated and at the same time it rejoices in the severance. The poem reaches its sexual climax when the political meanings of the familiar *isms* have been completely forgotten. Besides its antipolitical thrust, two other traits proclaim "Histoire" a New York School poem: It's a sestina, a form favored by the New York poets but considered old hat by Language theorists, and it's uproariously funny.*

American poetry at present seems to me vibrant with possibility, and the Language poets do not have the field to themselves in the area of experimental poetry. The renewed influence of the New York School is apparent in some of the freshest poems that

---

*According to Charles Bernstein in *A Poetics* (Harvard University Press, 1992), "A sestina, in almost anybody's / hands, seems artificial." So much for the sestinas of Pound, Auden, Bishop, Ashbery, Justice, Merrill, and Hecht.

are being published today. You can see it in the sestinas of James
Cummins with their gamesmanship ("Gary Snyder" is an end-
word in one of them), their mischievous wit, and their narrative
motion:

> Afterward, they were awkward, shy, trying to be funny.
> They couldn't get any more mileage out of Gary Snyder.
> "Some fling," he said, and she flung back, "Some fling!"
> But mostly they were quiet. Outside, the big yellow moon
> Yawned. He made a mental note to send her some tulips.
> She stared out the window, thinking about the word "neat."

You can hear it in the abstract music of Susan Wheeler's poems,
such as "Shanked on the Red Bed," whose quatrains owe as much
to early Auden as to early Ashbery:

> The envelopes were in the slots and paperweights were
>   flung.
> When I came down to seek you out the torrents had begun
> To rip the pan from handle and horizons from their shore,
> To rip around your heady heart looking there for more.

The new generation of New York School poets has revitalized
old forms and discovered new ones in odd places. Charles North
has written a series of poems in the form of baseball lineups. (On
the philosophers' team, Wittgenstein plays left field and leads off,
followed by Heidegger at second base and Aristotle at first.) Paul
Violi's "Index" takes the form of an index to an unwritten biography about a nonexistent painter; the index successfully conveys
the full contours of an egomaniacal life, making the writing of
the actual book a needless indulgence. Violi's recent poem "On
an Acura Integra" shows there is life left in the insincere apology

as a rhetorical ploy. Violi has a very specific reader in mind, a person who is asked to

> welcome this as a poem,
> Not merely a missive I've slowly composed
> And tucked under your windshield wiper
> So that these onlookers who saw me bash
> In your fender will think I'm jotting down
> The usual information and go away.

In Amy Gerstler's "A Fan Letter," the debased epistolary form named in the title is used to dramatize a psychotic personality. The author of the fan letter talks exclusively about herself, not at all about her idol, but she is never less than entertaining:

> The voice of your thoughts
> woke me like a rooster announcing
> the end of the world, or maybe
> a raven who'd grown teeth and learned
> to warble bawdy songs. Your seething words
> cured me—reading each was like swallowing
> leaf after leaf of a blessed, healing salad
> made from ambrosia and ragweed.
> I think we should meet. . . .

The form Aaron Fogel creates in "The Printer's Error" is a witty blend of testimonial and talmudic argumentation to advance the thesis that all misprints are heaven-sent. The poem's speaker, a typographer, argues for the abolition of all editorial work, "except insofar as editing / is itself an error, and / therefore also divine."

The device of the inventory or catalogue, a staple of Kenneth Koch's poetry, is used daringly in Paul Beatty's "Old Yeller Dreams of Days When They Wasn't Just Whistlin' Dixie," where

the ghost of Allen Ginsberg may also be discerned. Beatty lists
varieties of "coons," such as

> first coon on the moon coons
> *coon by yah my lord, coon by yah, oooh lord coon by yah*
> shut the fuck up censorship coons
> ACLU freedom of speech at any cost, americans have a
>   constitutional right to call you nigger bitch wop wasp
>   honky faggot kike coons
> folks who secretly like to be called nigger bitch wasp honky
>   faggot kike coons

and so on for two and a half pages. Catherine Bowman, too, seizes
upon the satirical possibilities of the catalogue form. In her poem
"No Sorry," the words named in the title are used to answer a
child's request for scissors or knife, a request that proliferates
and escalates into a list of weapons ranging from "lethal multipurpose stilletos" and "an axis bolt-action repeating rifle with
telescopic sight for sniping" all the way up to submarine-
launched cruise missiles and hydrogen bombs.

Behind Hal Sirowitz's *Mother Said* (1994), the reader detects
the methods and style of Joe Brainard's *I Remember*. Sirowitz's
book is composed of verse poems beginning with the words
"Mother Said" as a recurrent motif. His deadpan humor is Jewish, tender, self-mocking and yet infused with strong feeling.
The portrait of the mother in these poems is as affecting in its
way as the portrait of Portnoy's mother in *Portnoy's Complaint*:

> Don't swim in the ocean while it's raining,
> Mother said. Lightning can hit the water,
> & you'll be paralyzed. You don't like
> to eat vegetables. Imagine having
> to spend the rest of your life being one.

The naïveté animating *Mother Said* succeeds because it is so clearly genuine and not sentimental or willed.

The irony that is perhaps the signature motif of the New York School—irony that checks sentimentality while leaving plenty of room for sentiment—is evident in Billy Collins's poems, such as "Canada," in which the "scene of my boyhood summers" is evoked as that country is addressed:

> You are the moose in the clearing and the moose head on
> the wall.
> You are the rapids, the propeller, the kerosene lamp.
> You are dust that coats the roadside berries.
> But not only that.
> You are the two boys with pails walking along that road,
> and one of them, the taller one minus the straw hat, is me.

Another sort of irony is at work in the prose poems of Nin Andrews, whose *Book of Orgasms* marries the ironic and the erotic in a way one might not have thought possible. In a more recent poem, "A Philosophical Inquiry into the Nature of the Human Cock," the incongruity between the form of the discourse and its content reaches sublime heights. In the poem, five goddesses, "permanent residents of the land of pure bliss," apply Plato's ontology and Aristotle's rebuttal of it to a consideration of the male sexual organ. "A man knows not his own cock," one goddess opines. "So a man can only imagine it. And what he imagines can never be a cock, but is only an idea of a cock. What a poor substitute for reality illusion, or the cock, is. A cock removed from the pussy is little more than a thought removed from a mind." The poem can be deconstructed for its hidden sexual politics, but that might spoil the fun.

Many more examples could be proffered. When I think of writers whose work has been enriched by the New York School influence, I think immediately of such poets as L. S. Asekoff, John Ash, Star Black, Tom Breidenbach, Tom Carey, Maxine Chernoff, Andrei Codrescu, Marc Cohen, William Corbett, Douglas Crase, Connie Deanovich, Tom Disch, Denise Duhamel, Elaine Equi, the English poet Mark Ford, Gerrit Henry, Paul Hoover, Wayne Koestenbaum, John Koethe, Ann Lauterbach, Eileen Myles, Wang Ping, Carter Ratcliff, Eugene Richie, David Shapiro, Tony Towle, the Australian poet John Tranter, David Trinidad, Rosanne Wasserman, Marjorie Welish, Terence Winch, John Yau, and Dean Young. The list could easily be twice as long, but I think the examples I have given suggest the gathering strength of the New York School's influence in contemporary poetry. My own debt to the New York School is considerable, not only in my poetic practice but in my work as a teacher (where I have borrowed liberally from Koch), as a journalist (where I have kept Ashbery's example in mind), and as an editor (where O'Hara's curatorial labors have been an inspiration).

After reading Ashbery and Koch, O'Hara and Schuyler, one will turn away dissatisfied from any conception of poetry that would limit it to the autobiographical lyric, invariably plaintive in tone, usually in the first person, with maybe a little Surrealism to give it some edge, and with sincerity as the ultimate criterion. The New York poets showed that poems could be comic, satirical, absurdist, dramatic, discursive, and occasional, with no loss of true aesthetic seriousness. In a world of writing workshops, where there is always the danger that poetry will be too neatly identified with the compulsive rites of confessionalism, the New York School's conception of what a poem might be and do seems nearly as liberating for younger poets now as when O'Hara wrote his "I do this I do that" poems, Koch threw his hilarious antiacademic tantrums, Schuyler recorded what he saw out the window, and Ashbery crafted poems so bizarre and so resistant to paraphrase that mainstream critics maligned him as a "professional mindblower" presiding over a "Technicolor waste land."

It might be thought that in the course of this book I have made, or repeated, a convincing argument that the avant-garde is finished as a vital concept or ideal capable of stimulating new art into existence. But if as O'Hara once remarked, "the avant-garde always exists in the state of idea," there may still be hope for it. "The avant-garde has been made up, I think, completely, and all through history, with people who are *bored* by other people's ideas," O'Hara said. "Now, you do not have to have the Russian Revolution or the French Revolution or the Civil Rights Movement in order to get irritated by other people's ideas. All you have to do is be one individual who is tired of looking at something that looks like something else." This book is dedicated to that one individual.

INTRODUCTION

p. 1 "artistic underground": Roger Shattuck, *The Banquet Years: The Origins of the Avant Garde in France, 1885 to World War I*, rev. ed., pp. 24, 28, 29, 274–75.

p. 2 "New York poets": James Schuyler, "Poet and Painter Overture," in Donald Allen, ed., *The New American Poetry*, p. 418.

p. 4 "Youth wants": Frank O'Hara, *Art Chronicles: 1954–1966*, p. 94.

p. 5 "John and Frank": Carl Little, "An Interview with James Schuyler," *Agni Review*, no. 37 (1993), p. 161.

p. 5 "like the members": Kenneth Koch, "An Interview with Jordan Davis," *The Art of Poetry, Poems, Parodies, Interviews, Essays, and Other Work*, p. 213.

p. 5 "There was no": John Ashbery, quoted in Richard Kostelanetz, "How to Be a Difficult Poet," *New York Times Magazine*, May 23, 1976.

p. 11 "For a long time": Gertrude Stein, "Composition as Explanation," in *Selected Writings of Gertrude Stein*, ed. Carl Van Vechten (New York: Vintage Books, 1972), p. 515.

p. 12 "Secretly": Letter from James Schuyler to John Ashbery, October 13, 1959. John Ashbery Papers, AM-6, Box 17, Houghton Library, Harvard University.

p. 13 "That was the year": John Cheever, *The Journals of John Cheever* (New York: Knopf, 1991), p. 117.

CHAPTER 1

p. 20 "The idea was": Peter Stitt, "John Ashbery: The Art of Poetry," *The Paris Review*, no. 90 (Winter 1983), p. 39.

p. 21 "We were all": Larry Rivers, quoted in John Gruen, *The Party's Over Now*, p. 135.

p. 21 Clement Greenberg told Myers: "Clem said, 'You want to be a serious gallery dealer, this is what you need to do.' And he gave him a list of artists he should show. Larry Rivers, myself, Grace Hartigan, Bob Goodnough, Harry Jackson, Helen Frankenthaler were on the list. That was Clem's stable. And it went to Tibor de Nagy all in one fell swoop." Interview with Al Leslie, June 14, 1995. See also John Bernard Myers, *Tracking the Marvelous: A Life in the New York Art World*, p. 147.

p. 21 "Every artist": Virgil Thomson, quoted in Myers, *Tracking the Marvelous*, p. 147.

p. 22 "vast paper murals": John Bernard Myers, *The Poets of the New York School* (Graduate School of Fine Arts, University of Pennsylvania, 1969), p. 14.

p. 23 "John and Herbert wanted": James Merrill, *A Different Person*, pp. 253–54.

p. 23 "Frank O'Hara is": John Bernard Myers, quoted in Carl Little, "An Interview with James Schuyler," *Agni Review*, no. 37 (1993), p. 159.

p. 23 " 'Sweetie,' he cried": Merrill, *Different Person*, p. 254.

p. 23 "I asked Elaine": Myers, *Tracking the Marvelous*, p. 136.

p. 24 "No gathering was": Ibid., p. 147.

p. 24 *Kenneth Koch: A Tragedy*: See Larry Rivers, with Arnold Weinstein, *What Did I Do?*, p. 276.

p. 24 "John came out of": Interview with Barbara Guest, November 11, 1995.

p. 24 "He was a marvelous": Larry Rivers, quoted in Gruen, *Party's Over Now*, p. 136.

p. 25 "Whether the Tibor": Hilton Kramer, "De Nagy, Secret Banker, Charmed City Bohemians," *New York Observer*, January 17, 1994, pp. 1, 19.

p. 25 "static and classical": Renato Poggioli, *The Theory of the Avant-Garde*, trans. Gerald Fitzgerald, p. 20.

p. 26 "designates a place": John Ashbery, Statement at the National Book Awards symposium "Poetry Now," St. Regis Hotel, New York, March 5, 1968. John Ashbery Papers, AM-6, Box 31, Houghton Library, Harvard University.

p. 26 "where everybody is": Interview with John Ashbery, October 17, 1977.

p. 27 "experimental approach": John Tranter, "An Interview with John

Ashbery," *Scripsi* 4, no. 1 (1986). The interview took place on April 20, 1985.

p. 27 "We also got": Ashbery, Statement at the National Book Awards symposium. Ashbery Papers, AM-6, Box 31, Houghton Library.

p. 28 "We were": Peter Stitt, "John Ashbery: The Art of Poetry," *The Paris Review* no. 90 (Winter 1983), p. 40.

p. 28 "It wasn't": Anne Waldman, "Paraphrase of Edwin Denby Speaking on the 'New York School,' " in Bill Berkson and Joe LeSueur, eds., p. 32.

p. 30 "can sort of": Robert Thompson, "An Interview with James Schuyler," *Denver Quarterly* 26, no. 4 (Spring 1992), p. 121.

p. 30 "In our own": Letter from Frank O'Hara to Larry Rivers, June 27, 1953. Donald Allen Papers, University of Connecticut Library, Storrs. Used with permission.

p. 31 "Art does not": Fairfield Porter, "American Non-Objective Painting" (1959), *Art in Its Own Terms: Selected Criticism 1935–1975* (Boston: Zoland Books, 1979), pp. 55–57.

p. 32 "New York City had": Anatole Broyard, *Kafka Was the Rage: A Greenwich Village Memoir*, pp. 7–8.

p. 33 "Along with so much": Louis Kronenberger, *Company Manners: A Cultural Inquiry into American Life* (New York: New American Library, 1955), p. 14.

p. 34 "the silliest idea": Kenneth Koch, "A Note on Frank O'Hara in the Early Fifties" (1964), in Berkson and LeSueur, *Homage to Frank O'Hara*, p. 26.

p. 37 "Wigging in": From "Trip," in James Schuyler, *Collected Poems*, p. 252.

p. 38 "I often wish": Frank O'Hara, *Early Writing*, ed. Donald Allen (Bolinas, Cal.: Grey Fox Press, 1977), pp. 97–110. Entry of October 17, 1948.

p. 39 "Recklessness is": John Ashbery, *Reported Sightings*, p. 391.

p. 39 "I grew up": Kenneth Koch, "Educating the Imagination," *Teachers and Writers Collaborative*, March/April 1994, p. 4.

p. 40 "probably the most": Frank O'Hara, "Service Experience," Harvard College Application for Admission, June 22, 1946.

p. 41 "I did stand by": Robert Thompson, "An Interview with James Schuyler," *Denver Quarterly* 26, no. 4 (Spring 1992), p. 111.

p. 42 "never figured out": Interview with Kenneth Koch, October 29, 1994.

p. 42 "We were supposed": Ibid.

p. 43 "the army had done": Kenneth Koch, Harvard College Application for Admission, May 20, 1946.

p. 44 "Frank [O'Hara] one night": Rivers, *What Did I Do?*, p. 233.

p. 44 "East Fifties queen": Schuyler, "Dining Out with Doug and Frank," *Collected Poems*, p. 249.

p. 45 "It's / not that I": From "Saturday Night," in Schuyler, *Collected Poems*, pp. 188–89.

p. 47 "exemplary": John Asbery, "R. B. Kitaj," *Reported Sightings*, pp. 303, 308. Originally in *Art in America*, January 1982.

p. 47 "an abyss of glamour": Frank O'Hara, "Jackson Pollock," *Art Chronicles: 1954–1966*, pp. 38–39.

p. 48 "We were arrogant": Interview with Robert Bly, March 26, 1998.

p. 49 "I went into": Interview with Donald Hall, December 2, 1992.

p. 49 "misjudged": Daniel Ellsberg, "The Playgoer," *Harvard Crimson*, March 1, 1951, p. 2.

p. 50 "I don't know where": Interview with Kenneth Koch, October 29, 1994.

p. 51 "To read them": Kenneth Koch, on the occasion of the Poetry Society of America's presentation of the Frost Medal to John Ashbery, New York Public Library, April 28, 1995.

p. 51 "I just read": John Asbery, quoted in Kenneth Koch, "Educating the Imagination," *Teachers & Writers* newsletter, March/April 1994, p. 3.

p. 52 "You won": Interview with Kenneth Koch, October 29, 1994.

p. 52 "a ridiculous remark": John Ashbery, "A Reminiscence," in Berkson and LeSueur, *Homage to Frank O'Hara*, p. 20.

p. 52 "been having a terribly": Letter from Frank O'Hara to James Schuyler, February 11, 1956, in William Corbett and Geoffrey Young, eds., *That Various Field: For James Schuyler*, p. 13.

p. 52 "terribly literary": Letter from Donald Hall to David Lehman, November 29, 1993. Other quotes are from interviews with Donald Hall, November 1992, January 1994, December 1995, and June 1996.

p. 53 "the best parties": Donald Hall, *Death to the Death of Poetry* (Ann Arbor: University of Michigan Press, 1994), p. 146.

p. 54 "I refuse to be": O'Hara, *Early Writing*, pp. 108–9.

p. 55 "I never enjoyed": Interview with Kenneth Koch, June 30, 1993.

p. 55 "Kenneth was a cutup": Interview with Nell Blaine, March 30, 1994.

p. 56 "I had come down": Ashbery, *Reported Sightings*, p. 241.

p. 57 "I thought he": Frank O'Hara, "Larry Rivers: A Memoir," in *Standing Still and Walking in New York*, ed. Donald Allen, pp. 169–70.

p. 57 "We shook hands": Larry Rivers, quoted in Gruen, *Party's Over Now*, p. 141.

p. 57 "a demented telephone": O'Hara, "Larry Rivers: A Memoir, pp. 169–70.

p. 57 "charming madman": Rivers, *What Did I Do?*, p. 228.

p. 58 "The lights went on": Interview with Kenneth Koch, June 30, 1994.

p. 58 "Kenneth Koch words": Letter from Frank O'Hara to Jane Freilicher, July 6, 1951. Donald Allen Papers, University of Connecticut Library.

p. 58 "Alack aday": Letter from Frank O'Hara to Jane Freilicher, June 6, 1951, in "Frank O'Hara Letters transcribed by Allen. Volume I: 1951–1960." Donald Allen Papers, University of Connecticut Library.

p. 59 "in memory": Interview with Kenneth Koch, February 10, 1994.

p. 59 In a home movie: Myers, *Tracking the Marvelous*, p. 136.

p. 59: "I just stepped": Letter from John Ashbery to Kenneth Koch, April 13, 1955.

p. 59 "locked in": Letter from John Ashbery to Kenneth Koch dated "Nov 13," headed 33, rue de Varenne; probably 1960.

p. 59 "the Irene": Letter from Jane Freilicher to John Ashbery, October 2, 1962.

p. 59 "Please write again": Letter from Jane Freilicher to John Ashbery, December 5, 1958.

p. 59 "my summer": Letter from Jane Freilicher to John Ashbery, July 18, 1960.

p. 59 "I know I am": Letter from Jane Freilicher to John Ashbery, April 12 and 13, 1962. Ashbery Papers, AM-6, Box 9, Houghton Library.

p. 60 "At moments": Letter from Alfred Leslie to John Ashbery, February 25, 1979. Ashbery Papers, AM-6, Box 11, Houghton Library.

p. 60 "like a high school": Joe LeSueur, *Nothing to Lose*, unpublished manuscript, p. 196. Courtesy Joe LeSueur.

p. 60 "I published": Interview with Barbara Guest, November 11, 1995.

p. 60 "After a week": Rivers, *What Did I Do?*, p. 34.

p. 61 "had more integrity": Ibid., pp. 246–47.

p. 62 "Somehow, you": Larry Rivers, quoted in Gruen, *Party's Over Now*, p. 142.

p. 62 "our Joan": Interview with Jane Freilicher, March 31, 1994.

p. 62 "I maintain": Interview with Arnold Weinstein, April 1, 1994.

p. 63 "Nell made me feel": Rivers, *What Did I Do?*, p. 109.

p. 63 "Larry Rivers was": Interview with Nell Blaine, March 30, 1994.

Chapter 2

p. 65 beautiful art groupie: Lee Hall, *Elaine and Bill: Portrait of a Marriage* (New York: HarperCollins, 1993), pp. 196–200.

p. 65 "play the game": Ibid., p. 196.

p. 65 "a decade-long": Mark Stevens, "De Kooning's Master Strokes," *Vanity Fair*, May 1994, p. 176.

p. 66 "We go there": Ad Reinhardt, quoted in Lionel Abel, *The Intellectual Follies: A Memoir of the Literary Venture in New York and Paris*, p. 212.

p. 66 where Elaine's husband: Ibid., pp. 212–13.

p. 66 where Jackson Pollock: Steven Naifeh and Gregory White Smith, *Jackson Pollock: An American Saga*, p. 749.

p. 66 "always got there": Larry Rivers, quoted in Ibid., p. 749.

p. 66 "Interrogation green": Stevens, "De Kooning's Master Strokes," p. 176.

p. 66 The smoke-filled: Naifeh and Smith, *Jackson Pollock*, p. 748.

p. 66 "This is the place": B. H. Friedman, "Art World Details: Journal Excerpts," *Grand Street*, no. 51 (Winter 1995), p. 148.

p. 67 "it was something": Frank O'Hara, *Standing Still and Walking in New York*, ed. Donald Allen, p. 169.

p. 67 "I sat for hours": Robert Creeley, "On the Road: Notes on Artists and Poets, 1950–1965," in *Poets of the Cities: New York and San Francisco, 1950–1965* (New York, Dutton, 1974), p. 59.

p. 67 "Well, look": Franz Kline, quoted in Robert Creeley, "An Interview with Linda Wagner," in Martin Lammon, ed., *Written in Water, Written in Stone: Twenty Years of Poets on Poetry* (Ann Arbor: University of Michigan Press, 1996), p. 60.

p. 67 Somebody at the Cedar: Mark Stevens, "Power and Melancholy," *New York*, January 16, 1995, p. 58.

p. 67 "it's like an empty": Willem de Kooning, quoted in William Barrett, *The Truants: Adventures Among the Intellectuals*, p. 144.

p. 68 The painter, pleased: Letter from Kenneth Koch to Frank O'Hara, March 22, 1956.

p. 68 "De Kooning blinked": Barrett, *Truants*, p. 144.

p. 68 "I used to go": Interview with John Ashbery, April 29, 1997.

p. 68 "unliterary": James Merrill, *A Different Person*, pp. 3, 255.

p. 69 "the rhythm": Allen Ginsberg, *The Village Voice*, November 12, 1958.

p. 69 "You were headed": Ronald Sukenick, *Down and In: Life in the Underground*, pp. 18–19.

p. 70 "the battle": Mary McCarthy, quoted in Ibid., p. 36.

p. 70 "It is hard": William Weaver, "Remembering Frank O'Hara," *Southwest Review*, Winter 1994, pp. 140, 143.

p. 72 "Collabortion": Peter Schjeldahl, "Frank O'Hara: 'He Made Things & People Sacred,' " in Bill Berkson and Joe LeSueur, eds., *Homage to Frank O'Hara*, p. 141.

p. 72 "If I have a hero": Joe Brainard, "Frank O'Hara," in Berkson and LeSueur, *Homage to Frank O'Hara*, p. 168.

p. 72 "become blind drunk": Brad Gooch, *City Poet: The Life and Times of Frank O'Hara*, p. 416.

p. 73 "be frank": Letter from James Schuyler to Bill Berkson, July 24, 1969. Bill Berkson Papers, University of Connecticut Library, Storrs. Used with permission.

p. 74 "It was easy": Interview with Kenneth Koch, October 19, 1994.

p. 74 "James Schuyler is": Interview with John Ashbery, October 17, 1977.

p. 76 "Don't forget that": Letter from James Schuyler to John Ashbery, December 29, 1970. John Ashbery Papers, AM-6, Box 17, Houghton Library, Harvard University.

p. 77 "In both art": John Ashbery, "The Invisible Avant-Garde," *Reported Sightings*, pp. 393–94.

p. 78 "Each one was different": Norman Bluhm, "Twenty-Six Things at Once," *Lingo*, no. 7 (1997), pp. 11–13.

p. 78 "If my words": Kenneth Koch, *The Art of Poetry: Poems, Parodies, Interviews, Essays, and Other Work*, pp. 168–69.

p. 78 "They were all": Edward Lucie-Smith, "An Interview with Frank O'Hara," in O'Hara, *Standing Still and Walking in New York*, pp. 18–19.

p. 79 "One of the most": Interview with Kenneth Koch, February 28, 1994.

p. 81 "How can we": David K. Kermani, *John Ashbery: A Comprehensive Bibliography*, pp. 23–24.

p. 81 "strangeness and": John Lawrence Ashbery, "Three Novels of Henry Green." Master of Arts Thesis, Columbia University, June 1950, pp. 72–73.

p. 82 "poetry is not": T. S. Eliot, "Tradition and the Individual Talent," in *Selected Prose of T. S. Eliot*, ed. Frank Kermode (New York: Harcourt Brace, 1975), p. 43.

p. 82 "It was written": Carl Little, "An Interview with James Schuyler," *Agni Review*, no. 37 (1993), pp. 163–64.

p. 83 "I liked your": Letter from John Ashbery to James Schuyler, August 31, 1966. James Schuyler Papers, MSS. 78, Archive for New Poetry, Manderville Special Collections Library, University of California at San Diego.

p. 84 "I was attracted": Interviews with Kenneth Koch, June 20, 1993, and February 28, 1994.

p. 84 Kenneth Koch on the writing of *When the Sun Tries to Go On*: "I wrote five 24-line stanzas of it and thought maybe it was finished, and I showed it to Frank O'Hara and he said, 'Listen Kenneth, it's very good, and since you're doing this kind of thing so well now why don't you just go on with it as long as you can.' Therefore I decided to write 100 stanzas. So I really owe the existence of the work to Frank." Kenneth Koch, interview with Mark Hilringhouse, *Joe Soap's Canoe*, no. 12 (1989), n.p.

p. 84 "John wrote": Interview with Kenneth Koch, February 29, 1994.

p. 85 "EUROPE is so": Letter from Kenneth Koch to John Ashbery, January 23, 1960. Ashbery Papers, AM-6, Box 11, File 2, Houghton Library.

p. 85 "Frank says": Letter from Kenneth Koch to John Ashbery, n.d. (typed on thin, small stationery from Hotel Nacional de Cuba, Havana), probably January 1960. Ashbery Papers, AM-6, Box 11, File 2, Houghton Library.

p. 86 "just beautiful": Postcard from Kenneth Koch to John Ashbery, February 17, 1961.

p. 86 "writing an article": Letter from Kenneth Koch to John Ashbery, January 21, 1962. Ashbery Papers, AM-6, Box 11, File 2, Houghton Library.

p. 86 "If, like Marianne": F. W. Dupee, "Kenneth Koch's Poetry," *The King of the Cats* (New York: Farrar, Straus & Giroux, 1965), p. 188.

p. 88 "were all but": John Ashbery, "A Reminiscence," in Berkson and LeSueur, *Homage to Frank O'Hara*, p. 20.

p. 89 "didn't think": Letter from James Schuyler to Kenneth Koch dated "Jan. 57."

p. 90 "an enshrinement": Pauline Kael, *5001 Nights at the Movies* (New York: Holt, 1991), p. 210.

p. 90 "Y'know": James Dean, quoted in David Halberstam, *The Fifties* (New York: Villard, 1993), p. 485.

p. 91 "James Dean is": Kael, *5001 Nights at the Movies*, p. 209.

p. 91 "I have seen": Letter from Frank O'Hara to Janice Koch, July 14, 1955.

p. 92 "I've decided": Letter from John Ashbery to Frank O'Hara dated "7 decembre 1956."

p. 92 "My father had": John Ashbery, quoted in Dinitia Smith, "Poem Alone," *New York*, May 20, 1991, p. 49.

p. 92 "I was always: John Ashbery, interviewed by Michael Gizzi in *Lingo*, no. 2 (1993), p. 9. Mary Butts was a writer Ashbery recommended to Koch in these terms: "Very weird, rather like Djuna [Barnes], but tight-lipped and suppressed hysterical." Postcard from John Ashbery to Kenneth Koch dated "Sept. 13" (early 1950s).

CHAPTER 3

p. 94 "It is often": Wallace Stevens, *The Necessary Angel* (New York: Vintage, 1951), p. 121.

p. 94 "My own biography": Rose Labrie, "John Ashbery: An Interview," *American Poetry Review*, May/June 1984, p. 29.

p. 97 "How about": Interview with John Ashbery, October 17, 1984.

p. 99 "I learned my lesson": Telephone interview with John Ashbery, September 29, 1997.

p. 102 "In a line": From interview with Bill Berkson, 1969. Undertaken for *The Paris Review* but unpublished.

p. 104 "I am reminded": Letter from Karen Pepper to David Lehman, April 1, 1997.

p. 107 "I think that": John Ashbery, quoted in David Lehman, *The Line Forms Here* (Ann Arbor: University of Michigan Press, 1992), p. 170.

p. 107 "I thought": Both examples of colloquialism are from "At First I Thought I Wouldn't Say Anything About It," in John Ashbery, *Can You Hear, Bird*, p. 13.

p. 107 "sacred for me": John Ashbery, quoted in Lehman, *Line Forms Here*, p. 171.

p. 110 "Mayberry the 22nd": Letter from Kenneth Koch to John Ashbery [1960]. John Ashbery Papers, AM-6, Box 11, File 2, Houghton Library, Harvard University.

p. 111 "Popeye has": Telephone interview with John Ashbery, February 28, 1994.

p. 111 There is a portrait: From the Larry Rivers exhibition at the Robert Miller Gallery, New York, November 1977.

p. 117 "negative capability [is] acting up again": The poem is "From Such Commotion," John Ashbery, *Wakefulness* (New York: Farrar, Straus & Giroux, 1998). As read at the Morgan Library, New York, November 10, 1997.

p. 117 "Hotel Laundromat": John Haines poem published in *The Hudson Review*, Fall 1993.

p. 118 "John Ashbery": Jeffrey Skinner poem published in *Poetry*, March 1997, pp. 326–27.

p. 119 "Best of Poets": Letter from Harold Bloom to John Ashbery, 1975. Ashbery Papers, AM-6, Box 3, File 1, Houghton Library.

p. 121 "One of my earliest": John Ashbery, "Wallpaper," *Reported Sightings*, p. 383; originally published in *New York*, September 8, 1980.

p. 121 *The Book*: "Just Say Know," *Voice Literary Supplement*, February 1992.

p. 122 "I resemble": John Ashbery, quoted by Anna Quindlen, *New York Post*, February 7, 1976.

p. 122 "kind of took over": John Ashbery interview with Michael Gizzi in *Lingo*, no. 2 (1993), p. 9.

p. 123 "If you at times": Letter from Henry Lawrence to John Ashbery, September 29, 1944. Ashbery Papers, AM-6, Box 11, File 2, Houghton Library.

p. 123 "has the gloomy": John Ashbery, "The Poet's Hudson River Restoration," *Architectural Digest*, June 1994, p. 40.

p. 123 "I had a crush": Interview with John Ashbery, March 31, 1998.

p. 124 "he wanted": "Craft Interview with John Ashbery," in William Packard, ed., *The Craft of Poetry* (New York: Doubleday, 1974), p. 122.

p. 125 He played: Ibid., p. 114.

p. 125 "until they were": "A Conversation" (John Ashbery and Kenneth Koch), in Anne Waldman, ed., *Out of This World: An Anthology of the St. Mark's Poetry Project 1966–1991*, p. 26.

p. 125 "one part shimmer": John Ashbery, Frost Medal Lecture, New York Public Library, April 28, 1995.

p. 126 "I pored": Sue Gangel, "An Interview with John Ashbery," *San Francisco Review of Books* 3, no. 7 (November 1977), p. 8.

p. 126 "Dear Montcalm": Letter from John Ashbery to Kenneth Koch, n.d., from 10, rue de Vaugirard, Paris 6. Courtesy Kenneth Koch.

p. 126 What the Surrealists: John Ashbery, Statement at the National Book Awards symposium "Poetry Now," St. Regis Hotel, New York, March 5, 1968.

p. 126 Marcel Duchamp: See Calvin Tompkins, "Duchamp and New York," *The New Yorker*, November 25, 1996, pp. 92–100, for an excellent discussion.

p. 126 "What would a musical": Ruth Duskin Feldman, *Whatever Happened to the Quiz Kids?* (Chicago: Chicago Review Press, 1982), p. 14.

p. 127 "had managed to": J. D. Salinger, *Franny and Zooey* (Boston: Little, Brown, 1961), pp. 53–54.

p. 128 "The first ten": Interview with John Ashbery, February 7, 1994.

p. 129 "was a superb": Unsigned front-page article, *Deerfield Scroll*, December 9, 1944.

p. 129 "John Ashbury [sic]": Stuart I. Repp, letter of November 1984 to the Deerfield class of 1945, announcing the reunion scheduled for June 14, 15 and 16 (1985).

p. 129 "Poetry today": John Ashbery, "Recent Tendencies in Poetry" (paper written at Deerfield 1945). Ashbery Papers, AM-6, Box 31, File 2, Houghton Library.

p. 130 "Lost Cove": John Ashbery poem published (under the name Joel Michael Symington) in *Poetry* 66 (November 1945), pp. 66–67.

p. 131 "mystical imagination": Letter from David Morton to Marion Strobel, May 11, 1945. *Poetry* magazine, 1936–1953, Box I/XVII, Folder 12, Department of Special Collections, Joseph Regenstein Library, University of Chicago.

p. 131 "permanently blackballed": John Ashbery, *Poetry* nos. 1–2 (October/November 1987) 75th Anniversary Issue, p. 203.

p. 132 "Sestinas are": Letter from John Ashbery to Kenneth Koch, June 18, 1948. Courtesy Kenneth Koch.

p. 132 "with furious": Letter from John Ashbery to Kenneth Koch, August 7, 1948. Courtesy Kenneth Koch.

p. 133 "her surreal": John Ashbery, quoted in Gary Fountain and Peter

Brazeau, *Elizabeth Bishop: An Oral Biography* (Amherst: University of Massachusetts Press, 1994), p. 337.

p. 133 "Be sure to read": Letter from John Ashbery to Kenneth Koch, June 18, 1948. Courtesy Kenneth Koch.

p. 134 "I am unable": John Ashbery, "The Complete Poems," *New York Times Book Review*, June 1, 1969; reprinted in Lloyd Schwartz, ed., *Elizabeth Bishop and Her Art* (Ann Arbor: University of Michigan Press, 1983), p. 204.

p. 134 In March 1997: At the New School for Social Research, March 13, 1997. The reading was sponsored by the poetry center of the 92nd Street Y and by the Academy of American Poets. The anthology is entitled *Earth Took of Earth*.

p. 136 "Right here and now": John Ashbery's diary (1942). Ashbery Papers, AM-6, Box 31, File 2, Houghton Library.

p. 137 "Point of Departure": John Ashbery poem published in *The Advocate* 131, no. 1 (October 1947), p. 9.

p. 137 "But we don't": Kenneth Koch, introducing John Ashbery's Frost Medal Lecture, New York Public Library, April 28, 1995.

p. 137 "I was amazed": Interview with Robert Bly, March 26, 1998.

p. 137 "Creeley was much": John Ashbery, introduction to a poetry reading by Robert Creeley and Charles Tomlinson, New School for Social Research, New York, April 25, 1995.

p. 138 "sophisticated": Interview with John Ashbery, December 8, 1994; interview with Alison Lurie, December 9, 1994.

p. 138 "Since I heard": Handwritten letter from John Ashbery to Kenneth Koch, n.d.

p. 138 "Put a simile": Letter from John Ashbery to Kenneth Koch, June 18, 1948. Courtesy Kenneth Koch.

p. 139 "The theatre is not": Roger Oliver, "Interview: John Ashbery, Poet in the Theatre," *PAJ* 3, no. 3 (Winter 1979), p. 16.

p. 139 *The Heroes*: In John Ashbery, *Three Plays*, pp. 4–7.

p. 141 "the hit": James Merrill, *A Different Person*, p. 255.

p. 142 "John's play": Letter from James Schuyler to Kenneth Koch, June 3, 1955.

p. 143 "and was": Oliver, "Interview: John Ashbery," p. 23.

p. 146 "The place has": Henry James, *A Little Tour in France* (New York: Farrar, Straus & Giroux, 1983), pp. 153–54.

p. 146 "Most of the time": Letter from John Ashbery to Fairfield Porter, March 2, 1956. Ashbery Papers, AM-6, Box 25, File 2, Houghton Library.

p. 147 "just couldn't": Lawrence G. Blochman, quoted in David K. Kermani, *John Ashbery: A Comprehensive Bibliography*, p. 9.

p. 148 *A dark horse:* Given as an instance of the rhetorical figure called amphiboly, in Karl Beckson and Arthur Ganz, *A Reader's Guide to Literary Terms* (New York: Farrar, Straus & Giroux, 1960), pp. 7–8.

p. 148 *"Locus Solus"*: Letter from John Ashbery to Kenneth Koch ("Dear Alumnus"), June 11 [1958]. Courtesy Kenneth Koch.

p. 149 "insisted on": John Ashbery, "A Note on Pierre Reverdy," *Evergreen Review*, 1962.

p. 150 "A friend of mine": Bill Berkson, unpublished interview with John Ashbery, 1969.

p. 151 "power": Letter from Harry Mathews to John Ashbery, March 25, 1978. Ashbery Papers, AM-6, Box 13, Houghton Library.

p. 152 "French and English": "John Ashbery Interviewing Harry Mathews," *The Review of Contemporary Fiction* 7, no. 3 (Fall 1987).

p. 152 "You have [a]": André du Bouchet, quoted in Christopher Sawyer-Laucanno, *The Continual Pilgrimage: American Writers in Paris, 1944–1960* (New York: Grove Press, 1992), pp. 253–54.

p. 152 "an atmosphere": Letter from Harry Mathews to John Ashbery, April 9, 1970. Ashbery Papers, AM-6, Box 13, Houghton Library.

p. 152 "Americans can": John Ashbery, introduction to Ellsworth Kelly, *Plant Drawings* (New York: Matthew Marks Gallery, 1992), unpaginated.

p. 152 "The Americans in": John Ashbery, "American Sanctuary in Paris," originally published in *Art News Annual*, 1966; reprinted in Ashbery, *Reported Sightings*, pp. 88, 90–91, 96–97.

p. 153 "personal reasons": John Ashbery, "Joan Mitchell," originally published in *Art News*, April 1965; reprinted in Ashbery, *Reported Sightings*, p. 98.

p. 153 "I found my poetry": Ashbery, introduction to Kelly, *Plant Drawings*.

p. 154 Ashbery and Pierre Martory: John Ashbery, "Introduction" to Pierre Martory, *The Landscape Is Behind the Door*, trans. John Ashbery, pp. ix–x.

p. 154 During the last: Harry Mathews, "Introducing John Ashbery and Pierre Martory," DIA Center for the Arts in New York City, October 5, 1993 (unpublished).

p. 154 "was the ideal": John Ashbery, "Introduction" to Martory, *Landscape Is Behind the Door*, p. x.

p. 154 "I remember when": Rosanne Wasserman, "Pierre Martory: An

Interview," *American Poetry Review*, September/October 1993, p. 14.

p. 155 "crypt words": John Shoptaw, *On the Outside Looking Out: John Ashbery's Poetry*, pp. 65–66.

p. 160 "There's a Métro": Bill Berkson, unpublished interview with John Ashbery, 1969.

p. 162 "Having lived": John Ashbery, quoted in a letter from Harry Mathews to Ashbery, April 9, 1970. Ashbery Papers, AM-6, Box 13, Houghton Library.

p. 163 Now, for the first: In 1957–58, when Ashbery interrupted his Paris sojourn with a one-year stint in New York, Kenneth Koch was spending the year in Florence.

CHAPTER 4

p. 165 O'Hara's broken nose: Alice Neel, quoted in Bill Berkson and Joe LeSueur, eds., *Homage to Frank O'Hara*, p. 96.

p. 165 "gave him the look": John Ashbery, "A Reminiscence," in Berkson and LeSueur, *Homage to Frank O'Hara*, p. 20.

p. 166 "When I painted": Elaine de Kooning, *Art in America* (1975); reprinted in Berkson and LeSueur, *Homage to Frank O'Hara*, p. 97.

p. 166 "He was thin": Larry Rivers, with Arnold Weinstein, *What Did I Do?*, p. 228.

p. 166 "I remember Frank": Joe Brainard, *I Remember*, p. 14.

p. 166 "Oh I hate": Harold Brodkey, "What Going Out Without Ora Is Like: Johnno: 1956," *Partisan Review*, no. 4 (1985), pp. 361–97.

p. 167 *The Killing Cycle*: See Marjorie Perloff, *Frank O'Hara: Poet Among Painters*, pp. 1–3.

p. 167 In "The Accident": Judith Stein, "Introduction and Chronology to the Killing Cycle," in *Alfred Leslie: The Killing Cycle* (St. Louis Art Museum, n.c.), p. 43.

p. 169 "unquenchable inspiration": James Schuyler, quoted in Frank O'Hara, *Collected Poems*, ed. Donald Allen (New York: Knopf, 1971), p. 536.

p. 170 "alcoholism was so": Interview with James Schuyler by Raymond Foye, March 9, 1990, Chelsea Hotel, New York. James Schuyler Papers, Mss. 78, Box 26, Folder 28, Archive for New Poetry, Mandeville Special Collections Library, University of California at San Diego.

p. 170 "always felt that": Grace Hartigan, quoted in Brad Gooch, *City Poet: The Life and Times of Frank O'Hara*, pp. 467–68.

p. 171 "causing at least": J. J. Mitchell, "The Death of Frank O'Hara," in Berkson and LeSueur, *Homage to Frank O'Hara*, p. 145.

p. 171 "if he had wanted": Perloff, *Frank O'Hara*, p. 5.

p. 172 "Frank O'Hara was not": Interview with Joe LeSueur, June 9, 1994.

p. 172 A few weeks before: Interview with Patsy Southgate, September 23, 1994.

p. 173 "Frank O'Hara was a": Edward Denby, quoted in John Gruen, *The Party's Over Now*, p. 166.

p. 173 "the last stage": Kenneth Koch, "All the Imagination Can Hold," in Berkson and LeSueur, *Homage to Frank O'Hara*, p. 208. Originally published in *The New Republic*, 1972.

p. 173 "To us he seemed": Morton Feldman, "Lost Times and Future Hopes," in Berkson and LeSueur, *Homage to Frank O'Hara*, p. 13.

pp. 174–75 "a pattern of": Gooch, *City Poet*, pp. 194–97.

p. 175 "Is it my memory": John Ashbery interviewed by Michael Gizzi, *Lingo*, no. 2 (1993), p. 7.

p. 176 "If I had my way": Frank O'Hara, quoted in Joe LeSueur, *Nothing to Lose*, unpublished manuscript. Courtesy of Joe LeSueur.

p. 176 "went to extremes": Brainard, "Frank O'Hara," p. 167.

p. 176 "was a very great": Barbara Guest, interview with Mark Hillringhouse, undated typescript, 1982, p. 20.

p. 177 "If this all seems": Letter from Frank O'Hara to John Button, November 4, 1960. Berg Collection, New York Public Library.

p. 177 "As for your thing": Letter from Frank O'Hara to Joseph Caravolo, 4 March 1966. Donald Allen Papers, University of Connecticut Library, Storrs. Used with permission.

p. 178 "Suddenly": Letter from Frank O'Hara to Barnett Newman, 15 July 1966. Donald Allen Papers, University of Connecticut Library.

p. 178 "You do what": Frank O'Hara, "To Larry Rivers," *Collected Poems*, p. 128.

p. 179 "Pollock is": Frank O'Hara, *Jackson Pollock*, p. 24.

p. 179 "best criticism": Charles Baudelaire, "The Salon of 1846," trans. P. E. Charvet, in *Selected Writings on Art and Literature* (New York: Penguin Books, 1972), p. 50.

p. 189 "what his work": Frank O'Hara, *Collected Poems*, p. 515.

p. 189 Take that lady: At P. J. Moriarty's, on Sixth Avenue and Fifty-second Street, a short stroll from O'Hara's office at the Museum of Modern Art, the diners might have had a martini, a shrimp cocktail, and a filet mignon dinner for less than ten dollars.

p. 190 "Holy mackerel": J. Alfred Adams. "Speaking of Books," *New York Times Book Review,* April 12, 1959.

p. 191 "these *were* children": Diana Trilling, *Claremont Essays,* p. 162.

p. 192 "a dogged woman": Alfred Kazin, *New York Jew* (New York: Vintage, 1979), p. 68.

p. 192 "Except when": Diana Trilling, *The Beginning of the Journey,* p. 162.

p. 194 "move on": LeRoi Jones, "Bop," in Robert Gottlieb, ed., *Reading Jazz: A Gathering of Autobiography, Reportage, and Criticism from 1919 to Now,* p. 879; originally in LeRoi Jones, *Blues People* (1963).

p. 195 "was original": Letter from Jamie Katz to David Lehman, October 20, 1996.

p. 196 "to smash": Amiri Baraka, "Like—This Is What I Meant!" in Charles Russell, ed., *The Avant-Garde Today: An International Anthology* (Urbana: University of Illinois Press, 1981), p. 226.

p. 196 "inclusiveness": Yusef Komunyakaa, in Richard Howard, ed., *The Best American Poetry 1995* (New York: Scribner, 1995), p. 261.

p. 197 "I consider": Frank O'Hara, "Answer to Voznesensky and Yevtushenko," *Collected Poems,* p. 468.

p. 201 "the goatee": Jones, "Bop," p. 871.

CHAPTER 5

p. 204 "continuing celebration": John Hollander, "Kenneth Koch," in Harold Bloom, ed., *Contemporary Poets* (New York: Chelsea House, 1986), p. 157.

pp. 204–5 "If it's funny": Charles Simic, "Cut the Comedy," *Orphan Factory* (Ann Arbor: University of Michigan Press, 1977), p. 40.

p. 208 "The little I knew": Tom Andrews, "Into What a Delicious Riot of Things Am I Rushing?," *Poetry East,* no. 34 (Spring 1992): in *The Self-Avoiding Random Walk,* unpublished manuscript, p. 35.

p. 209 "Frank comes out": Kenneth Koch, "A Time Zone," *One Train,* p. 23.

p. 209 "The Boiling Water": Kenneth Koch, *On the Great Atlantic Rainway: Selected Poems 1950–1988,* p. 188.

p. 210 "where there's": Letter from Frank O'Hara to John Ashbery, February 1, 1961. Courtesy John Ashbery.

p. 210 "ruled with": Koch, *On the Great Atlantic Rainway*, p. 72.

p. 213 "The first page": Kenneth Koch, "Educating the Imagination II," *Teachers and Writers Collaborative*, 1994.

p. 214 "I did not have": Kenneth Koch, "Inspiration and Work: How Poetry Gets to Be Written," *Comparative Literature Studies* 17, no. 2 (June 1980), p. 211.

p. 214 "That's very good": Katherine Lappa, quoted in Ibid., pp. 212–13.

p. 214 "instance of": Entry on Kenneth Koch in *Current Biography*, 1978.

p. 215 "feel the buildings": Kenneth Koch, *Seasons on Earth*, p. 92.

p. 215 "I remember the *Bysshe*": Interview with Kenneth Koch, October 29, 1994.

p. 216 "an intelligent": T. S. Eliot, "The Use of Poetry and the Use of Criticism," in *Selected Prose of T. S. Eliot*, ed. Frank Kermode (New York: Harcourt Brace, 1975), p. 81.

p. 216 "I was trained": Interview with Kenneth Koch, February 10, 1994.

p. 217 "Poem for My Twentieth Birthday": Kenneth Koch poem published in *Poetry* 67 (November 1945), p. 80.

p. 218 "What's this all": Interview with Kenneth Koch, February 10, 1994.

p. 219 "With hoarded": Dorothy Alyea, "There's Margaret," *Poetry* 67 (November 1945), p. 81.

p. 219 "bright, affable": Transcript for Jay Kenneth Koch, Registrar's Office, Harvard University. Courtesy Thurston Smith, Associate Registrar, Harvard University.

p. 219 "My reason": Transcript for Jay Kenneth Koch.

p. 219 "The Koch": Letter from John Ashbery to Kenneth Koch, November 17, 1948.

p. 221 "And you will": Kenneth Koch, *The Art of Poetry: Poems, Parodies, Interviews, Essays, and Other Work*, pp. 98–99.

p. 221 "My poetry": Kenneth Koch, quoted in Donald Allen, ed., *The New American Poetry*, pp. 439–40.

p. 221 *"Comme"*: Kenneth Koch, interview with Mark Hillringhouse. Courtesy Mark Hillringhouse.

p. 222 "Sweet are": Kenneth Koch, "Days and Nights," *On the Great Atlantic Rainway*, p. 104.

p. 224 "swan of bees": Kenneth Koch, *Wishes, Lies and Dreams: Teaching Children to Write Poetry*, pp. 148–55.

p. 225 "The dancing wagon": Kenneth Koch, "Lunch," *On the Great Atlantic Rainway*, p. 109.

p. 229 "It was the time": Kenneth Koch, "Seasons on Earth," *On the Great Atlantic Rainway*, p. 310.

p. 230 "the geography": Kenneth Koch, "The Pleasures of Peace," *On the Great Atlantic Rainway*, p. 134.

p. 230 " 'A wonder!' ": Ibid., p. 140.

p. 232 " 'Hello, Jim' ": Kenneth Koch, "The Railway Stationery," *On the Great Atlantic Rainway*, p. 104.

p. 232 " 'Professor!' ": Koch, "Pleasures of Peace," p. 133.

p. 233 "He said that": Interview with David Shapiro, October 31, 1996.

p. 235 "It's like being": Interview with Mitch Sisskind, June 7, 1994.

p. 235 "Koch made us": Interview with Aaron Fogel, May 9, 1994.

p. 236 "part of what": Koch, *Art of Poetry*, p. 212.

p. 236 "a happy Sisyphus": Kenneth Koch, "Presenting John Ashbery," *The Art of Poetry*, p. 50.

p. 237 "There was this": Interview with David Shapiro, October 31, 1996.

p. 237 "The Lost Golf Ball": David Shapiro, remarks at a poetry reading in Barnes & Noble (Chelsea store), New York, November 21, 1996.

p. 237 "Kenneth Koch / could": James Schuyler, "I sit down to type," *Collected Poems*, p. 241.

p. 239 "What is death": Kenneth Koch, "The Circus," *On the Great Atlantic Rainway*, pp. 51–52.

p. 241 "I remember when": Ibid., p. 154.

CHAPTER 6

p. 243 "It seems that": Letter from Ted Berrigan to James Schuyler, January 30, 1964, in Anne Waldman, ed., *Nice to See You: Homage to Ted Berrigan*, p. 8.

p. 245 "Freely Espousing": James Schuyler, *Collected Poems*, pp. 3–4.

p. 246 "I have always": James Schuyler, *A Few Days* (New York: Random House, 1985), p. 73.

p. 246 "a calm secret": James Schuyler, "December," *Collected Poems*, p. 13.

p. 249 "It seems so": Rae Armantrout in conversation, March 17, 1997.

p. 249 "Current Events": James Schuyler story published in *Locus Solus*, no. 1, pp. 34–35.

p. 250 "Some observers": Ibid., pp. 43–44.

p. 251 "Granny came": James Schuyler, *Alfred and Guinevere*, p. 56.

p. 251 "Mother's mad": Ibid., p. 82.

p. 251 "Hello, daughter": Ibid., p. 57.

p. 252 *"Alfred and Guinevere* does": Kenneth Koch, "Poetry as Prose," *The Art of Poetry: Poems, Parodies, Interviews, Essays, and Other Work*, p. 30; originally published in *Poetry*, February 1959.

p. 253 "It was Alfred's": Schuyler, *Alfred and Guinevere*, p. 147.

p. 254 "Some days": James Schuyler, *The Diary of James Schuyler*, ed. Nathan Kernan, pp. 100–1.

p. 255 "Not only": John Koethe, "Freely Espoused," *Poetry*, October 1970, p. 54.

p. 255 "I am going": Letter from Elizabeth Bishop to John Ashbery, March 5, 1973. John Ashbery Papers, AM-6, Box 3, Houghton Library, Harvard University.

p. 255 "one of the few": Letter from Elizabeth Bishop to Charles North, April 1975.

p. 255 "precision of detail": Howard Moss, "Whatever Is Moving," *Minor Monuments: Selected Essays* (New York: Ecco, 1986), pp. 194, 200.

p. 256 "Just as Porter": Douglas Crase, "Plainsongs," *The Nation*, November 16, 1985, p. 506.

p. 256 "Nah, you're": Schuyler, "A Few Days," *Collected Poems*, p. 368.

p. 256 "a very hunting-and-shooting": Carl Little, "An Interview with James Schuyler," *Agni Review*, no. 37 (1993), p. 156.

p. 256 "Knowing Whitman": Ibid., p. 157.

p. 257 "I think you ought": Letter from James Schuyler to Kenneth Koch, typed, dated "Jan. 57." Courtesy Kenneth Koch.

p. 258 "disreputable American": Little, "Interview with James Schuyler," p. 160.

p. 259 "And / when": James Schuyler, "Wystan Auden," *Collected Poems*, pp. 242–43.

p. 259 "I would": Little, "Interview with James Schuyler," p. 161.

p. 259 "told / an": Schuyler, "A Few Days," *Collected Poems*, p. 368.

p. 259 "a hero": Schuyler, "Dining Out with Doug and Frank," *Collected Poems*, pp. 248–49.

p. 260 "John had come": James Schuyler, interview with Raymond Foye, March 9, 1990. James Schuyler Papers, Mss. 78, Box 26, Folder 28, Archive for New Poetry, Mandeville Special Collections Library, University of California at San Diego.

p. 260 "Dining Out with Doug and Frank": Schuyler, *Collected Poems*, p. 250.

p. 261 All his adult: See Anne Waldman's poem "I am blinded by a fiery circle," in William Corbett and Geoffrey Young, eds., *That Various Field: For James Schuyler*, p. 19.

p. 261 "eighty": Interview with Ron Padgett, March 27, 1997.

p. 261 "Can you imagine": Letter from James Schuyler to John Ashbery, September 25, 1971. Ashbery Papers, AM-6, Box 17, Houghton Library.

p. 262 "June 30, 1974": Schuyler, *Collected Poems*, p. 230.

p. 262 "the heaviest": James Schuyler, "The Painting of Jane Freilicher," in J. D. McClatchy, ed., *Poets on Painters: Essays on the Art of Painting by Twentieth-Century Poets* (Berkeley: University of California Press, 1988), p. 262.

p. 263 "This old hotel": Schuyler, *A Few Days*, p. 77.

p. 264 "jealous": John Ashbery, "Introduction to a Reading Given by James Schuyler," in *Denver Quarterly*, Spring 1990, p. 11.

p. 266 "Look out": James Schuyler, "Mike," *Collected Poems*, pp. 150–51.

p. 267 "When you": James Schuyler, "The Morning of the Poem," *Collected Poems*, p. 294.

p. 267 "The morning": James Schuyler, "A Few Days," *Collected Poems*, pp. 362–63.

p. 269 "if I did": "Ode," signed "Jimmy & Frank," dated April 16, 1956. Donald Allen Collection, Mss. 3, Archive for New Poetry, Mandeville Special Collections Library, University of California at San Diego.

p. 270 "I don't mean": Letter from Frank O'Hara to John Ashbery, May 1, 1961. Donald Allen Papers, University of Connecticut Library, Storrs. Used with permission.

p. 270 "After drinking": Letter from James Schuyler to Kenneth Koch, typed, dated "Jan. 57."

p. 271 "Epistle to Dr. Koch": Undated, signed "J.S.," probably 1969. Courtesy Kenneth Koch.

p. 274 "Sleek": James Schuyler, "A Stone Knife," *Collected Poems*, p. 112.

p. 275 "as they were": Letter from Charles North to David Lehman, March 14, 1997.

p. 276 "an image": Interview with Darragh Park, April 11, 1997.

p. 277 "The scale": Schuyler, "Painting of Jane Freilicher," p. 262.

p. 277 "Lesser artists": John Ashbery, "Jane Freilicher" (1986), *Reported Sightings*, p. 242.

p. 277 "superficial": Helen Vendler, "New York Pastoral," *Soul Says: Recent Poetry* (Cambridge: Harvard University Press, 1995), p. 62.

CHAPTER 7

p. 284 "The twentieth": Umberto Saba, quoted in Renato Poggioli, *The Theory of the Avant-Garde*, trans. Gerald Fitzgerald, pp. 69–70.

p. 286 "the whole": Poggioli, *Theory of the Avant-Garde*, p. 83.

p. 287 "As a style": Paul Goodman, *Speaking and Language: Defence of Poetry*, pp. 215–17.

p. 287 "No work": Lionel Trilling, "Art, Will, and Necessity" (1973), in *The Last Decade*, ed. Diana Trilling (New York: Harcourt Brace, 1979), pp. 134–35.

p. 288 "The spectacle": Janet Malcolm, "Forty-One False Starts," *The New Yorker*, July 11, 1994, p. 52. Ms. Malcolm makes it clear that her sympathies are with the painter. The quotation represents her paraphrase of "the common perception," not her own. "In the common perception, there is something unseemly about young people getting rich. Getting rich is supposed to be the reward for hard work, preferably arriving when you are too old to enjoy it."

p. 290 "if we define": Fairfield Porter, quoted in John Bernard Myers, "Jottings from a Diary (1952–1975)," in *Fairfield Porter (1907–1975): Realist Painter in an Age of Abstraction* (Boston: Museum of Fine Arts, 1982), p. 43.

p. 291 "Today one": John Ashbery, *Reported Sightings*, pp. 393–94. Epigraph to this chapter from same source, p. 392.

p. 291 "what might be": Poggioli, *Theory of the Avant-Garde*, p. 12. "Within the military connotations of the image, the implication is not so much of an advance against an enemy as a marching toward, a reconnoitering or exploring of, that difficult and unknown territory called no-man's land" (pp. 27–28).

p. 292 In the end: Poggioli, *Theory of the Avant-Garde*, p. 31.

p. 293 "No poem": Charles Baudelaire, trans. P. E. Charvet, *Selected Writings on Art and Literature* (Penguin Books, 1972), p. 203.

p. 293 The art historian: Linda Nochlin, "The Invention of the Avant-Garde, France 1830–80," Thomas B. Hess and John Ashbery, eds., *Avant-Garde Art*, pp. 20–21.

p. 294 "the joke": Noel Annan, *Our Age: English Intellectuals Between the World Wars—A Group Portrait*, p. 54.

p. 295 "Laughter is": Charles Baudelaire, "On the Essence of Laughter" ("De L'essence du rire"), in *Les Fleurs du mal et oeuvres choisies*, ed. Wallace Fowelie (New York: Bantam, 1964), pp. 176–77.

p. 296 "No matter how": Harold Rosenberg, "Collective, Ideological, Combative," Hess and Ashbery, eds., in *Avant-Garde Art*, p. 92.

p. 297 Italian Futurism: Richard Cork, *A Bitter Truth: Avant-Garde Art and the Great War*, p. 16.

p. 297 Some Surrealists went: Maurice Nadeau, *The History of Surrealism*, trans. Richard Howard, p. 303.

p. 298 "a maker": Charles Simic, "Negative Capability and Its Children," in Martin Lammon, ed., *Written in Water, Written in Stone* (Ann Arbor: University of Michigan Press, 1996), p. 203.

p. 300 "The artist must": Meyer Schapiro, "The Liberating Quality of Avant-Garde Art," *Art News* 56, no. 4 (Summer 1956), p. 42.

p. 300 "The poet must": Wallace Stevens, *Collected Poetry and Prose* (New York: The Library of America, 1997), p. 825.

p. 300 "ersatz culture": Clement Greenberg, "Avant-Garde and Kitsch," *The Collected Essays and Criticism*, vol. 1, ed. John O'Brian, p. 12.

p. 301 "It has been": Ibid., p. 8.

p. 302 "the most advanced": Clement Greenberg, "The Situation at the Moment," *Partisan Review*, January 1948; reprinted in Greenberg, *Collected Essays and Criticism*, vol. 2, p. 193.

p. 303 "the neurosis": Ibid. p. 194.

p. 303 "What can fifty": Clement Greenberg, "The Present Prospects of American Painting and Sculpture," *Horizon*, October 1947; reprinted in Greenberg, *Collected Essays and Criticism*, vol. 2, p. 170. It was in the *Horizon* article that Greenberg said that the only American artists he would consider major were Jackson Pollock and sculptor David Smith, and that the fate of art was in the hands of the fifty or so people for whom "Hofmann's presence in New York" was all-important.

p. 303 "isolation": Greenberg, *Collected Essays and Criticism*, vol. 2, pp. 192–96.

p. 303 "The main premises": Clement Greenberg, "The Decline of Cubism," *Partisan Review*, March 1948; reprinted in Greenberg, *Collected Essays and Criticism*, vol. 2, p. 215.

CHAPTER 8

p. 304 "Artists in any": James Schuyler, quoted in Donald Allen, ed., *The New American Poetry*, p. 418.

p. 304 "the upper classes": Interview with Kenneth Koch, February 28, 1994.

p. 304 "a way we baby": Interview with Kenneth Koch, February 10, 1994.

p. 304 "Painters had lives": Interview with Kenneth Koch, June 30, 1994.

p. 305 "argue and gossip": Frank O'Hara, "Larry Rivers: A Memoir," in *Standing Still and Walking in New York*, ed. Donald Allen, p. 169.

p. 305 "powers and personality": Frank O'Hara, in *Standing Still and Walking in New York*, p. 22.

p. 305 "not entirely because": John Ashbery, Statement at the National Book Awards symposium "Poetry Now," St. Regis Hotel, New York, March 5, 1968. John Ashbery Papers, AM-6, Box 31, Houghton Library, Harvard University.

p. 306 "the state of": Frank O'Hara, "Jackson Pollock," *Art Chronicles 1954–1966*, pp. 25–26.

p. 308 "Frank O'Hara's poetry": John Ashbery, "Frank O'Hara's Question," in *Book Week*, September 25, 1966.

p. 308 "We are in danger": Robert Lowell, quoted in Richard Tillinghast, *Robert Lowell's Life and Work: Damaged Grandeur* (Ann Arbor: University of Michigan Press, 1995), pp. 28–29.

p. 309 "had a bad press": Josephine Jacobsen, "Poet of the Particular," *Commonweal*, December 4, 1964; reprinted in *The Instant of Knowing: Lectures, Criticism, and Occasional Prose*, ed. Elizabeth Spires (Ann Arbor: University of Michigan Press, 1997).

p. 309 "complimented [O'Hara]": Louis Simpson, *The Nation*, April 24, 1967.

p. 309 "I was not 'sneering' ": Letter from John Ashbery to the editor of *The Nation*. Ashbery Papers, Box 25, Houghton Library.

p. 309 "while it is": John Ashbery, *Art News* 67, no. 3 (May 1968), p. 41. Quoted in John Shoptaw, *On the Outside Looking Out*, p. 187.

p. 310 "the loyalty-oath": "John Ashbery Interviewing Harry Mathews," *The Review of Contemporary Fiction* 7, no. 3 (Fall 1987), p. 46.

p. 313 "the Nixon White House": Stephen Paul Miller, "The Mirror's Backing Considered as a Major Trope of Watergate and Ashbery's *Self-Portrait in a Convex Mirror,*" *Staten Island Review,* Fall/Winter 1986–87, pp. 60–68.

p. 316 "I was spending": From Sue Gangel, "An Interview with John Ashbery," *San Francisco Review of Books* 3, no. 7 (November 1977), p. 11.

p. 318 "In those days": Interview with Larry Rivers, March 25, 1994.

p. 318 "queerdom was": Larry Rivers, quoted in John Gruen, *The Party's Over Now,* p. 133.

p. 319 "was just a way": Larry Rivers, *Drawings and Digressions* (New York: Clarkson N. Potter, 1979), p. 59.

p. 320 "Someone who": Letter from Frank O'Hara to Larry Rivers, June 27, 1953. Donald Allen Papers, University of Connecticut Library, Storrs. Used with permission.

p. 320 "Kenneth, read": Letter from Larry Rivers to Kenneth Koch, n.d., 1953. Courtesy Kenneth Koch.

pp. 320–21 "that's nothing": Larry Rivers, quoted in Alfred Friendly, Jr., "Lagos Frees American Artist and a Filmmaker," *New York Times,* January 9, 1968.

p. 321 "a farce": Larry Rivers, with Arnold Weinstein, *What Did I Do?,* p. 441.

p. 321 "Art gives him": Fairfield Porter, "Larry Rivers Paints a Picture," *Art News,* January 1954.

p. 321 "search for his life": Letter from Fairfield Porter to Richard Freeman, October 26, 1973.

p. 321 "the important thing": Fairfield Porter, quoted by John Bernard Myers, in *Fairfield Porter (1907–1975): Realist Painter in an Age of Abstraction* (Boston: Museum of Fine Arts, 1982), p. 43.

p. 322 "It was snowing": Fairfield Porter, quoted in an interview with Anne Porter, September 9, 1996.

p. 323 "No psychiatrists": Fairfield Porter, quoted by Kenworth Moffett in *Fairfield Porter (1907–1975): Realist Painter in an Age of Abstraction* (Boston: Museum of Fine Arts, 1982), p. 24.

p. 323 "Often in still lifes": Fairfield Porter, quoted by Paul Cummings, "Conversation with Fairfield Porter" (1968), in *Fairfield Porter (1907–1975),* p. 57.

p. 324 "it was impossible": Fairfield Porter, "Recent American Figure Painting," *Art in Its Own Terms: Selected Criticism 1935–1975* (Boston: Zoland Books, 1979), p. 70.

p. 324 "To say that you cannot": Ibid., p. 70.

p. 325 "If Jimmy likes": Fairfield Porter, "I Wonder What They Think of My Verses," *The Collected Poems* (New York: Tibor de Nagy Editions, 1985), p. 63.

p. 326 "I have no idea": William Arrowsmith, *The Hudson Review*, Summer 1956.

p. 326 "In Ashbery's poetry": Letters of Fairfield Porter, *Boulevard* 6, nos. 17 and 18 (Fall 1991), pp. 35–36.

p. 327 "Ashbery's language": Porter, *Art in Its Own Terms*, pp. 224–25.

p. 327 "The genius of Cornell": John Ashbery, *Reported Sightings*, p. 15.

p. 328 "strictly for domestic": Letter from John Ashbery to Kenneth Koch, August 4, 1955. Courtesy Kenneth Koch.

p. 329 "I want to do everything": Fairfield Porter, quoted in Frank O'Hara, "Porter Paints a Picture," *Art News*, January 1955; reprinted in O'Hara, *Standing Still and Walking in New York*, p. 52.

p. 330 *"Stanzas in Meditation"*: John Ashbery, "The Impossible," *Poetry*, July 1957, pp. 253–54.

p. 332 "An ambiguity": William Empson, *Seven Types of Ambiguity* (originally published 1930) (New York: New Directions, 1947), p. 1.

p. 332 "the language of poetry": Cleanth Brooks, *The Well-Wrought Urn* (New York: Harcourt Brace, 1947), pp. 3, 20–21.

p. 333 "In his early poems": Joseph Epstein, "Mistah Lowell—He Dead," *Hudson Review*, Summer 1996, p. 189.

p. 334 "As I often say": Robert Frost, "Maturity No Object," in Donald Hall, Robert Pack, and Louis Simpson, eds., *The New Poets of England and America: An Anthology*, p. 12.

p. 334 "one common characteristic": Donald Allen, "Preface," *The New American Poetry*, p. xi.

p. 335 The inclusion of: In fact, the New York poets were the one group—the only group—that could have plausibly fit in either anthology. Donald Hall reports that Ashbery almost slipped into *New Poets*. "I liked John's work when we were undergraduates [at Harvard] and I never stopped liking it," he wrote to me. "I got hold of some poems by John and brought them to [Robert] Pack and [Louis] Simpson. Pack thought they were absolutely terrible . . . Louis did not feel strongly. . . . He believed in my advocacy of [Ashbery's poems] and so they were put into the manuscript, two against one." When space limitations demanded that the editors prune back the manuscript by fifty pages, "we went through the list. Louis did not feel warmly about John, and so John was one of the poets removed in the last cut." Letter from Donald Hall to David Lehman, May 10, 1994.

p. 335 "I thought the common": Allen Ginsberg and Kenneth Koch, "From a Conversation," *Poetry Project Newsletter*, October/November 1995, p. 5.

p. 335 "and maybe a little": Ibid., p. 6.

p. 335 "it was quite a disaster": Letter from Frank O'Hara to John Ashbery and Pierre Martory, March 16, 1959.

p. 337 "a united front": Ginsberg and Koch, "From a Conversation," p. 5.

p. 338 "So many poems": Hayden Carruth, "Essay," *Collected Shorter Poems 1946–1991* (Port Townsend, Wash.: Copper Canyon Press, 1992), p. 146.

p. 339 "Allen Ginsberg thinks": Gore Vidal, "How I Survived the Fifties," *The New Yorker*, October 2, 1995, p. 64.

p. 340 "Idealism retreated": John Updike, "The '50s: Each Man Was an Island," *Newsweek*, January 3, 1994, p. 36.

p. 340 "In 1950 there was": Ashbery, *Reported Sightings*, p. 390.

p. 341 "Not only is": Kenneth Koch, review of *Spearhead*, ed. James Laughlin, in *The Advocate* 131, no. 4 (Winter 1948), p. 22.

p. 344 For Barbara Guest: Interview with Barbara Guest, November 11, 1995.

p. 346 "that of a Jeremiah": Josephine Jacobsen, "Poet of the Particular," *Commonweal*, December 4, 1964; reprinted in Jacobsen, *The Instant of Knowing*.

p. 347 "I don't think that": Edward Lucie-Smith, "An Interview with Frank O'Hara," in O'Hara, *Standing Still and Walking in New York*, p. 13.

p. 347 "Robert Lowell is": Richard Poirier, quoted in Tillinghast, *Robert Lowell's Life and Work*, p. 26.

p. 347 "It'll slip into": Frank O'Hara, quoted in Joe LeSueur, *Nothing to Lose*, unpublished manuscript, p. 21. Courtesy Joe LeSueur.

p. 350 "silliest and emptiest": Letter from John Updike to David Lehman, March 7, 1996.

p. 350 "a familiar O'Hara": Rudy Kikel, "The Gay Frank O'Hara," in Jim Elledge, ed., *Frank O'Hara: To Be True to a City* (Ann Arbor: University of Michigan Press, 1990), p. 338. Originally published in *Gay Sunshine*, no. 38 (Winter 1978).

p. 351 "a mode of aestheticism": Susan Sontag, "Notes on Camp," *Against Interpretation* (Farrar, Straus & Giroux, 1966), pp. 275–92.

p. 352 "One doesn't have to": John Updike, "Legendary Lana," *The New Yorker*, February 12, 1996, pp. 68–75.

p. 354 "Against the concept": Hilton Kramer, *The Revenge of the Philistines: Art and Culture 1972–1984*, p. 7.

p. 355 "completely baffled": Letter from Elizabeth Bishop to John Ashbery, typed, March 5, 1973. Ashbery Papers, AM-6, Box 3, Houghton Library.

Epilogue

p. 360 "What I had wasn't": Ted Berrigan, *On the Level Everyday: Selected Talks on Poetry and the Art of Living*, ed. Joel Lewis (Jersey City, N.J.: Talisman House, 1997), p. 70.

p. 360 "I like him": Alice Notley, "April Not an Inventory but a Blizzard," *American Poetry Review*, 1997.

p. 363 "Sex is a biologic": Ted Berrigan, "An Interview with John Cage," *Mother*, no. 7 (1966), p. 7.

p. 364 "The judges didn't": Interview with Ron Padgett, March 27, 1997.

p. 365 "a real New Yorker": Ted Berrigan interviewed by Mark Hillringhouse (1980) in *Joe Soap's Canoe*, no. 15 (1992), n.p.

p. 366 "There was a tremendous": Ron Padgett, *Ted*, pp. 49–50.

p. 367 "I remember Bunny": Joe Brainard, *I Remember*, p. 35.

p. 369 "preoccupation": Charles Bernstein, "From an Ongoing Interview with Tom Beckett," in *New American Writing*, no. 14 (1996), p. 29.

p. 370 "the ideological": Charles Bernstein, *Artifice of Absorption* (1987), quoted in Marjorie Perloff, *Radical Artifice: Writing Poetry in the Age of Media*, p. 45.

p. 371 "I wanted to stretch": John Ashbery, Frost Medal Lecture, New York Public Library, April 28, 1995.

p. 372 ". . . a newly laid": Barbara Guest, "Words," in John Ashbery, ed., *The Best American Poetry 1988*, p. 61.

p. 372 He likened one: Carl Little, "An Interview with James Schuyler," *Agni Review*, no. 37, p. 159.

p. 372 "The Language people": Interview with Barbara Guest, November 11, 1995.

p. 374 "Afterward, they": James Cummins, "Fling," *Portrait in a Spoon* (Columbia, S.C.: University of South Carolina Press, 1997), p. 34.

p. 374 "The envelopes were": Susan Wheeler, "Shanked on the Red Bed," *The New Yorker*, June 9, 1997, p. 94.

p. 374 On the philosophers' team: Charles North, "Lineups II," in David Lehman, ed., *Ecstatic Occasions, Expedient Forms* (Ann Arbor: University of Michigan Press, 1996), pp. 167–71.

p. 374 Paul Violi's: Paul Violi, "Index," in Lehman, *Ecstatic Occasions, Expedient Forms,* pp. 216–91.

p. 375 "welcome this as": Paul Violi, "On an Acura Integra," in *New American Writing,* 1997.

p. 375 "The voice of your": Amy Gerstler, "A Fan Letter," in James Tate, ed., *The Best American Poetry 1997* (New York: Scribner, 1997), pp. 75–76.

p. 375 "except insofar": Aaron Fogel, "The Printer's Error," in Richard Howard, ed., *The Best American Poetry 1995* (New York: Scribner, 1995), pp. 65–67.

p. 376 "first coon on the moon": Paul Beatty, "Old Yeller Dreams of Days When They Wasn't Just Whistlin' Dixie," in *New American Writing,* no. 14 (1996), p. 17.

p. 376 "lethal multipurpose": Catherine Bowman, "No Sorry," in Tate, *Best American Poetry 1997,* pp. 44–45.

p. 376 "Don't swim": Hal Sirowitz, "Damaged Body," *Mother Said* (New York: Crown, 1996), p. 13.

p. 377 "scene of my boyhood": Billy Collins, "Canada," in *Harper's,* August 1997, p. 33.

p. 377 "permanent residence": Nin Andrews, "A Philosophical Inquiry into the Nature of the Human Cock," in *Pearl,* 1997.

p. 379 "The avant-garde": Edward Lucie-Smith, "An Interview with Frank O'Hara," in O'Hara, *Standing Still and Walking in New York,* p. 9.

(PRIMARY)

John Ashbery. *And the Stars Were Shining.* New York: Farrar, Straus and
  Giroux, 1994.
———. *April Galleons.* New York: Viking, 1987.
———. *As We Know.* New York: Viking, 1979.
———. *A Wave.* New York: Viking, 1984.
———. *Can You Hear, Bird.* New York: Farrar, Straus and Giroux, 1995.
———. *Flow Chart.* New York: Knopf, 1991.
———. *Hôtel Lautréamont.* New York: Knopf, 1992.
———. *Houseboat Days.* New York: Viking, 1977.
———. *The Mooring of Starting Out: The First Five Books of Poetry.* Hopewell,
  N.J.: The Ecco Press, 1997.
———. *Reported Sightings.* New York: Knopf, 1989.
———. *Selected Poems.* New York: Viking, 1985.
———. *Self-Portrait in a Convex Mirror.* New York: Viking, 1974.
———. *Shadow Train.* New York: Viking, 1982.
———. *Three Plays.* Calais, Vt.: Z Press, 1978.
———, ed. *The Best American Poetry 1988.* New York: Scribner, 1988.
——— and James Schuyler. *A Nest of Ninnies.* Hopewell, N.J.: The Ecco
  Press, 1997.
Ted Berrigan. *A Certain Slant of Sunlight.* O Books, 1988.
———. *Selected Poems.* New York: Penguin, 1994.
———. *So Going Around Cities: New & Selected Poems 1958–1979.* Berkeley:
  Blue Wind Press, 1980.
Joe Brainard. *I Remember.* New York: Penguin, 1995.
———. *New Work.* Los Angeles: Black Sparrow, 1973.
Edwin Denby. *The Complete Poems of Edwin Denby,* ed. Ron Padgett. New
  York: Random House, 1986.
Kenward Elmslie. *Motor Disturbance.* New York: Columbia University
  Press, 1971.

——. *Moving Right Along*. Calais, Vt.: Z Press, 1980.

——. *The Orchid Stories*. New York: Doubleday, 1973.

Barbara Guest. *The Blue Stairs*. New York: Corinth, 1968.

——. *The Countess from Minneapolis*. Providence, R.I.: Burning Deck Press, 1976.

——. *Fair Realism*. Los Angeles: Sun and Moon, 1989.

——. *Moscow Mansions*. New York: Viking, 1973.

——. *Selected Poems*. Los Angeles: Sun and Moon, 1995.

Kenneth Koch. *The Art of Love*. New York: Random House, 1975.

——. *The Art of Poetry: Poems, Parodies, Interviews, Essays, and Other Work*. Ann Arbor: University of Michigan Press, 1996.

——. *The Burning Mystery of Anna in 1951*. New York: Random House, 1979.

——. *Days and Nights*. New York: Random House, 1982.

——. *The Gold Standard*. New York: Knopf, 1995.

——. *Hotel Lambosa*. New York: Coffee House Press, 1993.

——. *I Never Told Anybody: Teaching Poetry Writing in a Nursing Home*. New York: Random House, 1977.

——. *On the Great Atlantic Rainway: Selected Poems 1950–1988*. New York: Knopf, 1994.

——. *One Thousand Avant-Garde Plays*. New York: Knopf, 1988.

——. *One Train*. New York: Knopf, 1994.

——. *The Pleasures of Peace*. 1969.

——. *The Red Robins*. New York: Random House, 1975.

——. *Rose, Where Did You Get That Red?: Teaching Great Poetry to Children*. New York: Random House, 1973.

——. *Seasons on Earth*. New York: Viking, 1987.

——. *Thank You and Other Poems*. New York: Grove Press, 1962.

——. *When the Sun Tries to Go On*. Black Sparrow Press, 1969.

——. *Wishes, Lies, and Dreams: Teaching Children to Write Poetry*. New York: Random House, 1970.

Harry Mathews. *Armenian Papers: Poems 1954–1984*. Princeton, N.J.: Princeton University Press, 1987.

——. *Cigarettes*. New York: Collier Books, 1988.

——. *The Conversions*. New York: Random House, 1962.

Frank O'Hara. *Art Chronicles: 1954–1966*. New York: Braziller, 1975.

——. *The Collected Poems of Frank O'Hara*, ed. Donald Allen. Berkeley: University of California Press, 1995.

——. *Early Writing*, ed. Donald Allen. Bolinas, Cal.: Grey Fox Press, 1977.

——. *Jackson Pollock*. New York: Braziller, 1959.

——. *Selected Plays*. New York: Full Court Press, 1978.

——. *Standing Still and Walking in New York*, ed. Donald Allen. Bolinas, Cal.: Grey Fox Press, 1976.

Ron Padgett. *Great Balls of Fire*. New York: Holt, 1969.

Fairfield Porter. *The Collected Poems with Selected Drawings*. New York: Tibor de Nagy Editions, 1985.

James Schuyler. *Alfred and Guinevere*. New York: Harcourt Brace, 1958.

——. *Collected Poems*. New York: Farrar, Straus and Giroux, 1993.

——. *The Diary of James Schuyler*, ed. Nathan Kernan. Black Sparrow Press, 1997.

(SECONDARY)

Lionel Abel. *The Intellectual Follies: A Memoir of the Literary Venture in New York and Paris*. New York: Norton, 1984.

Donald Allen, ed. *The New American Poetry*. New York: Grove, 1960.

Noel Annan. *Our Age: English Intellectuals Between the World Wars—A Group Portrait*. New York: Random House, 1990.

Dore Ashton. *The New York School: A Cultural Reckoning*. Berkeley: University of California Press, 1992.

Gordon Ball, ed. *Allen Verbatim*. New York: McGraw Hill, 1974.

William Barrett. *The Truants: Adventures Among the Intellectuals*. Garden City, N.Y.: Anchor Books, 1982.

Martha Bayles. *Hole in Our Soul: The Loss of Beauty and Meaning in American Popular Music*. New York: The Free Press, 1994.

Bill Berkson and Joe LeSueur, eds. *Homage to Frank O'Hara*. Bolinas, Cal.: Big Sky, 1978.

Harold Bloom. *The Anxiety of Influence*. New York: Oxford University Press, 1972.

Anatole Broyard. *Kafka Was the Rage: A Greenwich Village Memoir*. New York: Crown/Carol Southern Books, 1993.

Peter Burger. *Theory of the Avant-Garde*, trans. Michael Shaw. Minneapolis: University of Minnesota Press, 1984.

William Corbett and Geoffrey Young, eds. *That Various Field: For James Schuyler*. Great Barrington, Mass.: The Figures, 1991.

Richard Cork. *A Bitter Truth: Avant-Garde Art and the Great War*. New Haven: Yale University Press, 1994.

Douglas Crase. "A Voice Like The Day," in *Poetry*, January 1994, pp. 225–238.

Miles Davis, with Quincy Troupe. *The Autobiography of Miles Davis*. New York: Simon & Schuster, 1989.

F. W. Dupee. *The King of the Cats*. New York: Farrar, Straus & Giroux, 1965.

Alan Feldman. *Frank O'Hara*. Boston: Twayne, 1979.

E. M. Forster. "Art for Art's Sake," in *Two Cheers for Democracy*. New York: Harcourt Brace, 1951.

B. H. Friedman. *Whispers*. Ithaca: Ithaca House, 1972.

Michael Gizzi, Interview with John Ashbery, in *Lingo: A Journal of the Arts* #2, 1993, pp. 4–14.

Laurence Goldstein. *The American Poet at the Movies*. Ann Arbor: University of Michigan Press, 1994.

Brad Gooch. *City Poet: The Life and Times of Frank O'Hara*. New York: Random House, 1993.

Paul Goodman. *Speaking and Language: Defense of Poetry*. New York: Random House, 1972.

Robert Gottlieb, ed. *Reading Jazz: A Gathering of Autobiography, Reportage, and Criticism from 1919 to Now*. New York: Pantheon, 1996.

Clement Greenberg. *The Collected Essays and Criticism*, vols. 1–4, ed. John O'Brian. Chicago: University of Chicago Press, 1986, 1993.

John Gruen. *The Party's Over Now*. New York: Viking, 1972.

Serge Guilbaut. *How New York Stole the Idea of Modern Art: Abstract Expressionism, Freedom, and the Cold War*, trans. Arthur Goldhammer. Chicago: University of Chicago Press, 1983.

Donald Hall, Robert Pack, and Louis Simpson, eds. *The New Poets of England and America: An Anthology*. New York: Meridian, 1957.

Thomas B. Hess and John Ashbery, eds. *Avant-Garde Art* (an *Art News* annual), Collier Books/Art News Series, 1968.

Richard Howard. *Alone With America*, enlarged ed. New York: Atheneum, 1980.

Robert Hughes. *Nothing If Not Critical: Selected Essays on Art and Artists*. New York: Knopf, 1990.

———. *The Shock of the New*, rev. ed. New York: Knopf, 1991.

David Kalstone. *Five Temperaments*. New York: Oxford University Press, 1977.

David K. Kermani. *John Ashbery: A Comprehensive Bibliography*. New York: Garland, 1976.

Jack Kerouac. *The Subterraneans.* New York: Grove, 1958.

Hilton Kramer. *The Age of the Avant-Garde.* New York: Farrar, Straus & Giroux, 1973.

——. *The Revenge of the Philistines.* New York: The Free Press, 1985.

V. R. Lang. *Poems and Plays with a memoir by Alison Lurie.* New York: Random House, 1975.

David Lehman, ed. *Beyond Amazement: New Essays on John Ashbery.* Ithaca: Cornell University Press, 1980.

Norman Mailer. *Advertisements for Myself.* 1959; rpt. Cambridge: Harvard University Press, 1992.

Pierre Martory. *The Landscape Is Behind the Door,* trans. John Ashbery. Riverdale-on-Hudson, N.Y.: Sheep Meadow Press, 1994.

J. D. McClatchy, ed. *Poets on Painters.* Berkeley: University of California Press, 1988.

James Merrill. *A Different Person.* New York: Knopf, 1993.

Howard Moss. *Minor Monuments.* New York: The Ecco Press, 1986.

John Bernard Myers. *Tracking the Marvelous: A Life in the New York Art World.* New York: Random House, 1983.

Maurice Nadeau. *The History of Surrealism,* trans. Richard Howard. New York: Macmillan, 1965.

Steven Naifeh and Gregory White Smith. *Jackon Pollock: An American Saga.* New York: Clarkson N. Potter, 1989.

Ron Padgett. *Ted.* Great Barrington, Mass.: The Figures, 1993.

—— and David Shapiro, eds. *An Anthology of New York Poets.* New York: Random House, 1970.

Marjorie Perloff. *Frank O'Hara: Poet Among Painters.* Austin: University of Texas Press, 1977.

——. *Radical Artifice: Writing Poetry in the Age of Media.* Chicago: University of Chicago Press, 1992.

Renato Poggioli. *The Theory of the Avant-Garde,* trans. Gerald Fitzgerald. Cambridge: Harvard University Press, 1968.

Carter Ratcliff. *The Fate of a Gesture: Jackson Pollock and Postwar American Art.* New York: Farrar, Straus and Giroux, 1997.

Larry Rivers, with Arnold Weinstein. *What Did I Do?* New York: Harper & Row, 1992.

Barbara Rose. *Autocritique: Essays on Art and Anti-art, 1963–1987.* New York: Weidenfeld and Nicolson, 1988.

Harold Rosenberg. *The Tradition of the New.* New York: Horizon Press, 1959.

Raymond Roussel. *How I Wrote Certain of My Books*, trans. Trevor Winkfield. New York: Sun, 1977.

Irving Sandler. *The Triumph of American Painting: A History of Abstract Expressionism*. New York: Harper & Row.

Peter Schjeldahl. *The Hydrogen Jukebox: Selected Writings of Peter Schjeldahl 1978–1990*, ed. Malin Wilson. Berkeley: University of California Press, 1991.

David Shapiro. *John Ashbery*. New York: Columbia University Press, 1979.

Roger Shattuck. *The Banquet Years: The Origins of the Avant Garde in France, 1885 to World War I*, rev. ed. Vintage Books, 1968.

John Shoptaw. *On the Outside Looking Out: John Ashbery's Poetry*. Cambridge: Harvard University Press, 1995.

Susan Sontag. *Against Interpretation*. New York: Farrar, Straus & Giroux, 1965.

Ronald Sukenick. *Down and In: Life in the Underground*. New York: William Morrow, Beech Tree Books, 1987.

John Spike. *Fairfield Porter: An American Classic*. New York: Abrams, 1992.

Diana Trilling. *The Beginning of the Journey*. New York: Harcourt Brace, 1993.

——. *Claremont Essays*. New York: Harcourt, Brace & World, 1964.

Helen Vendler. *The Music of What Happens: Poems, Poets, Critics*. Cambridge: Harvard University Press, 1988.

Anne Waldman, ed. *Nice to See You: Homage to Ted Berrigan*. Minneapolis: Coffee House Press, 1991.

——, ed. *Out of This World: An Anthology of the St. Mark's Poetry Project 1966–1991*. New York: Crown, 1991.

Geoff Ward. *Statutes of Liberty: The New York School of Poets*. New York: St. Martin's Press, 1993.

William Weaver. "Remembering Frank O'Hara," in *Southwest Review* (Winter 1994), pp. 139–146.

Jeffrey Weiss. *The Popular Culture of Modern Art: Picasso, Duchamp, and Avant-Gardism*. New Haven: Yale University Press, 1994.

acknowledgments

I incurred many debts during the course of writing this book. Bill Thomas, my editor at Doubleday, believed in this project from the start and helped shape the final manuscript. Douglas Bauer, Mark Bibbins, Douglas Crase, Roger Gilbert, Stacey Harwood, Phoebe Hoban, Charles North, Darragh Park, Mark Stevens, Paul Violi, and Susan Wheeler read portions of the manuscript in progress, and I am grateful to them for their suggestions. Nin Andrews, Marc Cohen, Laura Demanski, Robin Neidorf, Maggie Nelson, Scott Pitcock, Kate Fox Reynolds, and Suzanne Snider contributed to the research that went into the book. Major thanks are due to John Ashbery, Jane Freilicher, Barbara Guest, Kenneth Koch, Alfred Leslie, Joe LeSueur, Pierre Martory, Ron Padgett, Darragh Park, Larry Rivers, Patsy Southgate, and Arnold Weinstein, all of whom granted me interviews; I wish Nell Blaine were alive so I could thank her as well. I profited from extended discussions with Aaron Fogel, Mara Hennesey, David Shapiro, and Mitchell Sisskind, about studying with Kenneth Koch at Columbia. Bill Corbett, Mark Hillringhouse, Manly Johnson, Wayne Koestenbaum, Ted Leigh, Joseph Parisi, Rodney Phillips, Eugene Richie, Francine Ringold, Jane Uscilka, and Lewis Warsh helped me with archival and other matters. The Rodney G. Dennis Fellowship at the Houghton Library of Harvard University enabled me to spend the month of May 1994 reading the John Ashbery papers housed there. Thurston Smith, associate registrar of Harvard University, kindly let me read the academic dossiers of John Ashbery, Kenneth Koch, and Frank O'Hara. Stratis Haviaris and Joyce Wilson of the Poetry Room at the Harvard College Library made tapes of John Ashbery's Charles Eliot Norton lectures available to me. John Tranter provided me with a tape of an interview he had conducted with Kenneth Koch. Others who generously gave me their time, thoughts, and recollections include Lionel Abel, A. R. Ammons, Rae Armantrout, Mary Jo Bang, Bill Berkson, Robert Bly, Tom Carey, Caleb Crain, Robert Creeley, James Cummins, Ruth Duskin, Irving Feldman, B. H. and Abbey Friedman, Peter Gizzi, Jorie Graham, Donald Hall, Carolyn Harris, John Hollander, Paul Hoover, Richard Howard, Jamie Katz, David Kermani, Nathan Kernan, John Koethe, Hilton Kramer, John Lane, Alison Lurie, Alvin Novak, Maureen O'Hara, Karen Pepper, Robert Polito, Anne Porter, Liam Rector, Adrienne Rich, Charles Simic, Mark Strand, James Tate, Bill Wadsworth, and Trevor Winkfield. Upon learning that I was working on this project, Richard Snow, editor of *American Heritage*, gave it a push by commissioning articles on Abstract Expressionism and on Fairfield Porter. Arthur Vogelsang of *American Poetry Review* commissioned a piece on Kenneth Koch that formed the basis of Chapter Five of this book. I had the chance to try out my ideas in front of informed audiences at Bennington College, Brooklyn College, the New York Public Library, the Pollock-Krasner House, the Tulsa Arts and Humanities Council, the University of Cincinnati, Vanderbilt University, and Westminster College of Salt Lake City. For three consecutive spring semesters starting in 1995, I taught a graduate seminar on the New York School at Columbia University, and was inspired and sometimes instructed by my students. I owe, too, a profound debt to my literary agents, Glen Hartley and Lynn Chu.

For access to letters and other documents, I am grateful to the following libraries and librarians:

Houghton Library, Harvard University, for access to the

John Ashbery Papers (AM-6). Special thanks to Leslie Morris, Dennis Marnon, and Richard Wendorf. Note: This collection is still not fully cataloged. Therefore, the box references as given in the end notes will change.

Archive for New Poetry, Mandeville Department of Special Collections, University of California, San Diego, for access to the James Schuyler Papers (MSS 78), the Donald Allen Collection (MSS 3), and the Joe Brainard Papers (MSS 5). Special thanks to Bradley D. Westbrook, Manuscripts Librarian.

Archives and Special Collections, Thomas J. Dodd Research Center, University of Connecticut Libraries (Storrs), for access to the Donald Allen Papers and the Bill Berkson Papers. Used with permission. Special thanks to Rutherford W. Witthus, Curator of Literary and Natural History Collections.

Mark Bibbins, my literary assistant, worked overtime to help me assemble the pictorial insert in this book. Eric Brown of Tibor de Nagy Gallery and Betty Cunningham, formerly of Hirschl and Adler, provided valuable assistance. For photographs (and for permission to use them) I am grateful to Rudy Burckhardt, John Gruen, and Walt Silver; to Rodney Phillips, Curator, Henry W. and Albert A. Berg Collection of English and American Literature, New York Public Library; and to David Acton, Curator of Prints, Drawings and Photographs, Worcester Art Museum. Permission for Alice Neel's portrait of Frank O'Hara was arranged through Robert Miller Gallery and the National Portrait Gallery, Smithsonian Institution. Photos were also provided by John Ashbery, Jane Freilicher, Carolyn Harris, Alvin Novak, Hilde Ridenour, and Larry Rivers.

For use of copyrighted material, published and unpublished, grateful ackowledgment is made to the following:

Maureen Granville-Smith for quotations from the letters of Frank O'Hara. Copyright © 1998 by Maureen Granville-Smith. Used by permission.

City Lights Books for "Personal Poem," "Poem (Lana

Turner Has Collapsed!)," and "The Day Lady Died," from *Lunch Poems* by Frank O'Hara. Copyright © 1964 by Frank O'Hara. Reprinted by permission of City Lights Books.

Alfred A. Knopf, Inc. for "Autobiographia Literaria," "Today," "Why I Am Not a Painter," and excerpts from "Memorial Day 1950" and "For James Dean" from *The Collected Poems of Frank O'Hara*, edited by Donald Allen. Copyright © 1971 by Maureen Granville-Smith, Administratrix of the Estate of Frank O'Hara. Reprinted by permission of Alfred A. Knopf, Inc.

Georges Borchardt, Inc. for excerpts from "And You Know," "The Instruction Manual," "The Picture of Little J. A. in a Prospect of Flowers," and "The Painter" by John Ashbery from *Some Trees* (New Haven: Yale University Press, 1956). Copyright © 1956 by John Ashbery. Excerpts from "Into the Dusk-Charged Air" and "The Skaters" by John Ashbery from *Rivers and Mountains* (New York: Holt, Rinehart & Winston, 1966). Copyright © 1962, 1963, 1964, 1966 by John Ashbery. Excerpts from "Soonest Mended" by John Ashbery from *The Double Dream of Spring* (New York: Dutton, 1970). Copyright © 1970, 1969, 1968, 1967, 1966 by John Ashbery. Excerpts from "And Ut Pictura Poesis Is Her Name" and "The One Thing That Can Save America" by John Ashbery from *Houseboat Days* (New York: Viking, 1977). Copyright © 1975, 1976, 1977 by John Ashbery. Excerpts from "A Snowball in Hell" by John Ashbery from *April Galleons* (New York: Viking, 1987). Copyright © 1984, 1985, 1986, 1987, 1988 by John Ashbery. Reprinted by permission of Georges Borchardt, Inc. for John Ashbery.

University Press of New England for "They Dream Only of America" and excerpts from "America," "Europe," "The Tennis Court Oath," and "How Much Longer Will I Be Able to Inhabit the Divine Sepulcher . . ." from *The Tennis Court Oath* by John Ashbery (Wesleyan University Press). Copyright © 1962 by John Ashbery. Used by permission of University Press of New England.

Farrar, Straus & Giroux, Inc., for excerpts from "A Poem of Unrest" and "My Philosophy of Life" from *Can You Hear, Bird* by John Ashbery. Copyright © 1995 by John Ashbery. Excerpts from "A Few Days," "A Stone Knife," "December," "Dining Out with Doug and Frank," "February," "Freely Espousing," "Haze," "Hymn to Life," "June 30, 1974," "Korean Mums," "Mike," "The Morning of the Poem," "The Payne Whitney Poems," "Saturday Night," "Things to Do," "To Frank O'Hara," and "Wystan Auden" from *Collected Poems* by James Schuyler. Copyright © 1993 by the estate of James Schuyler. Reprinted by permission. Excerpts from the previously unpublished poetry and correspondence of James Schuyler are used with permission of Farrar, Straus & Giroux, Inc. on behalf of the Estate of James Schuyler. Copyright © 1998 by the Estate of James Schuyler.

John Ashbery for "The Battle," "The Koch," and "French Poetry"; for excerpts from the poems of "Joel Michael Symington"; for all prose and verse quotations from his unpublished correspondence and other unpublished documents; and for his translation of Max Jacob's "The Beggar Woman of Naples."

John Ashbery and Kenneth Koch for excerpts from "Gottlieb's Rainbow," "A Postcard to Popeye," "The Canary," and other verse collaborations.

Jane Freilicher for all quotations from her letters.

Kenneth Koch for all quotations from his poetry and his letters.

Anne Porter for permission to reproduce paintings by Fairfield Porter, for the use of quotations from his letters, and for "I Wonder What They Think of My Verses" from *The Collected Poems with Selected Drawings* by Fairfield Porter, edited by John Yau with David Kermani (New York: Tibor de Nagy Editions, 1985).

Larry Rivers for quotations from his letters.